THE LAST
BATTLEGROUND

THE LAST BATTLEGROUND

The Civil War Comes to North Carolina

PHILIP GERARD

THE UNIVERSITY OF NORTH CAROLINA PRESS

Chapel Hill

This book was published with the assistance of the
Fred W. Morrison Fund of the University of North Carolina Press.

Designed by Jamison Cockerham
Set in Arno, Scala Sans, Cutright, Irby, and Type No. 8
by Tseng Information Systems, Inc.

The University of North Carolina Press has been a member
of the Green Press Initiative since 2003.

This book originally appeared as a series of monthly narratives in *Our State: Celebrating North Carolina* from April 28, 2011, to April 7, 2015, fifty installments in all. They have been revised for inclusion in this book and are published here with permission.

Cover images: (top, left to right) Rose O'Neal Greenhow and daughter Little Rose (Library of Congress, LC-DIG-cwpbh-04849) (also p. vi); unidentified African American soldier in Union uniform (Library of Congress, LC-DIG-ppss-00410) (also p. i); Sister Mary Ignatius Grant (Institute of the Sisters of Mercy of the Americas, Mercy Heritage Center) (also p. xiv); Capt. John Newland Maffitt (State Archives of North Carolina) (also p. xiii); (bottom) Capture of Fort Fisher / J.O. Davidson; L. Prang & Co. (Library of Congress, LC-DIG-ppmsca-19925) (also pp. ii–iii).

LIBRARY OF CONGRESS CATALOGING-IN-PUBLICATION DATA
Names: Gerard, Philip, author.
Title: The last battleground : the Civil War comes to North Carolina / by Philip Gerard.
Other titles: Civil War comes to North Carolina
Description: First edition. | Chapel Hill : The University of North Carolina Press, [2019] | Includes bibliographical references and index.
Identifiers: LCCN 2018038993 | ISBN 9781469649566 (cloth : alk. paper) | ISBN 9781469666112 (pbk. : alk. paper) | ISBN 9781469649573 (ebook)
Subjects: LCSH: North Carolina — History — Civil War, 1861–1865. | North Carolina — History — Civil War, 1861–1865 — Personal narratives. | United States — History — Civil War, 1861–1865. | United States — History — Civil War, 1861–1865 — Personal narratives.
Classification: LCC E467 .G47 2019 | DDC 975.6/03 — dc23
LC record available at https://lccn.loc.gov/2018038993

for

Jill

Contents

Preface

This book is distilled from a series of narratives published monthly in the pages of *Our State: Celebrating North Carolina* during the four-year sesquicentennial of the American Civil War — fifty original installments in all. When Elizabeth Hudson, the editor in chief, approached me with the assignment, I argued that North Carolina is home to many of the best Civil War historians in the country, and perhaps one of them would be far more qualified to write the story of the war in this pivotal state.

But she did not want the settled perspective of an expert writing with perfect hindsight, knowing how the great tragedy turned out. I was born almost exactly on the Mason Dixon Line, but I began the project knowing little about the war — and in fact that was my chief qualification: not to bring any preconceived notions but to report the war as if I were there among those fighting and enduring it.

So we laid down three simple rules for the narratives:

First, each story would in some significant way connect to North Carolina — which was so central to the political, military, and social facets of the war that it turned out to be the perfect state to use as a lens for capturing the whole war.

Second, the stories would focus not just on generals and battles but, whenever possible, on the ordinary people entangled in their own particular theaters of war. The stories would not be sweeping accounts of regimental maneuvers in battle but personal tales of people making the hardest choices of their lives.

Third, all the stories would happen in present tense, using only the knowledge of the time, when the people embroiled in the struggle did not know how things would turn out, when all issues remained in doubt, and they endured a true and terrible suspense. I stretched this rule at times to provide a coda to the lives in these stories, completing their arcs.

The sound of cannons and muskets is never far from these pages — it was a vast war that descended like a great storm on the state — but more compelling to me are the words in penciled letters home, the lyrics of the wistful songs sung in family parlors and around winter campfires, and the funeral orations and sermons and memoirs of a time of desperate hope and suffering, words in which ordinary men and women tried to make sense of the cataclysm.

In writing the war, I found it hard to pin down even the most basic fact beyond a shadow of a doubt. Casualty figures were often just wishful thinking, propaganda, or mere estimates. Uniforms were anything but uniform. Names were spelled with many variations, ages noted disparately by different sources. Carolina regiments were reorganized with befuddling results. Even the flags changed. Legend and gauzy memoirs written long after the fact have sometimes obscured the clear truth.

To write about a single battle such as the one at Bentonville is to try to reduce three days of maneuvering by as many as 80,000 soldiers—with their horses, artillery, hospitals, and supply trains—over 6,000 acres of broken landscape, partly in drenching rain that obscured sight lines and impeded maneuver, including scores of blunders, miscommunications, and assaults, along with hundreds of individual acts of remarkable heroism, tracking the decisions of dozens of generals and more hundreds of subordinate officers, into a few paragraphs that capture some essence of its truth.

In the course of this challenging assignment, I read and pondered scores of published books, along with hundreds of letters, private diaries, narratives compiled by descendants, and official records. The firsthand accounts moved me in ways I never expected, searing their hard emotions into my memory. And I am grateful to the many readers who wrote me with their comments and suggestions and offered personal archives and family stories. I only regret that I did not have space or time to include them all.

Among other excursions, I walked the battlefields at Manassas, Fort Fisher, the Crater at Petersburg, Gettysburg, the Wilderness, Wyse Fork, Forks Road, Bentonville, and Averasboro and listened to the murmuring ghosts. I walked the ruins of the once magisterial Fayetteville Arsenal destroyed by Maj. Gen. William Tecumseh Sherman, saw the graffiti left by his soldiers in a church at Laurel Hill, and walked among the mass graves of Union prisoners of war at the haunting national cemetery in Salisbury.

I visited the ordinary clapboard house in Ohio where Sherman grew up, and in Richmond, Virginia, I explored the Confederate White House, with its dining room transformed into a war room graced by a portrait of George Washington—to many Confederates, the original rebel—and a shelf full of handmade mementoes presented to President Jefferson Davis by liberated Confederate prisoners of war. I toured the Tredegar Iron Works that made the cannon for Fort Fisher and the iron for armored rams like the css *Neuse* and css *Albemarle*. I handled the crude instruments of amputation at the Burgwin-Wright house and visited Chimborazo Hospital in Richmond, where thousands of North Carolina soldiers recuperated—or died.

I visited the serene woods at Shelton Laurel, where thirteen men and boys were massacred by Confederates, and the site in downtown Kinston where Gen. George Pickett hanged twenty-two captured U.S. Army soldiers from North Carolina.

At the mountain retreat of Gen. Wade Hampton, I listened to a Civil War reenactor band, using 1860s-vintage brass instruments, play the mellow old music of the 26th North Carolina, rescued by the Moravian band that first played it and brought it home from the war.

I stood in the parlor of the restored McLean home at Appomattox Court House and also in the rebuilt Bennitt farmhouse—family places where the savage fighting turned into sentences of surrender and mercy.

To understand the long march of events in North Carolina from secession to surrender is to understand the entire Civil War—a personal civil war waged by Confederates and Unionists, free blacks and their enslaved counterparts, farm women and plantation belles, rivermen and blockade-runners, railroaders and spies, prisoners and jailors, surgeons and chaplains, Sisters of Mercy and Moravian musicians, Cherokee braves and mountaineers, ruthless bushwhackers and equally ruthless Home Guardsmen, conscripts and volunteers, and gentleman officers and poor-bocker privates.

The war formed a moving quilt of river battles, skirmishes in mountain passes, ambushes on lonely country lanes, coastal assaults, set-piece battles, secret spy missions, garrison duty, prisons, hospitals, railroads, arduous physical labor on farms and in factories, and all the rest.

And in its complex loyalties, its intimate savagery and routine heroism, its complicated racial legacy of slave catchers and Underground Railroad conductors, its martial religious zeal and obstinate pacifism, its sprawling geography of coastal plains and rugged mountains, its dual role as a home front and a battlefield, North Carolina captures the essence of the whole epic struggle in all its terrible glory.

I consulted some of the many extraordinary historians in the state and gratefully accepted the help of dozens of dedicated archivists, interpreters, reenactors, and site managers. And after six years of all this reading and research and writing, it might be supposed that I became something of an expert. But in fact the opposite is true. I am more aware than ever of the complexity of the war, its sheer expanse—geographically, ideologically, and morally—and my own limited ability to comprehend it, and the eternal difficulty of trying to parse it with mere words, however artful.

Whatever the grand political causes for war, whatever great battles decided its outcome, however abstract it might seem to us a century and a half later, the greatest truth I know is this: the war was always personal. In this way it ceased to be a historical abstraction and become intimately personal to me, too. Every reader of the accounts of soldiers and civilians must come to personal terms with its meaning, test his or her beliefs against the reality of that struggle for the national soul. Somewhere in the causes and chaos of the Civil War lies our identity as Americans—and as North Carolinians.

THE LAST BATTLEGROUND

JANUARY 1865

In Virginia, once the main theater of the war, stalemate has settled in.

Gen. Robert E. Lee's Army of Northern Virginia, no longer invincible and missing its best generals, has been beaten back to Petersburg, where it hunkers down in trenches—half-starved, uniforms in tatters, and running out of bullets, powder, and hope. The army is melting away: hordes of deserters drift south, infesting the western counties of North Carolina, finding refuge in the woods and rugged country, living off the land and preying on civilians.

The Shenandoah Valley of Virginia has been ravaged by Gen. Phil Sheridan's demolishing army and no longer can supply food for the Confederacy.

The theater of war in the East has shrunken, collapsed south on North Carolina, as Union armies converge on the state from east, south, and west. The last stage of the drama will play out in the parlor of a plain clapboard farmhouse—not at Appomattox Court House, Virginia, but on the Hillsborough road just west of Durham Station.

By now, the Confederacy has sacrificed many of its ablest leaders:

Thomas "Stonewall" Jackson, its most audacious field commander, has been dead for more than two years, mistaken for a Union officer and shot in the dark by his own North Carolina troops.

Dead, too, is Brig. Gen. James Johnston Pettigrew, the scholar-soldier from the University of North Carolina. He led Heth's Division of North Carolinians to the stone wall at Gettysburg in the infamous futile slaughter known as Pickett's Charge. He made it to the wall, was wounded, and was killed days later in the retreat.

J. E. B. Stuart, the dashing cavalry general, is also dead, fallen at Yellow Tavern the following year. Albert Sidney Johnston, Bishop Leonidas Polk, Ambrose Powell Hill, William Dorsey Pender, Stephen D. Ramseur, Lewis Armistead, and more than sixty other generals have fallen.

While Lt. Gen. Ulysses S. Grant holds Lee at bay in Virginia, his old friend Maj. Gen. William Tecumseh Sherman invades the Carolinas from the south, bypassing Charleston but taking and destroying Columbia, the capital of South Carolina, then moving fast through the rain and mud, his pioneer corps laying corduroy roads. With Sherman's blessing, his troops leave a trail of devastation in South Carolina, the Cradle of Secession, so indelible that one witness claims that the Union army's progress can be marked by the blackened chimneys left standing in its wake.

Sherman crosses the Pee Dee River and enters North Carolina, bivouacking his troops near Laurinburg. In the belfry of the white clapboard Laurel Hill Presbyterian Church there, his troopers scribble their names and regiments into the plaster. One of them, J.M Lcca, writes, "O when will this cruel war end and we poor soldiers go home," echoing the refrain of a popular sentimental song: "When this cruel war is over."

Sherman orders his men to respect private property in North Carolina—which has always harbored a large Unionist faction. He is done with vengeance.

In North Carolina, the new main stage of the war, one in three citizens relies on government food subsidies. The economy of the state—like that of the whole South—has collapsed. Citizens are starving. In Salisbury, Charlotte, and other cities, women have rioted for bread.

Even harder to bear, one in four men of military age has died of battle wounds or disease. The fabled 26th North Carolina—the largest and most storied regiment in the Army of Northern Virginia—was virtually wiped out in three days of vicious fighting at Gettysburg, far from native soil.

The 10,000 members of a secret society operating out of Raleigh, who call themselves the Heroes of America, sabotage the Confederacy at every turn. Now the Peace Party, led by William W. Holden, a Raleigh newspaper editor, holds mass rallies across the state, agitating for a separate peace between North Carolina and the U.S. government that will leave Richmond and General Lee isolated.

U.S. Army and Navy forces hold the coast from Virginia down to New Bern and Beaufort. Gen. Edward Wild's "African Legion" of U.S. Colored Troops has been raised at the Freedmen's Colony at Roanoke Island and raids the plantations along the tidal creeks—the former slaves avenging themselves on their onetime masters.

A blockading fleet patrols the waters off the mouth of the Cape Fear River, where massive Fort Fisher still holds out, guarding the fairway through which blockade-runners bring in precious food, ammunition, and other cargoes to Wilmington, the last open port of the Confederacy, to be shipped by rail to Lee's beleaguered army.

Just before Christmas, the fort endured the largest sustained naval bombardment in history. An even more powerful armada carrying 9,000 assault troops is sailing south for another try. Meanwhile the Confederate department commander, Gen. Braxton Bragg, pulls back most of his troops from the fort and issues contradictory and confusing orders.

If Fort Fisher falls against the seaborne onslaught, so must Wilmington. With Wilmington goes the flood of foreign supplies and foodstuffs and the Weldon railroad to carry it north to Lee's army in Virginia. So how much longer can Petersburg hold out? If Petersburg falls, Richmond will become untenable, and the Confederate government will abandon the city.

Meantime, from over the mountains in Tennessee, Maj. Gen. George Stoneman, abetted by thousands of Unionists in the North Carolina mountain counties, leads a force of 6,000 hard-riding cavalry troopers—called cossacks for their colorful uniforms—into the heart of the state, intent on freeing Union prisoners from the notorious prison at Salisbury. He is too late—they have been evacuated—so he burns the prison and many other buildings, igniting a pyre that burns all night long and lights up the sky for thirty miles around.

At New Bern on the coast, Maj. Gen. John M. Schofield prepares to move his brigades inland to join up with Maj. Gen. Alfred Terry's regiments attacking Wilmington. They both plan to rendezvous with Sherman's army of 60,000 marching up from Georgia through South Carolina, bound for the railroad junction at Goldsboro. From there Sherman can refit his troops and march north, hammering the Army of Northern Virginia against Grant's anvil.

When Sherman gets to Fayetteville, he intends to destroy the great arsenal there and torch the *Observer*, a newspaper that has championed the Confederate cause. The 25,000 liberated slaves from Georgia and the Carolinas accompanying Sherman's army will soon be sent downriver to captured Wilmington, to be processed though the Freedman's Bureau.

Standing between Sherman's army and his objective, led by Gen. Joseph E. Johnston, Lee's classmate from West Point, is the Army of Tennessee—a ragged ghost of the once-great army of the West, now reduced to fewer than 20,000 men cobbled together from decimated regiments, coastal garrisons, artillery units, and state militia. They will make their last stand at Bentonville.

When Lee's army evacuates Richmond, the Confederate government flees south and west, first to Danville, then to Greensboro.

The Great Surrender will take more than a week to negotiate at the Bennitt farm on the Durham-Hillsborough road. It will constitute the political as well as the military end of the war in the East, leaving only isolated Confederate armies in Alabama and Texas still in the field. The Alabamians—the last Confederate troops east of the Mississippi—will surrender on April 29, and Maj. Gen. E. Kirby Smith, his army melting away, will surrender the remnants of his troops on May 26.

And a Raleigh native—Andrew Johnson—has already ascended to the presidency after Lincoln's assassination and will make a political and social tragedy out of Reconstruction.

As the hard winter of 1865 warms into spring, virtually everything that will affect the outcome of the war—and the coming peace—is happening in North Carolina.

And each of the public events is also deeply personal, full of private longing, fear, expectation, desire, suffering, triumph, and heartbreak.

THE PAGEANT AND THE GLORY

Parading Off to War

May 21, 1861: It's a sweltering spring day in Raleigh.

One by one, the 120 delegates to the special convention called by the General Assembly pen their names to an ordinance of secession from the United States of America and then ratify the Constitution of the Confederate States of America (CSA).

Outside the capitol the waiting crowd, signaled by a handkerchief waved from a high window, goes delirious. Cannons blast out a 100-gun salute, church bells peal, and a marching band blares into full throat. Across the city, crowds erupt into spontaneous, manic celebration.

All over North Carolina, the war begins in a pageant of silk banners and marching men, young and eager, a jubilee of parades with brass bands and snappy drummer boys beating the step with a light tattoo, handsome officers in middle age outfitted more in costume than uniform — blue and gray and red and buff tunics striped with yellow and gold and black, buttoned in brass and leather and bone, festooned with sashes and braid and gilt badges and hand-sewn epaulettes, their caps emblazoned with crossed rifles, bugles, swords, and cannon barrels, wide-brimmed hats tilted rakishly on heads, plumed and feathered and brushed and banded, swords swinging from hips on brass saberhooks, hilts dangling gold and red braid, boots spit-shined to a mirror gloss by body servants, beards and moustaches trimmed and oiled in the manner of true cavaliers.

The officers' horses are a wonder — sleek and spirited, coats shiny from the comb and brush, manes and tails braided, saddle leather oiled to a rich sheen over handsome blankets.

The enlisted men wear the various uniforms of their local militia regiments: gray or butternut homespun battle shirts made by a mother or a wife, blue or gray frock coats, trousers made from "slave-cloth," a practical cottonwool weave. Their shoes are plain lace-up brogans.

In Raleigh, Kinston and Kenansville, Wilmington, Mocksville and Goldsboro, Wilkesboro, Boone, Asheville, and a score of other cities and towns from the wind-scoured coast to the piney Sandhills, through the rolling Piedmont and into the fastness of the western mountains, the troops turn out on brilliant parade, jubilant at the prospect of glory, certain of a quick victory. They call themselves colorful names that honor their home-places and resonate with bellicose confidence: the Duplin Rifles, the Scotch Boys, the Rough and Readies, the Cape Fear Rifles, the Wilmington Light Infantry, the Burke Rifles, the Cabarrus Troopers, the Lexington Wildcats, the Rockingham Invincibles.

From the Franklin Military Institute near Faison come the young and eager Confederate Greys, cocky boys with something to prove. From Davie County—every family of which will give a son, brother, or father to the Confederate army—march the Davie Grays, the Davie Sweepstakes, and three additional volunteer companies. Boone musters the Watauga Marksmen and the Watauga Minute Men. When news of secession reaches Edgecombe County, supporters raise a lone-star flag at Rocky Mount and fire a fifteen-gun salute. The population of just 7,000 sends six companies of volunteers, more than 600 men, including the Edgecombe Guards and the Edgecombe Spartans. Hillsborough fields the Orange Guards and the Orange Light Artillery, jokingly called the Church Bell Battery—two of its large howitzers are fashioned from church bells donated by the town.

In Greensboro, on the eve of war, the 180-strong Guilford Greys muster near the Revolutionary War battlefield where Continental troops under Gen. Nathanael Greene forced Lord Cornwallis to abandon his campaign in the Carolinas. A cadre of young ladies presents to their commander a beautiful blue silk flag with yellow fringe, 5 feet 4 inches by 6 feet, elaborately designed. One side features a wreath of acorns and oak leaves encompassing the North Carolina seal painted in oil: a tableau of two female figures, Plenty and Liberty. Liberty's right hand clutches a scroll labeled "Constitution," and her left hand holds a pole with a liberty cap perched atop it. Plenty is seated to her right bearing three heads of wheat in her right hand, her left hand resting on an upturned, overflowing cornucopia.

Above the seal an eagle holds fast a ribbon on which is painted in gold, "E. Pluribus Unum": Out of many, one. Below it another ribbon proclaims, "Greensboro, North Carolina."

The obverse side mirrors the state seal but carries more specific inscriptions: "Guilford Greys" above, and below, "Organized March 15th, 1860."

Centered inside the wreath is another legend: "Presented by the Ladies of Edgeworth Female Seminary, May 5th, 1860."

Mary Harper "Mamie" Morehead, niece of a former governor, on this day the queen of the May, dedicates the banner with romantic and thrilling words:

> Feign would we have it "a banner of peace" and have inscribed on its graceful folds "peace on earth, good will to man," for our womanly natures shrink from the horrors of war and bloodshed.
>
> But we have placed upon it the "oak," fit emblem of the firm, heroic spirits over which it is to float. Strength, energy, and decision mark the character of the sons of Guilford, whose noble sires have taught their sons to know but one fear—the fear of doing wrong.

There is no talk about the true usefulness of the flag—to be raised aloft above the pall of gunsmoke on a battlefield amid the chaos of exploding cannonballs so that the unit can be identified by the generals in the rear—or that the man carrying it makes himself a coveted target for enemy gunners.

No one remarks, either, on the disquieting irony that, because local firms lack the machinery and expertise, the flag is signed by a Northern manufacturer, Horstmann—of Philadelphia.

The Albemarle Guards carry their own blue silk flag, presented by the ladies of Edenton. The white silk banner of the Forsythe Rifles bears the ominous and daring motto "Liberty or Death." Company M of the Bethel Regiment of the 1st North Carolina Infantry carries a red, white, and blue state flag labeled "Dixie Rebels." The flag of the Brown Mountain Boys of Stokes County, also given by local women, bears a white eagle encircled by a dozen stars.

Each unit will eventually carry, as well, the second national flag of the Confederacy: a white field with a red canton bearing the blue-and-white Southern Cross. This will be the "stainless banner," inspiring an almost sacred devotion. It will also prove completely impractical on a battlefield, too easily mistaken at a distance for a flag of surrender, and will be modified with a broad vertical red stripe.

But all this lies in the future. The present is an almost giddy whirlwind of galas, quadrilles, mass celebrations, and earnest ceremonies of honor.

Some observers, though, remark wryly on the flamboyant theatricality of the volunteer units. Thomas Fanning Wood, a young pharmacist and medical student in charge of the Committee of Safety in Wilmington, notes in his journal, "The Minute Men were organized as far back as Nov. of 1860, and were conspicuous on the streets with their badges of ribbon with a pine-bur rosette. They were of the impetuous sort, ready to secede if it could be done in a day, and take up the next day's excitement with the same relish.... These were not the men to sit in council on the grave questions of the day."

Citizens, including and especially formerly ardent Unionists, compete to show off their loyalty to the Confederate cause. Pinned over their hearts are cockades — cloth rosettes with a centered brass button and two swallow-tailed ribbons, blue or red for secessionist. The red, white, and blue Unionist cockades have largely disappeared. The cockades resemble state-fair prize ribbons. Wood writes, "Nearly every Northerner was suspected of not being truly Southern without he enlisted in some sort of military company." He cites the case of Dr. T. B. Carr, a dentist and native New Yorker:

> He was an officious "minute man," and he wore the blue ribbon, [on] his coat, a blue badge button "C.F.M.M." My father, seeing this one day, accosted Dr. Carr.
> "Well, Dr. What does all this mean?" pointing to his badge.
> "Why, don't you know" answered the doctor with importance, "that is Cape Fear Minute Men."
> "O," replied my father, "I thought it was Cape Fear Milk Man."

Wood himself enlists in the Wilmington Rifle Guards in April 1861.

Amid all the martial roistering, however, there are troubling harbingers of doom. As the Flat River Guards march out of Durham County to the war, they stop at Walnut Hall, home of William Preston Mangum, a young enlistee, so he can bid farewell to his family. His father, a former U.S. senator now crippled by a stroke, speaks to them haltingly, with his daughter Pattie interpreting: "Boys, God bless you every one, but you can't succeed. Their resources are too great for you."

Young Willie Mangum will survive for another month, until mortally wounded at the First Battle of Manassas.

Old William Mangum is more prophetic than he knows. North Carolina has not much of an armory to supply these enthusiastic troops. At the Fayetteville Arsenal, 7,000 muskets have been in storage from the War of 1812 — old, smoothbore pieces too dangerous to fire. Only a handful of cannons are available, and there is no cannon foundry in the state; to build one would cost in excess of $100,000, an unheard-of sum. Officers and cavalrymen supply their own horses and tack. But there are not enough tanneries to make replacement harnesses for horses, artillery trains, and wagons and also to supply leather for shoes and cartridge boxes, so ladies will fashion cartridge boxes out of cotton cloth. But even their sewing needles must be imported.

Many of the volunteers rely on personal weapons. One of the Davie County men, Peter W. Hairston, a volunteer aide to J. E. B. Stuart, writes his wife, Fanny, "I want you also to send me my Sharpe's rifle and Old John Brown's Bowie knife," along with a request for a leather sling to carry the rifle.

The romantic idyll continues a while longer. From his camp on Confederate Point, formerly Federal Point, at the mouth of the Cape Fear River, Wood writes, "Our camp life was more like a holiday excursion. . . . Sometimes we would fall in at reveille with a fishing line in hand, half dressed, and as soon as we broke ranks would dash across the sand dunes for the sea beach and fish for drums and whiting until breakfast time."

Wood's unit is a company of boys, six to a tent, and they behave like boys. "We shot marbles, danced, played cards, chess, back-gammon, drafts, etc." There is little swearing, no drinking or gambling, faithful letters home to mothers, and no women except the visiting wives of officers. Even the practical jokes are harmless boarding-school antics.

It is all so innocent.

Once encamped with thousands of other soldiers, far from home, up in Virginia or out on the coast, facing imminent battle, some of the soldiers begin to reflect on the gravity of their choice. From Richmond, Major Hairston writes again to Fanny: "We have just received marching orders in the direction of the enemy. Should we never return, I commend my children to your charge and care and remember if I fall my last farewell was to you and my last remembrance is my affection of true and devoted love to you my darling wife."

Only a handful of officers have any experience at war, and that was service in the brief, one-sided Mexican War, which ended in a heroic charge at Chapultepec, a rout, and total victory. And unlike most of the original thirteen colonies, North Carolina vanquished the British Redcoats during the American Revolution. Four crucial battles were fought on North Carolina soil or along its near borders: Moore's Creek, the Cowpens, King's Mountain, and Guilford Courthouse. The first three were stunning victories for the underdog Patriots, and the last was a strategic success. They have no cultural memory of defeat.

So the North Carolina volunteers are cocky, thrilling for adventure, immortal. One writes, "All we want is a pure open field fight and we will fight three to one our Col. [says] we will whip them and I do not doubt it at all." Another boasts, "Few in numbers but tho I say it myself we have the best drilled Regiment in the south."

They have not yet heard of such far-off places as Sharpsburg, Fredericksburg, the Wilderness, Cold Harbor, and Gettysburg.

They have not yet starved in a country of farms or walked barefoot in frozen mud or seen their fine uniforms rot on their backs.

They have not yet been ordered to shoot healthy horses pulling gun caissons in order to immobilize the enemy's artillery, or to sharpshoot teenaged drummer boys to disrupt the enemy's command and control on the battlefield.

They have not yet felt the concussion of a cannonball that takes off a man's head, or charged into a hail of grapeshot that mows down a dozen men at once.

They have not yet watched the surgeons sawing off legs and arms for hours on end at the rate of one every fifteen minutes, with nothing to dull the pain.

They have not yet held in their arms a young comrade dying of fever, or served on a burial detail to shovel sand over a mass grave of their boyhood friends.

They have not yet watched their comrades, caught trying to return to their suffering families, tied to posts and shot for desertion.

On the home front, Liberty has not yet given way to conscription and the suspension of habeas corpus by the Richmond government. Plenty has not yet yielded to starvation.

Their silk banners have not yet disintegrated to tatters on their staffs, replaced by sturdier, plainer wool bunting flags, trophies to be captured on the field of glory and slaughter.

The 180 "sons of Guilford" have not yet been reduced, through death and dismemberment, to just a lucky 13 whole, surviving "heroic spirits."

They are not yet veterans. But for that distinction they will not have long to wait.

A HOUSE DIVIDED

Dr. Bellamy's Mansion

At last from Charleston to Wilmington has come the dramatic news that Dr. John D. Bellamy has been ardently wishing for: South Carolina has seceded from the Union. The date is December 20, 1860.

For twenty years Bellamy has been the head of the regional Democratic Party, a fierce supporter of secessionist John C. Calhoun. Now at age forty-three, he is in the prime of his life. Bellamy is not a handsome man but rather an imposing one, with fierce eyes and a thick dark beard, as befits a patriarch of his social standing. He is willful, completely self-assured, convinced of the rightness of his politics and moral stance. He is a strict temperance man and will not serve spirits in his house.

He has abandoned medicine for the lucrative career of a planter. Bellamy owns the plantation he was born on near Georgetown, S.C., and two others: Grovely, consisting of 10,000 acres on Town Creek, a western tributary of the Cape Fear River, and Grist's, a turpentine plantation farther west in Columbus County. In Wilmington, he owns a store and, nearby, what will soon be the grandest home in the city, sited on half an acre of prime real estate on Market Street five blocks up from the river.

Bellamy will not be pushed around by Yankees who do not understand the more genteel and honorable ways of the South. Bellamy descends from one of the original settlers of Charles Town in 1669.

He is one of the wealthiest men in North Carolina. His wealth is the fruit of slave labor. When his father died, Bellamy inherited 750 slaves. Now he owns nearly 1,000. Most work in gangs harvesting crops such as corn, rice, and peanuts. Other slaves operate the dairy, raise livestock, build barrels, make shoes and clothes, mend tools, and drive teams of mules and horses. At Grovely alone, Bellamy has 2,400 acres under cultivation by fifty mule teams; 1,500 head of cattle and sheep roam the meadows and corrals, and each year 1,500 hogs are slaughtered.

A few luckier slaves work indoors cooking, cleaning, waiting table, and tending the younger of Bellamy's eight — soon to be nine — children: Ellen, eight; John Jr., six; George, four; and Chesley, an infant.

The unluckiest slaves are assigned to remote camps in the pine woods of Grist, later to be known as Chadbourne, where they "box" longleaf pine trees with special axes to collect turpentine gum. It's hazardous work that exposes the enslaved to asthma, dizziness, "griping" of the bowels, "dead" limbs, mental impairment, skin rashes, and even blindness from the fumes, in addition to snakebite, heatstroke, malaria, drowning in bogs, tick fever, and being burned in the makeshift kilns. The men live in crude shacks or lean-tos without women or families.

Some of the most skilled — carpenters, stonemasons, plasterers — are at work on Bellamy's new home, carving the elaborate scrollwork and filigree, finishing the ornamental cornices and moldings, and fabricating the Italian marble fireplace mantels in the two great parlors.

When the news of secession arrives, Bellamy is vexed that his fellow Wilmingtonians receive it in such a subdued manner. Businessmen fear it might ruin commerce, which depends on a sea ruled by the Federal navy — Wilmington is a harbor city, after all. To force a celebration, three days before Christmas 1860, Bellamy buys up every barrel of tar he can find and organizes a torchlight parade, complete with brass band. The torches line Front Street paralleling the river and extend from the city limits at Ninth Street down Market to the open-air slave market on the river. There the parade rallies in front of a bonfire, and Bellamy proudly holds his six-year-old son's hand.

And early in the new year, Bellamy moves his family, complete with a retinue of nine house slaves, into the mansion and outbuildings on Market Street. In the two formal parlors hang oil paintings by his eldest daughter, named Mary Elizabeth but called by everyone "Belle" — romantic landscapes of mountain lakes and sentimental portraits, including that of a boy resting against a large shaggy dog.

Belle drew the design for the house based on a home she admired in Columbia, S.C., where she was attending the Barhamville Academy, a women's college with a classical curriculum. At twenty, dark-haired and pretty, she is already an accomplished artist. The Bellamys' new home is a grand structure, twenty-two rooms in four stories, capped by a belvedere at the very top. The signature of its Greek Revival style is the fourteen massive Corinthian pillars lining three sides of the white house. Only the rear, opening onto the four-room slave quarters and the carriage house, lacks them.

Dr. Bellamy's Mansion

Bellamy boasts that he is paying the cost of this house, including the $4,500 lot, with just one year's profits from the Grist turpentine plantation.

The port of Wilmington is enjoying a boom. On any given day, the harbor is crowded with ships from Greece, Russia, England, and Germany loading peanuts or cotton or naval stores — turpentine, tar, pitch, and rosin. Bellamy's son and namesake, John Jr., will never forget the sight of a "million" barrels of turpentine stacked up on both sides of the river for nearly half a mile, awaiting shipment. The ships off-load cargoes of mahogany, molasses, bananas, oranges, and linens.

In this year of 1860, Eliza Bellamy is fourteen. She and three friends have been sewing and selling bibs and aprons to raise money to buy a Bible for the new First Presbyterian Church that will be dedicated next year. Like other young ladies of her class, including her own sisters, she is educated, courteous, morally upright, compassionate, and refined. Yet she — and they — exist in a strange moral bubble, oblivious to the lifelong bondage of so many others that makes their opulent way of life possible.

The city, like the Bellamy family, is on the verge of a very promising year — and also on the verge of calamity.

Like the rest of North Carolina, the city is divided on the question of secession. Despite the energetic efforts of John Bellamy and others like him, such as Governor John W. Ellis, North Carolina stubbornly refuses to secede for another five months, until after Lincoln calls for 75,000 volunteers to put down the Southern insurrection. Then the abstract question of honor gives way to the stubborn, practical determination to defend home ground.

The Piedmont and western counties, along with a swatch of the northeastern part of the state, are firm Unionists; the southern and coastal counties, where slaves are kept in large numbers, are betting their future on secession, for a very practical reason, as expressed by the 169 delegates in South Carolina who initiated secession: the nonslaveholding states "have denounced as sinful the institution of slavery."

Some 22,000 people reside in New Hanover County, 10,000 of them in Wilmington alone. More than half are enslaved. Slaves are valuable. A strong female useful in the kitchen might fetch $300, and a male field hand in good health might cost as much as $1,000. A slave trained in the arduous, skilled work of harvesting and distilling turpentine might cost well over $2,000. John Jr. will later recall being a spectator at the slave market: "An auctioneer would cry out the age, sex, and capability of the slave, just as they sold livestock, then and now."

John Bellamy Sr., like other prominent southern planters, rules an empire, and it is not a democracy. He belongs to a select group of fewer than a hundred men in the state who each own at least 100 slaves. He is known as hard-nosed but not cruel, and he expects toughness and resilience from slaves, hired workers, and family alike. In the cold months to come, he will insist that his young son John Jr. go barefoot all winter, even in snow and sleet, to toughen him up for later life.

In March, the Bellamys host a double wedding reception for Mrs. Bellamy's brother George Harriss and his bride, Julia, and another relation, Hattie Taylor, and her husband, Dr. Edward S. Tennent, a surgeon in the Confederate army. Ellen Bellamy will never forget the spectacle: "I can remember how beautiful everything was, especially the long table set in the dining room laden with everything conceivably good!"

Tennent is fated to die in battle in Marion, South Carolina.

Meanwhile, Wilmington is thrown into a tumult by the war. Soldiers encamp at Delgado Cotton Mills and at Camp Lamb. Sailors and speculators crowd the filthy wharves. Prostitutes suddenly appear in great numbers, along with gamblers, soldiers of fortune, and every kind of petty criminal. It's no longer safe for women to walk the streets unescorted. Bellamy volunteers the services of a contingent of male slaves to join the nearly 500 — including conscripted Lumbee Indians — who will soon labor in the brutal heat to construct a chain of sand forts to guard the Cape Fear River. As a patriotic gesture, he will accept no compensation from the Confederate government.

Sleek side-wheeler steamers with shallow bottoms — blockade-runners — dare the shoals at night to bring war materiel from the West Indies: powder, cannon, muskets, and all the industrial products the South cannot manufacture in necessary quantities. But they also bring in silks and champagne, among other luxuries, and the captains become both heroic and rich. They hold poker games and cockfights and trade currencies and gold.

And indeed there is a kind of gold-rush, frontier boomtown feel to the port, raucous and violent, noisy and vulgar. Time is suspended in an eternal present tense while men scramble to make their fortunes not knowing how long the boom will last, how long it will take for the war that seems so far away to make it this far south.

But the improbable yet somehow inevitable war begins with the bombardment of the U.S. Army garrison at Fort Sumter, in Charleston Harbor, on April 12. By summer there is fighting up in Virginia. Marsden Bellamy, the eldest son, has enlisted in the 3rd North Carolina Cavalry. His younger brother William, just seventeen, has joined the 18th Regiment of North Carolina Infantry. Still the war remains distant. The children cheer news of victories, and whenever they learn of setbacks or of friends or relatives killed in battle, they hide behind the house and weep into their caps.

Babe Sims, a school friend of Belle's, writes from South Carolina inviting Belle to bring her whole family down to Columbia should they need refuge. She writes in a careful, small cursive with a minimum of loops and curlicues, "How many beloved ones have 'fought their last battle and now sleep their last sleep.' . . . Pa was in the Battle of Manassas. We have a good many trophies from the battle field."

There are no Yankee invaders to repel, not yet. Then on August 6, 1862, the enemy steals upriver in a different guise aboard the blockade-runner *Kate*: yellow fever. Almost overnight, a handful of infections become an epidemic. Five hundred cases. One thousand. More than 1,500. Wagonloads of corpses are drawn down Market Street to Oakdale Cemetery, the first of more than 600 who will die. One of them is the superintendent of the cemetery himself. Five of the city's ten doctors fall victim to the fever.

The Bellamy family has inhabited their grand new home for scarcely six months. Bellamy is a doctor and knows there is no cure for yellow fever. The only certain way to save his family is to get them out of the city in time. As they prepare for flight, Bellamy is hailed from the street by an old friend, James S. Green, secretary and treasurer of the Wilmington and Weldon Railroad, on whose board Bellamy serves. "Dr. Bellamy, aren't you afraid to be here while the fever is raging?"

"Yes, we are preparing to leave," Bellamy replies. Though a physician, he does not intend to remain and minister to the sick, exposing himself to fatal infection. "Are you going to stay?"

"Yes, I am immune and not afraid."

Leaving a trusted slave in charge of the house, the Bellamys take the rest of their household slaves with them more than 100 miles into the hinterland to Floral College. Behind them, in the city they and some 6,000 of their fellow Wilmingtonians abandon, their first wholesale casualties of the war of secession are being lowered into a mass grave in Oakdale Cemetery. Bellamy's old friend, James S. Green, does not live out the week.

3

UNFLINCHING LEADER

This new war—which Gen. Robert E. Lee is already calling a civil war—quickly produces fools and giants. Some of the giants have legendary, even biblical names worthy of the cataclysm over which they will preside. For victory, the North will look to men such as Ulysses, Tecumseh, Philip, and of course, Father Abraham. The South will entrust its deliverance to the likes of Jefferson, Judah, Jubal, Raphael, and a host of more prosaic Johns, Thomases, Jameses, Georges, and Roberts. One of the Roberts, derided early in the war as "Granny," will become a lion of the battlefield.

Some will earn colorful nicknames that bespeak the affection and admiration of their comrades: "Stonewall," "Fighting Joe," and "Uncle Billy."

In the eastern theater of war, one fact becomes clear almost from the start: against a succession of timid, unprepared, unimaginative, or just unlucky Union commanders, the Confederate army fields a cadre of brilliant, resourceful, aggressive commanders; meanwhile, the Confederate government in Richmond drafts mediocre men of limited vision and combative personalities to fill its ranks.

The result is a series of astonishing Confederate victories on the battlefield accompanied by a confused muddle of policies that, right from the start, seriously impair the army's ability to be fed, supplied, and deployed and turns popular sentiment in North Carolina against the government in Richmond. For the duration of the war, North Carolina will not only fight the Federals, but it will also fight Richmond—with speeches, newspaper editorials, impassioned letters, court rulings and legislative decrees, and sometimes in a literal clash of arms.

At the outbreak of war, in the Old North State, weak leadership is quite a literal term. The governor who presides over the secession convention, John W. Ellis, suffers from consumption. His health steadily deteriorates until in his final months he is overseeing the government from a sickbed. The son of a plantation owner from Salisbury, he is a strong defender of slavery. But knowing how divided the state is on the question of secession, he has been reticent to express public support for a total break with the Union. Privately, in January 1861 he writes to Governor Joseph E. Brown of Georgia, which has just seceded: "I trust that this event is the beginning of a future of prosperity, peace and happiness for the people of Georgia and my earnest desire is that North Carolina will unite her destinies, by a formal act, as they are now in fact united with the Seceding States."

When President Lincoln requests troops from North Carolina, part of the 75,000-man army he is mustering, to help put down the rebellion, Ellis telegraphs him on April 15, 1861: "I can be no party to this wicked violation of the laws of the country, and to this war upon the liberties of a free people. You can get no troops from North Carolina."

Ellis lives to convene the secession convention in Raleigh later that spring, but by summer he is failing fast. He vacates the governor's office to acting governor Henry T. Clark, the speaker of the state senate, and tries one last remedy. He makes the difficult journey north to the public tuberculosis facility at Red Sulphur Springs, Virginia, but he is too far gone to be helped by mineral springs. He dies there on July 7, 1861. He is just forty-one years old.

Clark, another scion of the plantation class from Edgecombe County, succeeds formally to the governor's office. Clark is a proficient administrator. He sets in motion the machinery for moving troops by railroad to the front in Virginia. He establishes salt works to provide the army with the precious food preservative. He builds a gunpowder mill, establishes trading connections across the Atlantic, and authorizes the first and only Confederate prison in North Carolina at Salisbury.

Thanks to his efforts—including a special arrangement with the CSA Quartermaster Corps that the state will provide its own uniforms in exchange for funds—North Carolina troops are among the best clothed and equipped in the Confederate army. A timely investment in blockade-runners by his successor will continue to make this possible.

But Clark is overwhelmed by circumstances and is not really cut out for the treacherous political landscape that comes with the war. As the troops head north to Virginia, they leave the northeastern coast unprotected. Soon U.S. Army troops have taken Hatteras Island, New Bern, and other coastal territory, and politicians across the state, egged on by newspapers such as the *North Carolina Standard*, raise an uproar.

On every hand lurk radicals of all stripes, including armed Unionists who will try to foil every effort to support the war. And the Confederate government in Richmond quickly proves to be inflexible and authoritarian.

It institutes a draft and sends squadrons of conscription agents into North Carolina to round up men between the ages of eighteen and thirty-five. The upper age limit will be raised again, to forty-five, and by war's end, the Confederacy will forcefully conscript men as old as fifty and accept junior reserves as young as seventeen.

There is a loophole: an eligible man may buy his way out of the army by hiring a substitute, paying as much as $5,000 — a cost only the wealthy plantation class can afford. And the law exempts one white man of military age — usually the owner or overseer — from any plantation with twenty or more slaves. Owners divide their property into twenty-slave holdings so their sons can be exempted from service. For North Carolinians, this lends a galling irony to the war: the small plantation class lobbied loudest for secession in order to protect its economic interests, and now members are able to use the very money gotten from the proceeds of their slaves' labor to sit out the fighting in safety.

Throughout the Confederacy, the equivalent of more than fifty regiments of rich Southern men buy their way out of the war they worked so hard to bring about. Meanwhile, the Old North State supplies one-sixth of all the men in the Confederate army, enough to fill more than eighty regiments of regulars.

Richmond issues one after another draconian pronouncement and seems deaf to requests from North Carolina. It automatically prolongs all militia enlistments from six months or a year to a full three years. Clark goes along and does his best to please Richmond, but though his constituents hate Washington, they begin to hate Richmond even more. Jefferson Davis and his cabinet are perceived to act with disdain toward North Carolina and will not detail troops to defend its vulnerable coast. They commandeer all the troops and all the resources for the defense of Virginia.

A special election is called for August 1862, and Clark isn't even nominated.

The man who replaces him doesn't campaign for the office. He is propelled to a landslide victory by the relentless support of two newspapermen, William W. Holden of the *Standard* and Edward Hale of the *Fayetteville Observer*. Holden in particular has been a savage critic of the administration in Richmond and its treatment of North Carolinians — and of Governor Clark's perceived complicity. The campaign takes place within the pages of the newspapers, and the victor's margin is almost three to one, by far the largest mandate in the state's history.

At last, North Carolina has found its giant: Zebulon Baird Vance.

A battlefield hero becomes governor without a campaign: the formidable Zebulon Baird Vance is captured in a photo "made when he was inaugurated as Governor, 1862." (Courtesy of the State Archives of North Carolina)

He is in fact a physically formidable man, 6 feet tall and 230 pounds. He is handsome, easily recognizable by his black moustache and shock of long unruly hair swept back from his forehead. He is known as a practical joker, a canny politician, and a stubborn fighter.

Vance is outraged by the policy allowing wealthy planters to hire substitutes to fight on their behalf, deriding the practice as "a rich man's war and a poor man's fight." He comes from a political family in the mountains, not from the eastern plantation class. His ancestral roots are in Ulster, Ireland, as well as Scotland and Germany. Trained as a lawyer, he gravitated toward politics practically before he had finished his schooling. In his early twenties, he was elected to a series of local offices. He is popular, likable, and a gifted orator who weaves humorous folksy stories into his speeches to make his points.

But he is by no means a simple man. He believes in the inferiority of blacks: "We are opposed to negro equality. To prevent this we are willing to spare the last man, down to the point where women and children begin to suffer." Yet he remains an ardent Unionist. He writes to a friend in the state legislature, urging him to "make haste slowly": "We have everything to gain and nothing on earth to lose by delay, but by too hasty action we may take a fatal step that we *never* can retrace—may lose a heritage that we can never recover 'though we seek it earnestly and with tears.'"

In 1860 in Raleigh, in a two-hour-long speech, he ridicules the claim of two secessionist congressmen that an independent South would enjoy the protection of England—a protection, Vance says, "our forefathers waged a seven years war to escape."

Yet he favors a secession convention, arguing that the people have the right and responsibility to make this momentous decision, and "after such mature and *decent* deliberation as becomes a great people about to do a great act, if *they* choose to undo the work of their wise and heroic ancestors, if *they* choose to invite carnage to saturate their soil and desolation to waste their fields, they can not say their public servants *precipitated* them into it!"

By age thirty, when war breaks out, he is serving his second term in the U.S. Congress, actually canvassing his native state on behalf of the Union. He recalls the watershed moment when his allegiance to the Union falters: "I was addressing a large and excited crowd, large numbers of whom were armed, and literally had my arm extended upward in pleading for peace and the Union of our fathers, when the telegraphic news was announced of the firing on Sumter and the President's call for 75,000 volunteers. When my hand came down from that impassioned gesticulation, it fell slowly and sadly by the side of a Secessionist."

Two weeks before North Carolina formally secedes, Vance raises a company of Buncombe County men in Asheville, the Rough and Ready Guards, and now a captain, leads them off to war. In the confusing scramble to align volunteer regiments into a cohesive army, Vance's cohort is renamed Company F of the 14th North Carolina Regiment. Encamped near Statesville, he writes to his wife, Hattie, "I am quite well but in rather low spirits at the way things are managed in Raleigh. I see a pretty determined purpose there to carry on affairs under a strict party regimen; none but Locos and Secessionists will be appointed to the Offices: the old Union Men will be made to take back seats and do most of the hard work and make bricks with straw. So be it. I am prepared to serve my country in spite of the small men who control its destinies — But many persons are disgusted. Companies are disbanding."

In June 1861, resplendent in new uniforms, his regiment entrains to Suffolk, part of the defensive perimeter around Norfolk. By August, Vance is a colonel commanding the 26th North Carolina Regiment stationed at Fort Macon on Beaufort Inlet. Roanoke Island falls to the U.S. Army in February, forcing a retreat.

It is not until March 1862 that Vance leads his troops into battle for the first time. Maj. Gen. Ambrose E. Burnside with 11,000 troops is pushing down the Neuse River toward New Bern. For more than five hours, Vance's troops hold off an attacking enemy that outnumbers them about three to one. They hold the extreme right flank for a full hour after the rest of the Confederate line has buckled and retreated, and they are the last to leave the field to regroup in Kinston.

Vance describes, breathlessly, the thrill of first action in a letter to his wife: "Balls struck all around me, men were hit right at my feet — My men fought gloriously — the first fire was especially magnificent — It was a dark foggy morning and the men were situated in small half moon redans, they fired by company beginning on the left, and the blaze at the muzzle of the guns was bright and glorious — Many of the Yankees tumbled over & the rest toddled back into the woods — For five hours, the roar of the small arms was uninterrupted, fierce and deafening."

Their retreat across Bryce's Creek takes as long as the battle. In typical heroic fashion, Vance swims seventy-five yards across the swollen creek to procure boats for his men. It's a deep creek with a strong current, and three of the men who follow him across drown. Then follows a forced thirty-five-mile march to Kinston.

In an after-action letter to his commander, Brig. Gen. Lawrence O'Bryan Branch, Vance underplays his own valor: "I cannot conclude this report without mentioning in terms of the highest praise the spirit of determination and power of endurance evinced by the troops during the hardships and sufferings of our march. Drenched with rain, blistered feet, without sleep, many sick and wounded, almost naked, they toiled on through the day and all the weary watches of the night without murmuring, cheerfully and with subordination, evincing most thoroughly those high qualities in adversity which military men learn to value still more than courage upon the field."

Later, at Malvern Hill outside Richmond, Vance leads his men into the withering fire of Federal guns. The charge is valiant but futile, the kind of charge that will soon become all too familiar: a slaughter of onrushing, exposed lines of men by cannons and massed musketfire entrenched behind earthworks. Vance's courage is beyond question now, his unflinching leadership a settled fact. He makes it to within a stone's throw of the cannon's mouth before being forced back. Zebulon Vance, the Unionist, is now a bona fide Confederate war hero.

When the newspapers begin clamoring for his nomination for governor, from Kinston Vance cagily replies in a letter to the *Fayetteville Observer*, "If, therefore, my fellow-citizens believe that I could serve the great Cause better as Governor than I am now doing, and should see proper to confer this responsibility upon me without solicitation on my part, I should not feel at liberty to decline it, however conscious of my own unworthiness."

At his inauguration, the 26th regimental band, made up of Moravians from Salem, performs "Governor Vance's Inauguration March" in honor of the occasion. Vance delivers his inaugural address with all the charismatic vigor his listeners have come to expect. It is an oddly hopeful moment, a short lull amid the opening shock of war. Vance's wife, Hattie, has just delivered their fifth child, a son named Thomas Malvern. But Vance's speech, uncharacteristically short, is for once lacking his celebrated humor. There are no laugh lines. He admonishes his audience, "To prosecute this war with success, there is quite as much for our people as for our soldiers to do."

They applaud heartily a truth that has yet to manifest itself in all its terrible majesty.

4

RIVER RUNAWAYS

In the rainy darkness at the foot of Orange Street on the east bank of the Cape Fear River, eight runaway slaves crouch in the shadows, careful to conceal themselves behind barrels and bales, listening hard against the patter of rain on wharf and river for the sound of patrols. They wait long into the night until the streets are deserted and the river is an inky black smear at the edge of their vision, more heard than seen.

Their leader is a twenty-four-year-old master brickmason and plasterer named William B. Gould. The son of a white English father and an enslaved mother, he is slightly built and stands 5 feet 5½ inches tall, but he is strong and, more important this night, he is bold. Gould is one of sixty-nine slaves owned by Nicholas Nixon, a peanut farmer with a plantation north of the city at Porters Neck and a stalwart of St. John's Episcopal Church in Wilmington. Gould, like many of the skilled artisans, lives in Nixon's slave quarters, just four blocks away on Chestnut Street.

Tonight—September 21, 1862—he plans to leave Wilmington and the South forever. His companions are William Chanse, John Mitchell, Charles Giles, George Price, John Mackey, and brothers Andrew and Joseph Hall. In the government census, their names have not been recorded. Each man is just three-fifths of a human being, under the compromise hammered out by the aristocratic gentlemen—many slaveholders among them—at the constitutional convention that created the governing document of the United States of America.

Collectively, the eight men add up legally to a mathematical remainder, four and four-fifths human beings. They are considered a quantity of property, an economic asset to be used and disposed of like any other. Gould has always chafed under his bondage and has done all he can to prepare himself for freedom. He has learned to read and write, although for a slave, such education has been against the law since before he was born. He can recite Shakespeare, speaks passable French, and knows a smattering of Spanish.

He is not a man to remain anonymous. When he worked on the fine interior of the John D. Bellamy mansion, he signed his initials in the wet plaster. He will be remembered.

Gould and his seven companions are bound for a place where their names will matter. Fourteen other slaves huddle in the darkness nearby. Gould's contingent is part of a wave of blacks seizing the chaos of war to escape to freedom. When the yellow fever struck Wilmington, affluent families fled, leaving their homes and businesses in the charge of trusted slaves. But many of those slaves take advantage of the opportunity and make their way to the river, thence to the sea, where they are welcomed into the ships of the U.S. Navy blockaders. The shoreline has become the new boundary between slave and free states.

At last it is time. Gould and his party steal aboard the small boat tethered to the wharf. It has oars and a sail, but they will not risk raising the sail until they are in the estuary, some twenty miles downriver, for it can be too easily spotted by the lookouts of the nine forts they will pass or the slave patrols that will soon be scouring the city and countryside for them once they are missed. The other slaves slip into two boats, and soon all three are out on the wide dark river.

The water—not just the coast, with its limitless ocean vista, but the rivers as well—has always been a tantalizing lure to the enslaved.

A generation ago, a slave named Peter, one of many black river pilots, helped to guide fugitive slaves downriver to Smithville, a small settlement at the mouth of the river. There he arranged clandestine passage aboard oyster sloops owned by two Quakers named Fuller and Elliot, for Quakers have long been opposed to the practice of human bondage. From the sloops, the fugitives could be transferred to outbound schooners. They were all part of the nautical Underground Railroad. But it isn't just Quakers and other white people of conscience who aid runaways. Indeed, their help comes mostly from their own community: other slaves, runaways hiding out in the swamps, and free blacks willing to take a chance.

There is the plantation culture that the white owners see—the opulent household of the master, the seemingly obsequious "darkies"—the one Northern audiences know from the comic minstrel shows. But there is another culture on the plantation as well, a culture that encompasses larger areas and takes place at night, in remote places, far from the prying eyes of overseers and their agents. Slaves move back and forth among plantations, visiting family, making alliances and friends, laying up supplies and precious cash, trading in forbidden commodities such as weapons and books, exchanging information and news, and mapping escape routes.

In North Carolina, there are more than 331,000 slaves and another 30,000 free blacks. Despite the draconian laws, the curfews, and the prohibitions against travel, there is just no way to control the movements of so many able-bodied beings with their own desires and needs. Slavery is their curse. Their survival requires constant vigilance, the ability to seem like what they are not, and the discipline to keep secrets. Even if they are legally free, there is always the risk of being taken for a runaway. They subvert the system quietly every day.

The most subversive black man of all was probably David Walker, son of a black man and a white woman and therefore, according to the peculiar calculus of racial inheritance, a freedman. He went north from Wilmington at the earliest opportunity, and from Boston in 1829 he issued his famous — or infamous — *Appeal,* in which he urged slaves to rise up against their masters. The pamphlet was sewn into clothing sold to sailors at Walker's shop, smuggled into the Cape Fear region, and passed hand to hand up and down the Southern coast, creating a panic. It was rumored that a general uprising was planned for Christmas. Just a year later, Walker died mysteriously; many suspected that proslavery agents poisoned hum.

The plantations along the Cape Fear River — like those all up the coast as far as the great Dismal Swamp — are far flung and full of difficult terrain: bogs, tidal creeks, pocosins, marshes, rivers, and blackwater swamps. The overseers depend on slaves who can handle boats, navigate treacherous creeks and rivers, and find their way to remote turpentine works in blind forest. The slaves often must rove far from their overseers, working in small teams too scattered to be supervised closely. They get used to a certain amount of mobility, a small degree of freedom.

So there has grown up a strong clandestine tradition of black watermen helping their fellow slaves navigate the soggy maze of coastal waterways to freedom — in flatboats, dugout cooners, flatties, punts, and periaugers. They travel by night, trusting only one another.

Among their most reliable allies are small pockets of runaways who have made a life in the remote fastness of the pine woods, river canebreaks, and swamps. They are known as Maroons and live beyond the pale of slave law. The Maroons exist invisible to white society, out in places no one else seems to want, but they provide a temporary oasis for other runaways.

On the Pasquotank and Chowan Rivers and in the Great Dismal Swamp, some bands number thirty or forty people and have been established for generations. Even if they could find their hideouts, the slave catchers know better than to go up against them; they are well armed and will fight if provoked. There is strength — and determination — in numbers.

But the life is hard. Some of the Maroons hire out as day laborers at the turpentine camps, boxing pines for their rosin, or find work at the Dismal Swamp Land Company cutting shingles or sawing wood. The foremen look the other way; they need the hands. The pay is $2 per month, a pair of rough trousers, a shirt, and plain food.

From the rice and turpentine plantations, the runaways follow the Cape Fear to Wilmington. From tobacco and cotton plantations in the Piedmont, they journey down the Neuse and Trent to New Bern. The Tar River takes them to Washington; the Roanoke, to Plymouth. Each port city is a doorway to a new world, but a dangerous one. Any sailor or ship's master can betray them to earn the bounty. Any port inspector can discover them. Examiners sometimes fumigate the ships' holds just to drive out stowaways by burning pitch or brimstone between decks — the same method they use to drive out rats.

If captured, runaways are turned over to the slave patrols to be whipped and sent back into bondage. So they must have enough money for both bribes and passage, and the passage may cost many times what a white passenger would pay.

Some runaways wait for months for their chance, others years. A thirty-four-year-old carpenter named Henry Gorham hides out in the forest for eleven months before he can arrange safe passage. Ben Dickenson bides his time for three years. Harriet Jacobs tucks herself away in an attic in Edenton for a full seven years before being taken aboard a schooner bound for Philadelphia.

This rainy September night, Gould and his companions row hard and are swept downriver past the moored ironclad and blockade-runners; past the sleeping sprawl of Orton Plantation and the mouth of Town Creek, where Bellamy's 10,000-acre plantation Grovely lies; past the artillery post on Sugar Loaf Bluff and Battery Anderson; past the guns of Fort Anderson and Fort Johnston on the opposite shore; and past the sweeping bend at Smithville, Fort Fisher looming to the left on Confederate Point, and Fort Caswell, an old masonry fortress, on the right.

It takes all night to make the passage. Now it is past sunrise.

Out beyond Smith's Island, the open sea beckons. They hoist the sail and scud along in the fresh morning breeze. Before long they are spied by lookouts aboard the USS *Cambridge,* one of the blockading Union squadron, which records the event in its log: "Saw a sail S.W.S. and signaled same to other vessels. Stood for strange sail and at 10:30 picked up a boat with 8 contrabands from Wilmington, NC."

"Contraband" is the new word for an escaped slave. Maj. Gen. Benjamin F. Butler coined the term: "Contraband of War," meaning they are assets to the enemy, so capturing them deprives the enemy of one more resource with which to wage war. Outside the Confederacy, the Fugitive Slave Law no longer applies. The future of black slaves is very much at issue in this war.

Indeed, almost at the very hour that seamen are taking Gould and his companions aboard the *Cambridge,* President Abraham Lincoln summons his cabinet to brief them on a speech that will restate the Union war aims. He calls it the Emancipation Proclamation. It will declare that "all persons held as slaves within any State or designated part of a State, the people whereof shall then be in rebellion against the United States, shall be then, thenceforward, and forever free."

Gould is not finished with his adventure. He enlists in the Union navy and now, as a serving hand on the *Cambridge* and, later, on the *Niagara,* chases blockade-runners, sinking them or running them aground. His ship takes aboard a dozen contrabands from a small boat in October, a month before a freak snowstorm kills off the mosquitoes vectoring the epidemic.

The proximity of the beach leads to a vexing security problem for the Confederates as they conscript hundreds of slaves and "free persons of color" to turn Fort Fisher from a few gun batteries into an impregnable fortress that can successfully stand off the U.S. Navy blockade and keep the port of Wilmington open. The port is vital to supply Lee's army via the 162-mile-long Wilmington and Weldon Railroad, the longest railroad in the world when it was built, and one of the few north-south railroads in the state.

The U.S. Navy ships patrol just offshore, which means that if a slave can swim or paddle a boat out far enough, one of the smaller picket boats can pick him up. And on several occasions, longboats land brazenly on the beach and pick up runaway slaves, many of whom then enlist in the fight.

Col. William Lamb, the young commander and architect of Fort Fisher, loses one of his own slaves in this manner, with momentous consequences. In May 1864, Charles Wesley slips out to the beach and is picked up by sailors from the USS *Niphon.* Having helped to build the fort, he proceeds to brief the Federals on its layout; its fluctuating garrison of 800-odd artillerymen, regular soldiers, and junior reserves; and its armaments.

Though the fort will stand for eight more months, its security is now undermined. Thus an escaped slave is credited with helping engineer the downfall of the mighty fortress. Altogether, eighty-two African American men from the Wilmington area run away and join the Union army or navy, and a dozen of them will return to fight in the final battle of Fort Fisher.

GLORY BOUND

In the brilliant summer of 1861, when he marches off to war from his beloved home in the Yadkin River Valley, Capt. William Henry Asbury Speer does not expect to be captured. He will fight, and with the Lord's help, his side will prevail. Or he will die valiantly on the field of honor. Either way, he believes he is bound for glory. In this, he is exactly like so many soldiers on either side.

He is a reluctant soldier, an opponent of secession who loves his home-place deeply enough to defend it. He descended from Ulster Scots who inter-married with pacifist Quakers. His family has farmed land in the Yadkin for more than a century, and like all Speers, he is deeply tied to the land. The land and family are inseparable. The Yadkin Valley is a Unionist stronghold, forced into war by the slaveholding plantation class—so he believes. Of the secessionists, he writes to his father, "They are the 'cause' of the war. I do not believe God had any more hand in bringing the war than the 'child un-born' did."

A photograph of Speer in his Confederate uniform shows a ruggedly handsome man with thick hair and beard, high forehead, and eyes intently staring at the camera with a fixed expression at once proud and conflicted. He is tall, well regarded by the ladies, and deeply religious.

He works as the superintendent of a tannery in Jonesville, where he lives. In 1856, he is elected for a two-year term in the North Carolina House of Commons. For ten years before the outbreak of war, he serves as colonel of the Yadkin Valley Militia. Astride his powerful horse and outfitted in a tailored tunic with rows of gold brocade and brass buttons, elaborate gold epaulettes and shoulder boards, and a cocked hat, sword hanging at his side, he is the very incarnation of martial leadership.

So when the volunteers muster to oppose the Federals, he is the natural choice to be elected captain of Company I, 28th Regiment of North Carolina Troops. They call themselves the Yadkin Stars—ninety-odd soldiers, according to the Salem *People's Press*, which describes them as "a fine company of able-bodied men."

From High Point they entrain for Wilmington and then, in the spring of 1862, rush to the defense of New Bern. But they arrive too late to stop a Union victory and are forced to retreat to Kinston. At last, on May 27, 1862, the Yadkin Stars are tested in battle at Hanover Court House, north of Richmond, Virginia.

Entrenched in muddy positions, backed up against the Chickahominy River, they weather a night of chilling rain. Dawn brings an attack by an overwhelming force of Federals. After a hot running fight that lasts more than three exhausting hours, Speer and fifteen of his company are trapped against the river. They are desperate, outnumbered four to one, and outgunned. He records the moment of truth in his diary: "I could have swam the river but my men could not & they begged me to stay with them. With tears in their eyes, told me they had stuck by me all day & would have died around me to have saved my life. How could I leave such men?"

The unthinkable happens: they are all captured together.

Under guard, they march sixteen miles to White House Landing through the wreckage of battle — smashed wagons, broken artillery, dead horses, and the corpses of soldiers. They pass a field hospital shrill with the cries of the wounded. Speer gets a glimpse of the awful might of the Union war machine. He writes, "As we marched along the road we were continually meeting troops, Redgts., Brigades, etc. Artileory after artileory was hurrying on with numerous cavelry & every now and then we would pass long lines of Bagage wagons, emence tranes of them drawn by the best horses and mules I ever Seen."

They also pass the grave details. In one place, fifty of their own dead are laid out for burial, and a band of U.S. Army Zouaves in baggy red trousers is busy rifling their pockets for money and other valuables.

All along the route, they are flanked by crowds of Union soldiers who are seeing "dirty rebels" for the first time. "We were gazed and Stared at as if we had been live Devels," he confides to his diary. "They seemed to be amazed to see that we were human beings as same as themselves." Some of the Yankees taunt them, while others merely stare, transfixed.

They embark on the transport steamer *Star of the South* bound for New York.

This early in the war, as an officer, Speer is treated with a modicum of dignity. Though he and his men spent thirty-six hours marching and sleeping in the rain without a meal, now he is given plenty to eat and a cabin in which to sleep. Seasickness plagues the prisoners, many of whom have never been aboard a ship. Three days later the *Star* arrives off Governors Island. "Now our steamer casts anchor and here comes the N.Y. Yankees to see the bloody Seceshes," he writes. "'Look, Pa,' says a very pretty little girl, 'they have got no horns and tails as I can see.'"

The officers are separated from the men and taken to Fort Columbus, half an acre of parade ground surrounded by barracks and thick masonry parapets mounting cannon. Having been given his parole, like the other Confederate officers, Speer is allowed the run of the fort and is quartered in one of the comfortable barracks. "We are very well treated by all officers, privates, men, women, children, even a dog called Sport," he records, and he spends his days watching out over the busy harbor, an alert spectator to steamers and clipper ships, ferry traffic, and yacht races. From the top of the fort, he can see Manhattan, Brooklyn, Staten Island, and Long Island—even Hoboken and Jersey City in New Jersey. He writes copious letters home and passes the time reading and making jewelry from scraps of fabric, metal, and gutta-percha.

But then comes the disconcerting news that he is to be moved farther north. He writes home of his disappointment at hearing the "grape," or rumor: "I did hope to be paroled & come home as I am tired of war and its destruction."

He is moved to Johnson's Island on Lake Erie, sixteen and a half acres enclosed by a fifteen-foot-high nail-spiked palisade, and there he endures much harsher treatment. On August 8, 1862, he records in his diary the cold-blooded murder of a fellow prisoner: "The poor man told the Sintinel that he was going to his quarters but yet the murderous centinel firred and Killed him. He was a young man, very peaceable quiet fellow. . . . It was one of the most horable things I ever Seen in life."

In late September, Speer is mustered for exchange and returns south to Vicksburg to rejoin the fight.

At the outset of the war, which everybody on both sides expects to last only a few weeks, no long-term provisions have been made for holding prisoners of war. It's a complicated business: prisoners have to be accounted for, transported, housed, fed, kept warm, and supplied with fresh water and clothing, and their wounds and sicknesses have to be attended to.

Above all, they have to be guarded. Virtually no one volunteers for guard duty—tedious, confining, lonely, lacking the chance for glory. Especially in the South, being a prison guard is considered unmanly.

Initially, after a battle has been decided, commanders merely parole their prisoners. That is, the captured soldiers give their word of honor neither to attempt to escape nor to rejoin the hostilities, and they are trusted to remain available until an exchange can be worked out. Once they are exchanged, usually for a like number of men on the other side, they are free to rejoin their units.

These arrangements are informal, and the U.S. Army refuses to formalize them, because that would mean, in effect, recognizing the Confederacy as a sovereign nation. But as time goes on, a growing number of prisoners on both sides became stranded in a limbo of confinement. Lee, commander of the Army of Northern Virginia, and Maj. Gen. George B. McClellan, commander of the Army of the Potomac, press for a more formal arrangement on both humanitarian and practical grounds: the Confederacy, in particular, just does not have the resources to feed and house prisoners, and increasingly it cannot afford the manpower to guard them.

Thus is born the Dix-Hill Cartel, named for the two officers who negotiate it: Maj. Gen. John A. Dix, USA, and Maj. Gen. D. H. Hill, CSA. The cartel creates a uniform process whereby captured soldiers will be repatriated and spells out equivalencies — that is, a brigadier general is worth twenty enlisted men, a captain six, a sergeant three, and so on.

This system of parole and exchange dates back two millennia to the Carthaginian Wars and was continued through the Crusades, the Napoleonic Wars, and the War of 1812. It has a whiff of nobility about it, the trust of armies reposed in words of honor. In practice, though, it sometimes means that weary troops allow themselves to be captured by the enemy for a period of rest and recuperation before being returned to the rigors of battle.

Captain Speer once again takes his place in the 28th Regiment, but his ambivalence about the war haunts him. He fights fiercely and with great courage in battle yet tirelessly schemes for a way to get out of the army. For him, service in a morally ambiguous cause has become its own kind of confinement. He determines to resign his commission, but a new order from Richmond decrees that any officer who resigns his commission may not go home but must be conscripted into the ranks as a private soldier. Even furlough is denied him; as the toll of dead and wounded mounts, there just isn't another officer available to take his place.

Speer campaigns with equal vigor to keep his younger brother, James, out of the war, and in this he succeeds. He rises to the rank of major. He fights at Fredericksburg and is wounded at Chancellorsville and again at Gettysburg, where he charges Cemetery Ridge with Lane's brigade under Pickett. He writes, "We charged the batteries 1½ miles over a plain. O such slaughter never was seen. We lost 2/3 of our Regt. O my God, where will this slaughter end?"

Nonetheless, in February 1864, his entire regiment signs a pledge to "never lay down our arms or abandon the struggle." Speer survives ten more major battles, including the killing grounds of the Wilderness, Spotsylvania Court House, and Cold Harbor. A year after Gettysburg, he is promoted to colonel in command of the regiment.

But the shortages of clothing, food, and arms remain a constant reminder that the cause is now becoming unwinnable. In May 1864, Speer writes a poem in eight stanzas for his family, ending,

> I am dying, comrade, dying.
> Tell my heart's last fitful swell,
> Tell the cold dew gathering o'er me,
> Father, Mother, friends — Farewell.

Scarcely three months later, at the battle of Ream's Station near Petersburg, the blast of shrapnel from an artillery shell catches him in the head. He lingers four days and dies at the age of thirty-eight. Friends cart his body home in a wagon across the Yadkin River and bury him among his ancestors.

THE NEW NATIONAL
PASTIME AT WAR

On July 4, 1862—the eighty-sixth anniversary of American Independence Day—Confederate soldiers in Salisbury Prison yard cheer on Union troops as they battle to the finish on the grassy plain. But the troops wield no weapons, just bats and balls. The contest is a friendly one: a game of base ball.

Dr. Charles Carroll Gray, a prisoner at Salisbury, notes in his diary that the occasion is "celebrated with music, reading of the Declaration of Independence, and sack and foot races in the afternoon, and also a baseball game."

The players are Union prisoners of war who have brought to the prison yard game their "New York" rules, adopted at the first Base Ball Convention of sixteen clubs in 1857: the playing field is a diamond, not a square, and behind the first and third baselines lies foul ground; all nine strikers on each side must bat in a regular rotation; each inning continues until three outs—not just one—are made; no throwing the ball at the runner to get him out, as in the Massachusetts rules; likewise a fielder must catch a fly ball in the air, not on a bounce, to make an out.

And the contest continues until nine innings have been played, no matter the number of "runs" or "aces" scored by either side. Older rules specified 21 or 100 as the winning total.

Among the prisoners is a forty-six-year-old commercial artist, Capt. Otto Boetticher of the 68th New York Volunteers. He sketches the scene and, after he is paroled a few months later, immortalizes the game in a colorful lithograph. The players in the field wear dark blue trousers and forage caps, except the "hurler," who wears tan trousers and a homemade straw hat. A red rosette adorns each of their white shirts above the left breast. The players on the batting team wear red or blue shirts. They are lean and rangy, young men in the prime of their lives.

The hurler is frozen in time, with his long right arm at the apex of his

Otto Boetticher, *Union Prisoners at Salisbury, N.C.*, 1863. The new national pastime goes to war: Union prisoners at Salisbury are depicted playing base ball in this hand-colored lithograph based on a painting by Capt. Otto Boetticher, from sketches he made as a prisoner. (Courtesy of Reynolda House Museum of American Art, affiliated with Wake Forest University)

windup as he prepares to "pitch" the ball toward the striker, underhanded, in the manner of horseshoes. Behind him, an alert runner, cap in hand, breaks down the baseline, bound to steal second base, forever balanced on his left foot, his momentum carrying him forward as if he were charging into battle.

Prisoners and captors surround the diamond, standing shoulder to shoulder, sitting cross-legged on ladder-backed chairs, or lounging on the shady lawn. Some are neatly uniformed, while others are dressed in a motley of civilian and military garb. In the foreground, their backs to the game, a cadre of officers huddles deep in discussion, while two large dogs gambol nearby. Behind home plate, separated from a gang of spectators by an orderly row of white peaked canvas tents, young men play a game of jacks.

In the distance rises the three-story brick edifice of an abandoned cotton factory, now the main prison barracks. Neat rows of outbuildings stretch along the wooden palisade, and far beyond right field, gray-clad soldiers march and drill. But for most of the hundreds of men on the scene, the base ball game is clearly the center of interest.

In fact, Salisbury Prison has become a prime venue for base ball. On nearly every day except Sunday, prisoners form up sides and play. The guards watch and sometimes even join in. In this regard, the prison activities are merely an extension of the pastimes soldiers have gotten used to in bivouac. In the camps of both armies, commanders encourage base ball games as a way to keep their men physically fit and mentally alert. Because the Southerners are not familiar with the New York rules, at least one of them—a hurler from Texas—is ejected from a game for deliberately hitting runners with the ball and "badly laming" several of them.

But mostly the games provide amusement, exercise, diversion, and even camaraderie among prisoners and guards alike. One prisoner, Sgt. William H. Crossley from Rhode Island, records in his memoir that the "great game of baseball" offered "as much enjoyment to the Rebs as to the Yanks, for they came in hundreds to see the sport." Of one game in particular, played between teams of prisoners who were previously held at Tuscaloosa and New Orleans, respectively, he writes, "I have seen more smiles today on their oblong faces than before since I came to Rebeldom, for they have been the most doleful looking set of men I ever saw, and the Confederate gray uniform really adds to their mournful appearance." That game ends in a tie, 11-11.

As in most wars, the fierce episodes of battle are tempered by long periods of inaction: training and drill, the long preparation for battle, and the exhausted period of recovery and refit that follows. But there is also winter quarters, the four-month season when campaigns are suspended due to bad weather and worse roads, and soldiers simply wait in their tens of thousands at camps far from home, passing the time as best they can.

They gamble at cards and dice, stage amateur theatricals, attend Sunday services, and congregate to enjoy regimental brass band concerts. They engage in trials of physical prowess: wrestling and boxing matches, swimming and foot races, and pole-climbing contests. They race horses. They carve pipes and write letters. They paint and draw, read newspapers, and stage tournaments of chess and drafts. They chase greased pigs and, in winter, battle each other in lively snowball fights. But there is so much "time to kill"—the ironic idiom expressing bemused detachment from the war.

For more than a generation, base ball in some form has been sweeping across the land. First played in the Northeast—in big cities like New York and Boston—it has spread west and south. Now even small-town boys in North Carolina have become familiar with some version of "town ball," "bat ball," or "base ball."

Seasoned amateur players, most of them in the Union army, carry their equipment with them to the war: finely turned ash or hickory bats, factory-made base balls covered in horsehide stitched with the new figure-eight pattern, and even natty uniforms bearing their proud logos: Excelsiors, Eagles, Mutuals, and Atlantics.

Confederate soldiers make do with a whittled tree branch or the single-tree from a wagon, batting any kind of ball they can fashion, even if it is just a walnut wrapped tightly in yarn.

The game has five major advantages for soldiers.

First, it is portable, requiring just a bat and ball and no carefully groomed sporting grounds, as does cricket. Any pasture or town square will do.

Second, any reasonably fit man can learn the basics in a few minutes—catching throwing, running, and hitting.

Third, it keeps the men active and in good physical shape, unlike cards, dominoes, or dice.

Fourth, it occupies many men at once. Though regulation teams consist of nine to a side, other men can join in so long as the teams remain roughly equal, and many more can participate as spectators, cheering on their favorite nine.

And fifth, a game can last as short or long a time as the players wish. Pressed to move out, they can shorten a game to a matter of a few innings. Given a long period of inaction, they can play extra innings. Because the armies are at their idlest in the winter, waiting for good marching weather, most camp games are played between late fall and early spring.

And it's no accident that the Union prisoners at Salisbury should choose to celebrate Independence Day with a game of base ball. Almost from its inception as a sport organized into amateur leagues with formal rules, base ball has been imbued with patriotism. As early as the 1830s, the Philadelphia Olympics, Excelsiors, and Athletics celebrated the Fourth of July by reading the Declaration of Independence, singing patriotic songs, commissioning a speech on the virtues of the Stars and Stripes—and playing a game of base ball.

In 1860, a New York sporting journal called the *Clipper* declares unequivocally that base ball "may now be considered the National game of ball."

At the front in Virginia, soldiers of both armies can watch their enemy counterparts across the battle lines playing base ball games—close enough that they can cheer on the action as a runner is thrown out, a batter swings and misses, or an outfielder snags a long fly ball. Writing home in 1862, one private from an Ohio regiment marvels at the sport's popularity: "It is astonishing how indifferent a person can become to danger. The report of musketry is heard but a very little distance from us. . . . Yet over there on the other side of the road is most of our company, playing Bat Ball and perhaps in less than half an hour, they may be called to play a Ball game of a more serious nature."

Before long, base ball has become a metaphorical construct for the war itself. A newspaperman from Rochester, New York, reports that "many of our first class players are now engaged in the 'grand match' against the rebellious 'side,' and already have made a 'score' which, in after years, they will be proud to look upon."

A ball-playing Union soldier observes in 1864, "If General Grant does not send them to have a match with Gen. Lee, they are willing to have another friendly match, but if he does, the blue coats think that the leaden balls will be much harder to stop than if thrown by friendly hands on the club grounds."

The prisoners depicted in Boetticher's festive lithograph will soon be liberated from Salisbury Prison under the conventions of the Dix-Hill Cartel. Many will find themselves marched into the thick of the terrible battles still to come: Second Manassas, Sharpsburg, Fredericksburg, the Wilderness, Cold Harbor. Maybe a sense of foreboding afflicts the senior officers in the painting—the reason they seem to remain deaf to the cheering crowd and the chatter of the ballplayers, aloof from a friendly game of hitting and catching and running fast toward home.

Soon enough the Dix-Hill Cartel will be rescinded by the Union to keep the enemy from sending the same troops back to fight time and again. After that, prisoners unlucky enough to be sentenced to Salisbury will languish there until the war is nearly over.

But on this Fourth of July, the sun shines brightly, the clamor of battle is yet far off, the captors behave humanely and with honor, and the prisoners are healthy and well fed, full of banter and ready laughter, alive with the pure joy of outdoor play.

You can see it on their faces: they are enjoying themselves, intent on their game of Base Ball, having good wholesome fun in the open air. And why not? Most of them are, after all, just boys.

The New National Pastime at War

THE "DARK HOLE" AT SALISBURY

The war, begun with noble pronouncements, sentimental loyalties, rash heroism, and codes of gentlemanly honor, soon takes a turn. For two years of war, prisoners are captured on the battlefield and paroled according to conventions as old as wars between nations, formalized in the summer of 1862 in an agreement called the Dix-Hill Cartel. But the process has one glaring flaw.

After he captures Vicksburg on July 4, 1863, Lt. Gen. Ulysses S. Grant is appalled to learn that his 37,000 rebel prisoners—all exchanged according to the cartel—have returned to their regiments. He expresses his frustration succinctly: "If we commence a system of exchange which liberates all prisoners taken, we will have to fight on until the whole South is exterminated." He refuses to fight the same men over and over until they are all wounded or killed.

U.S. Secretary of War Edwin M. Stanton heeds Grant's wisdom: there will be no more prisoner of war (POW) exchanges. Grant has effectively condemned many captured soldiers to suffering and death—ironically for the most humane of reasons, to end a greater suffering and death as quickly as possible.

Early in the war, Lee recognizes that the exchange program is untenable in the long term and argues for a system of prisons to hold Union captives. Richmond appeals to state governments, and North Carolina proposes locating a prison at Salisbury, fifty miles southwest of Greensboro—one of the first of thirty that will be established throughout the Southern states. Salisbury is a railroad hub in bountiful farm country. For $15,000, the Confederate government buys the Old Cotton Factory, a vacant three-story brick structure on sixteen acres, with six brick tenant cabins, a blacksmith's shop, a small hospital, and assorted outbuildings. Workers erect a stout wooden stockade encompassing six acres of lawn shaded by oak trees.

In 1861, forty-six Federals captured at Manassas, Virginia, are the first tenants. Soon they are joined by seventy-three sailors from the USS *Union*, which grounded off the coast. For these first prisoners, Salisbury is a pleas-

Salisbury Prison depicted early in the war as a neat, sanitary holding pen for prisoners expecting exchange. Later it becomes notorious—a crowded hellhole of misery and death. (Courtesy of the State Archives of North Carolina)

ant, almost restful place. They spend their time playing base ball in the yard, reading under the trees, gambling at poker, staging amateur theatricals, and trading buttons and pocket goods with the locals for delicacies such as fresh vegetables and tobacco. They print and distribute their own newspaper, the *Stars and Stripes in Rebeldom*. And in due time they are exchanged for their counterparts in gray.

For a long year, the prison remains largely vacant, housing only some escaped slaves, Confederate deserters, and civilian felons. The first commandant is Dr. Braxton Craven, president of Trinity College in Durham, and his congenial Trinity Guards are mostly students from the college.

All that changes in 1864, as fighting intensifies on all fronts. As the year opens, the prison population swells to 2,500, more than the total population of Salisbury at the outbreak of war. By October 1864, the number of POWs approaches 9,000.

The large brick building has been taken over by the wounded and ill, except the top story, which is occupied by the worst of the worst, the so-called muggers. All the other prisoners live outdoors in burrows dug into the glutinous clay of the main yard. A Confederate preacher, Dr. A. W. Mangum, records the strange and inhuman village that honeycombs the prison

The "Dark Hole" at Salisbury

grounds: "They were queer-looking holes, dug some three feet deep, with mud-thatched roofs, a hole being punched through the surface at one end and a little chimney built out of baked earth." A man has to sit or lie down inside.

The prisoners petition the new commandant, Maj. John H. Gee, for permission to use pine logs to build dry cabins, but he refuses, giving no reason.

The prisoners include those taken on the battlefield but also deserters from both armies, captured runaway slaves, and so-called political prisoners—a catchall term that includes Unionists; Quakers and other pacifists; civilians with suspect loyalties; at least two war correspondents from the *New York Tribune*, Junius H. Browne and A. D. Richardson; and saboteurs of the Confederate war effort who call themselves the Heroes of America. There is also a hard core of ruthless criminals.

Into this prison marches Pvt. Benjamin F. Booth on the cold, drizzly afternoon of November 4, 1864. It is his and his comrades' special misfortune to be captured at the Battle of Cedar Creek in the Shenandoah Valley of Virginia. Booth is twenty-six years old, a large, robust man of 181 pounds, a two-year combat veteran who can handle himself in a brawl. His outfit, the 22nd Iowa Volunteer Infantry, is part of Gen. Phil Sheridan's army of "barn-burners," who are systematically destroying farms in the Shenandoah Valley to starve out Lee's troops and end the war.

The Confederates spend all night of October 18 stealthily moving into position, then attack out of the predawn fog. Booth and his detail of sharpshooters are caught in the open by an overwhelming force of the enemy. Rather than surrender, they shoot off a single volley to sound the alarm, and the enemy returns a devastating fire. More than fifty U.S. soldiers fall dead. Their commander, Col. Harvey Graham, reports, "In this stand the enemy was so close to our ranks that their fire burnt the clothes of our men, and while falling back many were captured."

Because of Sheridan's tactic of hard war in which civilians are made to suffer for supporting insurrection, Booth and his twenty-two companions are among the most reviled of the Yankee prisoners. Despite the rules of engagement agreed upon by both sides, their captors strip them of their clothes, their blankets, their hats, their shoes, and even their canteens. One is bayoneted along the march. First they are taken to Libby Prison in Richmond, where the guards shoot them for sport if they come too close to a window.

Booth writes in his diary, "With these facts before us, who will dare say that the Union soldiers were engaged in fighting chivalrous and brave men?"

Then the prisoners are removed to Salisbury, what one prisoner calls the "dark hole," and their trials truly begin. At Salisbury, the prisoners die in droves. They are stricken by dysentery from poor sanitation and pneumonia from living outdoors in mud warrens during the long wet winter. Smallpox passes quickly among men so closely confined, and dengue or "break-bone" fever is carried by the ubiquitous lice. Wounded men, as well as men whose limbs have become frostbitten, succumb to gangrene, and their limbs rot off their bodies. Starved of protein and fresh fruit, they ulcerate with scurvy.

Gangs of muggers—many of them from the crowd of deserters who have taken over the top story of the main building, now known as Devil's Den—attack the new prisoners at night. The prisoners retaliate, hunting down the worst and killing them in reprisal.

Seventy-three men are shot to death by guards.

In his diary, faithfully kept from the day of his enlistment forward, Booth records that one poor fellow has nothing at all wrong with him physically, but he dies anyway "from sheer despondency." And it is true: the most virulent epidemic sweeping the prison is despair.

The blacksmith shop has been turned into the dead-house, where bodies are collected for burial. Their clothes are stripped off by their comrades, so they go to their graves naked. The dead are hauled out each day, eight to a wagonload, to be thrown into open pits.

The prisoners are so starved that they climb the oak trees in search of acorns, and fish for scraps of food or bone in the open sewers running through the camp. They trade scarce uniform buttons, hand-carved trinkets, homemade rings, anything at all, for food.

Booth keeps a death log in his diary, tabulating the cost of incarceration in bare numbers carefully inked beside dates: November 29—46 dead. December 1—58 dead. January 12—40 dead.

Beyond hunger and disease, beyond physical pain and bone-chilling cold, the worst torture is confinement itself. The men constantly plot their escape, plan elaborate ruses, and forge complicated alliances. At any given time, some gang of men is digging an escape tunnel. They hold their secrets close, since other men will betray them for rations or money or simply favor with the guards.

Some men make a break over the palisade while the guards are sleeping or derelict. Others bribe the guards to let them out. The two newspaper correspondents escape in this manner, taking a cohort of loyal friends with them all the way to Tennessee. A prisoner named Sheehan, who makes it out with them, writes later, "After thirty-four days of travel through the wilds

The "Dark Hole" at Salisbury

of western North Carolina and east Tennessee, on the morning of February 27th we beheld the bright folds of our starry banner as it floated on the breeze. Oh, Comrade, I cannot describe to you our feelings at that moment. I fell on my knees and thanked God for my deliverance, as it was out of the House of Bondage and the land of Egypt."

But most of the escapes are foiled, and even when a man breaks free of the stockade he is likely to be rounded up before he can make it to the fastness of Unionist country in the western Piedmont or the mountains.

The hellish plight of the prisoners leads them to a bloody uprising just weeks after Booth enters Salisbury. On November 25, 1864, a mob of prisoners storms the gate. They overpower a handful of guards and seize their muskets, then push out of the stockade. But the other guards turn artillery on them—three cannon loaded with grapeshot, canisters full of metal slugs the size of rivets—at point-blank range. A troop train at the nearby depot unleashes a wave of reinforcements, who add their massed fire.

Booth's diary tells the awful tale: "The desperate men acted solely on the impulse of the moment. It was an ill-advised, futile attempt. It lasted but a few moments, nevertheless, in that short time eighty-one were killed and as many wounded. The enemy were so enraged that they kept up the firing long after the prisoners surrendered."

It is a horrible slaughter. In the aftermath, two surgeons enter the prison to carry out the grim task of amputation. Though Salisbury is home to a large whiskey distillery commissioned by the Confederate government for the express purpose of making strong spirits to be used as anesthetic in field hospitals, the commandant claims there is no anesthetic available for use on prisoners. The amputees have nothing to dull their pain.

The dead are hauled directly to the burying ground and heaved into a pit. Later, affidavits from prominent citizens of Salisbury affirm that at least two of the men are still alive when dirt is shoveled over their faces. They try feebly to climb out of the pit but are covered up with the rest.

Most of the dead are buried anonymously in unmarked graves. But inquiries from the State Department in Washington turn up the name of one casualty of the uprising, perhaps the most famous prisoner to be held at Salisbury: an imposter who enlisted under the alias Rupert Vincent. He turns out to be Robert Livingstone, son of the famous African missionary Dr. David Livingstone. Before capture, he writes to his father, "I am convinced that to bear your name here would lead to further dishonoring it." He goes on, "I have never hurt anyone knowingly in battle, having always fired high."

Salisbury earns a notorious reputation in the North as a death camp.

On April 12, 1865, Maj. Gen. George Stoneman assaults Salisbury with 6,000 cavalry troopers with the aim of liberating the Union prisoners. In short order, Stoneman's troopers overwhelm the few hundred boys, elderly men, and invalid troops who stand in their way and enter the town. But only a few prisoners too ill to travel remain. The rest have already been evacuated to Wilmington or Richmond. Stoneman's troopers burn the infamous prison, the original hospital, the outbuildings, the railroad depot, the distillery, and other buildings containing stores for the Confederacy: 10,000 rifles, 17,000 uniforms, 25,000 blankets, and more than 200 tons of food and other supplies.

The fire at Salisbury burns all night, the flames visible in Statesville, thirty miles distant.

Though he leaves Salisbury four months before the end of hostilities, Major Gee—the most notorious of the ten commandants to oversee the prison—is arrested and put on trial for war crimes. He is acquitted.

All told, the Confederacy has held more than 200,000 Union prisoners. Some 15,000 of those have passed through Salisbury. An estimated 5,000 have died there—a fatality rate much higher than that of battlefield troops. Only about 300 have managed to escape and remain free.

When the POWs are released on February 22, 1865, Booth smuggles his diary out of the prison wrapped in a scrap of tent canvas. He has lost more than ninety pounds in captivity, half his body weight. He and his cohort are marched to Greensboro, then loaded onto trains to Raleigh and Goldsboro by stages. On March 2, at the Northeast Cape Fear River, their train halts, for the railroad trestle has been destroyed by Confederate sappers fleeing the Federal invasion of Wilmington. They are ferried across the river.

He writes, "Those who were able to stand marched to the city, where, within a mile of headquarters, the old flag was proudly to welcome us home. . . . The climax was reached when we drew near to headquarters and saw that poles had been erected on each side of the road which were wreathed in evergreens and a banner drawn across the road from pole to pole, on which was inscribed, in large gilt letters, WE WELCOME YOU HOME OUR BROTHERS."

The first troops to receive the prisoners are U.S. Colored Infantry, who give them shirts, pants, blankets, shoes, food, and water in a gesture of fraternal generosity that Booth will remember for a lifetime. A band strikes up the familiar strains of "Home, Sweet Home." Booth records: "This was more than we could bear."

Union headquarters is housed in the spacious confiscated mansion of Dr. John D. Bellamy.

THE HEROES OF AMERICA
RISE FOR THE UNION

From Randolph County, square in the middle of the state, John A. Craven pens a letter of bitter complaint to Governor Zebulon Vance in October 1862: "On Saturday night last an officer that lives within a mile of me arrested a conscript a neighbor of His. The Next Night the officers Barn with all its Contents Except His Horses was burned to the ground."

North Carolina is in rebellion against the Union, but the heart of the Old North State is already edging toward rebellion against the Confederacy. Almost as soon as the church bells toll the hour of secession, a new organization rises up among the discontents in the northern Piedmont. The strong pacifist tradition among the Quaker and Moravian communities there, along with a moral abhorrence of slavery, creates ripe ground for Unionists.

The so-called Quaker Belt stretches nearly 5,000 square miles across nine counties—Alamance, Chatham, Davidson, Davie, Forsyth, Guilford, Randolph, Surry, and Yadkin—and includes such key cities as Salem, Asheboro, Lexington, and Greensboro. These counties form a kind of no-man's-land nearly the size of Connecticut located just west of Raleigh, effectively splitting the state in two. The Quaker Belt is hostile ground for the Home Guard, dangerous territory for the conscription patrols sent to round up able-bodied men.

The stealthy members of the new order call themselves the Heroes of America. Their goal is simple and audacious: to bring down the Confederacy. To that end, the Heroes harbor spies. They guide escaping Yankee prisoners over the Blue Ridge Mountains into Tennessee and Kentucky. They spirit runaway slaves and fellow Unionists alike to free states. Through pamphlets and clandestine meetings in cantonments, they convince Confederate soldiers to desert their units, then help them hide out from the conscription patrols. Some resort to violence. Secret and effective, the Heroes of America are Jefferson Davis's worst nightmare come true: a fifth column bent on destroying the Confederacy from within.

They style themselves after the Freemasons, adopting signs and countersigns, special handshakes and symbols, and above all, an oath of loyalty unto death to fellow members — and to protect the secrets of the organization.

Their motto: "Truth, Virtue, Honor, Fidelity, Justice."

Their password: "United we stand," answered by "Divided we fall."

The Heroes take their inspiration from the Book of Joshua, the story of the two Israelite spies who infiltrate Jericho in advance of an attack. The king learns of their presence and sends agents to capture them. But a harlot named Rahab shields them, misdirects the king's agents, and then lowers them from her window down the face of the city wall by a scarlet cord. Her only condition for saving their lives is that, when they return to sack the city, they will spare her family. They assure her, "Behold when we come into the land, thou shalt bind this line of scarlet thread in the window which thou didst let us down by: and thou shalt bring thy father, and thy mother, and thy brethren, and all they father's household home unto thee."

Likewise, the Heroes display a red cord on a doorjamb or windowsill, or sew a red string into their lapels to signal initiates that they have come to a safe haven. Upon meeting, they give the code word "Three" and await the correct answer: "Days" — signifying the length of time Rahab cautioned the Israelite spies to lie low in the mountains before returning to their camp.

Emulating the Freemasons, the Heroes first initiate a candidate into the lowest of three degrees, progressing to increasing levels of responsibility and knowledge of the order. First-degree Heroes might know only one other member, the best insurance against betrayal. The initiate swears to eight promises, "binding myself under no less penalty than to have my head shot through." He finishes the initiation ceremony by kissing the Bible.

The Heroes of America organize themselves into small bands and work with the traditional pacifists and "stationmasters" on the Underground Railroad. One of the earliest bands operates in Davidson County and is led by John Hilton, a buggy maker from Thomasville. Hilton's neighbor, James H. Moore, betrays him to Governor Henry Clark, confiding that "there are five hundred men in Davidson and other counties around ready to strike for the old Union." Worse, Moore tells the governor, Hilton has been bragging that "certain secessionists in the neighborhood . . . would 'feel the rope' in a short time."

Clark dispatches the Trinity Guards to High Point to put down the imminent uprising. The sheriff of Davidson County arrests Hilton near

Thomasville for threatening violence. But the Heroes are not daunted, only driven deeper underground.

Out on bail, Hilton reappears on March 7, 1862, leading a peace rally at the Kennedy School House near Thomasville — one of many such Unionist "night meetings." Hilton is also hatching a scheme to rescue Yankee captives from Salisbury Prison. Alerted in advance to the rally, tipped off that Unionists are also stockpiling arms and powder for an uprising, Governor Clark sends 300 troops to High Point and orders the entire 33rd Regiment of North Carolina Troops to converge on the rally. The soldiers take many prisoners, but Hilton eludes them, crosses the mountains into Tennessee, and eventually enlists in the U.S. Navy.

Most newspapers are reluctant to report the lively Unionist activity for fear of demoralizing troops fighting far from home. Only in 1864 will the Heroes of America be publicly revealed as a complex, secret organization with more than 10,000 sworn members.

Among the founders is Dr. John Lewis Johnson, a native Philadelphian who moved to North Carolina in his boyhood, studied medicine in Lexington, and practices in Forsyth County. He enlists in the Confederate army — probably under threat by Confederate agents — is captured under suspicious circumstances during the Sharpsburg Campaign, and returns south on parole. He now becomes an apostle of the Heroes, proselytizing for the order all over the state.

Another — surprisingly — is Henderson Adams of Davidson County, who serves as state senator from 1862 until the end of the war. The appeal of the Heroes is greatest among small farmers and working-class whites who feel pushed into war by the plantation class. In April 1862, this resentment turns to outrage in some quarters when the Confederate government passes the Conscription Act. Under its terms, all men between the ages of eighteen and thirty-five must serve in the army when called. Men who have volunteered for a year now are required to serve two additional years — but the twenty-slave rule exempts a privileged few.

A soldier named O. Goddin writes the governor, "The Govt. has made a distinction between the rich man (who has something to fight for) and the poor man who fights for what he will never have. . . . Now Govt. do tell me how we soldiers who fight for the 'rich mans negro' can support our families on $11 month?"

The effect on troops in the field is immediate and devastating — especially North Carolina troops, fierce fighters but also among the most ambivalent in the Confederate army. Davis and many of his senior advisors are dubious of the loyalty of North Carolina troops and are accused of consistently bypassing their talented officers for promotion—a source of bitter tension for the duration of the war. Many of the troops consider themselves pro-Union and volunteered only out of loyalty to the honor of their home state. The rate of desertion becomes a crisis. Not only do the desertions weaken the fighting army; in addition, other units and companies of the Home Guard must be dispatched to round up the deserters and bring them back.

Gathering strength from their founding base west of Raleigh, the Heroes move into Raleigh itself and establish the Grand Council of the Heroes of America practically on the front lawn of the capitol. After the initial fervor of secession dies down, the city is so pro-Union that the garrison troops there remain on guard as much against attacks from their fellow citizens as from the U.S. Army.

From the Quaker Belt, the Heroes spread out east to Kinston, Goldsboro, and the coast. They create chapters in Charlotte, Greensboro, and even Salisbury. They gain a foothold in the openly pro-Union mountain counties. They recruit in Virginia, South Carolina, and Maryland and establish a satellite headquarters in Washington, D.C.

When the state builds a salt works on Masonboro Sound near Wilmington, Unionists and Quakers from the Piedmont—nearly all Heroes of America—fill the jobs. Maj. Gen. William H. C. Whiting, in command of the Wilmington District, complains openly to Governor Vance, "I have at length positive information that at least two thirds of the conscripts at the State Salt Works belong to the treasonable organization called the 'H.O.A.' . . . I recommend strongly that the whole force be turned over to the conscript camp for distribution in the Army and their places be supplied by free negro or slave labor."

While the Heroes foment a rebellion within a rebellion, the war comes to North Carolina. By the end of August 1861, Hatteras Island falls. Citizens on the Outer Banks line up to swear a loyalty oath to the United States of America, forsaking the Confederacy. The governor responds by sending the 7th Regiment of North Carolina State Troops to Hyde County to forestall the "evil influence" of Unionism and stem Yankee infiltration.

Six months later, Union troops capture and occupy Roanoke Island. They establish a Freedmen's Colony that becomes a magnet for runaway and emancipated slaves, as well as a staging ground for Union spies. The settlement flourishes, with its own schools and churches. Soon it provides fertile ground for recruiting black troops to fight for the Union. All along the northern coastal plain, U.S. Army regiments press local militia troops.

In Richmond, Davis will not assign enough troops to hold the crucial seaports. By spring of 1862, Union forces seize New Bern, Beaufort, Morehead City, Havelock Station, and Carolina. Former slaves, acting as pilots, guide Union forces in a daring amphibious attack against Fort Macon, and the besieged rebel stronghold is taken. By the end of the year, U.S. troops win a fierce battle at Kinston.

Indeed, of the nine significant battles fought on North Carolina soil during the first two years, seven are Union victories and the other two are draws. The Federals have come, and they do not intend to leave.

As the war becomes ever more calamitous to the state, the Peace Movement gains momentum, championed by William Woods Holden, editor of the *North Carolina Standard* at Raleigh and once a staunch champion of Vance. Holden is a balding, earnest man of iron convictions who tends to speak his mind in plain terms. He himself is not a Hero of America, but they support him. He makes no secret of his plan: to negotiate a separate peace with the government in Washington before the state is totally devastated.

In July 1863 comes the news that breaks the back of Confederate loyalty in North Carolina: Gettysburg. The shock is not just that the great battle was lost, but the staggering casualty figures. Of the nearly 28,000 killed and wounded on the Confederate side, one in four is from North Carolina. Many die on the last day of battle in a valorous, suicidal charge against Cemetery Ridge.

In the following months, Holden mounts an all-out attack on Vance's government in Raleigh, preparing to challenge him for the governorship in 1864 on his peace platform.

Brig. Gen. Robert F. Hoke, a North Carolina native, is released from the Virginia front to push the Union forces out of Plymouth and to tamp down growing Unionist activity on the northeastern coast. So-called Buffaloes—working-class Unionists without the Quaker disdain for violence—have been doing the work of the Heroes, and the state is fracturing.

On July 2, 1864, in the run-up to the August election, one of Vance's supporters reveals startling news calculated to discredit Holden: a secret order calling itself the Heroes of America has been subverting both Vance and the Confederacy all along. More revelations follow. Duncan K. MacRae, coeditor of the *Daily Confederate*, infiltrates the organization and exposes one of its members, Rev. Orrin Churchill. Churchill then publicly confesses. Other coerced confessions and "outings" of H.O.A. militia officers and justices of the peace follow in the *Daily Conservative*, the *Fayetteville Observer*, and the Salisbury *Carolina Watchman*. In one blow, the Heroes are paralyzed.

A young sailor named Richard J. Bacot, stationed at Kinston aboard the css *Neuse*, writes his sister on July 18, 1864: "Every one expects a lively time about here, when the elections come off in August. A secret, treasonable league has been discovered by the state called the H.O.A.'s — (Heroes of America) they are all in league with the enemy & are all Holdenites. Since the disclosures, made by some members who became disgusted with the society, the remainder have kept remarkably quiet. I wish President Davis would have Holden & his entire *clan* taken up and hung; that would stop such radicals quicker than any *conciliatory* measures."

On August 22, incensed that Vance did not crush the Peace Movement and imprison Holden, Davis writes to Vance in a fastidious cursive hand that barely conceals his fury:

> *Dear Sir,*
>
> *I send you here with a sheet of the New York Herald which has been brought to my attention containing allusions to a recent article of the Raleigh Standard.*
>
> *It is apparent what encouragement such publications afford to the enemy, how they tend to cause our situation to be misunderstood to our prejudice abroad, and how they are calculated to mislead a portion of our own people.*
>
> *As you have been specially named as approving this publication of the Standard, I have thought it proper to bring the matter to your notice that you may take such action in regard to it as your judgment may suggest.*

On September 9, Davis gets his wish. Georgia troops disembarking at the railroad station march on the office of the *Standard* and wreck it. But their vandalism only incites retaliation. The following morning, a mob of citizens destroys the office of the rival *State Journal*, a stalwart Confederate newspaper. One citizen reports, "The city is quiet but fire smoulders underneath the exterior. An immense majority of the population are more anxious to fight for Holden than for the Southern Confederacy."

Holden spends the remaining days of the campaign season hunkered down with friends, sleeping in a succession of different homes, guarded by trusted men bearing loaded pistols. With the Heroes set back on their heels, Holden silenced under fear of arrest or assassination, and peace rallies shuttered by troops, Vance wins a crushing victory. But all too soon, Vance will be the one seeking a separate peace.

The Heroes of America Rise for the Union

FIRST DO NO HARM

The Apprenticeship of a Surgeon

To many North Carolinians, the war brings danger and death, hardship and want. To a fortunate few, it brings the opportunity of a lifetime.

Thomas Fanning Wood has aspired to be a doctor from his earliest boyhood in Wilmington. By the time he is a teenager attending the Odd Fellows School, run by Levin Meginney, he has acquired such a taste for scientific reading and experimentation that his teacher gives him his own set of chemistry apparatus. His heart is set on enrolling at the University of North Carolina to study medicine. But his father, a brickmason and builder, won't hear of it; he says the young men at Chapel Hill learn nothing more than how to "dress like gentlemen and act like rowdies." He wants Thomas and his brothers to become engineers and work alongside him.

In any case, the family can't afford the modest tuition. Thomas Wood's father and uncle came to Wilmington together from Nantucket after the whaling industry crashed in order to build a church, the soaring St. James Episcopal. They worked under Thomas U. Walter, the architect renowned for designing the new U.S. Capitol dome in Washington, D.C., which—at the time North Carolina secedes—has been under construction for more than four years. Flush with the success of the church project, the brothers start their own building firm. Among their commissions are the new city hall and the railroad line connecting Wilmington with Charleston, South Carolina. But by 1859, their firm is foundering, and they contract their services to U.S. Army captain William H. C. Whiting, who is building a lighthouse near Beaufort, South Carolina.

They stay at the plantation of a cousin, Thomas A. Coffin. Wood roams the Low Country, learning to identify plants and trees as an amateur botanist. His father contracts virulent dysentery. In that remote country, with no doctor on hand, Wood consults *Dunglison's Medical Dictionary* and concocts a treatment of Dover's Powder, which contains opium for pain and ipecac to make his father sweat out the fever. Based on his reading, Wood doses his father with five grams every three hours. The fever breaks, the pain subsides, and within days his father enjoys a full recovery. It is Wood's first medical success.

In 1861, his father and uncle join Captain Whiting, now a Confederate officer, in constructing a massive sand fort at the mouth of the Cape Fear River. Medical school is still out of the question, but after a stint as a rural schoolteacher, his friend and mentor, Dr. James McRee, secures Thomas a position at a pharmacy owned by Louis B. Erambert. Wood borrows medical textbooks from Dr. McRee and studies during every spare hour.

War is imminent. But Wood witnesses his first bloodshed right inside the pharmacy. A group of drunken University of North Carolina rowdies invades the pharmacy one evening. Two of them begin fighting. Erambert draws a pistol and orders them to leave the store. One of the young men jerks a pistol and shoots, and Erambert fires back. When the gunfight is over, one boy is badly wounded and Erambert himself lies with a gunshot in his shattered thigh. For the next six months, Wood runs the pharmacy on his own and teaches himself the art and science of mixing and dispensing drugs.

The war breaks over North Carolina like a fact of weather, a charging of the atmosphere like the ozone chill breezing across a meadow in advance of a thunderstorm. Wood's father is an avowed Unionist. Wood himself is proudly secessionist. Loyalties are being counted. Churches play a role in determining politics. St. James, whose pastor is from the North, remains conservatively pro-Union. The Methodist church, which Wood attends, is outspoken in its support for secession. Wood volunteers as secretary of the Committee of Safety, an organization modeled on such committees in the Revolutionary War.

Soon military companies begin to form. After secession, Governor Ellis orders the formation of ten regiments of state troops. But only in September 1861, when Erambert has recovered sufficiently from his wounds, can Wood join the Wilmington Rifle Guards. Even his Unionist father now drills with a mounted cavalry unit. The Guards become part of the 18th North Carolina Regiment, detailed to garrison Fort Fisher. The duty is easy, the atmosphere more like a boys' summer camp than a wartime garrison. The young men delight in defying the orders of their officers, like errant boys playing pranks on the teacher.

Wood bunks with five other young men in a canvas tent. Each tent squad invents its own rakish nickname. Wood christens his group Les Elites. He turns out to be anything but an elite soldier: inept at field drill, indifferent

The Apprenticeship of a Surgeon

to military protocol, even a hopeless cook. When his unit is mobilized north to Virginia, he finds himself marching for grueling miles on muddy, rutted roads toward battle at Hanover Court House, thirsty and exhausted from hauling a heavy, custom-made, patent-leather pack. "It was only suited for holiday soldiering," he recalls, "but I was too proud of the appearance it made to give it up for the poor rag of a thing the men had."

In it he carries two fine white blankets, his mother's parting gift. "As we were running into battle, my knapsack got too heavy—I was very thirsty—and confident that we would return by the same road when the fight was over, I threw my precious knapsack into a tangle of smilax vines and went on, now and then stopping to scoop up water from the cart-ruts which were running with muddy water."

Soon enough he is distracted from his thirst by the distant concussion of guns. "Just as we neared the battlefield, I saw the first wounded man I had ever seen in battle. . . . He had been shot in the bowels, and was a pale and horrible sight." He advances through a field strewn with dead and wounded horses and is ordered to lie down. The enemy encompasses them, and the din of battle seems to move around them in waves just beyond his sight. At nightfall, Wood and his company are ordered to retreat, by a different route. His knapsack and blankets are lost. But along the way he picks up a discarded Enfield rifle and casts away his old-fashioned percussion musket.

The dirty rut-water turns out to be more dangerous than the enemy. Soon Wood is stricken with fever and out of commission for weeks. When he recovers, he is ordered to report with other convalescents to the North Carolina hospital in Richmond, a converted tobacco warehouse near the James River named the Moore Hospital, after the Confederate surgeon general, S. P. Moore. The Confederate Medical Department has determined that men will recover more quickly and with better morale among comrades from their own states, so each state has its own facility. Moore is comparatively small, with just 120 beds.

Moore Hospital is just down the hill from the Chimborazo Hospital, a forty-acre complex with more than seventy-five wards and beds for 3,000 wounded and sick men. Seventy-six thousand patients pass through Chimborazo alone, and one in five dies there—the common rate. The largest hospital in the Confederacy is Winder Hospital, with six regular wards and a tent ward, 5,000 beds in all. By 1863, North Carolinians fill three of the wards, and by 1864, they fill five wards—3,500 of the beds.

In addition to Moore, Chimborazo, and Winder, there are twenty-five more large, official hospitals in Richmond, as well as two dozen private homes or boardinghouses converted to small hospitals. There are separate hospitals designated for prisoners of war, smallpox cases, and the insane. Yellow fever hospitals fly a yellow flag.

Even the many hospitals in Richmond are not enough. During the course of the four-year struggle, more than 75,000 Confederate soldiers are wounded on battlefields within a ninety-mile radius of the city. Thousands more arrive by train from more distant fields of carnage: Shiloh, Sharpsburg, Gettysburg. In nearly every railroad depot town throughout the South, boardinghouses and churches are turned into hospitals.

Both sides start the war confident that it will not last long. There is little planning for the treatment of the wounded, let alone the wounded by the tens of thousands. The Confederacy fields fewer than 8,000 doctors. Every regiment of 1,000 men has just two ambulances, spring wagons with no cots or bedding. The Union at least begins the war with a medical department, and the Confederacy scrambles to match it but always lacks essential medicines, supplies, mules for the ambulances, and surgical equipment.

It is common for the wounded to lie on the field untended for hours after a battle. Sometimes, as at the Wilderness and Cold Harbor, they lie all night in agony, calling out to their comrades for relief. On other battlefields, the soldiers are too exhausted to tend the wounded and sleep on their arms wherever the tide of battle has carried them. Sometimes the wounded remain under the fire of the enemy and cannot be safely removed without a truce.

Once the field is safe enough, regimental musicians, medical orderlies, and slaves attached to the army carry off the wounded on stretchers. They place them on two- and four-wheeled ambulances, rough conveyances that may be merely farm wagons pressed into service. Assistant surgeons rove the battlefield, treating some men on the spot, directing that others be carried to field hospitals. There, stewards divide the wounded into three categories: those who are going to die no matter what treatment they receive, those who will not die immediately without treatment, and those whom immediate treatment can save.

Most wounds of the stomach, chest, and bowels are untreatable. Wounds to the limbs often require amputation. The operating theater is a living room, a front porch, a barn, a shed. Surgeons operate on a kitchen table, the tailgate of a wagon, a door set across two barrels. Incredibly, if a man undergoes amputation within twenty-four hours of wounding, his chance for survival is almost 75 percent.

After initial treatment, the soldier travels by wagon or rail to a regular hospital for extended care and convalescence—to hospitals like Moore, Chimborazo, and Winder. The hospitals are laid out in pavilion-style wards, full of air and light, with beds placed in orderly rows, as in a barracks. A label pinned to the wall at the head of the bed identifies the patient and indicates his malady and prescribed treatment.

Wood is fortunate to have been assigned to Moore, run by Dr. Otis Frederick Manson, a handsome dandy of a man with jet-black hair and moustache who has an eye for talent. "When I reported at the hospital I expected to be examined and returned to my regiment," Wood writes. "Dr. Manson found out I was a medical student . . . and he put me to work." He also shares his considerable library with Wood, who douses himself with cold water to stay awake at night while studying reference works on pathology, fevers, fractures, and wounds.

Wood is named wardmaster of the second floor, in charge of fifty patients, most of whom are suffering from typhoid and malaria, with five nurses to assist. The nurses have had no formal training. They are volunteers who learn on the job. The women from poor and working-class backgrounds prove more useful, as a rule, than their more genteel sisters; their sensibilities are not so delicate.

One anonymous nurse writes, in a poem called "Hospital Duties,"

Fold away your bright-tinted dresses,
Turn the key on your jewels today,
And the wealth of your tendril-like tresses
Braid back in a serious way;
No more delicate gloves, no more laces,
No more trifling in boudoir or bower,
But come with your souls in your faces
To meet the stern wants of the hour.

Wood sleeps on a cot in the dispensary, separated by a partition from the ward. During the days, he attends lectures at the newly opened Medical College of Virginia. Before the war, a medical student would have been required to attend all the lectures twice, but not in wartime. It's a nine-month course, but Wood has time to complete only six.

Wood keeps his ward scrubbed and clean, and when Governor Vance visits, spitting tobacco on the floor, a black orderly is detailed to follow along behind him and mop up the spittle. Vance is treated like visiting royalty, for it is he who has made sure the hospital for North Carolina soldiers is the best equipped and supplied in Richmond—so well equipped, in fact, that the

Confederate surgeon general orders Manson to share his largesse with other hospitals. Outraged, Manson at first refuses to comply.

Wood, meantime, keeps meticulous records of the patients in his ward, noting similarities between typhus and typhoid, tracking the effects of quinine dosage on malaria, identifying a new virulent strain of measles that he calls Army Rubella—using his ward as a classroom and a laboratory.

Medical practitioners commonly accept that disease is caused by a miasma in the air, detectable by bad smells. But Wood, like many army doctors, understands early that cleanliness, proper sanitation, and good personal hygiene promote health. They don't know *why* this is so, but they respect empirical data and value results. Their remedies include a few that are helpful: for pain, laudanum, a mixture of opium and alcohol, and paregoric, or tincture of opium. They prescribe quinine, a South American import made from cinchona tree bark, the only reliable proof against malaria—so rare in the South as the war enters its second year that women spies smuggle it across the Mason-Dixon Line in hollowed-out dolls. Their pharmacy also includes many "medicines" that are useless, even harmful: most notoriously, calomel, a mercury-based substance used for purging the system, which is in fact a virulent poison.

For anesthesia, surgeons have ether, which is highly combustible and dangerous near flames and gunfire, and chloroform, which is not, and therefore is preferred. The Confederate army rarely has enough of either one.

Young men who have never ventured beyond their farming settlements are suddenly crowded into camps full of thousands of strangers, where contagion is easy; a single case of smallpox or measles becomes, overnight, an epidemic. Exposure and fatigue bring on pneumonia. The price of malnutrition is scurvy: open sores, collapsing joints, and teeth that loosen and fall out.

In the camps, sanitation is primitive and hygiene lax, ideal breeding grounds for dysentery. Lice carry typhus, which strikes almost every soldier before the end of the war. Contaminated drinking water spreads typhoid fever, which has a mortality rate of 60 percent and takes three agonizing weeks to kill a man. Of the slovenly habits of his own soldiers, General Lee comments with bitter sarcasm, "They are worse than children, for children can be forced to clean."

In the coastal Low Country and swamps, mosquitoes, "galli-nippers," become a foe more fearsome than the Yankees: they carry malaria and, worse, yellow fever. Known as the Scourge of the South and the Black Vomit, yellow fever kills half of those it infects. Soldiers who survived it in childhood are immune.

Of 750,000 or so who die in the war, some 500,000 are the victims of disease, and on their charts is noted simply, "D.O.D." — Died of Disease. Altogether some 10 million cases are recorded; many soldiers suffer multiple bouts of illness.

During the excruciatingly long course of the war, as many as 3 million men serve. A soldier's chance of dying in service is one in four. Nearly half a million suffer wounding, many more than once. There is no accurate accounting of the maimed, men who are missing limbs, hands, eyes, jaws.

As the war opens, Wood is just as experienced with gunshot wounds and other traumas as most veteran surgeons, which is to say, almost none of them have treated such wounds before.

But even country doctors know how to perform an amputation. Most carry a boxed surgical kit that hasn't changed since the American Revolution, when surgeons perfected the art of removing an arm or a leg in as little as ten minutes. The kit includes a screw tourniquet made of a canvas belt and an iron tightening screw; one long, straight bullet probe with a ceramic tip and another fashioned into pincers; a trepanning saw for boring a hole in the skull to remove pressure on the brain; sutures made of readily available horsehair, which is boiled to make it pliable and is often the cleanest item in the kit; a wooden or leather bite-strap for the patient's mouth; a multibladed fleem for bleeding off the bad humors; lances and scalpels; an anesthesia funnel; several amputation knives curved to fit around the muscle tissue of various limbs; and a rubber-handled capital or bone saw for completing the operation.

Wood sits before the examining board in February 1863 and then waits days to learn he has at last achieved the rank of assistant surgeon. He writes, "I was now 22 years old, rather an unripe specimen of a doctor, with but a young moustache, and not much external evidence of wisdom and skill, but my appointment was a great source of internal satisfaction."

To his chagrin, he is not ordered to return to duty at Moore but is sent into the field in snowy midwinter to join the 3rd North Carolina Regiment, marching toward a country crossroads in Virginia called Chancellorsville. Now officially Dr. Wood, he wears the distinctive gray uniform of a medical officer: collar and cuffs faced with black, black stripes down each trouser leg. Embroidered on his cap in gold are the letters M.S. flanked by the olive branches of peace. Each sleeve carries a double row of gold braid, and three gold bars adorn the collar.

He's a slightly built young man with swept-back dark hair, clean-shaven cheeks, and a cavalier's long moustache. After his brief stint in the infantry, for many months he has led an indoor life. Now his duty requires a robust vigor, physical stamina, and a hardy constitution.

Wood reports in February, tramping miles through deep snow to the medical director's tent several miles beyond Hamilton's Crossing, on the Richmond, Fredericksburg, and Potomac Railroad line, and settles into camp life. He writes his mother, "If I dared, I would look back at the comfortable old rocking chair, the blazing and cheerful hearth, and plenty of good books, far, far away. But I control such retrospective glances, and in a few hours after I got into camp I learned to look upon home and all its happy appliances as a romantic little spot, having existence only in the imagination."

In the spring, the North Carolinians move toward Fredericksburg as part of Lt. Gen. Thomas "Stonewall" Jackson's Second Corps of the Army of Northern Virginia to meet a colossal Federal army led by Maj. Gen. Joseph "Fighting Joe" Hooker pouring across the Rappahannock River. Jackson's corps of seventy regiments — 26,000 men marching four abreast, with wagon train and artillery — stretches out more than six miles.

The entire Confederate army enlists just 3,200 field surgeons, one for every 300 soldiers. Among them all, they have the use of just ten thermometers. "Surgical instruments were so scarce that it was not every Assistant Surgeon who had a pocket case," Wood writes in his memoirs, "so that having none myself, I secured a very poor one." He confiscates it from a Union surgeon captured in his field hospital at the Battle of Winchester.

Wood and the other surgeons in the 3rd North Carolina are assisted by an ambulance corps of twenty men, two from each company in the regiment. Wood recalls, "These men were selected with care, generally because of the physical strength and personal courage of the men." The ambulance corpsmen are excused from the routine duties of standing guard and conducting drill, but in battle they share much of the danger faced by fighting troops. Like the rest of the medical staff, they are far more likely to be captured when their position is overrun.

In addition, the regimental medical staff has its own cook and a designated "knapsack bearer," who carries the hospital pack in addition to his own. "Morton was my knapsack bearer," Wood writes. "He was a short, stout boy, about 23 and carried the hospital knapsack and his own with perfect ease, and was always ready to do extra duty when called upon. He was a picture of smiling good nature, under the most trying circumstances." On the campaign, Morton never strays far from Wood's side with his precious cargo of instruments, sponges, lint bandages, liniments, adhesive plaster, ligatures, and morphine. Bandages and sponges are scarce, so doctors reuse

The Apprenticeship of a Surgeon

them, sometimes after a brief rinsing, more often not. One of the ambulance men carries one canteen of water and another of whiskey.

The regimental ambulance corps has just two spring wagons, each drawn by a brace of sturdy mules, for transporting the wounded. When there is a lull in the fighting, an ambulance serves as Wood's quarters, a respite from soggy, cold ground.

In early May, one of their ambulances bears Jackson from the nighttime battlefield at Chancellorsville after he is shot accidentally by his own men and mortally wounded. The wounding of General Jackson is kept quiet, lest his men become demoralized. Jackson's guide in the ill-starred scout of the Union position, Pvt. David Kyle, recounts what happened:

> We went down that old Mountain road some four hundred yards when we came in hearing of the Federals. . . . We stayed there I should judge from two to four minutes when Gen Jackson turned his horse around and started back up the road we had come down. . . . When we were about halfway back . . . he turned his horses head toward the south and facing the front of our own line of Battle he started to leave the old Mountain road and just as his horses front feet had cleared the edge of the road while his hind feet was still on the edge of the bank there was a single shot fired. . . . In an instant it was taken up and . . . a volley as if from a regiment was fired.

The shots are fired by jumpy men of the 18th North Carolina Regiment who believe that the returning scouts are Union cavalry—a shame they will bear till the end of the war. Jackson is struck once in the right hand and twice in the left arm. The litter-bearers carry him by hand over the rough terrain under enemy fire, dropping him twice before reaching the ambulance. Surgeons take the arm, to no avail. He succumbs to pneumonia a week later, on May 10, 1863. For such a fierce, uncompromising warrior, his final words are surprisingly gentle: "Let us cross over the river and rest under the shade of the trees."

Wood's job is to follow the advance of the regiment and treat wounded men on the field. At Chancellorsville, as he is gently turning over one soldier to learn if he is dead or alive, a tremendous barrage of artillery erupts all around him. "The clear space on each side of the road was very narrow, perhaps no more than 100 yards—and all the artillery was concentrated there," he reports. "Shells and shrapnel rattled around us for awhile so that we were obliged to lie down until it was all over."

On another part of the field, a tangled forest is set ablaze by cannon fire, and Wood is sickened by the sight of the dead there, for "some of the badly wounded who could not get away were charred in the very agony of their contortions." For Wood, the aftermath of battle is a test of both nerve and faith. And he learns soon enough that he has the extraordinary stamina required of a field surgeon, who must work without pause for many hours, many days, regardless of his personal fatigue or the horrific nature of the work before him. That night he unrolls his bedding under a tree in the door-yard of a farmhouse, wounded soldiers lying all around him in the open. The next morning, Sunday, he awakens beside a corpse. But there is little time for shock or grief.

Wood has entered a violent world where ordinary human emotions must be set aside if he is to function. He is recalled to a field hospital in the rear, where the worst of the wounded have been collected, and the work is the most grisly he has yet faced. "My first case was amputation just below the shoulder joint," he recalls. "There was no escape from it and it was necessary to save the man's life."

Previously he has treated fevers, splinted broken bones, and bandaged bullet wounds and saber strikes, but never has he performed radical surgery on his own. Now, just ninety days after passing his board exam for assistant surgeon, without any supervision, he must perform his first battlefield amputation. He does not hesitate. He understands the procedure in theory and knows the awful sequence of his duty: chloroform, tourniquet, knife, saw, suture, and bandage.

The operation takes only a few minutes and seems to go fine. But he has no chance to follow up, to learn if the man survives beyond a few hours. The wounded are accumulating in staggering numbers, and soon Wood is an old hand at the bone saw. Water is running low, flies infest the wounds, men strip off their filthy shirts and socks to fashion bandages. Day after day, from sunup until long after dark, there is no respite from the stench of gangrene and the pitiful cries of the wounded. He works steadily, confident now in his own hands, filtering out all distractions, as focused as he has ever been in his life.

One minor piece of good news reaches him: after a spirited charge against an improvised earthworks at the Chancellor House, the regiment captured a large supply of medicine, including blessed chloroform and ether, bearing the brand of E. R. Squibb, Brooklyn, New York.

After a week of fierce fighting and shocking casualties, the commanders call a truce between the armies to exchange the wounded. At a crossing called United States Ford, Hooker's engineers expertly lay down a pontoon

The Apprenticeship of a Surgeon

bridge—planks secured to floats. For the next three days, a parade of 200 U.S. Army ambulances crosses the river back and forth, hauling away their own wounded and bringing across their wounded enemies. In addition, the U.S. Army sends over five wagons loaded with fresh beef, 50,000 rations, blankets, and medical supplies. Twenty-six Union surgeons remain behind to help care for the wounded of both armies. For Wood, it is a spectacular show of humanity on the part of the Yankees. It is also a dispiriting reminder of wealth and plenty, the nearly endless resources to be found north of the Mason-Dixon Line.

The butchery on both sides is about equal: altogether, more than 3,000 soldiers are killed and almost 20,000 are wounded in seven days of fighting that decides nothing—except that the war will go on.

Lee determines that only a second invasion of the North will force the Federal government to accept a conditional peace. He plans to march the Army of Northern Virginia up the Shenandoah Valley and maneuver behind Washington, panic the enemy, and dare him to attack the Confederates on Union ground.

In June, the North Carolinians cross the Potomac River at Shepherdstown, and the following day they bivouac at Sharpsburg, near Antietam Creek. The previous September, it was the site of the bloodiest single day of fighting in American history—during the first invasion of the North. President Davis justified that first invasion, because "we are driven to protect our own country by transferring the seat of war to that of an enemy who pursues us with a relentless and apparently aimless hostility."

Now at the site of that great slaughter, the North Carolinians march to the mass grave of their own regimental dead from that battle—a "victory" that nearly shattered the army. They salute their fallen comrades by reversing arms: pointing sword tips and rifle muzzles to the ground in the time-honored military expression of grief. The regimental chaplain, the Reverend George Patterson, consecrates the ground with a Christian burial service, and a color guard fires a salute over the grave.

For now, the roads are flat and make for easy marching, the weather is fine, and food is abundant. The troops marvel at the neatness of the Pennsylvania farms, the lush plenty of the countryside. "Every field here is groaning under the burden of immense crops, which we are in hopes to eat," Wood notes. Lee has issued strict orders that there is to be no looting, so the obliging North Carolinians pay for all the food and horses they take—in Confederate dollars.

For days on end, they march deeper into the heart of enemy country, but no enemy appears. Then the various columns of Lee's army converge on a picturesque country crossroads called Gettysburg, fringed to the south by hills: Seminary Ridge, Cemetery Ridge, Culp's Hill, Little Round Top. There they stumble into a battle that lasts for three days and nearly consumes the army.

The 3rd North Carolina arrives on the field after the first day's fighting has resulted in a stunning and almost accidental Confederate victory. For the next two days, they fight tenaciously but cannot dislodge the stubborn Federal regiments. On the third day, they attempt a final assault on Culp's Hill, trying to break the Union line on the right while Pickett's, Pettigrew's, and Trimble's forces attack the center. But the attacks are not coordinated. Pickett's troops step off late, and the North Carolinians are hit from all sides in a murderous crossfire.

More than 500 men charge into battle, and more than 200 fall killed or wounded. Only three officers are left standing. At a field dressing station set up in a farmhouse northeast of Culp's Hill, Wood and his small staff labor to exhaustion and beyond. And even then there is no rest: they fall back, first to a divisional hospital, then toward safety across the Potomac.

Wood writes, "The retreat from Gettysburg was begun in the rain which continued without cessation for some days. Every empty wagon was loaded with wounded men, and the roads leading toward the Potomac were full of troops, stragglers, slightly wounded men, making their way as best they could. But there was no panic." It is a fighting retreat, with skirmishes at every creek crossing until they reach the Potomac River.

Wood soldiers on through the bloody nightmares of the Wilderness Campaign and Cold Harbor and the long fight up the Shenandoah Valley toward Washington, D.C., in 1864. At last he finds himself, in April 1865, at Appomattox Court House with about thirty surviving members of his regiment. North Carolina troops fire the last volley of the Army of Northern Virginia before surrender. Wood signs his parole and begins walking home through 200 miles of ruined country. Along the way, he lingers to tend wounded and sick men.

When at last he reaches Wilmington, he finds that the great church his father and uncle built, St. James, has been taken over for a military hospital — for Union soldiers, many of them recently liberated from Salisbury and Andersonville prisons. The nearby Burgwin-Wright house at Third and Market Streets becomes a staging area. The house was built into the side of a hill in 1770 by John Burgwin, a wealthy planter and merchant, then used for

The Apprenticeship of a Surgeon

headquarters by British general Lord Charles Cornwallis in the days leading up to his final defeat at Yorktown.

In the basement, under the supervision of Union surgeon Dr. Henry Shaw, orderlies prep sick and wounded soldiers for surgery at the church. They lie in rows on the floor, their blood staining the wide heart-pine boards, remnants of the original New Hanover County jail, on the ashes of which Burgwin constructed his residence. No one records the irony that liberated prisoners once again languish helpless in jail.

Locally, the little Burgwin-Wright Hospital becomes known as the clearinghouse to the national cemetery, only a few blocks east on Market Street.

Years after he has settled into his peacetime medical practice in Wilmington, Dr. Wood strikes up a conversation with an old one-armed oyster monger named Everett who regularly peddles his wares in the alley behind Wood's house at Second and Chestnut. Wood inquires of him with professional curiosity, "Who amputated your arm?" Everett replies, "I think you ought to know, you done it yourself."

He was Wood's first amputation case at Chancellorsville, a hardy survivor and living testament to the skill of a "rather unripe specimen of a doctor."

10

THE BATTLE OF THE BANDS

As war fever spreads across North Carolina in 1861, a twenty-seven-year-old accountant named Julius A. Leinbach mulls his options. He's slightly built, stands 5 feet 5 inches tall, with brown hair, brown-gray eyes, and a fair complexion. He's a native of the Moravian community of Salem, where antiwar sentiment runs high.

Leinbach is already in the habit of confiding his thoughts to a pocket leather diary the size of a deck of playing cards, which tucks closed with a flap. In a miniature hand of elegant cursive script, the i's dotted with devil's teardrops, Leinbach writes, "Volunteers for both armies were being called for, and drafts were being made, and the indications seemed to be that all able bodied young men would sooner or later be compelled to enter military service."

A musician, Leinbach performs with his brother Edward in Salem's brass band, talented players trained from a rich heritage. The ensemble began a century ago as a quartet of trombones that played sacred music. By now, it has expanded to a mixed wind and brass ensemble, touring the state to receptive audiences.

Julius Leinbach finds an answer to his predicament. "I was not wanting to shirk any duty that called me; at the same time, I was not anxious to become a target for bullets fired by any one. I was open for some other engagement and therefore when an offer came to me to become a member of a band that was being organized in Salem, N.C. to go into service with some No. Ca. regiment, I accepted, resigned the situation I held as book keeper of Haw River Mills, in Alamance Co., came home, and became one of the 'Band boys.'"

The Band boys are attached to the 26th North Carolina Regiment, the largest in the Confederate army, commanded by Col. Zebulon B. Vance. With his fellow musicians, Leinbach departs Salem on March 5, 1862, for Camp Branch, at New Bern. Along with their heavy instruments, they haul with them a mess chest packed with cooking utensils, plates and forks, a coffee pot, knives, a stove, and other essentials for camp life. Leinbach boasts, "We had uniform suits of Frie's best Cadet jeans, with brass buttons, of which we were very proud."

The Band boys reach camp after two days of travel, bed down outside the guard lines to have freedom of movement after dark, and wake to a light dusting of snow. They are issued tents and buy capes to complete their handsome uniforms. As if to emphasize his privileged status in the regiment, each band member wears a custom gray uniform with double black chevrons on the lower sleeves of the coat, topped by a kepi-style forage cap.

The original roster is thin, just eight players, among the smallest in either army: Abe P. Gibson, Joe O. Hall, William H. Hall, Alex C. Meinung, August L. "Gus" Hauser, Dan T. Crouse, Leinbach, and Sam Mickey, who leads the band and arranged for its inclusion in the 26th. Later they are joined by Julius Transou, Charles Transou, Ed Peterson, Henry Siddall, James M. Fisher, Bill Lemly, Edward A. Briedz, and Gus Reich. Reich, who performs under the stage moniker Guss Rich, is known as "The Wizzard of the Blue Ridge" because he performs magic tricks in camp and during concerts.

Their instruments include a variety of B-flat and E-flat cornets, trombones, horns, and tubas, in tenor, baritone, and bass. Leinbach, the most diminutive man in the outfit, draws the bass saxhorn, a so-called Dodworth back'ard blaster, with a large bell facing over the shoulder for the benefit of marching troops. It travels in a long black box. In camp, he is hazed by one of the hospital orderlies, who inquires, with macabre wit, "if I had brought my coffin with me."

In a photo taken on furlough in the summer of 1862, the Band boys stand solemn and proud, backs ramrod straight, holding their brass instruments like weapons. Leinbach is lanky, moustachioed, dwarfed by Fisher and Crouse on either side. He looks hardly able to hold up his own instrument, the largest by far in the band. "It did not take me long to figure out that the big E flat bass horn was not the instrument for me," he confides. "I did not have sufficient lung power to fill it properly, and the large mouth piece was not suited to my lips, which, being somewhat chapped, would crack open and bleed, so that after every piece we played I could pour a spoonful of bloody water from my crook."

He trades with Joe Hall, and from now on, Leinbach is happier marching with the B-flat cornet. They set aside time in the afternoons for practice and marching drill, one of the special challenges of playing in a military rather than a concert band, as Leinbach wryly notes: "One of the most difficult requirements was to 'keep step' as we marched up & down the lines

This photo, taken in 1862 while the Band boys are on furlough, shows them standing tall and proud. (Courtesy of the Moravian Music Foundation and Old Salem Museum and Gardens)

at dress parade. Our natural gaits were very dissimilar, and as our attention must necessarily be given to the music, we would sometimes forget our feet."

The Confederacy fields more than a hundred military bands, and nearly every regiment in the U.S. Amy has its own band. The bands are essential to arouse patriotic spirit during recruiting drives. In garrison and in camp, they perform concerts to liven the tedium of repetitious training, drill, and guard duty. On the march, they strike the cadence and keep the troops moving together at the right pace for a long haul. On many occasions, they actually play the troops into battle.

In camp, the 26th band plays every morning at eight o'clock for the mounting of the guards and every evening at dress parade, when the regiment musters by companies. It performs a short concert every night and plays at regimental inspection on Sunday mornings, at brigade reviews, and on other special occasions. Like musicians in other regiments, the Band boys are the first awake and the last to sleep.

Some, but not all, of the band members in a regiment are considered "field musicians." These always include drummers, fifers, and buglers. The field musicians perform several crucial functions. Reveille is an ensemble performance of drums, horns, and fifes that begins with a single drummer calling out the other musicians. The bugler relays the commander's orders to the troops through a series of calls. In the infantry, the drummer controls the movement of troops into battle formation, then plays them through the evolution of loading and firing. Thus the field musicians become an integral part of the command and control system — and therefore high-value, usually stationary targets.

When the fighting begins, the regular bandsmen either keep playing to rouse the troops to greater exertions or else they retire to the rear to assist the surgeons. After the battle, they serve as stretcher-bearers, clearing the field of the wounded, acting as medics, and later picking up shovels and burying the dead. The bands also play the dead march, escorting fallen comrades to their graves with muffled drums. And they play for executions.

The drummer of the 26th is Harrison Miller, who enlists at the age of fifteen. He lies, telling the recruiter he is nineteen. Boys as young as nine years old run away to join regiments in both armies, and many have no musical training at all prior to enlistment. An instruction book teaches them the basic strokes and beats: the tap, the flam, the ruff, the flamadiddle, the roll. The left hand is Dada and the right hand Mama.

The 26th band soon becomes a favorite of Gen. James Longstreet and of Lee himself, who declares, "I don't believe we can have an army without music."

After the Battle of New Bern — the first engagement of the 26th — ends in defeat, the band evacuates to Goldsboro and soon is rejoined by the rest of the regiment. At Camp Rest, they play their first brigade review, a grand affair with six regiments, more than 7,000 men, mustered on a single field.

Many of the soldiers have enlisted for only twelve months, for it was unthinkable that the war would last any longer. Now the enlistments are almost up. Colonel Vance, a gifted orator, addresses his own regiment, urging them to sign on for three more years. The band provides rousing musical accompaniment, and in the end, nearly all the soldiers re-up. His superiors are impressed and ask Vance to make a similar plea to the other regiments in the division. Vance knows the crucial role of the band in exciting the patriotic emotions of the soldiers, and he requests their help. Leinbach records, with characteristic candor, "Of course we felt flattered, and gladly consented to blow as much war spirit into the men as we could, however little of it we had ourselves!"

The regiment moves on to Kinston, where the band serenades the ladies of the town as they present a new flag to a fellow regiment, Col. John Sloan's 27th North Carolina, including the Guilford Greys. When Hattie Vance visits her husband at his quarters five miles from town, they stage an impromptu concert in her honor.

With much of the division moving north to Hanover Court House, the band takes over a cabin at recently vacated Camp Magruder on the outskirts of Kinston. There they have all they want to eat, including hams and molasses, and pass their most pleasant interlude of the war, an idyll in advance of a storm to come. Leinbach waxes poetic in his description of the countryside: "The wild crab apple, with its pink and white blossoms, with other flowering shrubs, made the woods seem almost like a garden, while the snow-white bloom of the Bay-tree or bastard Magnolia filled the air with a fragrance we had never known before."

The band offers a series of benefit concerts at the Methodist church. The opening night brings a packed house, and when soldiers outside can't get in, a near-riot ensues. Only when an officer assures them that there will be repeat performances do the men retire to their quarters. Three concerts net $420, equally divided among the six regimental and the one brigade hospital.

The band plays the regiment into battle at Malvern Hill with "The Marseilles." The losses in the brigade are appalling—more than 500 killed and wounded. After the battle, the bandsmen act as medics, help with the gruesome task of amputations, and work through the night to exhaustion. Leinbach walks the battlefield past dead horses and men. Many of the wounded are still lying where they fell, and the giant shells lobbed by the Federal gunboats on the James have left an astonishing scene of devastation: "In one piece of pine woods, the trees had been cut off by shells as though the ground had been cleared. It seemed miraculous that any one should have escaped annihilation."

One prized battle trophy is a Yankee brass horn, which is presented to the band. Its tone is of such a superior quality that the Band boys use it for the remainder of the war.

When Vance is elected governor, the band debuts a march in his honor composed by Leinbach's brother Edward, who plays along with the band and earns a warm notation from Julius: "He had drilled us in our first efforts to master our instruments, composed and arranged a great deal of music for us, and in every way did what he could for our comfort and welfare all through the weary and tiring years we spent in camp."

When the Band boys return to Petersburg, Virginia, Brig. Gen. James Johnston Pettigrew, the beloved brigade commander, gives them the piano sheet music for "The Rifle Regiment Quickstep," his favorite tune, so they can arrange it for brass. The band stages a hospital benefit concert at Phoenix Hall. The program is made up of fourteen pieces, including "Annie Laurie" and the polka "Carolina," finishing with a rousing medley of "Dixie" and "The Bonnie Blue Flag."

Also featured are "Guss Rich's quaint, queer, cute, and comical Magical Mystifications! Featuring Illusions and Metamorphoses, followed by comic singing!" and "concluding with mechanical fantocine figures — the whole enlivened with popular and elegant Music by the Band!"

All too soon the regiment moves north, bound for Pennsylvania. As they approach Gettysburg, a spirit of foreboding descends on the Band boys: "It was evident that there were two very large hostile armies in close proximity, and that there could, under the circumstances, be but one thing to be expected, a collision that would be terrible in its results."

The 26th North Carolina goes into action on the first day of battle and has fourteen color-bearers shot down. On the second day, the band plays to keep up morale. As it plays, British colonel Arthur James Fremantle, observing on the Confederate side, remarks, "When the cannonade was at its height, a Confederate band of music between the cemetery and ourselves, began to play polkas and waltzes, which sounded very curious, accompanied by the hissing and bursting of shells."

The following day, the remnants of the 26th North Carolina join the disastrous assault on Cemetery Ridge that will come to be known as Pickett's Charge. They reach the Union stronghold at the Angle, plant their colors, and are driven back with horrendous loss of life. Eight hundred men of the 26th go into battle on July 1, and by the evening of July 3, just sixty-four privates and three officers are left.

As the survivors of Pettigrew's brigade return from the slaughter of Cemetery Ridge, weeping bandsmen standing in the treeline greet them with a sorrowful rendition of "Nearer My God to Thee."

The beaten Confederates retreat south. Leinbach and his comrades endure the sustained bombardment of Petersburg, only to learn of Lee's surrender. Three of the Band boys succeed in escaping capture, though their instruments are confiscated or left behind. The rest march out of the city and are taken into custody by Federals. They are crowded aboard a steamer at City Point, Virginia, and taken to a prison camp in Maryland.

Leinbach and most of the others are moved to a more permanent camp soon after. "In a few days we were transferred to a larger pen, surrounded by a high board fence, at the top of which negro guards with loaded muskets marched back and forth," he writes with disgust. "Guarded by niggers!! Could anything be more humiliating?"

Conditions are squalid and unsanitary, the food is often rotten, and clean water is withheld from the prisoners despite the several nearby wells. Though the war is over, men despair and die every day.

One by one, the Band boys are freed. Julius Leinbach is the last. Finally, on June 28, 1865, he is granted his parole.

He proceeds by train to High Point, then falls in with an old friend from Winston. They are met on the road by Leinbach's brother James, who has come in a buggy to find him, bearing lunch. Julius Leinbach arrives home on July 1 to find his mother deathly ill, hanging on in hopes of seeing her son one last time. She embraces him. Three days later, on July 4, she falls into a deep sleep and slides into a peaceful death.

"And now, what of the 26th Band?" Leinbach wonders. "Where was it? The boys were here, but only two horns, Sam's and Alex's, had been saved. Should we never play together again?"

Long after the war, Julius Leinbach receives a letter from his old deputy commander, Col. John Randolph Lane, who reminds him, "We did not only have a good regiment, but we did have the very best band in all of Gen. Lee's great grand army. Gen. Lee said so on the 1st of May 1864, the night before we started out to meet Gen Grant at the Wilderness. Your band did its full whole duty."

The Band boys have accomplished one other feat, something no other band in the Confederate army has managed to do: they have brought home with them all their sheet music. It will be played again.

11

BANJOS AND BALLADS

A War of Songs

America in 1860 is enjoying a spirited musical age, and so its new war becomes a musical war. Music is played, sung, and heard everywhere: in the theater houses, in genteel parlors, on street corners, aboard riverboats, in churches and social halls, in slave cabins deep in the heart of the plantation South, on the crooked front porches of Appalachian homesteads, in lessons chanted in rustic schoolrooms, and at the fraternity sings of college chapter houses. North and South of the Mason-Dixon Line, choral groups are wildly popular. Men and women alike sing music arranged for a solo tenor or baritone melody, accompanied by a four-part harmony on the chorus.

Those who join the armies find no contradiction between the urge to sing and play songs and the urge to destroy the enemy. They are mostly amateur soldiers, trained for just a few weeks, if at all, before battle. Their average age is eighteen. They bring into the armies their civilian habits, their hobbies and pastimes, their base balls and banjos.

Above all, they carry with them their songs. Their families sing them off to war, and their own singing now unites them in their brotherhood of death.

One of every 1,500 Americans owns a piano, a prized possession in many North Carolina homes. Girls are trained to play after supper for their families and guests. Young women are also taught to sing—sentimental airs and ballads, story songs with numerous long, complicated verses punctuated by short, memorable choruses. The performances are private, meant to edify fathers, brothers, and male suitors. Musical training is thought to complete a well-bred girl's character, so long as she doesn't grow too proficient and come to crave a life on the stage.

The U.S. Census of 1860 identifies twenty-five pianoforte makers in North Carolina, more than the number of sailmakers or agricultural implement manufacturers. But in the whole state, only two men make other kinds of musical instruments and none builds guitars. Five-string banjos, adapted decades ago from the African gourd instruments, are mostly homemade, though they can be bought from a drum maker in Baltimore named William Boucher. The playing style is a syncopated clawhammer method originally learned from slaves, though a softer finger-style of pinching the strings between thumb and fingers is catching on.

Minstrel shows are the fashion on big city stages and travel with the riverboats into the hinterlands of the Midwest and South. The genre debuted in New York City in 1843, when the Virginia Minstrels promised their patrons a lively experience of "Ethiopian" entertainment showcasing the "oddities, peculiarities, eccentricities, and comicalities of that Sable Genus of Humanity."

The three-act productions are written mostly by white Northerners who have never set foot on a plantation. They feature jokes and slapstick routines, satirical speeches and ridiculous repartee, all spoken by stock characters in a thick dialect for comic effect, interspersed with plenty of musical numbers intended to mimic black slave ballads, spirituals, and songs of jubilation. White performers with faces blackened by burnt cork portray "Negroes" as shiftless and ignorant, hapless and prone to pratfalls, always exuberantly singing and dancing, happily ensconced on a benevolent plantation. Rarely do minstrel shows employ black performers.

The reality is that black slaves participate in a rich and complex tradition of songs that set the cadence for work, encode the map toward freedom, celebrate heroic stories and bemoan tragedies, praise the deity, woo lovers, and encapsulate a homeland history largely stolen away by the Middle Passage.

Strange to say, the mocking minstrel show creates a tenuous bridge between black and white musical cultures. Words from the West African–inspired Gullah language — a creole spoken by slaves from south of the Cape Fear River through the sea islands of South Carolina, Georgia, and Florida — percolate into the lyrics of white composers: goober peas (peanuts), cooters (mud turtles), bile (for boil), and gumbo.

The exaggerated dialect of the minstrel show is a fanciful distortion of a creole language that evolved in West Africa and was carried to the states. It allows enslaved blacks from a wide range of linguistic traditions to communicate with a shared grammar and lexicon. In mocking it as simply fractured English, the white performers display their ignorance of its true role in uniting the enslaved with a common language.

Even as war breaks over the nation, three white "songcatchers" are collecting melodies and lyrics among the Gullah: William Francis Allen, Charles Pickard Ware, and Lucy McKim Garrison. They will publish more than 130 of the songs they discover, noting "the rich vein of music that existed in these people."

"Michael, Row the Boat Ashore" and "Go Down, Moses" contain instructions to break the bonds of slavery disguised as biblical admonitions. "Let my people go" is directed at overseers much more local than Pharaoh, and "The Promised Land" lies just north of the Mason-Dixon Line.

As North Carolina troops mobilize for war, congregating in camps outside Raleigh, Goldsboro, Fayetteville, Wilmington, and a score of other mustering points, they entertain themselves by putting on minstrel shows — sometimes in camp clearings, other times on elaborately constructed stages. Their popularity never flags. Even in the grievous aftermath of battle, men gather in the pale of campfires to watch the silly antics of their blackfaced comrades and laugh along with the shopworn slapstick routines.

One popular minstrel ballad written for New York theatergoers, "Dixie" or "Dixie's Land," is penned over a weekend by Daniel Decatur Emmett, a banjo player, to be performed in blackface by Bryant's Minstrels. Emmett is a well-known songwriter of American favorites such as "Turkey in the Straw," "Old Dan Tucker," and "Blue Tail Fly." But his new tune is already familiar to some black slaves in the South, and as a child Emmett may well have heard a version of the song sung by Ben and Lew Snowden, two African American brothers born to slave parents in Maryland who emigrated to Emmett's hometown of Mount Vernon, Ohio.

Almost overnight, "Dixie" becomes by popular acclaim the anthem of the Confederacy, more ubiquitous even than "Bonnie Blue Flag," with its roll call of Confederate states. Emmett's song has six stanzas, but only one becomes well known in the South:

> I wish I was in de land ob cotton,
> Old times dar am not forgotten,
> Look away! Look away! Look away! Dixie land.
> In Dixie land whar I was born in
> Early on one frosty mornin'
> Look away! Look away! Look away! Dixie land.

The song's success is no doubt due to the rousing, infectious spirit of the chorus:

> Den I wish I was in Dixie, Hooray! Hooray!
> In Dixie Land I'll take my stand,
> To lib and die in Dixie!

When a Union officer just back from the front encounters Emmett in a Manhattan bar, he tells him that every night, across the distance separating the armies, he could hear Confederate bands playing "Dixie." Is Emmett aware that the song has become the battle hymn of the South? Emmett tells him, hardly disguising his anger, "Yes, and if I had known to what use they were going to put my song, I will be damned if I had written it!"

Up in Pittsburgh, Stephen Foster has written another universally popular, sentimental valentine to plantation life, "Old Folks at Home":

> Way down upon de Swanee Ribber,
> Far, far away,
> Dere's wha my heart is turning ebber,
> Dere's wha de old folks stay.

Foster has never laid eyes on the Suwannee River. He picked the name out of an almanac after rejecting "Yazoo" and "Pee Dee" as not sonorous enough.

In North Carolina, mountain boys pick up old hand-me-down fiddles or make their own, slipping the dried, cut tail from a timber rattlesnake inside the soundbox to dehumidify the precious wood during the warm, rainy months. Poor farmboys make cigar-box banjos or play the "bones," a percussion instrument common in minstrel shows carved from the shinbones of oxen or of a hardwood such as ash or maple.

Some lucky few men can afford a store-bought guitar, portable enough to carry into the army. A rosewood parlor guitar made by C. F. Martin & Co., neck bound in elephant ivory and with a pretty abalone rosette encompassing the soundhole, can be ordered from the factory in Nazareth, Pennsylvania, at a cost of $45, nine weeks' salary for a factory hand or three months' profit for a small farmer.

All brass band instruments are manufactured in the North, so captured band instruments become prized battle trophies for Confederate regiments.

In the plantation slave cabins on "the line," musical instruments abound: African drums with animal-skin heads, fretless banjars made from gourds and strung with waxed horsehair or twine, violins made from scrap pine, one-string African fiddles, flutes, and all manner of percussion idiophones fashioned from bone, wood, and scrap metal. The songs mingle Christian hymns with rhythms from the West Indies and Africa in a wide variety of dialects. Sometimes the only instrument is the voice, chanting words and melodies that fall strange on the ears of white listeners, an ecstatic group clamor that goes on for hours and is called only "the shout."

These men, too, carry their instruments and their songs into the army—the Union army, after they bolt for freedom or are liberated by advancing Yankee troops—and it becomes an item of curiosity among their white officers that they sing almost constantly. Moreover, their style of singing is new to their officers' ears. As the team of songcatchers notes, "There is no singing in *parts*, as we understand it, and yet no two appear to be singing the same thing—the leading singer starts the words of each verse, often improvising, and the others, who 'base' him, as it is called, strike in with the refrain, or even join in the solo, when the words are familiar."

Improvisation is rampant in both armies, among all classes of men. If they don't know the verses, they make them up as they march. They substitute lyrics for the other army's tune. They turn a straight song satirical, so John Brown's body mouldering in the grave turns into Jeff Davis hanging from a sour-apple tree.

Only a handful of music publishers exists in the South—in Richmond, Charleston, and New Orleans. When war comes, Southern music publishers reap a bonanza. The Confederate government no longer recognizes United States copyright, so they pirate whole catalogs of popular songs and sheet music, selling them under their own trademarks. Sheet music for the piano becomes ubiquitous throughout the Confederacy—love songs, ballads, and classical numbers, written for amateur piano players with arrangements for two, four, or even six hands.

Songwriters churn out new material as fast as they can rhyme new words to traditional melodies—not just professional songwriters like Emmett and Foster, but lawyers, housewives, clerks, and of course, soldiers. The tunes are often complicated and recursive, the lyrics spooling into epic stanza counts and a rousing chorus calling on honor, God's protection, victory, and freedom.

Early in the war, the songs are full of martial boasting, heroic sentiments, and braggadocio. "Maryland, My Maryland" is adapted from a broadside by James Ryder Randall, written after secessionist radicals attack a Union regiment crossing Baltimore between trains. The mayhem leaves four Massachusetts soldiers and twelve civilians dead. Though Maryland never joins the Confederacy, the song becomes a favorite even in North Carolina regimental camps, because of its bloody call to vengeance:

Avenge the patriotic gore
That flecked the streets of Baltimore

And be the battle queen of yore
Maryland! My Maryland!

The soldiers already know the tune, taken from the familiar German Christmas carol "O Tannenbaum." Gen. J. E. B. Stuart, Lee's flamboyant cavalry commander, enjoys the song so much that he names one of his favorite horses My Maryland. He travels with his own banjo player and a mixed-race servant who sings and plays the bones.

The hymns and ballads sung by the marching ranks goad the men on to greater exertion, instilling a sense of heroic purpose into their endless marching. Walter Clark, whose unit is ordered from Virginia to Garysburg, in his home state of North Carolina, reports on the effect the music has on the footsore marching column: "Our men almost began to believe the rumor that we were being carried to North Carolina to hunt up deserters. Unpleasant as such duty would have been, there was rejoicing at the thought of being nearer home, and with a pathos that cannot be described, the men sang Gaston's glorious hymn:

Carolina, Carolina, Heaven's blessings attend her,
While we live we will cherish, protect and defend her."

William Gaston's chorus to "The Old North State" is typical of the ebullient spirit of such marching songs:

Hurrah! Hurrah! The Old North State forever!
Hurrah! Hurrah! The good Old North State!

Every battle, it seems, provides material for the hawkers of sheet music. "The Battle of Roanoke Island: Story of an Eyewitness" features bugle calls and stirring anthem chords, finishing with a death march in C minor. Manassas, Port Royal, Sharpsburg, and New Orleans all inspire ballads. There are marches dedicated to artillery units, quicksteps for the infantry, rousing charges for the cavalry. Even the signal corps is memorialized in song.

"The Star Spangled Banner" has long been the unofficial national anthem of the United States. Southerners now reject its lyrics but will not relinquish the melody. In March 1861, George Tucker renames it "The Cross of the South" and endows the anthem with Confederate words that finish in a patriotic crescendo:

'Tis the CROSS OF THE SOUTH, which shall ever remain
To light us to freedom and glory again!

As the war wears on, churning out little but death and want, the songs grow sadder and commemorate particular beloved fallen comrades.

In camp, North Carolina troops relax to the plaintive lyrics of "Lorena," "Kathleen Mavourneen," and "Aura Lee." Like their Yankee counterparts, they sing "The Girl I Left Behind Me," as American soldiers have been singing it since the War of 1812.

They sing in groups, by companies, around the campfire, and in ranks. One Confederate regiment sings for three straight hours, standing in the pouring rain to allow the army's baggage train to pass. They dance to fiddle tunes and sing parodies of Yankee marching songs and sentimental favorites. "Hard tack, hard tack, come again once more," they sing with empty bellies.

The war becomes, strangely, a war of songs. Just as the regimental brass bands play off against one another across the deadly space between slumbering armies, the men of both armies fortify themselves with communal singing and can be inspired to heroism or brought to tears merely by a scrap of a beloved tune. One Confederate soldier, Carlton McCarthy, complains that he and his comrades must fight against the Yankees' more forceful songs— "John Brown's Body," "Rally Round the Flag," "The Stars and Stripes," "The Star Spangled Banner," "Hail Columbia," and "all the fury and fanaticism that skilled minds could create—opposing this grand array with the modest and homely refrain of 'Dixie,' supported by a mild solution of 'Maryland, My Maryland.'"

Not all the singing and dancing is pleasant diversion. Margaret Thornton of Four Oaks, North Carolina, never forgets the day the war arrives at her home and later records her impressions: "I wus jist five years ole when de Yankees come, jist a few of dem to our settlement. I doan know de number of de slaves, but I does 'member dat dey herded us tergether an' make us sing a heap of songs an' dance, den dey clap dere han's an' dey sez dat we is good. One black boy won't dance, he sez, so dey puts him barefoot on a hot piece of tin an' believe me he did dance."

By war's end, the music has turned wistful, even mournful. The words anticipate going home, rejoining family and friends, getting on with life. Charles Carroll Sawyer and Henry Tucker's sentimental ballad "Weeping Sad and Lonely" or "When This Cruel War Is Over" is sung plaintively in the camps of both armies, and Sawyer's lyrics weigh so heavily on morale that commanders on both sides ban it from being played or sung. Still, it sells more than a million copies in sheet music, making it the best-selling American song of all time.

Oft in dreams I see thee lying
On the battle plain.
Lonely, wounded, even dying,
Calling but in vain.

The heartbreaking chorus offers a sorrowful prayer for the living and the dead:

Weeping sad and lonely
Hopes and fears, how vain.
When this cruel war is over,
Pray that we meet again.

On April 9, 1865, with the slaughter nearly done, General Grant rides toward the McLean house at Appomattox Court House, Virginia, to the strains of a Union band playing "Auld Lang Syne." Grant himself has made it plain that he does not enjoy music and is tone deaf. "I know only two tunes," he is fond of saying. "One of them is 'Yankee Doodle,' and the other isn't." He has come to dictate terms of surrender, and there is no song in either army for that.

Gen. Robert E. Lee emerges in silence from the house. There is no brass band playing, no lusty singing by victorious troops. Grant will not allow even cheering. For now, the music has stopped.

12

THE WOMEN'S WAR

Nancy Leigh Pierson Bennitt has absolutely nothing to gain from the war.

She and her husband own no slaves. She has expressed no public political convictions. The federal government in Washington is virtually irrelevant to her life in the Piedmont of North Carolina, which is defined by hard work and a close-knit family. The compass of her life is limited. She does not travel and has no financial holdings affected by the tariff wars or lofty debates about states' rights.

Indeed, the war intrudes on her life at a moment when she and her husband, James, are finally making a decent living for themselves and their three grown children. When the war overtakes them, they have already been married thirty years. He was her second chance. She came to him a widow, already thirty—five years younger than James. During the early years of their marriage, they struggled. James labored as a tenant farmer who did not own the home they lived in. Those were lean years of borrowing and getting by, always just one dry season ahead of ruin and one bumper crop away from a more secure life.

In 1846, when he is forty years old, James purchases a 325-acre farm on the Raleigh-to-Hillsborough road, about ten miles east of Hillsborough. Once again the couple takes on debt, but this time they pay off the mortgage by reselling half their land. By the time the war overtakes them, they own the remainder of the property free and clear.

Their farm is not much: a small, unpainted wood-frame homestead with a substantial stone chimney, a separate cookhouse, a couple of outbuildings, a well, fertile acreage for gardens and cash crops, a small orchard of cherry trees, and an oak-shaded dooryard enclosed by a neat fence. Nancy keeps a tidy house. A visitor later describes it as "scrupulously neat, the floors scrubbed to milky whiteness, the bed in one room very neatly made up, and the few articles of furniture in the room arranged with neatness and taste." The furniture includes a handsome drop-leaf table, a treasured possession.

They are now yeoman farmers, part of the respectable backbone of their community. James is elected orderly sergeant in the local militia, but the weekend soldiers have not much to occupy themselves except drill and socializing.

Meanwhile, he and Nancy grow potatoes, melons, corn, and oats for horse feed. They raise chickens and hogs and keep two milk cows. Because their farm is located on the main east-west thoroughfare, it's a natural stopping place for travelers. Nancy lodges them and cooks their meals. One dollar buys a bed, breakfast, and supper. James sells them tobacco plugs and whiskey.

It's not an easy life, but they are making a go of it. Using store-bought patterns, Nancy sews trousers, vests, and coats for sale in order to augment the family income. At the general store, a coat sells for $10, but she can make a profit at $1.50. Their two sons, darkly handsome Lorenzo and bookish Alphonso, work in the fields with their father until they are grown, trudging behind an old-fashioned mule-drawn Dagon plow.

Lorenzo marries Martha Shields in 1858, and the couple have two children, a boy and a girl. He goes into partnership with his brother-in-law, Charles Shields, operating Alpha Woolen Mills on the nearby Eno River, where they oversee the work of five women and three men. In 1860, they turn out 1,200 yards of "jeans etcetera."

Nancy and James's daughter, Eliza, helps her mother until she marries Robert Duke in October 1861 and bears him a son.

Always alert to a new opportunity, James builds a wagon in which to haul their goods to market. From time to time, the wagon functions as an omnibus, carrying young scholars to the University of North Carolina at New Hope Chapel Hill, fifteen miles away. The Bennitts have not achieved prosperity, but they have built a stable life, unencumbered by debt, with a thriving family, all of whom can be counted on to help out when the seasons demand it.

When war comes to North Carolina in May 1861, their fortunes turn. Lorenzo and his partner, Robert Shields, enlist in the Hillsborough Orange Guards. Eliza's husband, Robert Duke, joins the 46th North Carolina Infantry, which will see some of the heaviest fighting of the war. Before long, all the young men are absent, and the Bennitt farming clan is reduced to an aging couple and their daughter. Nancy's life has suddenly become much harder, both physically and emotionally.

For women in North Carolina, as for women throughout the South, the war brings privation and want. But for every class of woman, it is a different war.

Women of the plantation class are buffered in several ways. First, many of their husbands stay home from the war, exempt under the terms of the Conscription Act. In addition, their properties hold storehouses of meat, flour, coffee, wine, and other foodstuffs, so it takes much longer for shortages to affect them. They still control slaves to perform any additional physical labor required for the war, including the building of defense works. When invasion is imminent, they can pack up and go to someplace safer, traveling if not in style, at least in comfort, under the protection of a trusted escort of slaves and family. But eventually the shortages reach even the moneyed class. All the textiles in the state are commandeered for uniforms, so clothing is suddenly scarce, even for the well-to-do.

Middle-class women raid their attics for discarded dresses, blankets, and baby clothes. They laboriously pull out the stitching, recut the cloth, and fashion new dresses, shirts, or uniforms. Carpets and drapes are unraveled and made into blankets and coats. And no wonder: the price of any fabric is dear. Alice Campbell, a young upper-class woman from Fayetteville, laments, "I had a calico dress for State occasions for which I paid ten dollars a yard and shoes that cost one hundred dollars a pair." By war's end, a new pair of shoes will cost as much as $500; a gentleman's overcoat, $1,500.

Further down on the social scale, the shortages hit early and hard—and only get worse.

One by one, the small amenities that make life bearable disappear into the cataclysm of the war. At the time of secession, a barrel of flour costs $8. Less than four years later, it costs $500. The price of coffee rises from 15 cents a pound to more than $100 a pound, and then it simply becomes unavailable. A writer in the *Greensborough Patriot* reports, "Where the blockade rendered coffee so scarce . . . my wife began to cast about for a substitute and we tried . . . okra seed."

Wheat and rye are also ground for coffee. Sorghum is substituted for sugar. Hats are woven from palmetto leaves, and buttons are made from persimmon seeds. Leather goods disappear into the quartermaster's stock, so an enterprising firm in Raleigh, Theim and Fraps, offers a line of wooden shoes.

Many women across the state go to work in the thirty-nine cotton and nine woolen mills, the first time in their lives most have worked outside the home. Numerous others work in "cottage" factories—private homes. Patriotic women form sewing circles and fashion cartridge boxes from layers of precious linen painted with varnish. They spin rabbit fur with wool and make socks for men at the front. They fashion "helmets" or "smoking caps"—colorfully decorated head-warmers—for soldiers to wear while sleeping outdoors.

The women are resourceful and game, but their industry is no substitute for the bounty of trade goods cut off by the U.S. Navy blockade. Blockade-runners manage to slip their cargoes into the few open ports, but corruption takes its toll. Unscrupulous traders and speculators hoard staples such as bread and cloth and charge astronomical prices. Tea and sugar now cost $10 a pound, then disappear altogether from the market, for ordinary people.

"Talk about Yankees worshipping the almighty dollar!" writes a Confederate officer describing the speculators' trade in cotton, tobacco, silks, tropical produce, and spirits at the port guarded by Fort Fisher. "You should have seen the adoration paid the Golden Calf at Wilmington during the age of blockade running."

Hardest hit of all white women are the farmwives, especially sharecroppers. Not only do they survive from season to season on their crops, with little or nothing stored up against shortages, but they also rely on their men to do the backbreaking physical labor of plowing and harvesting, digging and hauling, chopping and splitting. When the army takes their men, their lives, already precarious, teeter on the verge of starvation and ruin.

One farm woman seeks help from Governor Zebulon Vance: "I am a pore woman with a pasel of little children and i wil have to starve or go naked."

Another pleads to Vance for "mearcy" and provisions: "I have plowed & hoed and worked in the field like a negro I have . . . no relations near me that is able to help me now."

With most of her men gone from the farm, and hired men scarce, Nancy Bennitt—like women all over the South—is forced to work in the fields. At least she has her husband at her side. Other women are not so fortunate, left behind by husbands, sons, brothers, and fathers. For the first time in their lives, they must not only plow, plant, and harvest; they must also make crucial decisions about what and when to plant and how and where to bring their goods to market during a turbulent time—all the while fending off corrupt local Home Guardsmen, roving gangs of deserters, and later Yankee "bummers" who come to pillage and vandalize their property.

Often alone and isolated, in a region where loyalties are at best divided, they face the ever-present risk of being assaulted or burned out by neighbors who suspect they favor the other faction. They are also easy targets for the lawless men set adrift by the war.

Women of the plantation class have very few practical skills to fall back on. On many plantations whose masters have gone to war, the women are not able to control their slaves. Some slaves help themselves to the bounty of the plantation, the fruit of their own hard work. More and more slaves run away to Roanoke Island to join the Freedmen's Colony. At first, it is mainly the male slaves who take the dangerous chance to run away, leaving behind their wives and children, all too often to face reprisal at the hands of their masters.

Whatever the hardships facing white women, the ones faced by black women—especially those in bondage—are magnified many times over. Some whose husbands have run away to join the Union forces are punished with beatings or turned out of their homes. Increasingly, female slaves take the gamble of running to the Union lines. But all too often, they are not welcome there and are treated as whores and beggars. Too many are brutalized and raped by soldiers on both sides. If caught while escaping, they are whipped or even hanged. They know the risks. But freedom is precious, for themselves and their children, and they make the dangerous journey anyway. Once in the Union lines, many work as cooks and laundresses.

Some women, black and white, give clandestine aid to Union soldiers confined at the Salisbury Prison: food, medicine, clothing.

Some of the women of the educated class become teachers. Before the war, fewer than 7 of 100 schoolteachers in North Carolina are women. By the end of hostilities, women preside over more than half of the classrooms in the state.

Outside the plantation class, many white women initially are even more caught up in the martial fervor than their men and are called upon by President Davis to shame their male acquaintances into enlisting. But as the war goes on and the casualty lists grow, their zeal is tested, and the fighting becomes almost a natural disaster to be borne. Talk of glory fades; patriotic zeal, now tempered by long suffering, for many gives way to grim resignation.

In cities such as Raleigh and Salisbury, women openly revolt in so-called bread riots against the privations of war by raiding storehouses of supplies stockpiled by speculators.

On March 18, 1863, the Salisbury *Carolina Watchman* reports,

Salisbury has witnessed to-day one of the gayest and liveliest scenes of the age. About 12 o'clock, a rumor was afloat, that the wives of several soldiers now in the war, intended to make a dash on some flour and other necessities of life, belonging to certain gentlemen, who the ladies termed "speculators." They alleged that they were entirely out of provisions, and unable to give the enormous prices now asked, but were willing to give Government prices. Accordingly, about 2 O'clock they met, some 50 or 75 in number, with axes and hatchets, and proceeded to the depot of the North Carolina Central Road. . . . The agent remarked: "Ladies . . . it is useless to attempt it, unless you go in over my dead body." A rush was made, and they went in, and the last I saw of the agent, he was sitting on a log blowing like a March wind. They took ten barrels, and rolled them out and were setting on them, when I left, waiting for a wagon to haul them away.

The rioters in general are members of the poor and working classes, white and some black. Their lives hold nothing extra, no cushion against hard times, and these are the hardest of all times, getting harder every day.

But worse than shortages of food and clothing, worse than the sicknesses brought on by malnutrition, is the absence of the young men. Whole communities are made up mostly of women and children, with a few old men and maimed veterans to remind them of who is missing. The news from the front grows ever more dire.

None of the young men from the Bennitt clan will ever return. Lorenzo and Charles Shields die of disease and lie in Virginia graveyards. Their mill closes. Lorenzo's widow, Martha, is awarded $134.03 in back pay. Robert Duke also dies in a Confederate hospital. Alphonso succumbs to sickness in the spring of 1863.

On April 17, 1865, a beautiful, sunny day, Nancy is at home with her husband and their daughter, Eliza. She has lost two sons. They own the farm, it is true, but without the young men to help, she and her aging husband are having a more difficult time making it pay. Soon Nancy and James will have to make a bargain with sharecroppers to work the farm and sell off more acres just to survive.

She hears the hoofbeats of a party of riders approaching, the jingle of tack, the clamor of voices as they dismount in her dooryard. Someone calls a greeting to the house, and she opens the door to an officer clad in gray. Behind him, she can see a retinue of other soldiers in blue and gray uniforms, a white flag of truce. Two men stand out from the others, clearly in charge. One wears gray, the other blue. The gray-uniformed man wears a silver beard and has big sunken eyes and an angular face below a balding head. He is thin to the point of gauntness. The other visitor has a darkness around the eyes, the weariness of a soldier after long, hard service. His red hair is thinning. He moves with a compact energy.

The war has taken her sons, has taken her daughter's husband, has taken her modest prosperity, and now the generals have come to call. Johnston and Sherman. Confederate and Yankee. Joseph E. Johnston was at the outbreak of war the premier commander in the Confederacy, was exiled in disgrace, and now has been recalled to duty to play out the war's final act. William Tecumseh Sherman rides at the head of an army even his enemies compare to Caesar's legion, 60,000 battle-hardened men who have torched warehouses, destroyed railroads, burned bridges, wrecked telegraph lines, and commandeered herds of livestock and the fodder to maintain them across a broad track of Georgia and the Carolinas. Thirty thousand more troops have joined him from the coast.

They are two men who have fought across many battlefields but have never met face-to-face before this day. Now they request to use Nancy Bennitt's parlor to conclude the fate of the Confederacy. She could protest, send them away, vent her crushing grief on these two men who have been in charge of so much death.

Instead, she offers them a pitcher of cool buttermilk. Then she retires with her husband and daughter to the cookhouse. She will do what women like her have done all through the war: wait for the men to be finished.

13

ATROCITY AT SHELTON LAUREL

It all begins with salt. In Madison County, remote in the western mountains of North Carolina, hard by the rugged Tennessee border, salt has become as rare as gold. Salt is crucial to curing game, baking biscuits, and preserving food through the long winter. A sack costs almost $100.

Salt has become a staple of the Confederate war effort, hoarded by shopkeepers, guarded by troops. Governor Vance has decreed that no salt be exported from the state. Troops have been sent into the region by both Vance and the Confederate authorities in Richmond, and they refuse to allow any salt to get into the hands of "disloyal" mountaineers, including bushwhackers and deserters, but also self-declared Unionists, derisively called Tories—an echo of Revolutionary factions.

Madison County is a Unionist stronghold. Tight-knit communities like Shelton Laurel are Republican to the bone. People here defeated a ballot calling for a secession convention, 532–345. In Marshall, the county seat, a "secesh" sheriff started waving his pistol around and wounded a local boy. The boy's father hunted down the sheriff and killed him in front of his neighbors.

In the middle of a raw, snowy January 1863, a gang of Madison County Unionists, including many local deserters from the 64th North Carolina Regiment and an unknown number from Shelton Laurel, descend on Marshall, where Confederate commissioners store stockpiles of salt. The Unionists take all they can carry and then loot the town. A special target is the residence of Col. Lawrence Allen, commander of the 64th, who is off with his regiment in Bristol, Tennessee, guarding another stockpile of salt. The army relieved Allen of command for six months for falsifying the duty roster, part of a scheme that earns him kickbacks from well-heeled conscripts who want to buy their way out of service. The looters hack open his trunks and cabinets, steal anything of value, and terrorize Mrs. Allen and her three small children, two of whom are bedridden with scarlet fever.

Brig. Gen. W. G. M. Davis reports on February 2, "I think the attack on

Marshall was gotten up to obtain salt, for want of which there is great suffering in the mountains. Plunder of other property followed as a matter of course. Col. Allen's Sixty-Fourth North Carolina regiment and the men of his command are said to have been hostile to the Laurel men and they to the former for a long time — a kind of feud existing between them."

Rumors fly that a force of 500 men is forming in Shelton Laurel to fight the weakening Confederacy, by burning bridges, raiding depots and towns, and attacking loyal Confederates in their homes.

Allen learns of the depredations at Marshall and is outraged. He obtains the permission of his superior, Brig. Gen. Henry Heth, to accompany the 64th back to the Laurel Valley to put down the insurrection. The 64th is an ill-starred unit suffering an epidemic of desertion. Once numbering 300 men, it can scarcely field a third of that number now.

Allen assumes the role of supernumerary, and Lt. Col. James Keith, his cousin, takes command. Keith, the son of a Baptist minister, is a firebrand who holds the mountaineers in contempt. At thirty-five, he is one of the twenty wealthiest men in Madison County, a successful merchant and physician. He is tall, confident, and sharp-faced, with a prominent brow and high cheekbones, a mane of black hair, a black beard, a dark complexion, and keen, slatey eyes. His whole aspect inspires fear rather than trust. Marshall is his hometown, so for him the mission is also personal.

Shelton Laurel lies in the valley of Shelton Laurel Creek between mountain peaks, not far from Marshall. Brothers David and Martin Shelton settled it back in the 1790s. By the time the war comes to the valley, 137 Sheltons live there, along with a community of neighbors descended from a handful of other families. Their labor is their only asset, except for the rough, forested land where they are rooted. It is country of breathtaking beauty, full of tulip poplar, oak, chestnut, and almost impenetrably thick stands of pine girdled with wild laurel.

But the mountainous land can also break their hearts with its harsh, bone-cracking winters; its stingy, stony soil; and its steep, tortuous paths to and from anywhere. Of those Sheltons recorded in the 1860 census, only four have lived beyond forty years. Theirs is a hard life with slim margins.

The Sheltons and their neighbors are proud and self-reliant. Many remain indifferent to a sectional war and stubbornly resist any effort to draw them into it. They are not pacifists. They fight for their families and their land, and as in other mountain communities, they live in a tangle of long-standing feuds made more violent by the war.

Keith's command moves on Shelton Laurel from two directions. He leads a column down from the high crest at the head of the valley, while Allen — acting in some ambiguous capacity as Keith's subordinate — brings his men up the mouth of the valley. Mountaineers lie in ambush and pepper Allen's column with occasional gunshots. His soldiers return fire, killing eight men. At the home of Bill Shelton, they meet a stubborn force of more than fifty riflemen, and a hot fight leaves six of the defenders dead.

As the troopers make camp to wait for Keith's column, Allen receives the news that his six-year-old son, Romulus, has died of scarlet fever. He gallops home to Marshall to find that his daughter Margaret, four years old, is also dying. He blames the intruders who ransacked his house weeks before. How could a sick child survive that kind of terror? He buries his children the next day and returns immediately to Shelton Laurel, inflamed by grief and the desire for vengeance.

Under Lieutenant Colonel Keith, with Colonel Allen complicit, the 64th goes on a tear. They torture women — in vain — to make them reveal the whereabouts of their husbands. They hang up and whip Mrs. Unus Riddle, eighty-five years old. They hang two of the Shelton wives, Mary and Sarah, by their necks until nearly dead.

The *Memphis Bulletin* reports all this: "Old Mrs. Sallie Moore, seventy years of age, was whipped with hickory rods till the blood ran in streams down her back to the ground. . . . Martha White, an idiotic girl, was beaten and tied by the neck all day to a tree." Keith and Allen's men knock down houses or burn them. They slaughter livestock wantonly. Finally, the marauding force rounds up fifteen men. Allen persuades them not to resist, promising a fair trial. He knows from the start that most of these men are unlikely to have had anything to do with the raid on Marshall; witnesses have identified the raiders as mostly deserters from his own regiment.

But Keith jails them anyway for two days in Marshall. Two of the prisoners manage to slip their bonds and escape into the night. The remaining thirteen are ordered to march up the valley: Azariah Shelton, age about sixteen; William Shelton, age twenty; brothers David Shelton, age about forty-eight, and Roderick "Stob Rob" Shelton, age about fifty-one; Joseph Woods, age sixty; Halen Moore, age about twenty-four; Wade Moore, age about eighteen; Jasper Chandler, age sixteen; James Metcalf, age forty; Ellison King, age about twenty-five; James Shelton, age about thirty-six; and his sons James Shelton Jr., age about sixteen, and David Shelton, the youngest of the group, age about thirteen.

As the *Memphis Bulletin* relates the story, "They bid farewell to their wives, daughters and sisters, directing them to procure the witnesses and bring them to the court in Tennessee, where they supposed their trial would take place. . . . The poor fellows had proceeded but a few miles when they were turned from the road into a gorge in the mountain and halted."

Keith orders five of the men to their knees. Soldiers file into line ten paces in front of them and aim their rifles. Joe Woods, the eldest, cries out, "For God's sake, men, you are not going to shoot us? If you are going to murder us, give us at least time to pray." Keith responds that there's no time for praying. The kneeling prisoners raise their hands to their faces, futilely trying to fend off bullets with flesh. For a long moment, the soldiers hesitate, moved by the pleas of mercy from the helpless men.

Keith can hardly contain his fury. "Fire or you will take their place!"

The soldiers fire. Four of the men fall lifeless. A fifth is gutshot and must be finished off with a bullet to the head.

Five more are made to kneel, including thirteen-year-old David Shelton. "You have killed my father and brothers," he pleads. "You have shot my father in the face. Do not shoot me in the face."

The soldiers fire, and again four men die instantly. The *Bulletin* quotes young Shelton, wounded in both arms as he hugs the legs of one of the officers: "You have killed my old father and three brothers, you have shot me in both arms. . . . I forgive you all this—I can get well. . . . Let me go home to my mother and sisters."

But they haul him back to the place of execution and shoot him again, eight times. Then they execute the remaining three men. The soldiers dump all the bodies into a shallow trench scored out of the snow. One of the soldiers, Sgt. N. B. D. Jay of Virginia, bounds onto the heap of bodies. He cries out to his fellows, "Pat Juba for me while I dance the damned scoundrels down to and through hell!"

One of the escapees, Pete McCoy, carries news of the massacre back to the victims' families. The next day, when the women climb up into the gorge to claim the bodies, they discover that wild hogs have been at them.

On February 16, Augustus S. Merrimon, chief justice of the state supreme court, writes to Governor Vance, "I have no knowledge of my own touching the shooting of several prisoners in Laurel. I have learned, however, from a most reliable source that 13 of them were killed; that some of them were not taken in arms but at their homes; that all the men shot (13 if not more) were prisoners at the time they were shot; that they were taken off to a secluded cave or gorge in the mountains and then made to kneel down and were thus shot."

His letter goes on in painful detail: "One man was badly and mortally shot in the bowels, and while he was writhing in agony and praying to God for mercy a soldier mercilessly and brutally shot him in the head with a pistol. Several women were whipped."

And there is no doubt about who is to blame. He writes, "I learned that all this was done by order of Lieut. Col. James A. Keith. I know not what you intend doing with the guilty parties, but I suggest they are all guilty of murder.... Such savage and barbarous cruelty is without parallel in the State, and I hope in every other."

Vance is determined to get to the bottom of the atrocity. He orders an investigation that lasts four months.

There is the question of Colonel Allen's involvement. He was not officially in command, yet all witnesses place him squarely at the center of events. It is Allen who promised the men a fair trial in Tennessee and thus persuaded them not to resist arrest. The army suspends Allen for six months without pay, which scarcely troubles him, since he has other ways to make money. His substitute enlistment scheme nets him $20,000 — significant fortune.

Vance demands an accounting for the orders of Brig. Gen. Henry Heth, Keith's and Allen's superior. Heth, the son of a Virginia planter and a cousin of Maj. Gen. George Pickett, was the one who initially granted Allen permission to return to Laurel Valley after the Marshall raid in the first place. From Richmond, Secretary of War James A. Seddon responds, "In a communication to the Department by Lieutenant-Colonel Keith he claims that Brigadier-General Heth gave him a verbal order to the effect: 'I want no reports from you about your course at Laurel. I do not want to be troubled with any prisoners and the last one of them should be killed.'"

An enclosed deposition by a Doctor Thompson supports Keith's claim. Seddon goes on. Heth, he writes, "admits that he told Keith that those found in arms ought not to be treated as enemies, and in the event of an engagement with them to take no prisoners as he considered that they had forfeited all such claims, but he denies in strong terms the making use of any remarks which would authorize maltreatment of prisoners who had been accepted as such or to women and children."

In the end, Heth escapes censure of any kind. He has a powerful friend and ally in Robert E. Lee — indeed, he is one of only two generals that Lee addresses by his first name. He is promoted to major general and is first on the field at Gettysburg, where his division stumbles blind into two brigades of Union cavalry and opens a disastrous three-day battle.

Keith escapes to the mountains. Governor Vance vows, "I will follow him to the gates of hell, or hang him." For two years, Keith remains a hunted fugitive.

When Keith is finally caught, it is not by the families of the Shelton Laurel victims or even by Vance's North Carolina troops, but by U.S. Army troops. He is indicted on thirteen counts of murder and imprisoned for more than two years, while the war goes out like a flame and the state legislature haggles over an amnesty for all who served the Confederate cause. In the end, even the state supreme court cannot levy justice on Keith. He is acquitted of the first count of murder and appeals the other indictments on the grounds that he is covered by the 1866 amnesty law and escapes. Days later, the state supreme court rules in his favor. He moves to Arkansas and resumes the practice of medicine.

Shelton Laurel mourns its dead. With the help of Merrimon, now a U.S. senator, and with the support of the new governor, William Holden, five widows of the murdered men petition Congress for pensions. Their petition dies in committee. In the world beyond Shelton Laurel, the massacre is largely forgotten.

In Shelton Laurel, the bitter memory will burn for generations.

14

LITTLE WILL THOMAS AND THE CHEROKEE LEGION

A Love Story

PART I

By the time war breaks over the mountains of western North Carolina, William Holland Thomas has already found and claimed the two great loves of his life. The first is the small band of Eastern Cherokee — the Ocono-luftee — who have made him their champion. The second is a comely young woman fittingly named Sarah Love, less than half his age and just three years his bride. Now, to fight for the first, the "Lufty," he will have to leave the second. Thomas has already led an extraordinary life. By war's end, he will become a legend hounded by enemies and haunted by madness.

He is born in 1805 in a log house on Raccoon Creek in Haywood County, already an orphan — his father drowned before he was born, the body never recovered. He is a distant cousin to President Zachary Taylor. He is a small, blue-eyed boy with long brown hair, thin lips, and a wide forehead. He yearns for a father of his own, and he will spend his adult life trying to fill a fatherly role for others.

He is an independent boy, at home in the outdoors, physically strong, and already used to traveling alone through the rugged mountains on errands for his mother and family friends. By the age of thirteen, he is managing a trading post on Soco Creek, away from his mother's company. She has schooled him in the Bible, and he is both literate and smart, a charming speaker and a natural salesman who can write letters and possesses an uncanny ability to do arithmetic in his head, adding up accounts, calculating interest, and figuring profit and loss on complicated transactions.

The store is located just beyond the Cherokee settlement called Qualla-town, near the confluence of the Tuckaseegee and Oconoluftee Rivers. His customers are mostly Indians, trading ginseng, fur, and skins for store goods. From an Indian boy, he learns to read and write the Cherokee language as fluently as English. He begins a lifelong love affair with the Cherokee. In Cherokee culture, an individual is defined by his membership in a clan. Young Will has only his sternly religious mother, Temperance, and finds among the Cherokee acceptance and belonging. His own son later records that he has an "almost romantic fondness for the Cherokee tribe."

Because Thomas has no living father, it is customary among the Cherokee that an older member of his clan become his mentor. The aging local chief, Yonaguska or Drowning Bear, takes the boy under his wing, mentors him in the customs of the Oconoluftee, and endows him with a Cherokee name: Wil-Usdi, meaning "Little Will." It is not flattering, but in the Cherokee manner, it is accurate: in manhood, Thomas stands just 5 feet 4 inches tall.

The boy turns out to be a quick study, a born negotiator and dealmaker, politically astute, and an eloquent, inspiring orator. Even in a community accustomed to hard physical labor, his work ethic is astonishing. He commonly labors through the day and all night, educating himself about business, law, and real estate. Despite his diminutive stature, he impresses the Cherokee with his stamina for physical labor and his energy for trekking and riding long distances in rugged mountain country.

He prospers in his business ventures, opening more stores, buying interests in mines and tanneries, even acquiring slaves. He travels the region far and wide, trading for denim to supply the army, surveying land he wishes to acquire, and visiting friends and cousins. But his main business is the Cherokee band.

In the years that follow, he becomes an unwavering advocate for the Lufty in Washington. He follows a Spartan routine: he wakes up to a cold bath at 4:00 A.M. and labors until 10:00 P.M. He pursues two distinct aims with an almost religious devotion: gaining permission for the Lufty to remain in North Carolina and securing their share of funds that the federal government is treaty-bound to pay. He lobbies Congress and the Bureau of Indian Affairs, drafts petitions and affidavits, and presents the case of a loyal, peace-loving people who deserve to own their tribal homeland.

By the Treaty of New Echota, Georgia, in 1836, 17,000 Indians were coerced into giving up their eastern lands in exchange for $5 million and a parcel of land in the Oklahoma Territory adjacent to lands already occupied by the Western Band of the Cherokee. The Georgia Cherokee largely went west, but a band of North Carolina Cherokee remained in their mountain home, and that's where they want to stay.

Thomas writes of the Cherokee homeland, "Their lands are productive, their orchards supply them with fruit; springs and brooks of the purest water from the sides and base of the mountain; and the atmosphere is one of the healthiest on the globe. No local causes for disease; no chills or fever which are so prevalent in the South. And that country is endeared to those Indians by the graves and sacred relics of their ancestors—the bones of their children, sisters, brothers, fathers and mothers lie there; they say we cannot leave them; let us alone in the land of our fathers."

He succeeds in his first aim. Some 1,500 Oconoluftee are declared exempt from removal. But their money will be a long time coming. Thomas remains in Washington through April 1838, politicking on behalf of the Cherokee. Unbeknownst to Thomas, back home the old chief, Yonaguska, lies dying. He exhorts his people never to leave their mountains and to abstain from drinking liquor. Then, in an astonishing break with tradition, Yonaguska summons his councilors to a final meeting at which he names Thomas as the new chief of the Oconoluftee Cherokee.

Thomas becomes the only white chief of the Eastern Cherokee.

He is also elected to seven terms in the state senate, championing the building of a 129-mile-long plank road linking Fayetteville to Bethania, a Moravian settlement west of Winston. He argues passionately to extend the Western North Carolina Railroad beyond Asheville to Waynesville and on to Franklin, at last intersecting the Blue Ridge Railroad. He dreams of boom times in the mountains and declares his region is poised to become "The New England of the South." By his lights, development and trade in the mountains will lead to prosperity for the Lufty.

In winning his point, he makes a powerful enemy: Zebulon Vance, who just as passionately—and unsuccessfully—lobbies for a northwestern rail route. Vance, soon to be the most powerful governor in the state's history, will neither forget nor forgive.

All his adult life, Will Thomas has searched for a female companion. But he has spent so much time traveling rough and has been so tied up in business ventures and politics in Raleigh and Washington that he has managed only the most casual liaisons. He adopts an Indian boy and a girl but still pines for a companion. He is fifty-one years old when he is smitten with all the romantic zeal of a youngster. Her name is Sarah Jane Burney Love, the daughter of James Robert Love. She is pretty and poised, well-spoken and self-confident, the eldest of four daughters in a family of eight children.

Strangely, he has known Sarah all her life; James Love is one of his oldest friends. But something changes when she reaches maturity, and now, starry-eyed, he proposes marriage. He does not expect her to say yes to such an older man. She is just twenty-four, a strong-willed woman with long, dark hair and kind eyes. But she surprises him, for she, too, is in love with this rough, independent, self-made man.

Their betrothal creates a local sensation. Announcing the wedding, a Raleigh newspaper congratulates Thomas for at last finding a bride: "The attention of all bachelordom is particularly directed to the following deeply interesting item — There is no such word as fail in the vocabulary of the patient and persevering."

But now his frequent sojourns in Washington on behalf of the Lufty become agonies of separation. He writes long sentimental letters to Sarah, assuring her of his fidelity and his love for her. He buys her a piano and has it shipped home, along with sheet music by Stephen Foster for the song "Willie, We Have Missed You."

When he finally breaks away from official business, it takes him six days to make it home to her: on the steamer *North Carolina* from Baltimore to the Elizabeth River, by train and stage to Asheville, then overland by mail coach and horseback. She soon bears him a son, William Holland Thomas Jr., who is born while he is away in Raleigh.

Overcome with affection and homesickness, feeling guilty for not being present at the birth of their first son, and painfully aware of their age difference, he writes that he is hovering over their little cottage in spirit, watching over the one "who had promised 'tho time should whiten the locks, and bedim the eyes of her Willie she would still love him, still cling to him, still be to him the warm hearted and affectionate Sarah, should fortune and all the world beside desert him."

By 1860, Thomas is one of the wealthiest men in the western counties. He holds $27,500 in personal property, owns 150,000 acres of real estate valued at $122,725, and holds fifty slaves. He lives on a beautiful, remote farm, Stekoa Fields, in a five-room house on a ridge with a bold stream flowing nearby. His adoptive children are grown and live apart. He shares Stekoa Fields with his aged mother, his wife, Sarah, and their two sons. Soon a daughter joins the family.

As the election of Lincoln looms near and the state roils with arguments for and against secession, Thomas finds himself in a quandary. He is a slaveholder who does not favor secession, if secession means war. But he gradually arrives at the unlikely conclusion that the U.S. government will let the

Confederate states secede without war, that there will be two countries: the United States and the Confederate States.

From Raleigh, he writes Sarah that the "mountains of Western North Carolina would be in the centre of the Confederacy where the Southern people would congregate in the summer, and spend their money, instead of spending it in the north." Thomas's vision is fantasy, yet all his life he has relied on the force of his personality, coupled with relentless hard work, to achieve the impossible. His Cherokee people are poor, working subsistence farms, hunting for their meat, bedding down in log cabins. Investment in the mountains will surely mean a better life for them.

He is one of four legislators elected to the secession convention, and like all the others, he votes enthusiastically to leave the Union. But the Lincoln administration will not allow a separate Confederate country without a fight. War comes, interrupting all routine commerce, dashing his dream of an economic boom in the mountains.

It is time to choose sides, and the Cherokee are caught in the middle. They are not considered legal citizens of the state, but they cannot remain neutral if they ever hope to become citizens. And by treaty, their allegiance is to the United States of America.

They must fight for one nation or the other in order not to lose their own. The only question is, which one?

PART II

Almost from the firing of the first guns at Fort Sumter, the Confederacy works hard to recruit allies among other nations — England, France, even Mexico. But one of the only nations that allies itself with the Confederacy has not yet been recognized as sovereign and is contained entirely within the boundaries of North Carolina: the Eastern Band of the Cherokee.

Some observers find it strange that the Cherokee should put their lives at hazard on behalf of a state in which they have always been — as free persons of color — second-class citizens. But it was the U.S. Army under Gen. Winfield Scott that made war on the peaceful Cherokee and, carrying out President Andrew Jackson's removal order, drove them west in a deadly forced march onto strange lands far beyond their revered eastern mountains. Along the Trail of Tears, as the trek came to be known, 4,000 Cherokees perished. At the outbreak of war, Scott is the supreme commander of the U.S. Army.

The government of North Carolina, on the other hand, remained largely ambivalent about whether the Cherokee went or stayed behind, and its benign neglect has allowed them to build an independent nation in their homeland. Now they fear that a victory over North Carolina will result in the abolishment of their independent homeland, removal to the West, or worse.

In October 1861, at the capital of the Cherokee Nation in Tahlequah, Oklahoma, a great conference of Cherokees, Choctaws, Chickasaws, Seminoles, and Creeks convenes to determine their allegiance in the coming conflict. They adopt the "Declaration by the People of the Cherokee Nation of the Causes Which Have Impelled Them to Unite Their Fortunes with Those of the Confederate States of America." It is written in light of a crucial fact: in the early days of the conflict, after the Union debacle at Bull Run, the Confederacy is clearly winning.

The declaration invokes the spirit of the original Declaration of Independence, echoing the North Carolina ordinance of secession: "The Cherokee people had its origin in the South; its institutions are similar to those of the Southern States, and their interests identical with theirs. . . . Menaced by a great danger, they exercise the inalienable right of self-defense, and declare themselves a free people, independent of the Northern States of America and at war with them by their own act."

But despite the grand rhetoric of the declaration, many of the 1,500 Cherokees now living in North Carolina find the war mainly a cause for confusion or indifference. It is Thomas who champions their joining the Confederate cause. Not all of them are persuaded. Like the rest of the state, the Oconoluftee are divided. Most will support North Carolina and the Confederacy. Some will fight for the Union. And some will simply try to remain neutral.

Thomas organizes a company of 130 Cherokee recruits at Quallatown on April 9, 1862, and they elect him captain. His deputy commander is Lt. James Terrell, a close business associate of Thomas before the war. Two of his most trusted Cherokee subordinates are Peter Graybeard and John Astoogatogeh, grandson of legendary chief Junaleska. Along the road to Knoxville, the ranks swell with new recruits until the company numbers nearly 200. Those who watch the Cherokees pass remark on their hardy physiques. Physically, they are stronger and have far better stamina than the average white recruit. One observer records that an Indian sentry endured fourteen hours of guard duty in a freezing mountain pass without complaint.

Their physical stamina is due in part to their long practice of playing stickball, with hickory sticks and a ball made of a rock wrapped in hair and stitched in hide. The two-hour contests range over a 600-yard-long field as teams of up to thirty young men use sticks to score a goal. It is a rough and ready game of running, skill, and physical endurance.

Little Will Thomas quickly rises in the Confederate hierarchy, first to major and then colonel. The first company forms the nucleus for Thomas's Legion of Indians and Highlanders, officially commissioned on September 27, 1862, in Knoxville, Tennessee. It is a battalion of cavalry and ten companies of infantry comprising Love's thousand-man regiment, named for its commander, Lt. Col. James R. Love, Thomas's brother-in-law and now his second in command. Love is the grandson of a Revolutionary War hero, Col. Robert Love, patriarch of the largest landowning family in Haywood County.

Later, in 1863, a light artillery battery is added, commanded by John T. Levi, and throughout the war as many as 2,500 men serve in the legion. About 400 of the legion are Cherokees, nearly every able-bodied warrior in the band. They are joined by mountaineers descended from the very settlers who did their best for well over a century to exterminate the tribe. The legion is remarkable in its integration of white mountaineers with Indian warriors.

Thomas is fifty-seven years old when he organizes the legion. Because of his aristocratic connections, he manages to bypass the entire command structure in North Carolina and reports directly to Richmond. This almost proves disastrous. President Davis at first wants to use the Cherokees in the swampy lowlands of the East, in unfamiliar country rife with diseases for which they have no immunity. But in the end this plan, like so many other ill-advised schemes emanating from the Confederate White House, is abandoned.

Thomas is a reluctant soldier. He wanted to join the Confederate Congress, but political enemies blocked him. His long rambles through the mountains on trading journeys and Indian business have taken their toll on his body, leaving him with chronic aches and recurring illnesses. Hardest of all is being absent from his wife, Sarah. But to his mind, the Cherokees must prove themselves both loyal and capable soldiers, or they will lose the home they have held onto so tenaciously even as thousands of their tribe were driven away to the West.

Legionnaires carry an assortment of old squirrel rifles, revolvers, and sabers, but also steel-tipped spears, long-bladed Bowie knives, and tomahawks that can be hurled with accuracy up to thirty feet and open up a man's chest or skull. They are largely self-equipped and self-supplied.

Little Will Thomas and the Cherokee Legion

Thomas intends that his legion will serve close to home, in the rugged country they know so well, and indeed much of their skirmishing against Unionist bushwhackers and guerillas occurs in the western counties, notably Madison. Their primary duty is guarding the mountain passes, precious salt works, and railroad bridges. They erect earthworks across the Oconoluftee Pass to turn back Unionist raiders from Sevier County, Tennessee. But as a bona fide Confederate unit, they must go where they are ordered, and that turns out to be Tennessee. Before marching off to war, the Cherokee prepare with feasting and ritual, seeking spiritual guidance and conducting a war dance in full regalia. Even Thomas wears ceremonial feathers along with his officer's uniform.

During an early skirmish in East Tennessee, as two companies of patrolling Indian troops enter Baptist Gap, Union sharpshooters kill the lead officer, Lt. John Astoogatogeh, one of the most revered men in the legion. His comrades rush the marksmen before they can get off another shot and fall on the Yankees in a fit of killing rage. They bludgeon, spear, and bayonet the shooters, then, using their Bowie knives, scalp the wounded and the dead alike. The Indiana troops who witness this act of bloody retribution retreat in panic, spreading the infamous legend of the savage Cherokees.

Thomas is appalled by the viciousness of the act. He was not present during the action, but he takes it personally. For all these years, he insisted that the Cherokee are just as civilized and honorable as any whites. Now he returns the sack of scalps to the Union commander for proper burial. Nevertheless, reports of scalping follow the legion throughout the war, and accounts vary widely, depending on the source. Lieutenant Terrell claims, "Throughout the war they did scalp every man they killed, if they could get to him, which they generally managed to do." But he is thought to exaggerate, in order to strike fear into the hearts of their enemies.

Some of the outliers and bushwhackers they fight have committed atrocities of their own, and the mountain war is fought with a sense of personal vendetta, which amplifies its savagery. Witnesses tend to be fiercely partisan, and documentation is sketchy at best. Whether the reports of scalping are truth or only legend, the legion achieves a reputation for efficiency and esprit de corps and are called by one newspaper "the best scouts in the world."

A spate of cross-border raids has the legion scrambling to defend railroad bridges and passes. By the autumn of 1862, Thomas has concocted a brilliant plan to secure the whole mountain border with just 5,000 men manning a series of outposts connected by new roads and supplied by a central depot. Yet President Davis, still chasing glory in Virginia, remains silent on such a practical plan to be carried out in a remote theater of the war.

In 1863, Maj. Gen. Ambrose Burnside takes Knoxville by storm and now controls eastern Tennessee. The legion fights a pitched battle at a railroad depot called Telford against an Ohio regiment, routing the Federals with just twenty casualties of their own and capturing hundreds of new rifles. But in their winter encampment at Gatlinburg, the legion is caught in a surprise attack by Col. William Palmer's veteran 15th Pennsylvania Cavalry. The battle is a draw, but it drives the legion back into the North Carolina mountains.

Other smaller battles follow, along with constant skirmishing against bushwhackers. The country is becoming rotten with outliers and deserters. One of the legion's most popular officers, Lt. Col. William C. Walker, gravely ill with typhoid fever, returns home on leave to Cherokee County. In the dead of night on January 3, 1864, his wife hears a hard knocking at the front door. She answers the door to strangers. Walker emerges from his bedroom, dazed with sleep. One of the men in the doorway draws a large revolver and fires into him point-blank, killing him instantly, then retreats into the freezing night. He might be a local man with a grudge or a Unionist assassin from across the border. Either way, the killing is personal—not war but plain murder.

Governor Vance laments, "The warfare between scattering bodies of irregular troops is conducted on both sides without any regard whatever to the rules of civilized war or the dictates of humanity."

The Confederacy, always outnumbered, needs fighting men in Virginia. The legion is deployed to the Shenandoah Valley in 1864 in support of Gen. Jubal Early's unsuccessful attempt to drive out the Federals. The valley is a crucial breadbasket of the Confederacy, and the Federals under Maj. Gen. Philip H. Sheridan have been systematically destroying crops and farmsteads.

Thomas is relentless in his efforts to have his dwindling command returned to their native state; but his troops are kept in action at Cedar Creek, Winchester, and Staunton, and the casualties mount. After the exhausting and costly campaign, which leaves fewer than 100 legionnaires on active duty, Confederate brigadier general Gabriel C. Wharton writes to Thomas, "The gallant conduct of your command rendered your efforts to rejoin your command in North Carolina abortive, and the constant refusal to your many applications for transfer is complimentary evidence of the esteem in which you were held, and a grateful acknowledgement of the services you could render."

But Thomas is imprisoned in Goldsboro, awaiting court-martial on charges that he did "knowingly entertain and receive deserters into his command." It is his third court-martial; the others never came to trial. But the charge is basically true: he has long since given up prosecuting deserters, and when they return, he simply reintegrates them into his unit. For doing the practical — rather than the rigidly honorable — he is found guilty.

Thomas gets no support from his old political nemesis, Vance. The governor writes, "Col. Thomas is worse than useless. He is a positive injury to that country." Vance calls the legion "a favorite resort for deserters."

So Thomas travels to Richmond to visit his cousin, the president. Davis not only reverses the verdict but orders the remainder of the legion home to North Carolina. Thomas's legion remains in the field even after the surrender of Confederate troops at the Bennitt Farm in April 1865.

On May 6, 1865, a company of Thomas's legion commanded by Lt. Robert E. Conley blunders into Lt. Col. William C. Bartlett's Union 2nd North Carolina Mounted Infantry Regiment in the woods near White Sulphur Springs. Conley's men form a skirmish line and drive off the enemy, killing one, the last man to die in action east of the Mississippi: James Arwood. Conley claims after the war, "I still have Mr. Arwood's gun as a relic." It is the last fighting between regular troops in North Carolina, an accidental clash that changes nothing.

The legion boldly surrounds the Union garrison at Waynesville, a settlement of twenty homes, threatening to attack, in order to negotiate its own surrender. By now it can field just 200 Cherokees and about 400 mountaineers. Thomas comes down from the hills in the company of Colonel Love and the district commander, Brig. Gen. James G. Martin, to present his terms for surrender. U.S. colonel Bartlett receives them, in command of a force that is clearly outnumbered.

Theatrical to the last, Thomas is arrayed in full Cherokee war regalia, complete with bare chest and feathers. He is dwarfed by his handpicked escort of twenty tall Cherokee warriors in full warpaint armed with tomahawks.

Over two contentious days of palaver, something comes unhinged in the man. He rants manically and threatens to scalp every man in a blue uniform. Bartlett is taken aback, argues awhile, then at last persuades Thomas that, though he can probably capture the Union force, it would be only a matter days before massive reinforcements arrived to annihilate the legion.

Thomas's superior, Martin, keeps a cool head and bows to the inevitable. Thus the legion surrenders on May 9, 1865, the last Confederate unit in the state to lay down its arms. Thomas's escorts are allowed to keep their weapons as they return home. And Bartlett's Federals soon depart.

In the wake of the surrender, a smallpox epidemic sweeps through Quallatown and the surrounding area, carried home by a deserter to the U.S. Army who returns to find, like others who fought for the Union, that he will be ostracized by his fellows. Over the winter of 1865–66, 125 of the Lufty Cherokee die of the disease. For such a small community, the toll is devastating.

The state recognizes the right of the Oconoluftee to remain on their lands, but it will not grant them citizenship.

During the last years of the war, the "productive lands" once celebrated by Thomas have not been productive enough to stave off hunger. The Cherokees left behind—mostly women, children, and the elderly—have been reduced to eating bark and leaves. Now Thomas spends $9,000 of his own money to procure cornmeal, flour, and bacon from South Carolina to feed his people. It is not enough. Thomas himself does not fare much better. Now sixty years old, his health broken by strenuous service, he returns to Sarah and their three children. President Johnson—who, as provisional governor of East Tennessee, once accused the Cherokee of cutting off the ears of their enemies and wearing them as trophies—formally pardons him for his role in the rebellion.

But the war has left Thomas deeply in debt, his multifarious business dealings a muddle of lawsuits and counterclaims. Businessman, land speculator, state senator, Cherokee chief, and war hero, he gradually lapses into incoherence and occasional violent outbursts. The crisis comes one day in 1867 when he raises a hatchet over Sarah's head and commands her to play the piano, his sentimental gift to her back in the sweet early days of their marriage. She summons her brothers, who arrive with the sheriff, and soon a judge declares William Holland Thomas legally insane. He is committed to Dix Hill, the state asylum for the insane at Raleigh.

Sarah brings him home after only a month and stubbornly tries to care for him between his most violent periods, when he must be returned to Dix Hill. She lives alone at Stekoa Fields, her children all farmed out to relatives. "I have not a home free of embarrassments in which to lay my head," she writes to her sister. "My heart aches within me, when I think of the coming future."

Thomas has no choice but to resign as chief of the Oconoluftee Cherokee. He is succeeded by Salanitah or Flying Squirrel. The following year,

Little Will Thomas and the Cherokee Legion

Congress at last recognizes the sovereignty of the Eastern Band of the Cherokee Nation.

Meantime a complicated lawsuit unfolds in which Thomas is accused of having used Cherokee funds paid out by the federal government for his own enrichment. The truth, as determined by an arbitration board after years of testimony and studious parsing of deeds, mortgages, and bills of sale, is that Thomas did indeed buy land with that money—and also with his own money—and gave most of that land to the Cherokee. But because they are not legally citizens of North Carolina, the titles remained in his name. When a bankruptcy court ordered his assets to be sold to satisfy creditors, that land was also sold.

In the end, a tract of 73,000 acres is deeded to the Cherokee upon payment of a small balance. The creditors are also paid. Thomas is ruined. He retains the family farm only out of the generosity of his chief creditor, his old lieutenant, James Terrell. Terrell looks with pity upon his old friend and commander: "When the trial began in Quallatown in August 1874," he writes, "the mildest description that can be given of the state of Col. Thomas' mind was that he was a raving, furious maniac."

For the rest of his days, Little Will is gripped by debilitating pain in his legs, skin lesions, and mental illness. He shuttles back and forth between the asylum and home. It is possible he is suffering from tertiary syphilis. It is whispered among their neighbors that Sarah has built a stone room in which she keeps her husband safely chained. But the truth is that she is keeping something else: the promise he asked of her in the glow of their honeymoon days, that "she would still love him, still cling to him, still be to him the warm hearted and affectionate Sarah, should fortune and all the world beside desert him."

Caring for her husband breaks Sarah's health. She dies suddenly after a brief illness in May 1877, just forty-five years old.

Thomas is transferred to a new asylum in Morganton, where he can look out over the mountains he once roved, settled, and defended. There he bestows one last gift on his beloved Cherokee.

In 1890, he is visited by a young ethnologist from the Smithsonian Institution named James Mooney. On Mooney's first visit the year before, the doctors warned him that Thomas was out of his mind—and violent—and he went away. Now he has returned to find Thomas enjoying a rare period of lucidity. For days, Little Will Thomas recounts his tales of life among the Oconoluftee, outlining their customs, telling their history and the exploits of the legion, humanizing the Indians for a white audience steeped only in myths of savagery. Making them — and himself — immortal.

William Holland Thomas, Wil Usdi, chief of the Oconoluftee Cherokee and Confederate veteran, a widower who never expected to outlive his true love, a man who straddled two worlds, dies on May 10, 1893, one day past the twenty-eighth anniversary of his theatrical surrender.

15

THE BURDEN OF WAR

True, the war is a cause and a struggle, a clash of ideologies and armies, but for the private soldier it also has heft and weight and substance, a physical presence that requires muscular strength and bodily endurance, sound limbs and good wind.

The war is not simply *there* in the offing—up in Virginia, out at the coastal forts, west along the Shenandoah Valley—as some complete phenomenon awaiting the soldier's participation. The war exists in pieces, each piece a part of a monumental work in progress. Every soldier must carry his part of the war to the great staging grounds of the war and there help to assemble it.

The phrase "to make war" is literally accurate, for the war is made by men manipulating objects across a landscape through the energy of their courage, their will, and their brute physical strength. Thus the soldier is a maker of war, a builder of destruction. He must carry his tools to the jobsite.

It falls to his lot to bear four kinds of burden. First are his own clothing and personal effects. These are both the lightest and the heaviest. Their weight depends on whether the wool coat on his back is rain-soaked or baked in sunlight, his haversack bearing a love letter from home or the news of a death in the family.

Second, he must bear the weapons with which to wage war. Many carry an 1853 model British Enfield rifled musket, smuggled through the blockade into Wilmington. It weighs nine and a half pounds unloaded and shoots a .577 caliber bullet more than half an inch in diameter. When a Confederate soldier faces a Union infantryman across that close deadly space of battle, the soldier in blue may be shooting back at him with exactly the same weapon, acquired in open trade by the U.S. government. A trained soldier can fire with accuracy three times per minute at targets 1,000 yards distant. The Minié ball can crush a limb or smash open a chest or abdomen. But to make it work, he must also carry powder cartridges, a belt pouch of percussion caps, and a ramrod, along with forty to sixty rounds of bullets—three to four pounds of grooved lead.

In addition to the rifled musket, many carry Bowie knives. The officers carry pistols—of many makes and calibers—secured in flapped leather holsters or stuck into sashes. Some carry multiple pistols. The artillerymen carry short Roman swords. Cavalrymen wield long, curved sabers. Some higher-ranking officers bear swords of exquisite design and quality, presentation pieces awarded them by their legislatures, their clubs, or their own troops.

The most devilish weapon any soldier carries is a socket-style bayonet that fits onto the muzzle of his rifle with a quick twist. It dangles from his belt in a stiff scabbard. Unlike his U.S. Army counterpart, whose flat-bladed bayonet inflicts a sharp cut that can be stitched, the North Carolina soldier mounts a triangular bayonet. It punches a hole in a man's flesh, making a puncture wound that cannot be repaired. In a war that quickly deteriorates into gruesome slaughter, the bayonet is the one weapon most soldiers on either side cannot bring themselves to use on another man. That is a burden they refuse to bear.

Instead, they carry it by the blade end on dark nights as they move around a camp safe behind the lines, for its round socket makes an excellent candle holder. They can stab it into the earth and fix a candle to it that will light the pages of the letters they are reading or writing.

Third, the soldier carries provisions to allow him to survive, almost always outdoors, through every mean season of the long struggle. Hardtack and bully beef, cornmeal, and coffee he carries in a special pouch inside his white cotton duck haversack, a shoulder-slung bag one foot square with a flap that buckles closed against the elements. The best ones are waterproof, but these are scarce in the ranks of the North Carolina men. At the start of the war, it is typical for each man to carry three days' rations, but many begrudge the weight and simply eat all of it the first day. And later in the war, rations are thin and spotty, and the haversacks hold wild berries, apples, persimmons—whatever can be scavenged from the countryside.

The fourth burden is the one that the soldiers rarely talk about, the one they bear in their arms off the field of battle. They bear the same burden, escorted by a brass band playing the sullen death march, to the graveyard: the fallen comrade, who is always heavier in death, who is weighted with their secret fears and grief and desperation, their homesickness and failing hope.

And as the war drags on for a year and then two and then longer, this particular burden gathers weight and presses on them like impending weather, a permanent gloom that no sun can dispel, a burden of absence, the absence of their loved ones and their departed fellows, and a foreshadowing of a day when they themselves will become the absent ones.

And so the boys from North Carolina trudge off to war bearing weight.

At first they carry knapsacks on their backs, stuffed with extra trousers and shirts and underwear, blanket roll and rubber groundsheet tied neatly on top. But the backpack grates on the shoulders and wearies the back, so gradually it is lightened, heavy clothes strewn by summer roadsides. Many discard even the packs themselves in favor of haversacks.

The soldiers wear an assortment of homespun jeans or wool trousers and cotton shirts, covered by slave-cloth or linsey-woolsey battle jackets and overcoats of brown or gray wool. By the second summer of war, they are issued shell jackets with proper insignia of rank and unit. On their heads they wear either a slouch hat with a wide brim or a leather-billed forage cap, modeled on the French kepi—a quartermaster's bargain at $2 apiece. The forage cap is often issued with a havelock, a linen cover with a long tail that keeps the sun off a man's neck, to ward off heatstroke. But most soldiers find them too hot to wear. Instead they use their havelocks to filter coffee grounds or to clean their rifles.

Cavalrymen wear riding boots, but the infantryman who must carry himself to the war on two legs prefers low shoes with flat heels, available free from the quartermaster when he has them or for $6 in town—until they become unavailable altogether. Shoes are the foundation of a marching army, and North Carolina, like all Confederate states, does not have enough shoes for an army that may cover hundreds of miles in a single campaign. The shoe factories, with their newly patented sewing machines for mass-producing fitted pairs, are all in the North. So dead men soon give up the right to wear shoes.

Foraging parties scout out stockpiles of shoes, and sometimes whole regiments go into battle to secure them, as at Gettysburg, where, it turns out, there are no shoes, only the rumor of shoes. Late in the war, while on their long marches, many soldiers carry their deteriorating, precious shoes in their haversacks or strung by the laces across the neck. Then, when they arrive at the place and hour of battle, they lace on their brogans for the charge.

They roll a spare shirt inside their double blankets and drape them diagonally across their bodies from shoulder to hip, the ends tied with cord or straps.

The Confederate canteen is wooden, closed with a cork stopper, based on the old U.S. Army canteen of Mexican War vintage. It holds just eight ounces of water—just half a pound of weight—never enough. Most would willingly carry a greater burden of water. If they are lucky, they capture Union army canteens, which hold one full quart and are covered with cloth. The cloth can be wetted, and the evaporation will cool the water inside, at least for a little while. On the cloth, they write their names or imprint the insignia of their company and regiment. Some of the U.S. Army canteens have reliable screw caps and are harder to spill.

Water is life, and whenever possible a line of march is planned to intersect with rivers and streams. Still the men suffer for long miles on dusty roads and when maneuvering for battle. At the Battle of the Wilderness in 1864, Lt. George H. Mills of the 16th North Carolina Regiment finds himself parched and lacking a canteen. He writes, "I met Tom Hayden with a canteen, and . . . asked him for a drink. Handing his canteen he said, 'Here is some pond water,' and without thought I took a big swallow before I found it was the meanest whiskey I ever tasted, and of course I was worse off than before I took it."

The men's haversacks and pockets transport all sorts of items: Corncob pipes and tins of tobacco. Paper and pencils. Inkwells and pens. Knives, forks, and spoons, plates and tin cups. Pocket diaries and Bibles enclosed in leather cases that button shut. Straight razors with ivory handles. Shaving brushes. Boar-bristle hairbrushes and combs made of ivory or wood. Soap and toothbrushes. Stubs of candles. Barlow folding knives. Pocket watches on gold chains handed down from father to son. Thick twists of good Southern chaw tobacco, looped and braided. Spare socks. Needles and thread. Playing cards. Dice and dominoes hand-carved from bone. Handmade banjos and factory-made bugles, flutes and whistles, fiddles and bows.

Ten-dollar bills minted in Richmond are inked with the figure of Hope with an anchor. Twenty-dollar Confederate bills bear the image of a sailing ship. Only an officer is likely to possess a $50 note, bearing the likeness of George Washington, or a $100 note, featuring a scene of slaves loading cotton bales onto a wagon, passing along their burden.

Through their letters home, the men share their pay and ease the burden on their families as much as they are able. Thus the most valuable burden they bear is also the most fragile: letters from home, creased from rereading. The husband of Caroline S. Alligood carries this letter from his wife: "I received A letter from you yesterday morning rote the 15 of December an was glad to here from you an here that you ware well an I recived one hundred dollars in it of Confederate. an I war glad to get it for I am in det for provision an it will take it all excepting five or ten dollars."

Sometimes the mail from home brings something more substantial than news. Lewis Warlick of the 1st Regiment of North Carolina Volunteers writes a note of thanks to his sweetheart, Cornelia McGimsey, back home in Burke County: "Tom and I got the cheese you sent us. You do not know how proud I was of it—to think that I had a friend among the fair sex of old Burke who thought enough of me to send at a distance of five hundred miles something that we poor soldiers could eat—a thousand thanks to you for it, and a long life of pure happiness is my sincere wish."

Photographs of loved ones are tucked into pockets or safely encased in ornate silver or leather frames. These are the one burden they will never cast off, except in death.

Outside Richmond, in one of the Seven Days Battles of summer 1862, soldiers of the 1st South Carolina Infantry find a wealth of discarded Yankee gear and trade up. Berry Benson reports, "The whole Confederate army refitted itself with blankets, rubber clothes, tent flies, haversacks and canteens, so that in the middle of the war and later, to see equipment of southern make was somewhat of a curiosity." The "rubber clothes" include ponchos, capes, and ground cloths for the tents, godsends in the rainy seasons.

The soldiers carry the burden of war on their backs and haul it in their wagons from Asheville and Salem. They drag it aboard steamboats at Wilmington and Fayetteville and lift it onto the splintery floors of boxcars at Goldsboro. They dig it out of the ground with spades and pickaxes and pile it high around the mouths of their heavy guns at Petersburg and Fort Fisher. They chop it from the forest with axes and stack it into palisades, then sharpen it with adzes into abatis to fend off charging cavalry.

And as the war wears on, one part of their burden lessens: provisions, especially meat, become scarce. When they overrun the Union camp at Chancellorsville, they are astonished at the bounty they discover. Capt. John Cowan and Capt. James I. Metts of the 3rd North Carolina Regiment report: "Rushing on toward the enemy's camp, the first scene that can be recalled is the abundant supply of beef and slaughtered rations cooking."

As the Confederate supply of beef, clothing, and shoes runs out, the deficiency has consequences on the battlefield. At Cedar Creek in the Shenandoah Valley in October 1864, it proves decisive. Capt. V. E. Turner and Sgt. H. C. Wall of the 23rd North Carolina Regiment write in their after-action report, "Meanwhile the tide of battle, so strongly in our favor in the morning, finally turned. The Confederate commands had been greatly weakened by men who left the ranks to loot the captured camps, so tempting to ill-fed, ill-equipped soldiers. . . . Then came disaster quick on the heels of disaster."

In March 1865, when William Tecumseh Sherman's battle-hardened army of 60,000 men marches into Cheraw, South Carolina, approaching the North Carolina border near Laurinburg, it moves like an army of ghosts in blinding sheets of rain. The men haul the war in their knapsacks and in 2,500 quartermaster's and commissary wagons drawn by 10,000 laboring mules. Their sixty-eight wheeled guns are harnessed to 272 stout horses, their wooden caissons filled with canisters of black powder and cannonballs weighing up to eighteen pounds each, atop two-wheeled limbers.

The cavalrymen thunder in advance on 4,400 fresh horses, which also carry their McClellan saddles, saddlebags, carbines, cartridge boxes, bedrolls, sabers, pistols, and personal effects. The buglers carry their instruments on cords slung across their shoulders or tucked into saddlebags. The officers carry brass field glasses and telescopes in stiff leather cases, and many of them also carry fat cigars buttoned into the pockets of their coats and strong whiskey in dented silver flasks.

The burden includes the wounded, who will ride in the 600 ambulances drawn by 1,200 horses. The ambulances also carry the medical corps, doctors and stewards and assistants and their boxes of bandages, saws, knives, tourniquets, medicines such as quinine and laudanum, and the precious chloroform no longer available to the wounded of the army they will face.

The collective burden of the massive army marches and rolls inexorably forward over corduroy roads — highways built out of forests. Pioneer troops fell the trees and lay them crosswise over the mud, building a road toward the final battle. By this time, after marching from Atlanta to Savannah and from there past Columbia, they are experts at their work: they lay down twelve miles of road every day. They carry each log to the road and fit it into the lengthening ribbon, physically hauling the war into North Carolina.

And as Sherman's army streams across the border, not just too big to stop but also too fast to catch, the country people who watch it pass feel the weight of war pushing over them like a slow landslide. The army fills every road in two vast wings fifty miles wide, the wagon trains snaking along behind it for miles. And it is clear that this army carries force. It simply has *more* — more guns, more horses, more food, more medicine, more ammunition. More confidence, more hope.

More *stuff* — a word that itself bears a weight of accumulated meaning in war: a body of soldiers, in Middle English. The baggage and munitions of an army. Food and stores. Items of value. The material of which something is made — a kettle, a saddle, a rifle, a soldier, a commander, an army. All of it, the whole burden that victory requires of strong backs and sturdy legs and willing hearts.

The Burden of War

The country people—farmers and slaves, the free and soon-to-be-free—watch miles of wagons and more miles of marching troops, which leave behind them a wake of discarded equipment, broken souvenirs of their passing: brass buttons, cracked pipes, leather cartridge boxes, worn-out harness, sole-less shoes, ragged overcoats no longer needed in the gathering spring warmth. Just the trail of what this army throws away amounts to a treasure for people who have been living on sawdust bread and chicory coffee and whatever they could hoard through the winter.

What they see is an army that cannot be defeated any more than you can defeat an earthquake or a hurricane. You can only endure it, wait for it to pass, and leave behind one final burden: the burden of defeat.

16

ABRAHAM GALLOWAY

From Cartridge Box to Ballot Box

In the mild spring darkness of April 1863, a white man in the civilian suit pauses before a dark house. It shows no lights, yet it is the right address, the home of a free black woman, Mary Ann Starkey, who teaches a reading and Bible school here for the many displaced black children who have been accumulating in this haven for runaways, New Bern.

His appointment is meant to take place at midnight. He has arrived a few minutes early—Edward W. Kinsley, businessman and partner of an import-export firm in Boston. Kinsley traveled south to Union-occupied North Carolina surreptitiously, posing in his official pass as servant of U.S. Army brigadier general Edward Augustus Wild, a fighting surgeon who was grievously wounded at the Battle of South Mountain, Maryland, by an exploding bullet that shattered his left arm. Wild supervised the amputation of his own left arm at the shoulder, an indication of the sand in his character.

But Kinsley is nobody's servant. He has strong features, a wide, set mouth and large, steady eyes. He is powerfully built, with a receding hairline and a square jaw framed by extravagant graying sideburns, facial hair made popular by Ambrose Burnside, the Union general who captured a large swath of the lightly defended North Carolina coast in March 1862 and held it until recently, turning over command to his replacement, Maj. Gen. John Gray Foster.

Kinsley does indeed work for Wild, as a special civilian envoy from the governor of Massachusetts—the abolitionist John Albion Andrew—and President Lincoln. They dispatched him to negotiate with the freed black citizens of North Carolina. Like Wild, Kinsley is a man of determination and conviction.

Kinsley's mission: to help Wild raise North Carolina regiments of black soldiers to fight for the Union. So far the meetings he has had with black leaders have proved inconclusive, and this has puzzled him. He and Wild had believed that after the successful formation of the 54th and 55th Massachusetts Regiments of Colored Volunteers, freed slaves in North Carolina would jump at the chance to take up arms against their oppressors.

The door cracks open, and a figure beckons Kinsley inside. In the dark of the hallway, hands wrap a bandage around his head, blindfolding him. He is urged onto a staircase, told to climb. He ascends to the second floor, keeps climbing, aware of the movement and press of other bodies around him. He reaches the attic and senses people crowding him close, hears their breathing, can smell the burn of a tallow candle. A long moment of silence ensues, then an authoritative voice orders the blindfold removed. Again he feels hands tugging at the lint fabric. His vision clears. The room is warm and close.

By the light of a single candle, he sees a formidable black man with a pistol in his belt. Beside the stranger, he recognizes a tall, well-built black man of light complexion: twenty-six-year-old Abraham H. Galloway. Behind them are pressed numerous other black men and women—expectant, curious, defiant, anxious, suspicious.

Before Kinsley can utter a word, Galloway slides a long, dull revolver out of his belt, cocks it, and places the muzzle to Kinsley's ear. Silence inhabits the attic room. This is no ambush, no crime at all. It is the final offer in a stalled negotiation.

Kinsley will always remember it as the most thrilling moment of his life. The gun to his head crystallizes his commitment to the cause of black enlistment. He does not hate Galloway for threatening him—on the contrary, the moment plants the seed of deep admiration for Galloway's uncompromising zeal. Kinsley will forever after count him a friend and a "man of more than ordinary ability."

Galloway acts as the chief representative of the more than 10,000 freedmen and freedwomen who have found refuge at New Bern or three nearby camps, notably James City, a tent and shanty town on the south bank of the Trent River, named for its founder, U.S. Army chaplain Horace James, appointed to supervise "contrabands" on Roanoke Island.

Galloway was born enslaved on the lower Cape Fear to a black woman and a white man—not his mother's owner, but another slaveholding neighbor. Galloway escaped in 1857 on a turpentine schooner. In Philadelphia he quickly fell in with abolitionists and took up clandestine work for the Underground Railroad, venturing as far as Canada. He does not hide his half-white parentage—indeed, he points it out publicly, outraged at a social system that can declare a human being to be the property of another based on such fine

Union spy, scout, and recruiter of U.S. Colored Troops, Abraham Galloway keeps his own counsel and is known to carry a pistol. (Courtesy of the State Archives of North Carolina)

distinctions of racial mixing. Once war was declared, he found his way back to North Carolina and, at last, to this attic room at midnight.

The U.S. Amy needs troops, and though many of its own officers have resisted recruitment of blacks — and few politicians have risked their careers to champion it — the wheel of history has turned. General Order Number 143 of the U.S. War Department, dated May 22, 1863, establishes a Bureau of Colored Troops to recruit and train freedmen and emancipated slaves to fight.

Here in North Carolina, 10,000 white troops are about to be transferred south to attack Charleston, and there are no replacements available. This is the chance for freed slaves to help liberate their brothers and sisters. The eloquent Frederick Douglass, an escaped slave with a wide following in the North, declares, "Once let the black man get upon his person the brass letters U.S., let him get an eagle on his button and a musket on his shoulder and bullets in his pocket, and there is no power on earth which can deny that he has earned the right to citizenship in the United States."

The plan brings the 55th Massachusetts Colored Volunteers to New Bern as the nucleus of Wild's Colored Brigade. Galloway has been adamant that four conditions be met before blacks in New Bern will enlist:

1. They must receive pay equal to that of the Massachusetts regiments.
2. While they are serving, the army must provide for their families, who are nearly all refugees.

Abraham Galloway

3. The U.S. government must set up schools to teach their children to read and write, so that they have a chance of advancing their prospects after the war.
4. Most crucial of all, the U.S. government must guarantee that, in the event they are captured, they will be accorded all the rights of legitimate military prisoners of war.

Now, holding Kinsley at gunpoint, Galloway demands his sacred oath to fulfill these conditions. This is the moment of truth. If blacks stand on the sidelines and allow others to give them their freedom, that freedom will never be complete; it will always be counted a gift, not a right. Their own blood must be part of the bargain, their investment in the cause, but they must be treated as equal partners. Galloway's goal is not mere grudging freedom from physical bondage but full political equality. "And if this should be refused them at the ballot box," he exhorts in public speeches, "they would have it at the cartridge box!"

In previous meetings, bound by the limits of his authority, Kinsley has not been able to offer his assurances. Now out of options, pistol barrel pressed to his head, Kinsley at last swears to honor all four demands. Whether he has been granted the latitude to make these guarantees is not clear. But in the months that follow, at least two of the promises — for schools and the support of families left behind — will be kept. Equal pay will remain a contentious issue until the end of the war, and the honorable treatment of prisoners of war lies in the fickle hands of the enemy.

Within days, hundreds of recruits queue up in the square fronting the Christ Episcopal Church. The frenzy of recruitment is captured in a vivid engraving published by *Frank Leslie's Illustrated Newspaper*. Galloway was not bluffing: he could deliver the recruits, for many of them have been training secretly all along in black militia companies.

The U.S. Colored Troops face an experience fundamentally different from that of their white counterparts. To start with, they enlist among freedmen's camps — communities of strangers — rather than in hometown or home county militias. Their families have been scattered or sold off, and they escaped their home counties. Except in rare cases, they don't enjoy the reassuring bonds of long friendships, of family ties to cousins and brothers. In this they are more like European conscripts than American volunteers.

In addition, they are rarely allowed to be led by men of their own race, no matter how brave, experienced, or capable. Wild does manage to appoint an African American chaplain, Rev. John N. Mars, but when he is invalided out of the army with severe rheumatism, a white officer takes his place. Likewise Maj. John V. De Grasse is appointed assistant surgeon. In 1864 he is cashiered for "drunkenness," though his actual offense was insubordination toward white officers.

To command the new regiment, designated the 1st North Carolina Colored Volunteers (later the 35th U.S. Colored Troops), Wild selects Col. James Chaplain Beecher, half-brother to Harriet Beecher Stowe, author of the incendiary novel *Uncle Tom's Cabin*. He chooses the remaining officers according to a simple, unvarying criterion. "Not one man have I taken who has not seen service (chaplain excepted)," he writes. "Most are real *veterans*. Not a few were discharged from the ranks crippled by wounds, but not disabled from using the sword or pistol, and again facing the enemy in his bitter mood." He wants a fighting outfit that can prove the worth of black soldiers.

The black volunteers suffer the endemic racism of both white soldiers and local civilians. Political leaders such as Edward Stanly, appointed provisional governor in 1862, consider the war to be "a war of restoration and not of abolition."

More importantly, they face the derision of their compatriots in blue. Many Union officers remain skeptical of their courage and discipline and don't think them smart enough to master the manual of arms and complicated battlefield maneuvering, let alone to handle artillery and make command decisions. Even many of their fellow soldiers in the white 45th Massachusetts, also stationed in New Bern, are but reluctant comrades. Writes one to his father, "I hope ere many years to be able to celebrate the emancipation of the slaves in the U.S. I wish they would be colonized though."

Another writes bluntly to a friend, "You who are at home are as ignorant of the position and qualifications of the Negroes, as they are of education."

Black volunteers come to the army inherently divided by their experience — slave or free man — bringing all sorts of complicated attitudes about class, color, and talent toward one another. There are no automatic loyalties to kin, neighbors, old friends, the flag, or especially, white officers. Alliances must be formed from scratch, trust earned through deeds.

They must fight not only the military enemy but their own army — for equal pay, decent uniforms, and rifles that will fire when their lives depend on it. Finally, they fight the racial codes of the Confederacy. If captured, they will be treated according to the state laws in force in the territory of their capture: summary execution as slaves in insurrection or a return to bondage. The *Wilmington Journal* makes this plain and adds, "All commissioned officers who shall be captured in command of negroes, shall suffer the penalty of death." So even their handpicked white officers are risking more than their counterparts in other regiments and have reason to resent the duty.

The wonder is that they take up the challenge at all, a bold, manly gamble to claim their rights as citizens. But Galloway is no naive freedom fighter trusting in the U.S. government to repay his loyalty with some unspecified goodwill when the war is all over. He is hardheaded and pragmatic.

Already he is a prominent leader of some fifty black men who have fought as night pickets, guarding Union camps from raiders. He and his cohort helped guide Burnside's assault force and have since served as guides for numerous Union sorties. They know the back trails, the swamps, the fords in the rivers. Now they also scour the countryside as recruiters, bringing in likely prospects to be signed up and sworn in. The superintendent of Negro affairs in New Bern writes admiringly of their exploits: "Upwards of fifty volunteers of the best and most courageous were kept constantly employed in the perilous but important duty of spies, scouts, and guides." He further reports, "They went from thirty to three hundred miles within the enemy lines." He calls them "almost indispensable."

It is not long before two black men bearing the papers of U.S. Army recruiters are captured by a Confederate patrol and hanged, to great local fanfare.

This is the world inhabited by the colored troops: a netherland in which the rules are never quite clear, laws are slanted toward white people, and the same action can be deemed either a heroic use of initiative or gross insubordination.

Galloway is a secretive individual who crosses the lines with seeming impunity. He routinely walks the streets of New Bern with the butt of his revolver sticking out of his belt. He confides in no one; he leaves no written account of his activities as a scout for Burnside and Foster, as night picket, recruiter, or spy. Galloway is naturally suspicious of leaving behind any record that might later be used against him. And the plain fact is, he can neither read nor write. He is a man with many followers, numerous loyal colleagues, but few intimate friends.

Galloway manages to slip into Wilmington in November 1863 and rescue his mother, Hester Hankins. He is so respected by Wild that he declares, "I would like to do all I can for Galloway, who has served his country well," and arranges for Hankins to receive safe passage to Boston.

The 1st North Carolina Colored Volunteers participate in the siege of Charleston. Their first real test of fire comes at Olustee, the largest battle in

Florida, in February 1864. Fighting alongside the 54th Massachusetts, they stem the rout of Union troops and leave 250 of their own on the field.

Kinsley, Wild, and Galloway eventually raise three regiments of colored infantry. Sherman raises a fourth during his final march through the Carolinas. By the end of the war, 5,000 North Carolina men of African heritage, most of them former slaves, fight alongside 174,000 other blacks in 175 U.S. Army regiments. More than 68,000 of those lay down their lives.

It is impossible to know whether the colored troops turn the tide in a military sense. But it is clear that their blood is part of that sacrifice that, as Lincoln affirmed at Gettysburg, consecrates the American battleground "far above our poor power to add or detract." Beyond their labor and bondage, they have now paid a new price in blood for their homeland.

After the fighting is over, one by one the contraband camps are disbanded. But James City endures, its inhabitants refusing to vacate the land that they have turned into a self-sufficient community.

Back home in Wilmington, Galloway makes it clear that his war is far from over. With familiar passion, he mounts the markethouse, once an auction block for slaves, and exhorts a torchlight procession of fellow black citizens: "My people stand here tonight fettered, bound hand and foot by a Constitution that recognizes them as chattel." He is elected a delegate to the constitutional convention, where he helps to fashion a new state compact that includes all citizens. He goes on to election as state senator and in 1868 is named the first black elector to a presidential convention in the state's history. He remains a passionate advocate for civil rights — including women's suffrage — a spellbinding orator and political force, a daring leader who battles the Ku Klux Klan with fists and clubs and who walks the streets with a horse-pistol tucked into his belt, always wary of assassins.

Then suddenly on September 1, 1870, Galloway is stricken with fever and jaundice and dies at his mother's home. He is just thirty-three. His crusade for justice has left him poor, and he leaves behind no financial legacy. He never did learn to read and write, which matters not to the 6,000 mourners who file up Market Street two days later to pay their last respects at St. Paul's Episcopal Church and escort Abraham H. Galloway to his final, unmarked resting place.

Abraham Galloway

INDIVISIBLE

The Siamese Sons Go to War

War comes to the ordinary citizen—the yeoman farmer, the tradesman, the tenant farmwife who works the fields, the child born into slavery. But it also overtakes the wealthy and famous. Robert Todd Lincoln, the U.S. president's eldest son, eventually escapes Harvard and his mother's protective custody and serves on the wartime staff of General Grant.

Col. Paul Revere, grandson of the famous rider who rallied the farmers of Middlesex to resist an incursion of Redcoats in 1775, is wounded and captured at Ball's Bluff in 1861. Repatriated, he leads the 20th Massachusetts Volunteers—the Harvard Regiment—at Gettysburg, where he is mortally wounded and dies on the Fourth of July 1863. The regimental surgeon writes of him, "Brave, chivalrous, self sacrificing, gentle and generous, he set a noble example of private virtues."

His brother, Assistant Surgeon Edward Hutchinson Robbins Revere, is killed at Antietam on September 17, 1862, while dressing another soldier's wounds.

Sampson Decatur "Sam" Sweeney is the last survivor of the famous Virginia Minstrels from Appomattox. He toured the United States and Europe along with his brothers, Joe and Dick. Now he enlists in Company H, 2nd Virginia Cavalry, in early 1862. Gen. J. E. B. Stuart recruits him to be his personal banjo player, and he accompanies Stuart on his daring campaigns until 1864, when he succumbs to smallpox.

In rural Surry County, North Carolina, the war comes to a pair of world-renowned celebrities living quietly out of the limelight on their farms: Chang and Eng Bunker, the famous Siamese Twins.

Of Chinese heritage and conjoined at the diaphragm by a ligature of skin and cartilage, the twins are discovered at the age of eighteen by an enterprising sea captain named Abel Coffin in the village of Meklong, Thailand. For a payment of $500, Coffin secures permission from their mother to take them abroad until they are twenty-one. He senses opportunity. Thus the twins embark on their first theatrical tour.

Both are quick studies. They pick up rudimentary English from deckhands on the voyage and learn the game of checkers so well they can beat any man on board. They speak and write in the singular first person: "I, Chang Eng."

But they are distinct individuals. Chang, 5 feet 5½ inches tall—an inch shorter than Eng—is quick to anger, impetuous, and dominant. Eng has a more congenial personality. They achieve remarkable physical prowess, walking, running, swimming, rowing boats, and even chopping down trees, in tandem. To amazed onlookers, their movements seem almost miraculously synchronized, as if they can sense each other's every muscle contraction in advance. In truth, they rarely speak to each other, yet the precision of their communication is uncanny.

Only once in childhood did they ever come to blows. Their mother rescued them from each other, warning them that because they are inseparable, they cannot harm either without harming both. They must live in perpetual harmony with each other.

Soon they are seasoned world travelers, feted by royalty and high society, at home in Boston, New York, Paris, Berlin, Antwerp, Dublin, Edinburgh, and London, where 100,000 people line up to see them and they are presented to the Duke of Wellington. At P. T. Barnum's American Museum in New York, they entertain Albert, Prince of Wales. They banter with audiences in perfect English, mimicking local accents, performing feats of acrobatics, and defeating local checkers champions. They pose for photographs and sign autographs and shake thousands of hands. In their off-hours, they develop a fondness for the outdoors—hiking, fishing, and hunting.

Convinced they have been exploited under Coffin's management, they engage a variety of new managers, growing ever more famous. Always, they strive to maintain their dignity. They refuse to participate in carnivals and "freak" shows, presenting themselves on stage as indeed they are in life: extremely intelligent, thoughtful citizens of the world, each with a lively personality, a ready sense of humor, a keen sense of self-respect, and a great capacity for compassion. They grow ever more individual in their tastes, demeanors, personalities, and opinions, yet they remain indivisible.

In New York, they are admired for refunding the fifty-cent admission price to patrons who are missing arms or legs. In Philadelphia, a man squeezes Chang's hand too hard and Chang decks him, but he avoids jail because Eng is innocent. In Alabama, when a doctor dares to try to examine them on a public stage, Chang and Eng simultaneously punch him, and both pay a fine.

Everywhere they travel, renowned doctors turn out to examine them, always in private, at the brothers' insistence, and usually in advance of a performance in order to drum up curiosity and interest. Dr. John Collins Warren, professor of anatomy and surgery at the Harvard Medical School, determines that Chang and Eng share exactly the same respiration and pulse: seventy-three beats per minute.

Another doctor experiments with poking one to learn if the other feels the stab—he does. Another attempts to strangle the cord between them and succeeds in making both twins sick.

Part of the public's enduring fascination with them resides in the question of whether they can ever be separated and survive. What exactly is connected through that two-inch-thick, sinuous cord? Just how vital is the link? Can each survive on his own, a loving brother but physically separate? Or are their fortunes forever entangled, their lives inextricable from each other's, their bond truly indivisible? The answers are contradictory and inconclusive. The doctors cannot agree. Early in life, neither twin can bear the thought of physical separation. On several occasions they almost dare it, but always they back off, reasonably afraid that any attempt to cut their bond might kill them both.

At last the Bunker twins tire of the endless travel and yearn for a more permanent home. In their dressing room at Peale's New York Museum, they meet Dr. James Calloway of Wilkesboro, North Carolina. "The doctor told them that Wilkes County was replete with clear streams teeming with fine fishes; that the hills and mountains abounded with deer and wild turkeys," an acquaintance records in his private memoir. "He invited them to come to Wilkesboro on their next vacation, assuring them the abundant courtesies of the town and country."

In 1839, they take up the doctor on his offer. In Wilkes County, they find both welcoming neighbors and the privacy they crave. Here they can make a life free of gawkers and the constant fatigue of travel. Before long, they have made the area their permanent home, and on October 1, in state superior court, they swear allegiance to their adopted country. They are now Americans. And they join their fortunes to those of the South.

Ten years of constant touring have netted them $10,000—a modest fortune. They invest in farmland and purchase Trap Hill House. They have installed an extra-wide stairway so they can navigate the second floor. Settled at last, they turn their thoughts to companionship and family. It is not long before love finds them, and they begin to yearn for separation to pursue romance. But the surgery is still out of the question. So in 1843 their double wedding to the Yates sisters from nearby Wilkesboro provokes a minor sensation. Adelaide, nineteen, becomes the bride of Chang, and Sarah, a year older, marries Eng. For a wedding present, their in-laws present the twins with a slave named Aunt Grace Yates.

The unlikely marriages will last more than thirty years, and between them the twins will father twenty-one children.

As the families grow, so does the need for space. The Bunkers move to a large farm in Mt. Airy in nearby Surry County and divide it into two farms with two houses, scarcely a mile apart and separated by Stewarts Creek. They donate land for the White Plains Baptist Church—a community-minded gesture, as neither of them is known to be especially devout. They set up a rigid schedule of alternating their lives between the two homes. In each, one of the twins is absolute master. Every three days, they switch houses.

They farm the profitable bright leaf tobacco, along with corn, beans, peas, potatoes, and fruit. They raise cows, sheep, and chickens; keep bees; press their own chewing tobacco for sale; and invest much of their profits in slaves. By the eve of war, they own twenty-eight slaves in all, ranging from small children to forty-year-old field hands, with a total net worth of almost $30,000.

They have thoroughly adopted the culture of the region and record no sense of irony at being slave owners, although they themselves complained bitterly about being sold away from home for the profit of a sea captain.

Chang's eldest son, Christopher Wren Bunker—just sixteen at the outbreak of war—is a slender, confident young man with a shock of dark hair combed back from his forehead and a rakish, neatly trimmed moustache. His features are a handsome blend of Chinese and European—a strong nose and chin below steady, intelligent eyes.

As soon as Christopher turns eighteen, he slips across the nearby state line and enlists in the 37th Virginia Cavalry. He is joined by his cousin Stephen Decatur Bunker—Eng's eldest son—smaller in stature, with a rounder face and a plain, friendly countenance. Both are accomplished riders after long practice roaming the rural hinterland of Surry County. Like other Confederate cavalry volunteers, they must supply their own mounts.

In a letter to his younger sister Nancy Adelaide, affectionately called "Nannie," Christopher recounts the details of hard duty in Tennessee in the autumn of 1863:

Chang and Eng Bunker with their eldest sons. Left to right:
Christopher Wren Bunker; his father, Chang; his uncle Eng; and
his cousin Stephen in a carte-de-visite made before the war.
(Courtesy of Wilson Special Collections Library,
University of North Carolina at Chapel Hill)

About two weeks ago we all went out on a scout and was gone about five days we travelled three nights and days before we made a halt. The seccond night got me it rained all night as hard as it could pour and we had to travell over the rockyest and the muddyest road that I ever saw and the next morning we ran up on the Yankee pickets and captured them and went on to a little town call Rogersville and there we saw a little fun catching Yankees, we captured about 150 Yankees and started back about twelve o'clock and travelled all night that night and in the whole scout we did not take our saddles off of our horses but once or twice and did not feed but once or twice a day and when we got back to camp every horse in the battalion had the scratches so bad that they could hardly travel.

Winter is coming on, and the Confederate quartermaster has mostly run out of uniforms and other necessities. So, like other troopers, Christopher requests them from home, where things are hardly better. "You must knit me two or three pare of socks and a pare of gloves," he writes. "I lost my gloves in that charge after the Yankees. . . . You must make them and try and send them out here if you can for I do not think I will come home this month and you must send me another blanket for the weather is getting very cold out here."

And they have run their horses into the ground with constant skirmishing and scouting in rugged country: "We had a hard time running of them and they running of us. My horse corked himself and became very lame and I had to leave him with a gentleman who lives five miles this side of Lexington . . . and if I should get killed or captured on this raid you can send and get him."

The following summer, the 37th moves across the Potomac into Pennsylvania under the command of Gen. John McCausland and captures a quiet crossroads called Chambersburg. McCausland's aim is to retaliate for U.S. general David Hunter's sacking of several towns in Virginia. McCausland demands a ransom of $100,000 in gold or $500,000 in U.S. currency, but the citizens cannot produce such a fortune. McCausland then orders the burning of the city.

McCausland's own outraged subordinate, Brig. Gen. Bradley T. Johnson, reports what happened then: "At Chambersburg, while the town was in flames, a quartermaster, aided and directed by a field officer, exacted ransom of individuals for their houses, holding the torch in terror over the house until it was paid. These ransoms varied from $750 to $150, depending on the

The Siamese Sons Go to War

size of the habitation. Thus the grand spectacle of a national retaliation was reduced to a miserable huckstering for greenbacks."

Johnson records numerous instances of robbery and theft of civilians: "Every crime in the catalogue of infamy has been committed, I believe, except murder and rape."

The Confederates fall back on Moorefield, West Virginia, confident they are safe from any pursuing Federals. But they underestimate the resourcefulness of the Union commander, Brig. Gen. William W. Averell, who is determined to avenge Chambersburg. His troopers disguise themselves in Confederate gray, then move in pretending to be a relief column. They ambush and rout the unwary Confederates. Christopher is shot out of his saddle.

His letter to Nannie has proven all too prescient, though she does not need to journey to Lexington to claim his mount. A friend escorts Christopher's horse, still spattered with his rider's blood, home to Mt. Airy. It takes some time before the family is reassured Christopher has survived the fight and is a prisoner of war.

In 1864, Christopher Wren Bunker finds himself at Camp Chase, a tract of flat, muddy ground that collects rain in standing pools, on the outskirts of Columbus, Ohio. Uncovered sinks funnel rainwater to the cisterns containing the drinking water for more than 1,000 prisoners of war. He shares a barracks with 200 other prisoners, who sleep on straw mats crawling with lice and endure periodic outbreaks of typhoid.

Early in the war, Camp Chase housed Confederate officers, who were allowed to swear a parole, their word of honor not to escape or commit violence. This allowed them to come and go at will in full uniform, attending shows in town and even carrying sidearms and swords. They frequented the best hotels, and more than a hundred of them were attended by the slaves they had taken with them to the war.

But by the time Christopher arrives, such scandalous practices have been stopped. The officers are gone to special camps, lest they organize their captive troops into an uprising. Likewise, the regulation daily ration has dwindled. In 1861 it included three-quarters of a pound of bacon or a quarter-pound of beef per day, augmented by bread, beans, potatoes, coffee, sugar, molasses, vinegar, and even a candle. But Camp Chase becomes notorious for the gristly slop provided by corrupt army contractors.

To stay alive, Christopher and his fellows catch and roast rats. Later, his family sends money to be used on his behalf, and with it he buys rations and a pocketknife. To pass the endless hours of captivity, he carves boats and musical instruments. His other solace is reading from a small Bible. Small-pox sweeps the camp, and Christopher, already wounded when he arrives, is stricken, along with several hundred others. He survives, as did his father and uncle when smallpox ravaged the twins' Thai village during childhood.

On October 12, Christopher writes a plaintive letter home. The penman-ship is carefully penciled on lined paper, limited to a single page as prescribed in prison regulations: "I was captured the 7th of last August and brought to [t]his place. I have no news of interest to write to you as there are none al-lowed to come in prison. . . . I see no chance for an exchange. I have not seen many well days since I came to this place. I have had the smallpox and now got the diareea but I hope that I wil be well in the course of a week. . . . We are drawing very light rashions here just enough to keep breath and body."

Stephen Decatur Bunker escapes the ambush at Moorefield, but he, too, is later wounded at Winchester. A surgeon cuts out a .44 caliber ball from his shoulder.

Meanwhile, in April 1865, Maj. Gen. George Stoneman raids North Carolina from the mountains at the head of 6,000 cavalry troopers. After the war, locals will recount the story of how Stoneman sought to bolster his ranks with conscripts chosen by a lottery wheel from a roster of local men over eighteen. Eng Bunker's name is drawn, but not Chang's. And Chang re-fuses to go. The befuddled troopers leave both twins behind as they gallop toward Salisbury, intent on liberating the Union prisoners there. It makes a wonderful tale and reinforces the inseparability of the twins, no matter their differences of opinion or politics or luck. It is such a good story that a Phila-delphia newspaper prints it.

But the tale is an utter fabrication. Stoneman has all the troopers he needs to burn Salisbury and ravage Virginia, and no authority to conscript anybody.

A few weeks later, the war at last spasms to a close.

Both Christopher and Stephen return to Mt. Airy to a joyful reunion, tempered by the painful reality that Chang and Eng are all but financially ruined. Their land remains; but their investment in slaves is gone, and their combined savings now amounts to just $2,100. The state's economy is wrecked, its currency worthless, its markets in chaos. Aunt Grace and some of the former slaves remain, working for wages.

Chang and Eng, seasoned troupers, set out to recoup their fortune. At the age of fifty-four, the Siamese Twins go back on tour—really a series of tours—sometimes taking along their wives and some of the children, re-turning home for brief respites. But age and life on the road take their toll.

Chang starts drinking heavily. Eng plays poker to all hours of the night when Chang wants to rest. Their lives, once so harmonious, now tug against the bond that unites them. No longer do they share the same rhythm of breathing, the same pulse. One night, in a drunken rage, Change grabs a knife and threatens to cut their bond himself.

Chang suffers a stroke in 1870, and their show business days are over. Now both are preoccupied with mortality. If one should die, the other will also be doomed. They make a pact with the local doctor that, in the event of the death of either one, the other will immediately be cut free, whatever the risk.

Alas, at four o'clock on the frigid morning of February 17, 1874, Chang dies in his sleep. Eng awakes in a cold sweat, terrified, and complains of excruciating pain. His wife rubs his legs and arms, but nothing she tries can assuage his pain or dull his terror. Before the doctor can arrive, Eng utters his final, agitated words: "May the Lord have mercy upon my soul."

Then he slips away.

Doctors from the Mütter Museum in Philadelphia persuade the family to allow them to perform an autopsy. They determine that what the twins always knew in their hearts was, indeed, true: they could not have been separated in life without fatal hazard. Their livers are connected through the band that has held them no more than five inches apart for sixty-three years. Thus they remained inseparable unto death. Their livers are preserved in formaldehyde for exhibit at the Mütter Museum.

Amid wild speculation that the bodies of Chang and Eng will be sold as medical curiosities, Christopher Wren Bunker and Stephen Decatur Bunker demand that the bodies be shipped home to Mt. Airy. The Philadelphia surgeons honor their request.

But the family cannot run the risk of "resurrection men" looting the grave for profit. They place the bodies in a single walnut coffin and carry it across the creek to Chang's house, where they hide it in a locked cellar for a full year before burying it under a holly tree in the front yard. Forty-seven years later, in 1917, their coffin is dug up and reburied on the grounds of White Plains Baptist Church, the church that was the twins' gift to their neighbors.

Christopher Wren Bunker and Stephen Decatur Bunker recover completely from their wounds and live long, full lives. In his colorful, plaintive, vivid letters home, Christopher created the only known account written by a Chinese American veteran of the war.

18

THE STOCKARD FAMILY'S WAR

Whenever a North Carolina regiment marches into battle, it is as if the entire community from which it was assembled has formed up in ranks, shoulder to shoulder, and is charging the guns of the enemy. The man to the right or left might be a brother, a cousin, or an in-law. Lieutenants and captains are likely uncles, fathers, or neighbors. The colonel is probably a local man of some reputation who, before the fighting, served as magistrate, militia commander, or political leader.

When a regiment takes heavy losses in a great battle, win or lose, back home it leaves empty pews at the Sunday service, widows and fatherless children, absent faces at the general store. The loss never seems individual, a lone soldier killed in the company of strangers. It feels collective, a small town or country crossroads suddenly emptied of able-bodied men. And as the war carries on with its own unstoppable momentum, the younger brothers and sons emulate their elders. They sign up with men they trust, then trek to a mustering station near a railroad.

On May 21, 1861, the day after secession is tolled from the bell towers of North Carolina churches, Judge Thomas Ruffin holds a recruiting barbecue in Alamance County. Originally from Virginia, Ruffin graduates from the College of New Jersey (later named Princeton) and then achieves great success and wealth in North Carolina, becoming speaker of the house in the General Assembly and rising to chief justice of North Carolina's supreme court, a position he holds from 1833 to 1852. He retires from the court for good in 1859. On his prosperous Haw River plantation, he employs about 100 slaves.

Judge Ruffin is notorious for his cruel treatment of slaves. A neighbor, Archibald Murphy, charges that Ruffin's overseer has been "literally barbecuing, peppering, and salting" some of them. Ruffin himself, ever fearful of runaways, is known to beat his slaves. Ruffin actively trades slaves for a profit. He sells Winny, a nine-year-old, to an Alabama slaver for a profit of $70. He sells "Little Charles, 10 and 2 cisters younger," for a profit of $325. Another adult slave, Noah, is married to an enslaved woman on Ruffin's plantation. Despite the man's pleas to remain with his wife, Ruffin sells him to a neighbor for $150.

Judge Ruffin, who has written opinions on 1,400 cases, is famous—or infamous—for one decision in particular: *State v. Mann*. The case reached the state supreme court in 1829 and defines Ruffin's loyalties to the slave-holding Confederacy more than thirty years later. John Mann was convicted of shooting a slave named Lydia as she tried to flee from a whipping. Mann did not own the slave but was only renting her. The court overturned Mann's conviction. Ruffin wrote, "The power of the master must be absolute to render the submission of the slave perfect. . . . It will be the imperative duty of the Judges to recognize the full dominion of the owner over the slave."

Ruffin opposes secession—he does not believe that the U.S. Constitution permits it—yet when the break comes, the imperious seventy-two-year-old judge embraces it as a revolutionary act against the United States. He declares, "I say fight, fight, fight!"

Now he is determined to fill the ranks of the 5th Regiment of North Carolina Volunteers (later changed to the 15th). Among the many young men who show up to hear the judge's rallying speech is John Williamson Stockard, a twenty-three-year-old farmer: slender, of medium height, with dark eyes, a pale complexion, and light-colored hair. Later his daughter, Sallie, will recall how the judge exhorted the boys to sign up to whip the Yankees. "Come on, boys! Enroll! Volunteer! We want as long a list as possible here today. Johnny Stockard, how about you?"

John Williamson Stockard answers the call. So does his uncle, thirty-three-year-old John Richard Stockard, who leaves behind a pregnant wife and two small children. The young ladies who are present loop a wreath of red roses over the head of each volunteer, and John Williamson is still garlanded with roses as he plods homeward at sundown and passes the home of his grandfather, who happens to be sitting on the porch. His grandfather knows he has been to Judge Ruffin's.

"I see you are wearing a wreath of roses," his grandfather observes. "Did you get those at the barbecue?"

John Williamson tells him yes, and relates what the judge said in his speech. "He could wipe up all the blood shed in the Civil War with his white handkerchief and not stain it."

His grandfather is skeptical. "This will be a bloody war," he predicts. "You should not have signed up. This is a rich man's war. As certain as there is a war, the South will lose."

But John Williamson has already signed on, and he musters in at Garysburg, near the railroad terminus of Weldon. He takes his place with 117 other enlisted men in Company H, commanded by his uncle, Capt. John Richard Stockard.

By summer, the 5th Regiment, 800 strong, is ordered to Yorktown, Virginia. Nearby is camped the 3rd (later 13th) Regiment of North Carolina Volunteers, the Alamance Regulators. Judge Ruffin's son, Capt. Thomas Ruffin Jr., commands Company E of the Regulators, which includes more relatives: John Williamson's younger brother, Robert J. Stockard, and his first cousin, Samuel Stockard. Also serving in Company E is Samuel Stockard's best friend and first cousin, Joseph Long.

Samuel's brother, William J. Stockard, has meanwhile enlisted in the 57th Regiment, and soon Samuel's cousin, the youngest Stockard, twenty-one-year-old Joseph S., enlists in the 1st North Carolina Infantry. Thus the war takes seven men from a single extended family:

Three Stockard brothers, John Williamson, Robert J., and Joseph S.
Their uncle, John Richard Stockard
Their cousins, brothers Samuel and William J. Stockard
And Samuel and William's first cousin, Joseph Long.

They are ordinary men. Tens of thousands like them also take up arms. Many come from small settlements made up of extended family. Camp life is a series of family reunions, as cousins and uncles are brought together in the mass of men assembled for war. They are mostly not political zealots or slaveholders. Their loyalties tend to be simple and local: to their families, one another, and their state. And they have no idea what they are in for.

At Yorktown, disease courses through the army. Hundreds of soldiers of the 5th Regiment, hill country men suddenly crowded together in the summer Low Country heat, fall victim to fevers and malaria. By September, only 10 percent of the men are well enough to report for duty. By late autumn, the regiment recovers, and by February it moves on Suffolk, then redeploys to Goldsboro. The only casualties so far die from fever.

In March 1862, John Williamson Stockard succumbs to "Icterus" — jaundice — and spends nearly two full months recovering at the General Hospital in Petersburg, Virginia. By September, he spends three weeks at Winder Hospital in Richmond, complaining of diarrhea, rampant in the army and symptomatic of a variety of ailments. Twice more he is hospitalized, at Chimborazo in Richmond, stricken by "Debliitas" — weakness and exhaustion.

The Stockard Family's War

He returns to his regiment just in time to join the evacuation from York-town of Maj. Gen. Joseph E. Johnston's Army of Northern Virginia, 56,000 men clogging two muddy roads. By now all volunteer regiments have been renumbered by adding 10, to avoid confusion with regular regiments. The 5th — now the 15th — acts as rearguard, skirmishing all the way to Williams-burg, living on parched corn. At last John Williamson and his regiment cross the Chickahominy River and camp.

In July 1862, the regiment, now down to 700, joins the first line at Malvern Hill and endures heavy fire all day; 164 men fall dead or wounded.

The regiment receives 250 new recruits and moves north, part of Lee's invasion of Maryland. The 15th fights alongside the 13th at South Mountain, losing 62 killed and wounded and another 124 men captured. After the battle at Antietam Creek near Sharpsburg, just 133 officers and men are fit for duty.

But for John Williamson Stockard, the war goes on. At Marye's Heights above Fredericksburg, the 15th stays in action for five hours, expending 35,000 cartridges. At Bristoe, John Williamson survives a charge against Union troops forted up in a railroad cut. The regimental historian records, "Confederate lines were mowed down like grain before a reaper."

Altogether, he fights in twenty-one engagements. He soldiers on through the horrific slaughter of the Wilderness and the relentless nine-month-long bombardment of Petersburg. As Confederate forces retreat west in April 1865, the 15th again acts as rearguard, and at last John Williamson is captured by Union forces. He is one of the lucky Stockards. After ten weeks in cap-tivity, he is "turned out half-starved with a sore leg and plenty of body lice," as his daughter, Sallie, records. But he makes it home.

John Williamson's uncle, John Richard Stockard, is granted a furlough back to Alamance County in July and August 1861 because of illness. The leave allows him to be present for the birth of his namesake son. When he rejoins his regiment, he is again stricken with debilitating fever and spends the winter "absent sick." On February 28, 1862, he is dismissed from service and returns home to his wife and three children. He, too, is one of the lucky Stockards.

Samuel Stockard, twenty-three years old, was the first of the clan to en-list, on May 13, 1861, even before secession was declared, recruited by Capt. Thomas Ruffin Jr., son of Judge Ruffin, into Company E, the Alamance Regulators, of the 3rd (later 13th) North Carolina Volunteers. After a bout of illness, Samuel writes from Suffolk, Virginia, on June 1, "The God of the Universe will be with us on every battlefield. He has been in our camp since we left our homes."

Still at Suffolk when other troops move on Harpers Ferry, he is champing at the bit for action. In his typical jaunty style, he writes to "Father & Family" later the same month, "Though I don't believe we are going to have any of the fighting to do, for any small no. of Southerners can slash the yankies every pop, why they cant fight a bit hardly."

He notes that he received a letter from his uncle and his cousin, John Williamson. "I read one from Cousin John also, he says he don't like the eating doings a bit, he said some droll remarks about the soldier's life. I don't think he likes it much."

But before he can fight the "yankies," Samuel is felled by illness again: "I have been in the hospital for a few days, afflicted with Diareah. You see this water down here don't agree with a feller and we have the *Belly-Ache* once in a while." Still, he brags, "We are going to whip them and be home in a few days."

He adds, "Cousin Bob is a Regulator, he has no gun yet but he will get one."

Samuel's first cousin, Robert J. Stockard, joins the regiment in September 1861. Cousin Bob stands 5 feet 9 inches tall, with blue eyes, blond hair, and a fair complexion. He is twenty-two years old. Bob's letters home are dry and factual, grammatical and precise, as if he is holding himself at arm's length from the emotion of sudden violent death. "A sharp fight took place the other day between the 5th Reg't N.C.V. and a large Yankee force who attacked them in their entrenchments. The Yankees were driven back with great slaughter after two hours hard fighting. The Alamance boys fought well and lost three killed to wit Monroe Clendennin Seymour Wood and Ensley steel."

By November, Samuel Stockard writes home, "I am a little tired of war, it's hard work."

The regiment goes into winter quarters at Camp Ruffin in Smithfield, Virginia, but with spring comes a new campaigning season. With spring also comes the Conscription Act, extending enlistments, approved, Samuel writes, by "King Davis." He is still recovering from the mumps and laments, "Im in for the term of 2 more long years, and as you know with a constitution not strong enough to bear the hardships that are heaped upon a Soldier in camp life . . . and as to getting home on furlough, that is almost as impossible as for a man to drive a nail through the moon."

Samuel fights with the 13th at Seven Pines, but Cousin Bob has been stricken with typhoid. He is sent home in July and never recovers. Robert J.

The Stockard Family's War

Stockard dies at home on August 6, his exact age etched in his tombstone: "23 years, 2 months, 26 days."

Samuel Stockard survives the carnage at Fredericksburg in December 1862. Then in the spring, the 13th is ordered to Chancellorsville. On a beautiful Sunday morning, May 3, the regiment advances on defensive lines of Union soldiers barricaded behind railroad ties—and into a blinding blaze of massed musketfire. Samuel Stockard falls mortally wounded; he lingers for nine days before he dies. He is buried in the Providence churchyard in Graham, North Carolina. Beside him lies his cousin, Joseph Long, killed in the same attack.

William J. Stockard follows his brother into the army on July 4, 1862. He too joins a band of Alamance County men in Company I of the 57th North Carolina Regiment, enlisting "for three years or the duration of the War Between the States." In October, William is stricken with typhoid fever and bedridden. He rejoins his regiment at the end of January. In May he fights at Chancellorsville, in June at Winchester, and in July he charges Cemetery Hill on the second day of the battle of Gettysburg. The slaughter is appalling.

After Gettysburg, William writes home in despair, "I can say that we got out of heart as soon as we got in Penn. To see the men they have there that never been in war. They have more men that never been in than we ever had in the war so I can't see no use in fighting they would better settle it some way for I believe in my heart that we are whipped. Get all our poor men killed that is about all good we ever done yet."

His letter is all too prescient. At Winchester in the Shenandoah Valley, he is shot in the back, gravely wounded, and captured. He dies anonymously and is buried along with 828 other Confederate unknowns.

William and Samuel's cousin Joseph Stockard is captured in the same battle. He has survived sixteen battles, his regiment often fighting alongside those of this brother and cousins. Now he manages to survive almost seven months of captivity before parole.

Of the six Stockard men, all but one have been killed or captured or died of disease.

John Williamson Stockard comes home and settles on his grandmother's homestead, where he raises six children. His uncle, John Richard Stockard, returns to the family farm and fathers thirteen children by two wives. Joseph S. Stockard, John Williamson's brother, also returns to Alamance County to farm and raise three sons and a daughter.

They have returned to their homeplace, a place missing so many cousins, brothers, and neighbors. Their ghosts of the missing are joined by the spirits of their unborn children, and whatever mark they would have made as they matured into men is erased.

Judge Ruffin survives the war by five years. His son, now Lt. Col. Thomas Ruffin Jr., becomes an associate justice of the North Carolina Supreme Court.

After the struggle, the survivors enjoy the blessing that their jaunty cousin and nephew Samuel Stockard penned back when the war was still young, before he was struck down at Chancellorsville and his little brother William was shoveled into an unmarked grave at Winchester: "I hope that the time may come soon when this war shall close, and peace reign o'er a free and happy people."

19

ONWARD CHRISTIAN SOLDIERS

For most North Carolinians in 1860, the world is a place governed by the will of Providence. Good fortune is the result of an upright life, and calamity comes as a judgment from the hand of God. The war itself is a special trial in which the Almighty will test the honor and purity of those who fight—and the faith of those who are left behind.

Many of the aristocratic class—plantation owners and political leaders—are Episcopalians, a minority faith with influence far beyond its 3,000 members, spread out in fifty-three congregations.

By contrast, the Baptists comprise 65,000 members in nearly 800 congregations, but they are divided in their doctrine and practices, sometimes fiercely so. For more than a generation, the Regular or Primitive Baptists have been estranged from the Separate or Missionary Baptists.

Likewise, the Methodists first split with their Northern counterparts over the issue of slavery, from being an antislavery force to a defender of slavery as a Bible-sanctioned way of life. Further schisms have created Christian, Methodist Protestant, and Wesleyan Methodist churches. As an aggressively evangelical sect that relies more on boisterous camp meetings than on staid ritual, it has quickly grown to rival the Baptists, with more than 60,000 members in more than 900 congregations. Combined with the Baptists, Methodists make up 80 percent of churchgoers in the state.

The Presbyterian Church claims more than 15,000 members, solidly rooted in the rising middle class and the Scots tradition of the Cape Fear River Valley and areas of the Piedmont.

The antislavery Quakers are clustered in Guilford, Chatham, and Randolph Counties, fewer than 5,000 strong. In Salem are settled the Moravians, a German sect that owns slaves communally—that is, the church is the slaveholder, and the slaves are used to perform the work of the settlement. There are pockets of Lutherans in the Piedmont, Disciples of Christ in the East, and a few Roman Catholics and Jews, mainly in the cities.

Among many congregations, churchgoing is more prevalent among women, for whom it provides a welcome milieu for socializing. Pastors complain about this, but they are widely seen as less manly than either the patriarchs of the plantation class or the rough-and-tumble working men.

Slaves are preached to by itinerant ministers hired by owners, or by ministers among their own ranks. Some attend services at their masters' churches, and many are denied any religious instruction at all for fear it will lead to discontent and an urge to run away or rebel.

Before the war, the churches mostly steer clear of politics, wary of the consequences of secession. And it is difficult to reconcile the forced bondage of fellow human beings, often in cruel and dehumanizing circumstances, with Christian charity.

The solution is to cast slavery in Old Testament terms. The classic argument comes from the Book of Genesis. Slaves are the descendants of Ham, condemned to serve the righteous of God, as one minister writes: "God did not make all men free and equal. He has enslaved some by placing them in bondage to others. Ham manifested the wicked traits which afterward developed themselves in his descendants, and on this account Heaven forged the chains of slavery and placed them upon him, using his father, Noah, as His agent. Hear Him: 'Cursed by Canaan, a servant of servants shall he be to his brethren.'" Thus many evangelical churches become staunch defenders of the institution as a God-directed state of affairs in which mere humans should not meddle.

Northern theologians, of course, take issue with this self-serving invocation of Mosaic law. One, Professor Taylor Lewis, writes in the *New York World* that no Old Testament patriarch "ever *sold*, or thought of selling for money, the humblest of his dependent vassals." Lewis continues, "To be *owned* is degrading; to be *property*, and nothing more, is dehumanizing," and therefore damning evidence of a sin against the teachings of Christ.

Not all North Carolina preachers are convinced that slavery is sanctioned by God. Dr. Robert Hall Morrison, a Presbyterian minister, wrestles with his conscience over the contradiction between man as the image of Christ and the practice of holding some people as property: "I have long looked upon Slavery as a traffic in itself detestable and justified by no principle either of nations or nature." Yet his 200-acre Cottage Home Plantation in Lincoln County is worked by more than sixty slaves.

None of this sea change in religious sentiment happens overnight. It evolves over years of debate, reflection, prayer, and social pressure. By the time war comes, in the South only the Quakers remain institutionally on the side of abolition.

Onward Christian Soldiers

When North Carolina at last secedes and troops begin mustering in large camps in Raleigh, Goldsboro, and elsewhere, at first, the only chaplains to attend them are recruited by the individual commanders. The Confederate government considers chaplains an unnecessary expense. Late in the war, bowing to popular demand, it grudgingly enlists chaplains at the rank and pay of private. Only about fifty chaplains officially serve the entire Confederate army, though many more are sponsored by individual states, congregations, or generals.

The churches band together to form a "religious military press." It prints thousands of religious tracts—newspapers, pamphlets, pocket devotionals—and distributes them to the army in the field. The various denominations agree not to pursue their own doctrinal agendas. The editor of the *Army and Navy Messenger* proclaims, "Remember, we are not laboring to promote the interests of any party or sect, but simply to lead men to Christ, to make them disciples of the Saviour."

Another purpose becomes quite clear, expressed by a writer for the *Soldier's Friend*: "to prepare them, if possible, for the greatest of emergencies, *death*."

The *Soldier's Visitor* preaches that there is no contradiction between killing the enemy and serving the gospel. "The old time idea that a good Christian cannot make a good soldier, has been thoroughly exploded," it explains. "It has been proved, that other things being equal—the better Christian, the better soldier."

There are prayers for the hour before battle to calm the nerves and steady the heart: "Stir up thy strength, O Lord, and come and help us; for Thou givest not always the battle to the strong, but canst save by many or by few."

There are prayers to recite after a defeat, to rally the men once more to the sacred cause and search their hearts for any weakness of spirit or faltering of courage that might have caused them to be vanquished.

There are especially prayers to be rendered enthusiastically on the heels of great victory, giving thanks and assuring the Almighty of the humility of his servants: "O Almighty God, the Sovereign Commander of all the world in whose hand is power and might, which none is able to withstand; we bless and magnify thy great and glorious name for this happy victory, the whole glory whereof we do ascribe to thee, who art the only giver of victory."

There is also a prayer for a sick or wounded soldier, and there are plenty of funeral invocations.

The prayers and revival meetings serve two main purposes. First, they reinforce the sense of a soldier's duty to his country as a sacred duty, an obligation not just to a regiment or a political entity or even a community but to the Almighty himself. "The true Christian is always a true patriot. Patriotism and Christianity walk hand in hand," sermonizes John Paris, Methodist chaplain to the 54th North Carolina.

Second, they prepare a soldier to face death, steadied by his belief in a better afterlife in which he will be united with loved ones and free of suffering. Thus, a tract titled "Prepare to Meet Thy God" exhorts the soldier-reader, "Consider the *certainty* of the event. You *must* meet God. . . . This meeting *may take place soon*—it cannot be *very* far distant. . . . You may never see old age; you may never see another year; nay, another *day*, another *hour* may usher your soul into the presence of your Judge."

Thus are reinforced obedience to commanders and valor in the face of slaughter.

One North Carolina soldier writes that the tracts are "gladly received and closely read." He goes on, "Candor leads me to say that a Chaplain, as a general thing, is of but little benefit to the soldiers. . . . Often I have seen the Chaplain of a regiment preaching to a squad of fifteen or twenty, while others were lolling about their tents, yet others at a game of cards. . . . I think the Missionary will be received differently and more favorably." In any event, the tracts lead to private reflection, and "Reflection leads to resolves of reformation."

The fight against the forces of the United States takes on the character of a crusade, a holy war in which *honor*—cast in Old Testament allegiance to tribe, culture, and God—is sacred, to be defended to the death. In a very real sense, the Confederacy has defined itself as a Christian nation, its fight as a Christian war.

North Carolina fields perhaps the most famous Christian soldier of all. Leonidas Polk, a Raleigh native and University of North Carolina alum, graduates West Point and then, after just six months, abandons his military career for a clerical one. He rises to become the Episcopal bishop of Louisiana, presiding from a plantation worked by several hundred slaves. When war comes, he stuns his fellow clerics by—in the words of his ecclesiastical critics—"buckling the sword over the gown."

He goes to the fight bearing a battle flag presented to him by a wealthy Louisiana neighbor, Sarah Dorsey, emblazoned with the Cross of Constantine. She drives home the symbolism in a letter to him: "We are fighting the Battle of the Cross against the Modern Barbarians who would rob a Christian people of Country, Liberty, and Life."

Onward Christian Soldiers

Polk's old friend Jefferson Davis soon promotes him to lieutenant general. Throughout the war, he retains his evangelical fervor. He habitually dons his clerical robes over his uniform to perform religious services.

He is a tall, stately man with a full beard befitting his station, hounded by critics but lauded by General Lee "as a model for all that was soldierly, gentlemanly, and honorable." Polk's aide recalls with admiration, "In battle he was a daring old man, with his heart in the fray, and his best faith on the result; riding through shot and shell from point to point, unconscious of danger. . . . He was proverbial for getting into 'hot places'; and he seemed to be able to pass along a line of fire like the children through the fiery furnace, untouched."

But in the summer of 1864, at Pine Mountain, Georgia, Polk is cut nearly in half by a cannonball and dies on the field. In the left pocket of his coat, his aides find a copy of *The Book of Common Prayer*, and in his right they discover four editions of *Chaplain C. T. Quintard's Balm for the Weary and Wounded*. Now stained with his blood, they were intended as gifts to Gen. Joseph E. Johnston and Gen. John Bell Hood, both recently baptized by Polk.

The ministers who serve as chaplains energetically support the prosecution of the war, urging soldiers to fight bravely, to die willingly, and to kill without remorse an enemy they cast as the infidel, the minion of Satan. They baptize and bury, and sometimes they perform both rituals in the span of a single day.

As the war progresses, many denominations—especially Baptists—call for state-sanctioned religion. President Davis decrees numerous days of national fasting and prayer. At the outset of the war, evangelical Christian churches in the state and throughout the South were morally certain that the South would prevail, that God was indeed on their side. With great fervor, they anticipated the establishment of a Christian nation blessed by the Almighty. The string of early victories against such great odds excited an almost ecstatic tenor to their claim that God has ordained victory.

But as Confederate soldiers are slaughtered at Sharpsburg, Gettysburg, the Wilderness, Winchester—all over the map, it seems—a kind of bafflement sets in. The North Carolina Baptists' *Biblical Recorder* raises the issue. "Some white Christians of the Confederacy, in seeking to determine why God has not yet given victory to his chosen nation and instead is allowing the war to continue, have determined that the primary sin of the South is that of extortion." In other words, God is angry that merchants are gouging customers for scarce commodities.

On another occasion, the *Recorder* offers a different conclusion: "What mountains of guilt have we been heaping up by our Sabbath-breaking, our profanities, our intemperance, our haste to be rich, our self-exaltation and disregard of God. This last is indeed the chief root of our difficulty."

It occurs to no religious leader that the sin that is causing all the trouble might be slavery.

In his second inaugural address, delivered from the steps of the Capitol on March 4, 1865, amid a crowd of onlookers that includes an actor named John Wilkes Booth, Abraham Lincoln expresses the contradiction that religious fervor on both sides has brought to the conflict: "Both read the same Bible and pray to the same God, and each invokes His aid against the other. . . . The prayers of both could not be answered. That of neither has been answered fully. The Almighty has His own purposes."

Indeed. A few weeks later, Lincoln is struck down by the hand of the actor who was part of this audience for his haunting speech. And the actor himself is shot to death by a religious zealot who explains, "Providence directed my hand." He wears his hair long in imitation of Jesus and has castrated himself with a pair of scissors "for the kingdom of heaven's sake." He calls himself Boston Corbett, after the city where he was saved.

MINISTERING ANGEL

A Chaplain among the Troops

The war overtakes the enthusiastic and the reluctant alike, and sometimes they are both the same man. Rev. Alexander Davis Betts of Smithville, a quiet village on the estuary of the Cape Fear River, is a gentle man, just three months shy of twenty-nine years old. With a long, studious face; a high, bald brow with swept-back hair; dark chin whiskers but no moustache; resolute eyes; and a long, sharp nose, he looks every inch the preacher.

He records in the diary he will keep for the duration of the war and meticulously edit afterward, "One day in April, 1861, I heard that President Lincoln had called on the State troops to force the seceding States back into the Union. That was one of the saddest days of my life." Betts writes, "That day I walked up and down my porch in Smithville and wept and suffered and prayed for the South."

Betts and his young wife, Mary, have four small children. He has never imagined himself going off to war. As a farmboy growing up in Cumberland County, he once tried to ride a steer and was thrown, so badly injuring himself that performing physical labor remains difficult for him. He walks with a limp ever afterward.

As a student at the University of North Carolina, he is stirred by the evangelical enthusiasm of Methodism, and in 1853, on one of the red-letter days of his life, he converts. He soon feels himself called to the ministry, and long before graduating, Betts begins preaching. A classmate recalls that Betts "was older than the average college student when at Chapel Hill, and his influence on his fellows was correspondingly greater He was faithful to every duty and graduated with honor."

Betts is acquainted with Lt. Lorenzo Cain of Company C, 30th North Carolina Regiment, who was a teacher in Brunswick County before the war. Lieutenant Cain nominates Betts to be chaplain of the regiment. The governor agrees to the appointment. Betts is torn between strenuous duty and the comforts of home, between his family and his calling.

After praying over the matter, Betts accepts the position of chaplain, and during the months he spends waiting for his commission to become official, he suffers his first blow of the war: in August, the day before his own twenty-ninth birthday, his son Eddie dies. At least he is home, and his wife is not forced to "sorrow alone." On the anniversary of the awful event, he writes, "One year ago today, my dear little Eddie was cold in death in parsonage in Smithville . . . and I was almost dead." And later, "My dear sainted Eddie! Safe in Heaven! Your father hopes to embrace you by-and-by in your angel home."

At last Betts receives his commission on October 25, 1861, guaranteeing that he will see the worst of the entire bloody war: the Seven Days Battles around Richmond, and the epic clashes at Sharpsburg, Fredericksburg, Chancellorsville, Gettysburg, and Cold Harbor.

In the early encampment at Federal Point across the river, the family joins him in a rented house. Later in Richmond they manage to visit him; but for most of the war they are separated, and he endures the same pangs of longing as the other soldiers, the same anxiety for the safety of those left behind.

The post of chaplain is no sinecure. Betts could make it so—conduct regular prayer meetings on the Sabbath, comfort the sick and wounded where he is stationed, and generally keep his pious distance from hardship and the battlefield. He could refrain from knowing the men too well, many of whom he will have to minister to in their wounded agony or bless into their graves. But he does the opposite. His Methodist calling exhorts him to be out among the troops, witnessing the gospel in not just word but also action.

He studies the names of all the men in the regiment, the names of their loved ones, and their hometowns. He tends to the wounded, but he doesn't confine himself to prayers. He carries men bleeding from the battlefield, coaxes one soldier to allow his arm to be amputated, and follows the dire cases to Chimborazo or Camp Winder. He sleeps under wagons and in open fields and wears out horses in his constant travels to Richmond, Ashland, Mechanicsville, Winchester, Martinsburg, and Strasburg—in addition to campaigning across Maryland and Pennsylvania. Time and again he is laid low by exhaustion and fever, and once he falls off his horse unconscious and awakens in a meadow an hour later. He observes, bemusedly, "God could take a man out of this world without his knowing anything of it."

After the Seven Days Battles, he takes on one of the war's most heart-

A Chaplain among the Troops

breaking tasks: writing letters of condolence to the families of the fallen. Among the dead he recognizes old friends from Wilmington and school-mates from Chapel Hill. His diary soon becomes a roll call of sick, wounded, and dying friends: Captain Sykes of Bladen; Daniel McDugold, a school-mate at both Summerville Academy and Chapel Hill; Lieutenant Shaw, "one of the noblest men I ever knew"; Lt. Duncan E. McNair, "my classmate of many years"; another college classmate, Capt. S. A. Sutton; Capt. John Barr Andrews, the first person to whom, as a student, Betts confided his own religious conversion.

And Lt. Lorenzo Cain, the schoolteacher who nominated him for his post as chaplain.

Betts's little book quickly fills up with other words, describing his own physical trials: "Hoarse and feeble," "weary," "Suffer with cough," "In camp sick," "cough and cold very bad," "Fever all day. May the Lord restore me so that I may administer to others."

He is beloved by the men he serves, a man of faith and humility. On August 25, 1862, he writes, "My birthday! Thirty years old! And yet how little knowledge I have acquired! How little grace! How little good have I done! God help me in time to come! Get marching orders at nine at night."

On the road from Warrenton to Leesburg, Virginia, Betts encounters the enemy up close.

I found a wounded Federal sitting on the field — a broken thigh, a rifle ball through his arm and a bruised shoulder made him right helpless. . . . He said he had a wife and two little children in his northern home. He told me our men had been very good to him during the three or four days he had been there. . . . As I was about to hurry away to overtake my regiment he asked me to lay him down! How could I? Where could I take hold? I did the best I could. As I took him by the hand and commended him to God, I think my heart was as tender as it ever was. His bones may be in that field now. I hope to meet his soul in Heaven in a few years.

At Sharpsburg, Betts is again pressed into service as a nurse and medical assistant: "Sep 17 — Very heavy firing in morning. Wounded coming in. God help our men to fight! Have mercy on those who are to die!"

Meanwhile, back home his little daughter Mary falls critically ill. "May now be in Heaven," he writes, but he cannot leave the army. "Father, into thy hands I commend my child."

As the cold weather sets in and the fighting slackens, Betts is at last

Rev. Alexander Davis Betts practices his faith on the battlefield and
keeps a journal filled with the names of his fallen friends.
(Courtesy of Wilson Special Collections Library,
University of North Carolina at Chapel Hill)

granted a furlough to see his family. The travel is arduous: "Nov. 20 — Six miles on saddle, twelve on wagon, five on foot." The next day he jounces in an ambulance to a Baptist church at Mt. Crawford, where he spends the night with scores of wounded men. A stage takes him to Staunton, where he entrains for Richmond and Weldon. He misses the Wilmington train, finally reaches Wilmington by way of Raleigh. From there he walks to the home of a friend, where he hitches a buggy ride to the home of another friend, who loans him a horse.

After five exhausting days of travel, a final buggy ride brings him to his own front door. "Nov. 25 — Had not seen family since July 31. In going home from the army I met Lieut. E. Ruark, of Co. C. on his way home at Smithville, on sick furlough. We sat together for many, many miles, and parted at Wilmington. He went home and died of smallpox, spreading it and killing his mother and others. Narrow escape for me and mine. Neither of us thought of the danger."

The best news of all: Betts's daughter Mary has survived her fever.

Betts does not spend his furlough resting, however. Instead he preaches at every opportunity, even takes his family to Raleigh to the church conference. And soon enough he is back in camp. "March 28 — Rain all day. Finish writing to churches for Co. G. Note: I talked with each church member in each company about his spiritual condition as often as I could. Once a year I wrote home to each church about its members and sent any message anyone wanted to send, and asked the church at home to pray for us. This was expensive, laborious work, but it was for souls whom Jesus died to save."

March and April bring furious gusts of rain, snow, sleet, and wind, and the army suffers constantly from exposure to the harsh elements. In April he applies for a leave of absence to be with his pregnant wife during an "important crisis" and is heartbroken when General Jackson personally denies it. But the news from home buoys him: "Apr. 25 — Our fifth child, a son, is born at 3:30 a. m. Mother and child doing well. Thank God!"

The carnage has not shaken his faith or dampened his zeal. On the tenth anniversary of Betts's own conversion, Charlie Ruffin, who enlisted at seventeen and "perhaps, was the wildest boy in his Regiment," dies in his arms. "Just before he breathed his last . . . He sweetly smiled and said: 'Bro. Betts as soon as I die I shall go straight to my blessed Jesus!' That was a happy moment to me . . . the joy I feel pays me a thousand times for all the nights I ever slept on frozen ground, snow or mud."

Betts constructs temporary arbors for services, even a real wooden chapel at camp in Virginia. He fashions a log cabin for himself during the winter months of 1863, a place of reflection, where he can talk to one friend at a time and read in solitude. He continues writing for the *Recorder*, an inspirational tract distributed by the Religious Military Press. He conducts a round-robin of prayer meetings, each day addressing a different company in the regiment.

By 1864, the war has been grinding on for three years. It is astonishing the number of parishioners, old friends, and relatives of friends he encounters in the hospital camps and among the dead. Even the enemy no longer seem strangers. After a battle at Winchester, the regiment falls back on Strasburg. "Riding alone and very sad, at midnight, I overtake one or two thousand Federal prisoners. They began to sing, 'We are going home to die no more.' My heart was touched. I shed tears as I thought many of them would die in Southern prisons."

Another task of the chaplain is to act as a "convenient agent" to retrieve boxes of clothing and food sent from home to soldiers in the field. Betts collects them at the nearest railroad depot and attempts to deliver them. All too often, by the time he finds the intended recipient, the man is already a casualty.

Betts is on furlough in Chapel Hill when he hears the news of Lee's surrender. As Sherman's army invades from the south, Betts joins the Army of Tennessee under Johnston, until that army is surrendered just a few weeks later.

Betts writes wistfully,

> The night following the tidings of our contemplated surrender was a still, sad night in our camp. Rev. W. C. Willson, the Chapel Hill pastor ... and I walked out of the camp and talked and wept together. As I started back to my tent — to my mule and saddle, I should say, for I had no tent — I passed three lads sitting close together, talking softly and sadly. I paused and listened. One said, "It makes me very sad, to think of our surrendering." Another said, "It hurts me worse than the thought of battle ever did." The third raised his arm, clenched his fist and seemed to grate his teeth as he said, "I would rather know we had to go into battle tomorrow morning."

For the next half century, the Reverend Alexander Davis Betts preaches to congregations across the state, time and again meeting survivors from his old regiment, attended always by a company of ghosts.

A Chaplain among the Troops

21

DEAR MY BELOVED

In the spring of 1861, young men march off to war from a hundred cities and towns between the mountains and the sea. Their greatest fear is that the war will be over before they can win their share of glory. Their women cheer them off to war. They parade off to mustering camps outside Raleigh and Wilmington like knights-errant en route to a tournament—characters in a novel by Sir Walter Scott—set on winning the hearts of their beloveds through daring feats on the field of honor.

They are ignorant of death and maiming, have not yet felt the hollow weakness of hunger or suffered the leveling epidemics of measles, typhus, and malaria.

In camp, they enjoy the novelty of living in tents and roughhousing with comrades. After a long day of drill, alone at night by candlelight, they write romantic letters home to their wives and sweethearts, their affection sharpened by separation, their love crossing the distance of both geography and imagination. Their women reply with flowery assurances of undying love, admonitions to be brave but to be safe—as if the two could ever be true in the same moment on a battlefield.

They are playing at the melodrama of grief, thrilled by the frightful prospect of violence and sudden death, the hero's fall like that of the mythical Roland blowing his horn to the last. The thrill is titillating, because they do not yet believe in death.

But this romantic idyll does not survive the summer of 1861. The armies collide in the bloody melee at Manassas, a rail junction in Virginia, with terrible carnage. It turns out that there is no honor in cannon fire, no glory on the surgeon's sawhorse table. Soon the letters take on a different cast. Soon enough, the men are no longer volunteers but conscripts.

One of them is Francis Marion Poteet, a farmer, miller, and carpenter from Dysartsville in McDowell County. Francis Poteet knows about death: among his other trades, he is a coffin maker. He is named for the fabled Revolutionary War hero Francis Marion, the "Swamp Fox" who bedeviled Lord

Cornwallis's redcoats in the Low Country of South Carolina. But unlike his namesake, Francis is no firebrand. When war darkens the country, he is a settled husband and father, happily married for sixteen years to the love of his life, Martha Henley Poteet.

He is unremarkable, tall and broad, with a plain country face, kind eyes, and a chin beard but no whiskers. He looks like what he is: a steady man of limited schooling who works with his hands. Martha is pretty enough, slight of build, a practical woman used to the hard daily work of caring for husband and children, household and farm.

In the fall of 1863, Francis is conscripted into Company A, 49th Regiment of North Carolina Troops, for a term of three years or the duration of the war. Martha does not cheer her husband off to war; she is newly pregnant with their tenth child.

Francis is thirty-six years old, long past the age when living in tents and marching on dusty roads could ever seem a lark. Scarcely a month after being conscripted, on November 3, 1863, Francis writes Martha from Kinston, "Sumtimes I think that I Will Runaway. . . . Tha is Eight or ten will Come With me any time that I will."

He goes on, "you Rote that if I could be at home to go with you to the shucking that you would be very glad. If I could I would give Ever thing that I am worth to be with you." Before another week passes, he writes again: "it seems to me that my heart will Breake when I think of you and the little Children."

After more than two years of war, rations are thin and hardship is routine, and hunger sharpens his longing for home. He writes on November 15, "I want you to send me sum tobacco . . . and send me sum unions sum pork if you had it and Bake Me sum cakes, you now what to send as well as I can tell, you don't know how bad that I want to see you and My little babes." He sends Martha a ring that he made, for she has been constantly on his mind since he left home. He confesses, "I have shed many ateare sence that time."

Near the end of the month, like so many in his company, he has fallen ill. He writes, "I have got A very Bad Cold and A very Bad Cough. My Dear Wife I cant tell how much I would give to be at home this morning to go With you to Preachin and stay with you as long as I live."

Hard as the separation is, other troubles intrude as well. Those who owe him money for services rendered have not paid, and Martha sorely needs the cash for food — and so does he. He complains that he ate only cornbread for breakfast and that crackers now cost a dollar a dozen. "I want you to tell Joseph Landis to pay you for them coffins," he exhorts her. The very paper on which he writes his letter cost him thirty cents, and his army pay never arrives.

And there's worse. Without an income, Martha has been threatened with eviction, her family's place to be given to a paying renter. In barely concealed anger, Francis writes, "if I had of bin at home when Bill Rented you out of house and home I think that I would of heart him and I Dont now but what I will yet."

Again, he rankles at the law that keeps him in the army fighting for a cause that is not his own, wishing with all his heart to be back with Martha. "I dont now what to doo if I was to come home and then tha catch me. then I would have to go back but I think that I will try it sumtime."

Like so many women left behind, Martha does not use her letters to boost her husband's fighting spirit. To the contrary, her letters throb with heartache and the fear of not being able to provide for their children. Between the lines, she all but begs Francis to desert the army and rejoin his family, who are in dire need of him.

When he learns that his thirteen-year-old son, Alvis, is deathly ill, Francis does just that. At Weldon, he slips away, travels west across the Piedmont, beyond Morganton, to Martha. He arrives at the bedside of his dying boy and remains at home for just eight days—long enough to bury him. If leaving his family the first time was hard, now it proves excruciating.

But he does what he thinks he must: at the end of January, he returns to his unit.

As her husband makes his way back to his regiment, Martha writes, "I now seat myself to write you a few lines to let you know we are not well, the children is sick with bad colds and I haint seen a well day since you left. . . . Bill Cowen come hear a teusday and told me to get out as soon as I could and what am I to do I don't know. . . . I will sell the Mar and Cows and live while the corn and meat last for I don't see how I am going to get along with no one to help me. I have to pay tax on the cows."

The Confederate government takes 10 percent of the value of all property, but Martha has no cash with which to pay taxes. She is anxious to know how Francis will be punished for going absent without leave and confides, "O my dear husband you don't know how lonsom I am sins you left. I dread to see Night come."

When Francis reports for duty on January 12, he is arrested and confined to the guardhouse awaiting court-martial. In the dark days since Gettysburg, North Carolinians, like other troops, have been deserting the Confederate ranks by the thousands. To restore discipline, the generals have been executing deserters who are caught, even those who are "captured" returning to their units. Francis Marion Poteet now faces execution for the crime of leaving his company to visit his dying child.

Martha writes, "O Francis it dos seem like it will kill me to be parted from you with no one to protect me and your little helpless children. I pray the Lord to save your sole and body from harm." She is puzzled and angry that her husband has been arrested. "I thought wen a man went back with in themselves they did not put them in the gard house but George Taylor told he tuck you up and is to get thirty Dollars of your wages and I suspect that is the reason of you being punished. It is just one month today sins our little son died. And I don't think they ought to blame you for coming home to see him Die."

For reasons that go unrecorded, Francis's life is spared. He is sentenced to serve four months hard confinement at Castle Thunder Prison in Richmond, a converted tobacco warehouse notorious for the sadistic brutality of the guards; the vile, crowded living conditions; and rampant disease.

While Francis struggles to stay alive in prison, Martha faces enemies of her own back in McDowell County, where she is nursing a sick baby whom she does not expect to live long. In the same letter in which she berates George Taylor for betraying her husband to the provost marshal, she writes of roving bands of Home Guardsmen who are rounding up parolees and men on furlough, anybody between sixteen and sixty, and enlisting them. Meanwhile Bill Cowen, who evicted her, is hauling provisions out of the way of the expected "Yankey" advance.

Worst of all, the community is no longer safe from looters. "I went to the Cross roads last Saturday and got two dollars worth of salt and Sunday Night somebody stole about half of it and about a half bushel of beans and they hav taken a heap of my corn."

Nonetheless, Martha manages to send her husband "five pies five ginger Cakes one dozen unions two custerds 1 ham of Meat and three twists of tobacco." By the time he receives the parcel, all the pies, cakes, and custards have spoiled, but the ham, onions, and tobacco keep him going.

Martha is still fighting eviction by her landlord Cowen, who warns her that even if she will not leave, he will not allow her to plant so much as a kitchen garden. "I have walked my self down this week trying to get a place and hav got non. me and my children are bound to perish. All the honest men is gone and a set of speckalating dogs is left to press the lives out of the poor Women and children while the soldiers is standing as a wall between them and the enemy. They are standing between them and there wives to snatch evry thing they can get."

Martha is a strong woman, but now she comes close to breaking. "I told you when you left I was left to the Mercy of the people there is about as much mercy shown me as a dog would show apeace of meat but I hope it wont always be so."

Francis writes, begging her to send more food, since he is half-starved and has sold even his razor to buy what little he can. But she is in no better shape: "they say that the yankeys can come here at any time they please but they dont want to come for there aint any thing to come for but a parcel of half perished women and children. . . . how I am to get along God knows, I don't."

In May 1864, Francis is released from Castle Thunder in time to rejoin his regiment in the defense of Petersburg. Martha writes him to let him know their four-week-old baby daughter, whom he has never laid eyes on, is now doing better—what would he like to name her?

More pressing is the condition of the farm she has managed to sow with wheat, thanks to the kindness of a neighbor. She implores Francis, "I would like for you to show this to your Capt and tell him if he pleases to let you come home a few days the first of July to take Care of it for me. I have about 8 bushels sowed and no person to cut a straw of it."

In the trenches of Petersburg, Francis endures constant bombardment and skirmishing. He reports that he is nearly broken down from the trials of battle, exposure, prison, illness, and constant hunger. Fifty thousand comrades in the trenches and surrounding garrisons share the same plight. By August he lies in the hospital, fighting off camp measles and swollen legs, hoping to get a furlough home. The furlough is denied. By October, he is subsisting on a quarter-pound of meat per day, along with a handful of flour. Soon even that stops. He has received no pay since January. The rumor is that Lee can't hold Petersburg and they will soon evacuate the city. Francis's morale, already low, sinks to dark resignation. He does not expect to survive the war.

On October 6, 1864, Martha writes a desperate rambling letter: "My grief and troubles is Moor than I can bear. if you dont get to come I dont know what will become of Me and the children. . . . My heart is so full I cant think of what I ought to. oh God have Mercy on My husband and children and my self. Spar our lives to meet in this world once moor the 12th day of this Month is a year that we hav bin parted and it seems all most a life time.

do the best you can keep out of them fights as much as you can. . . . I would tell you Moor than I can write some times."

In another undated, distracted letter penned on both sides of a sheet of foolscap, she breaks the awful news that their baby has died. "I expect it was a tooth Canker that the baby had come by her not cutting her teeth sooner. it come from her jawbone and morterfied as it went . . . and she is ded and gone to heaven." She never mentions the baby's name.

Francis replies, "I cant Rite for cring."

Meantime, in McDowell County, the Home Guard is rounding up more deserters. Some of the deserters put up a fight, and men on both sides are shot—one of them is Francis's brother Sydney. Martha delivers the news in a letter. Indeed, throughout their correspondence, she takes care to report which neighbor has been drafted, whose son has come home wounded. For his part, Francis provides a running roster of the dead, wounded, and missing in his own company, and of relatives and neighbors in other nearby units.

By Christmas 1864, Francis is subsisting on five hardtack crackers a day, no meat. His shoes are falling apart. His hips and knees ache from the cold and damp. In a recurring dream, Martha visits him and offers comfort. Often in the dream, he is badly wounded in the hips.

The rumors prove true: Lee can't hold Petersburg. After nine months of trench warfare and more than 3,000 battle casualties, the city surrenders on April 3, and Richmond follows. A few weeks later, at long last, Francis Marion Poteet returns to his wife, Martha.

In the years to come, she bears him two more daughters. He opens a gristmill and once again takes up carpentry. They live quietly happy lives.

On the evening of April 2, 1902, at their home in Mooresboro, while working in the yard, Martha collapses with a fatal stroke. Eight hours later, Francis dies in his sleep. The doctor pronounces it a heart attack, but his family calls it simply a broken heart. Their love affair of fifty-four years ends peacefully, together, at home.

FROM SLAVE TO FREE WARRIOR

In 1843, William Henry Singleton enters the world enslaved.

His father is a white man, William Singleton of New Bern, the second-largest city in North Carolina, with nearly 5,000 residents, including a large free black population. His mother is a black slave named Lettis Nelson, her surname taken from the family that owns her. Henry's master is John Handcock Nelson, a proud and haughty man with whom the stubborn boy will engage in a battle of wills lasting years.

The limits of Henry's life are the boundaries of a 1,390-acre plantation in Craven County, on the Neuse River north of Beaufort. There he spends his first four years, with the other infants and toddlers, in the care of an elderly black woman at the central house. His mother chops cotton, digs potatoes, and harvests the cornfields along with more than 100 fellow slaves.

Though Henry is light-skinned, his world is, quite literally, black and white. "And because I was black it was believed I had no soul," he writes later in his memoir — a small miracle, because throughout his childhood, he is denied schooling. "For in the eyes of the law I was but a thing."

As a thing, he can be sold. And when he is four years old, a man shows up, offers him a stick of candy, then simply takes him south to Atlanta. His new owner, a widow, operates an entrepreneurial "slave farm" — buying enslaved children, training them, and selling them for a profit.

Henry sleeps "on the dirt floor by the fireplace in the house like a little dog." He is too young to work in the fields, so he is employed to run errands. After one whipping too many for dawdling, he determines to run away home to his mother. Fortunately, the first person he encounters on the streets of Atlanta — an elderly black gentleman — sets him on the road north to the Carolinas. He admonishes Henry, "But don't tell anybody your name."

The boy is clever and daring. When he spies a white woman holding a carpetbag, he politely takes the bag from her and carries it to the stagecoach. The driver assumes he is the woman's servant, so he lets Henry board. In this manner he makes it as far as Wilmington, the lady's destination. She has figured out he is a runaway, but she doesn't divulge his secret.

Henry walks most of the ninety-five miles to New Bern, catching an occasional ride on a farmer's wagon. Then he hikes forty miles farther on dirt tracks to the Nelson plantation. He knocks on the first cabin door he comes to. The woman who answers says, "What do you want, little boy?"

Henry announces, "I am looking for my mother."

Neither recognizes the other, until Henry's older brother Hardy appears and pronounces, "Mamma, that's Henry."

But the woman is not convinced. How could a seven-year-old boy make it home from so far away? But she finally identifies him by a burn scar on the back of his neck, made by her own glowing pipe when Henry was an infant. Henry has hardly begun to recount the tale of his journey when the slave patrol is reported coming up the line. His mother hustles him underneath the board floor into a kind of potato cellar. The cellar becomes his hiding place for three years.

All that time, his mother feeds him secretly, and Henry keeps watch through the cracks in the boards under the house. One Sunday, while she is away at a camp meeting, he spies an incredible sight: fresh biscuits cooling on the fence rail outside. This is an old trick to lure out hungry runaways in hiding, but Henry is far too young to comprehend such deviousness. At once a horn sounds, and the slave catchers grab him.

This time he is sold for $500 to a man in a neighboring county.

But left to gather up his belongings for the trip, Henry runs away again and hides out in the thick woods. For the next few weeks, he lies low during daylight and sneaks back home to his cellar hideaway at night. At last John Nelson tells his mother that if Henry will agree to work on the farm, he won't be sold again.

Henry comes out of hiding, only to be sold a third time, for a mere $50 to a poor white farm woman. At least she treats him kindly, but she, too, soon sells him. Henry refuses, once again, to "stay sold." He escapes his new owner and hides out in the last place anyone would look for him: the town of New Bern itself. There he hires out as a bellboy at the Gaston House Hotel. When asked his name, he says he doesn't know.

"They called me the 'Don't know' boy," he writes later, recalling his three years of grace from plantation slavery. He is paid $3 per week, a small fortune for a boy who has never owned even the clothes on his back. But at last his secret is discovered, and he flees back to his mother. By now he is thirteen, old enough to do a man's labor.

From Slave to Free Warrior

At his mother's insistence, he gives himself up to Nelson. "He was a tall, raw-boned, black faced man, quite old then, too old to go to war when the war came. He said, 'All right, go out to the barn and go to work and it will be all right.'"

Henry learns to plow behind a mule and takes his place in the fields. His master whips him regularly with a harness strap for any small infraction. Once, Nelson's son Edward accuses Henry of opening one of his school-books, and Henry suffers a severe whipping. Henry recalls, "If you looked cross at them, they would whip you."

But Nelson's wife, Eliza, is troubled by her position as a slave owner and often speaks of a coming day when black and white will live in equality. In 1860, Eliza Nelson falls gravely ill. She summons some of the family's slaves to her bedside and exhorts them, "Be good and do your work and the time will come when you will all be free." Shortly afterward, she dies, and more than seventy-five slaves trail her casket to the cemetery, mourning her as a friend. Within eight weeks, John Nelson remarries, and the new mistress is no friend of the slaves.

"It was about this time, too, that we first heard of a man named Lincoln," Henry writes. "They said he was a bad man and that he had horns. Another man we heard about was John Brown and the underground railroad. Of course we did not understand what the underground railroad was. We thought it was some sort of a road under the ground."

John Nelson is deeply religious and preaches at the local Adams Creek Methodist church, attended by both the whites and their slaves, who sit in the back. On this particular day, the presiding elder invites a slave named Ennis Delmar to ascend the pulpit and offer a prayer for the congregation. Ennis prays, "Send the time when Ethiopia should stretch forth her arm like an army with banners."

Nelson is outraged that a black man has been called on to pray publicly with whites. After the service, he accosts Ennis and demands to know the meaning of his prayer. Ennis has no reply; he can neither read nor write and was only repeating what he had learned by rote. Nelson has him whipped on the spot.

The elder protests. Why shouldn't any Christian man — white or black — pray in church? Nelson banishes the elder from the congregation. From now on, he himself will do all the preaching at this church.

Secession is coming, and with it war. Nelson's nephew Samuel Hyman enlists in the 1st North Carolina Cavalry, and Henry Singleton volunteers to accompany him as his manservant. Singleton is already keen to learn the ways of a soldier, for he has visions of fighting for his freedom. He becomes so adept at soldiering that he is often called upon to drill the Confederate company in his master's stead.

When the U.S. Army captures New Bern and drives on Kinston, Singleton runs away in the confusion and reaches the Union lines, joining 10,000 other escaped slaves. He acts as a guide for the troops moving on Wyse Fork, outside Kinston, and his horse is shot out from under him. He tells his colonel that he will not fight anymore unless he is armed.

The colonel tells him, "We never will take niggers in the army to fight. The war will be over before your people ever get in."

But the colonel underestimates Henry's determination. "The war will not be over until I have had a chance to spill my blood," he retorts. He takes his pay—$5—and proceeds to New Bern and sets up a recruiting station. "I secured the thousand men and they appointed me as their colonel and I drilled them with cornstalks for guns," he writes. "We drilled once a week. I supported myself by whatever I could get to do and my men did likewise."

Singleton has grown into a handsome, formidable man, strong and outspoken. He stands just 5 feet 6 inches tall, but he is tough, and he holds himself with a soldier's erect bearing, looking out on the world through steady, deep-set gray eyes.

Time and again, Henry implores Maj. Gen. Ambrose E. Burnside, in command of the New Bern district, to allow his men to fight. Burnside has no authority to raise colored troops, he explains. But working at headquarters at Fort Monroe, Virginia, one day, Henry recounts, he has one of the most memorable encounters of his life. The adjutant indicates a man conferring with Burnside in the next room. "Do you know that man in there?"

"No," Singleton replies.

"That is our President, Mr. Lincoln."

When the president and Burnside emerge, the general points at Singleton and says, "This is the little fellow who got up a colored regiment."

Lincoln shakes Singleton's hand. "It is a good thing. What do you want?"

"I have a thousand men," Singleton answers. "We want to help fight to free our race. We want to know if you will take us in the service?"

"You have got good pluck. But I can't take you now because you are contraband of war and not American citizens yet. But hold on to your society and there may be a chance for you." It's the only time Singleton ever lays eyes on the "tall, dark complexioned, raw boned man, with a pleasant face."

Singleton bides his time. In January 1863, news of Lincoln's Emancipa-

A sheet of cards created by James Fuller Queen depicts the odyssey of a slave from bondage to free U.S. soldier, honored by his ultimate sacrifice to the cause of freedom. (Courtesy of the Library of Congress, LC-DIG-ppmsca-05453)

William Henry Singleton stands with his beloved 35th Regiment of U.S. Colored Troops at a postwar reunion. (Courtesy of the State Archives of North Carolina)

tion Proclamation raises hope that he and his brothers in arms will be taken into the U.S. Army at once. But months pass, and still they wait.

At last, on May 28, 1863, the 1st North Carolina Colored Volunteers (later the 35th U.S. Colored Troops) is officially formed at New Bern. Singleton is enlisted as first sergeant of Company G. The regiment drills briefly and then sets off to Kenansville on a raid meant to season the troops. They burn a saber factory, rescue two prisoners from the courthouse, and sweep through Warsaw before returning to their camp in high spirits, unscathed.

Before long, they march south to Charleston. During the next two years, Singleton fights battles in South Carolina, Georgia, and Florida, where he is wounded in the right leg at the Battle of Olustee, one of 1,800 Union casualties. After the battle, Brig. Gen. Truman Seymour, the ranking U.S. commander on the field, praises his regiment: "The colored troops behaved creditably . . . the 54th and the 1st North Carolina like veterans."

In the army, Singleton learns the letters of the alphabet and how to spell simple words. Mustered out in Charleston in 1866, he buys a secondhand primer, travels north, and settles in New Haven, Connecticut. There he joins

From Slave to Free Warrior

the African Methodist Episcopal Church and learns at last to read properly. He notes with pride, "And in those days since I was whipped simply because it was thought I had opened a book. I have seen the books of the world opened to my race."

In 1938, half-blind and with an ailing heart, William Henry Singleton attends the seventy-second national encampment of the Grand Army of the Republic in Des Moines, Iowa. Stubborn to the last, the ninety-five-year-old veteran parades for fifteen blocks in blistering heat. Hours later, he collapses with a fatal heart attack. He dies a free man, wearing the uniform he earned.

23

THE GRAY GHOST

A Rebel on the High Seas

He is born in the middle of the ocean aboard a ship bound from Ireland to America, destined for a life at sea. In later years he will call himself "a son of old Neptune, and . . . in duty bound to offer his allegiance as such."

At age five, he is adopted out of his impoverished family in White Plains, New York, by his Uncle William Maffitt and taken to Ellerslie, William's estate near Fayetteville. At age thirteen, John Newland Maffitt, namesake of his Methodist minister father, leaves Fayetteville and secures a midshipman's commission in the U.S. Navy.

Maffitt's early service aboard the frigate uss *Constitution* — "Old Ironsides," patriotic icon of the War of 1812 — takes him to the far reaches of the Mediterranean, and he returns a seasoned officer. By 1846, he is assigned to the U.S. Coast Hydrographic Survey and undertakes the meticulous process of charting the harbors at Savannah, Charleston, and Wilmington, among others. He is married with two small children, Eugene and Mary. But his wife dies young, and soon he remarries a widow, Caroline Read, with three children of her own. She bears him two more sons.

On the Cape Fear River, he lives with fellow officer J. Pembroke Jones at Fort Johnson in Smithville, which affords a panoramic view of the channel past Fort Caswell and Smith's Island. He commands a contingent of surveyors who work from small boats and coordinate with a team ashore, fixing each shoal or bend in the channel by laborious triangulation with landmarks on either bank of the river, sounding the depth at regular intervals. His chart of the Lower Cape Fear is a masterpiece of precision. But the duty keeps him away from big ships.

For that reason, the Naval Retiring Board decides Maffitt should not advance as an active-duty officer and furloughs him. Only a formal hearing, at which an overwhelming number of Maffitt's fellow officers testify to his abilities and character, gets him reinstated to active service in the U.S. Navy.

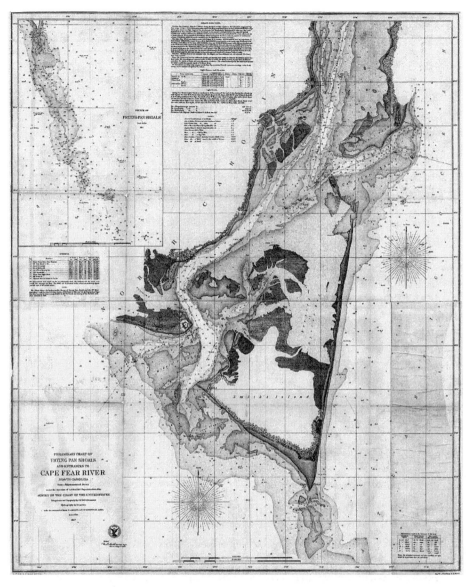

John Newland Maffitt's remarkably accurate chart of the lower Cape Fear River
and its approaches serves him well in running the U.S. Navy's blockade.
(Courtesy of the State Archives of North Carolina)

In 1857, Maffitt is given command of the brig *Dolphin* and ordered to the West Indies to intercept pirates and slave ships. His exploits in pursuit of the slaveship *Echo* make the *New York Times*: "The chase was a very exciting one, the *Dolphin* casting her shot exactly where the captain directed. The man-of-war deceived the Slaver by showing British colors. Several shots were fired over her to show what could be done if she did not hang out her flag and heave-to. At last she ran up the American flag, but still persisted in her flight. The moment she did so, the *Dolphin* hauled down the British ensign, replacing it with the stars and stripes, greatly to the horror of the fugitive."

Maffitt and his crew receive their share of the sale price of the vessel — and the prize money of $25 per slave for the 300 rescued. He becomes renowned for chasing down slavers. While captaining another vessel, the *Crusader*, he overtakes a French bark and liberates another 600 slaves. The slaves rejoice in their deliverance, Maffitt notes in his private journal: "They climbed up all along the rail, they hung on the shrouds, they clustered like swarming bees in the rigging, while rose from sea to sky the wildest acclamations of delight. They danced, and leaped, and waved their arms in the air, and screamed and yelled in a discordant but pathetic concert."

His wife, Caroline Maffitt, dies in 1859, leaving him twice a widower in the prime of his life.

Two years later, when secession strikes, he is living in Washington, D.C., pondering what course he should take. He considers the matter of choosing sides so sensitive that he does not even commit his thoughts to his private journal. In the end, events decide for him: "The Government had now commenced to taboo those suspected of Southern proclivities, and secret arrests were being made," Maffitt writes on April 29, 1861. "Being informed by a reliable friend that my name was on the list of those who were to be arrested, I concluded that my property had to take care of itself, and I made my arrangements to secretly depart."

When war comes to North Carolina, Maffitt knows the fairways and shortcuts of the three main eastern ports of the Confederacy perhaps better than any other man alive. He is forty-one years old, a charming Irishman with a thick mane of wavy dark hair and full whiskers, the dashing air of a seagoing cavalier, and a genial manner. Though it is customary when sitting for a photographic portrait to retain a stern and somber visage, Maffitt's portrait betrays the ghost of mischief in his eyes.

The U.S. Navy deploys more than forty warships, and before war's end it will have that many patrolling the mouth of the Cape Fear alone. The shipyards of New England and the Middle Atlantic states soon turn out scores of modern fighting ships to join the blockade of the 3,500 miles of Confederate coastline. The Confederacy has no fleet of seagoing warships. Instead, it depends on an improvised fleet of river gunboats and, later, ironclad rams, as well as coastal forts and "torpedoes" — containers of gunpowder rigged across channels and detonated by contact or electrical batteries.

The Confederate manpower shortage is even more severe: most of the U.S. Navy's 7,600 enlisted men remain loyal to the Union. Of its 1,554 regular officers, fewer than 400 go over to the rebel cause.

Maffitt is one of those few. He resigns his naval commission on May 2, 1861, and within a week receives a lieutenant's commission in the new Confederate navy. For a time he serves as naval aide to General Lee, constructing coastal defenses.

Without capital warships, the Confederacy soon resorts to the same strategy followed by the fledgling U.S. government during the American Revolution: it employs commerce raiders whose mission is to disrupt the enemy's shipping and thereby cripple its war effort.

Stephen R. Mallory, the Confederate navy secretary, dispatches agents to Liverpool, England, to acquire new or existing ships — fast side-wheel steamers that can be armed. It is an illegal business, so the ships must be purchased as merchantmen and then made lethal in less-regulated ports in the Caribbean or South America. Twelve such commerce raiders take to the high seas, hunting U.S. merchant ships.

Soon Maffitt commands the British-built *Florida*, a merchant raider propelled by sails and two steam engines and built on the lines of a British gunboat. It is sleek and fast; its propeller can even be folded to increase its speed. He and his crew of eighteen sail the ship unarmed to Nassau, the Bahamas, under a false Italian registry. There he outfits the vessel with a full complement of guns, then he sails for Cuba to pick up supplies.

But yellow fever sweeps the crew. With only five sailors fit for duty, his own sixteen-year-old stepson dead from the disease, and deathly ill himself, Maffitt runs the *Florida* through the blockade and into Mobile, Alabama, seeking refuge in a home port. He is a determined man, as his journal recounts: "I haven't got time to die now; there's too much for me to do."

Four U.S. Navy warships bar his way, but he steams right toward the harbor with all the speed his boilers can muster. He recounts the dramatic moment: "The loud explosions, roar of shot, crashing spars and rigging, mingling with the moans of the sick and wounded, instead of intimidating, only increased our determination to enter the destined harbor." He cons the fast *Florida*, both side-wheels churning furiously, straight at the USS *Oneida*. The

Union ship dodges out of the way to avoid a collision, and Maffitt slides his vessel past. He then steers for a patch of water squarely between two federal gunboats. They immediately cease fire, in order to avoid sinking each other. Miraculously, the *Florida* arrives in port without losing a single crewman in the encounter.

In Mobile, he enjoys a lively social life and is a favorite of the ladies. On another occasion, in Barbados, he dines with the governor. "He was in citizen's clothes, and excited considerable interest," reports the *New York Times*. "The ladies seemed to fancy this notorious pirate exceedingly." Maffitt is handsome and heroic in his tailored gray uniform, a swashbuckling character straight out of a romance novel.

Under cover of a violent storm on January 16, 1863, he runs the blockade outbound, eluding six pursuing warships. His daring escape from harbor earns accolades from his Union nemesis, U.S. rear admiral David Dixon Porter: "During the whole war there is not a more exciting adventure than this escape. . . . The gallant manner in which it was conducted excited great admiration. We do not suppose there was ever a case where a man . . . displayed more energy or bravery."

Maffitt takes to sea with a vengeance, capturing twenty-four U.S. merchantmen in the next nine months. Three of the captured vessels he outfits as raiders, and they capture an additional twenty-three ships. Maffitt's and the other Confederate raiders — such as *Alabama*, *Tallahassee*, and *Shenandoah* — are so effective at their trade that they destroy the supremacy of the U.S. merchant marine for good. Shippers and insurers around the world shun U.S. ships and transport their wares and raw materials in British bottoms.

Maffitt and his fellow commanders and their crews (including Maffitt's own son Eugene aboard the *Alabama*) sail under commission of the Confederate government, but the U.S. Navy considers them pirates. If captured, they are not to be accorded the status of prisoners of war but, rather, hanged outright. The Northern press christens Maffitt the Prince of the Privateers.

The former slave catcher now has become a staunch defender of a rebel nation founded on the slave economy. The onetime scourge of Caribbean pirates is now himself hunted as a pirate.

But Maffitt is no cutthroat. On the contrary, his captives often remark on his charm and sense of honor. "Captain Maffitt received me with great courtesy, invited me into his cabin, and said he regretted that it was necessary for him to burn my vessel, that the consequences of this war often fell most heavily upon those who disapproved of it," reports Capt. John Brown of the

A Rebel on the High Seas

brig *Estelle*. "Captain Maffitt and his officers were every inch the considerate gentlemen and attentive officers. . . . Generosity and courtesy on the part of enemies should not pass unheeded by."

After another capture, Maffitt surrenders his cabin for use by the wife of the merchant captain of the *Jacob Bell*, which he is about to burn after relieving the ship of its $1.5 million cargo of silks, spices, and tea. There she is confined for five days, and with the help of the ship's surgeon, she delivers her baby.

Maffitt tells a correspondent for the *Illustrated London News* in Brest, "We only make war with the United States' Government and respect little property. We treat prisoners of war with the greatest respect. Most of those we have captured have spoken well of us. To be sure we have met with some ungrateful rascals."

An English visitor to his ship describes Maffitt with some amusement: "Of the Captain himself I may say that he is a slight, middlesized, well-knit man of about 42, a merry-looking man with a ready, determined air, full of life and business — apparently the sort of man who is equally ready for a fight or a jollification, and whose preference for the latter would by no means interfere with his creditable conduct of the former."

In the spring of 1863, Captain Maffitt is promoted to commander. By August, he anchors the *Florida* off Brest, France, and waits a full week to be allowed to enter the harbor. Rumors fly ahead of the ship. He is called a sea wolf; his crew, desperate pirates. His ship, laden with captured gold, is adorned with "several corpses hanging from her masts." But in fact the *Florida* is badly in need of a refit. The ship has been at sea for eight months, with only four days in port, never more than twenty-four hours in any single harbor. "Yes, indeed, sir," Maffitt tells a reporter for the London *Times*, "two hundred and forty-five days upon solid junk, without repairs or provisions."

Like his ship, Maffitt is worn out and asks to be relieved of command. He writes to a fellow officer, "Am quite unwell, so much so as to be under the necessity of asking for a relief. Yellow fever, and a chronic affliction of the heart, with hard cruising, has used me up, so ere it be too late, I must try to build up again." He recuperates in Liverpool, England, alarmed at the dire news from Wilmington, where the blockade is slowly strangling Confederate shipping.

Without Maffitt in command, the *Florida* is soon captured. He recovers his health sufficiently to be named master of the *Lillian*, and his young purser is James Sprunt, who grew up on the Cape Fear River while Maffitt was charting it for the navy. Sprunt, the ambitious son of Scottish immigrants,

Capt. John Newland Maffitt cuts a dashing figure as
a blockade-running Confederate raider.
(Courtesy of the State Archives of North Carolina)

buys molasses, trades for cotton, and soon after war's end will control one of the most lucrative export firms in the South.

For a time Maffitt commands the ironclad css *Albemarle*, guarding the approaches to Plymouth on the Roanoke River, but his heart lies always on the open sea. He wants to take the ironclad into battle; but his superiors fear that losing the vessel would open the river to Union gunboats, and they order him to take no chances. Maffitt chafes at the dull work of defensive patrol, writing that he "cherished the sport of blockade running as others might women or fine bourbon."

He soon gets his wish of a new command. On October 3, 1864, Maffitt runs the steel-hulled British steamer *Owl* through the blockade out of Wilmington. The ship suffers nine hits from the blockading squadron but, in trademark Maffitt fashion, steams straight ahead, its commander and other crewmen wounded by the shellfire.

In April 1865, unaware that the city has fallen to Union forces, Maffitt attempts one last run into Wilmington with the *Owl*, fully loaded with mail and supplies for the Confederacy, but the concentration of U.S. warships proves too much. They drive him off, killing a dozen of his crew. Rather than surrender his ship, he sails to England and hands over the vessel to Confederate agents there. He has taken seventy prizes worth an estimated $10–15 million.

Eventually Maffitt returns to Wilmington, where he makes his home on a coastal farm called the Moorings, on Masonboro Sound. He spins his early seagoing adventures in the Mediterranean into a stirring novel, *Nautilus, or Cruising Under Canvas*. At age sixty-six, he is stricken with Bright's Disease, a painful malady that attacks the kidneys.

One day, half-deliriously remembering old voyages and lost shipmates, he remarks distractedly to his third wife, Emma, "The ship is ready, the sails are set and the wind is favorable; all we are waiting for is Mr. Lambert to come and ask God's blessing upon us; then we will heave anchor and away on the billows."

Bright's does what no Yankee commander could do in four years of war on the high seas: defeats him. A few days later he is dead.

Emma commits his adventures to the page, in a heartfelt memorial more lasting than the headstone at Oakdale Cemetery. In her preface she writes, "I commit this record of the life of a man whose watchword was ever *duty*, who shrank from no sacrifice in the fulfillment of what his conscience required of him, and who never made plaint of hardship or loss."

24

ROSE OF THE REBELLION

She is beautiful, beguiling, smart, haughty, politically adept, and willful. She is a slave owner and a socialite, a Catholic and a fierce anti-abolitionist, a mother of four daughters — one of whom died in her teens — and a widow in middle age. She is a confidante of the great men of her time, some of whom are now the enemy.

She was born Maria Rosetta O'Neale and was orphaned in childhood when a slave murdered her father. The slave was hanged, but she has never relinquished a fierce disdain for the "Negro" race. Now she calls herself Rose O'Neal Greenhow. By birth, she is a Marylander, but her dramatic journey will take her at last to the Old North State.

Greenhow is living in Washington, D.C., when secession brings on the war. She is forty-four, refined and charming, the six-year widow of the soft-spoken Dr. Robert Greenhow, a physician and historian who held a post with the U.S. State Department. As an orphan taken in by her aunt, proprietress of the Congressional Boarding House, she became familiar with many of the leading men in the government. Through her husband's contacts, she has deepened these bonds and come to be on intimate terms with many key players on both sides of the conflict: Senator Stephen Douglas, Lincoln's famous rival; Senators Thomas Hart Benton, William Seward, and Daniel Webster; Chief Justice of the Supreme Court Roger Brooke Taney (who authored the Dred Scott decision holding that an escaped slave could not be legally considered a U.S. citizen); and Presidents Martin Van Buren, John Tyler, James Polk, and James Buchanan.

Two of these men become crucial correspondents once her social circle is cleaved by war: Jefferson Davis and Gen. Pierre Gustave Toutant Beauregard.

An invitation to a Rose Greenhow dinner party is coveted. She resides on Sixteenth Street, between I and K Streets, in a tony section of the city, just a short distance from the dilapidated white mansion occupied by the president of the United States. The company is elite, the wine and spirits always the best, the conversation both witty and weighty. And the star attraction is always Rose Greenhow herself, her auburn hair fashionably gathered in a shimmering mass behind her head. When let down, it reaches below her knees.

She can console a friend with utter, guileless compassion. She can also cut a man off at the knees with a sly, biting remark. But though she speaks her mind freely, her greatest gift is that she knows how to listen. She listens to the chatter at the dinner table as the courses are served and the wine is poured from crystal decanters. She listens as the men smoke their cigars and sip their after-dinner brandies. Later, with some special man, she listens to pillow talk. The man is likely married, with a high position to uphold, but he can trust Greenhow to keep their secret. She is no more interested in scandal than he is.

One of those men is Col. Erasmus Darwin Keyes, aide-de-camp of Gen. Winfield Scott, who holds supreme command of the U.S. Army. In later years, he will defend his behavior in a half-mocking way: "Beautiful women ought to be considered contraband of war, and captured whenever found, and detained till after the fight under guard of a person of their own sex."

But it's clear to Greenhow's circle just who has captured whom.

A young lieutenant from Virginia, Thomas Jordan, recognizes her unique abilities, how perfectly placed she is to aid the Confederate cause. He recruits her as a spy. The role appeals to her patriotism as well as her vanity, and before long she has a chance to try it on.

"On the morning of the 16th of July, the Government papers at Washington announced that the 'grand army' was in motion, and I learned from a reliable source (having received a copy of the order to M'Dowell) that the order for a forward movement had gone forth," she records in her memoir, *My Imprisonment and the First Year of Abolition Rule at Washington*. "The heroes girded on their armour with the enthusiasm of the Crusaders of old, and vowed to flesh their maiden swords in the blood of Beauregard or Lee. And many a knight, inspired by beauty's smiles, swore to lay at the feet of her he loved best the head of Jeff. Davis at least."

But Greenhow has other plans. "At twelve o'clock on the morning of the 16th of July, I despatched a messenger to Manassas, who arrived there at eight o'clock that night," she writes. "The answer received by me at mid-day on the 17th will tell the purport of my communication — 'Yours was received at eight o'clock at night. Let them come: we are ready for them. We rely upon you for precise information. Be particular as to description and destination of forces, quantity of artillery, &c. (Signed) THOS. JORDON, Adjt.-Gen.'"

By return messenger, Greenhow outlines the U.S. Army's plan to cut the Winchester railroad and thus intercept Maj. Gen. Joseph E. Johnston, rushing in from the west to reinforce Beauregard at Manassas Junction, Virginia. The army acts on her intelligence, and the result is a staggering rout of Union troops under Brig. Gen. Irvin McDowell. They retreat in a panicked mob on Washington.

Just before the battle, Greenhow entrains for New York and does not return until July 23 at six o'clock in the morning. Even at that hour, she is thronged by friends anxious to congratulate her on behalf of the Confederacy. Among them is a secret courier: "A despatch was also received from Manassas by me—'*Our President and our General direct me to thank you. We rely upon you for further information. The Confederacy owes you a debt.* (Signed) JORDAN, Adjutant-General.'"

On August 11, 1861, Greenhow sends another—much longer—dispatch to Jordan. In precise detail, she reports the location and status of every fortification around Washington, including its armaments and garrison strength. She comments on the political views of key officers. She describes the defensive forces ringing the city: their dispositions, weapons, and even the number of mules and wagons.

But she has been a little too flamboyant in her role and has caught the attention of Thomas A. Scott, the assistant secretary of war. He engages a Scottish detective named Allan Pinkerton, who has been retained by Maj. Gen. George B. McClellan to gather military intelligence. Pinkerton writes, "She had now become an avowed hater of the Union, and it was feared, from her previous association with officers in the army, that she was using her talents in procuring information from them which would immediately be communicated to the rebel government in Richmond."

Accompanied by several detectives, he steals up on her house at night in a driving rainstorm. Two men hoist him high enough to peer through the parlor windows. He witnesses a scene straight out of a stage melodrama: a tall, handsome infantry captain, about forty years old, huddles in intimate conversation with Greenhow. He appears agitated, keeps shifting in his seat. After a few minutes, he draws a folded paper from his pocket and uncreases it for her: a map. Pinkerton recognizes the captain. He records, "I heard enough to convince me that this trusted officer was then and there engaged in betraying his country, and furnishing to his treasonably-inclined companion such information regarding the disposition of our troops as he possessed."

Pinkerton arrests Greenhow on August 23, 1861, and confines her to her own home. Detectives rifle through her correspondence but find nothing incriminating; she has used only noms de plume and writes in cipher. For instance, "Tell Aunt Sally that I have some old shoes for *the children*, and I wish her to send some one *down town* to take them, and to let me know whether she has found any charitable person to help her to take care of them" would be decoded by "Aunt Sally" to mean "I have some important information to send across the river, and wish a messenger immediately. Have you any means of getting reliable information?"

For five months, Greenhow languishes under house arrest with her youngest daughter, Little Rose. She is watched constantly, yet she manages to carry on a lively correspondence with her Confederate contacts right under the noses of her guards.

Her house is officially commissioned a federal prison, and other political captives arrive, not all of them to her liking. "A woman of bad repute, known and recognised by several of the guard as such, having been seen in the streets of Chicago in the exercise of her vocation . . . was brought to my house, and placed in the chamber of my deceased child adjoining mine," she complains in her memoir. "For what object I know not, but this woman was allowed unrestricted intercourse with me, the order being given that our meals should be served together."

Her long, impassioned epistles to her old friend William H. Seward, now Lincoln's secretary of state, are answered by matter-of-fact letters denying her freedom.

In January, things get worse: she and her young daughter are removed to the second floor of the Old Capitol Prison, where they sit for a Matthew Brady photograph. She writes of that time with loathing: "The walls of my room swarmed with vermin and I was obliged to employ a portion of the precious hours of candlelight in burning them on the wall, in order that myself and child should not be devoured by them in the course of the night. The bed was so hard that I was obliged to fold up my clothing and place them under my child; in spite of this she would often cry out in the night, 'Oh, mamma, the bed hurts me so much.'"

Strangely, in all the months of her imprisonment, Rose Greenhow has not been charged with any crime, let alone tried in a court of law. Despite Pinkerton's certainty that she is a spy, he can produce no direct evidence, no eyewitness testimony to corroborate what he is sure he witnessed. So Greenhow and her daughter remain under guard—too dangerous to release, too embarrassing to put on trial. At long last, she wears them down. The government will banish her south, never to return on pain of arrest.

Rose O'Neal Greenhow is confined with her daughter Little Rose to Old Capitol Prison, where they are photographed by Matthew Brady. (Courtesy of the Library of Congress, Brady-Handy photograph collection, LC-DIG-cwpbh-04849)

Thus on June 6, 1862, she and her daughter enter Richmond like royalty, cheered on by crowds of admirers. Now that she is known, her usefulness as a spy is over. She remains in Richmond, writing her memoir. In the summer of 1863, Jefferson Davis sends her abroad as a diplomatic emissary for the Confederate government.

On August 5, 1863, she sails out of Wilmington aboard the *Phantom*. The vessel is spotted by the watch of the *Niphon* off New Inlet, and a larger blockading ship, the *Mount Vernon*, gives chase; but it is no match for the speed of the *Phantom*.

Safely arrived in England and championed by the essayist Thomas Carlyle, Greenhow finds a publisher for her memoir. She presses the prime minister, Lord Palmerston, to recognize the Confederate States of America. In Paris, she argues military strategy with Napoleon III. She successfully negotiates with Charles Francis Adams, U.S. minister to France, to secure the release of a young 3rd lieutenant, Joseph D. Wilson, who is suffering severe mental distress. Wilson was captured when the *Kearsarge* sank the commerce raider CSS *Alabama* off Brest. After many months abroad, Greenhow says a heart-rending farewell to Little Rose at the Couvent du Sacré-Coeur in Paris, a safer place for her than aboard an inbound blockade-runner.

The vessel that carries Greenhow home across the Atlantic is the *Condor*, one of four Glasgow-built sister ships that are probably the largest and fastest blockade-runners on the seas. The sleek, powerful steamer is 270 feet long, with a beam of 24 feet, but draws just 7 feet of water. The *Condor* carries a crew of forty-five. Three funnels draft air to the engine room to fuel six boilers powering two double-expansion engines that use the steam twice, getting more and faster miles out of the smokeless Welsh coal.

The *Condor* is a seagoing marvel, many engineering generations beyond the early blockade-runners with their huge, ungainly boilers and "walking beam" engines that protruded high above the deck. The *Condor* is painted elusive white and casts no silhouette against the horizon. Its captain is a thirty-year-old British naval officer on half-pay, William Nathan Wrighte Hewett, who employs several aliases to avoid running afoul of British neutrality.

The *Condor*, fully loaded with a cargo of uniforms and supplies, puts in at Halifax to take on coal and pick up Confederate commissioner James P. Holcombe — and Lieutenant Wilson. When the *Condor* slips harbor, heading south, its departure is noted. Three U.S. Navy ships are ordered to intercept it: *Niphon*, *Alabama*, and *Kansas*.

In the dead of night on October 1, 1864, the *Condor* crosses the bar of Cape Fear. At 3:40 A.M., lookouts aboard the *Niphon* spy it and open fire. The *Condor* is now only 800 yards off Fort Fisher, which opens fire against the U.S. ships with long-range rifled artillery. Rockets flare overhead, lighting up the chase. It's a dirty night, with a freshening wind and a cold drizzle to spoil visibility.

All at once, dead ahead, Captain Hewett spots what appears to be a U.S. warship. He swerves the *Condor* hard to starboard to avoid a collision and runs right onto the shoals.

There was no warship, just the hulk of another blockade-runner, the *Night Hawk*, which ran aground two nights ago and is being worked by a salvage crew. The *Condor* lies close under the guns of Fort Fisher, and the Federal ships dare not venture any closer. But Greenhow demands to be put ashore at once. She is determined that she will never go back to prison, and she will not take the chance of being captured. At first Captain Hewett won't allow it, but at last he relents. A lifeboat is lowered into the frothing sea. Aboard it are Wilson, Holcombe, two seamen, and Rose O'Neal Greenhow. She carries a leather valise heavy with dispatches for the government in Richmond—and 400 gold sovereigns, about $2,000, royalties from her book sales that she intends to donate to the relief of veterans.

Almost the moment the lifeboat hits the water, it broaches to on a swell and capsizes. The occupants are tumbled into the sea. The men manage to cling to the overturned boat and are hoisted back aboard the *Condor*. But Greenhow is a forty-seven-year-old woman wearing a heavy silk dress and chained to seven pounds of gold and additional pounds of paper, satchel, and chain. She is carried under.

At daylight her bag of treasure washes up on shore, discovered by a 3-foot-11-inch-tall sentry who can hardly carry his enormous, unlikely name: J. J. Prosper For Me D. Doctor DeVowell Conner. A short while later, Thomas Taylor, on site to salvage the *Night Hawk*, finds Greenhow's body washing in the surf. Daisy Lamb, wife of Col. William Lamb, the commander of Fort Fisher, personally cleans the body and prepares it for its final journey upriver to Wilmington. At the wharf there, a somber crowd of hundreds meets her boat.

Eliza Jane De Rosset, president of the Soldier's Aid Society, cuts off Rose Greenhow's long hair, a legacy for Little Rose. Greenhow lies in state at the chapel of Hospital Number Four on a bier, her coffin shrouded by a Confederate flag. The chapel is redolent with candle wax and flowers—wreaths, garlands, crosses, bouquets.

Rose of the Rebellion

After a Catholic mass at St. Thomas the Apostle, the funeral cortege of eight carriages and scores of mourners on foot accompanies the coffin to Oakdale Cemetery in torrential rain. Mrs. De Rosset comments sadly, "Not a tear of affection was shed at the grave, for no one in the midst of all the trappings of sacred honor and cherished tradition really knew Rose Greenhow."

The local newspaper reports that, at the moment Rose Greenhow's coffin is lowered into the grave, the rain quits and the sun bursts out of the gray sky. But the weight of her treasure, the legacy of her imprisonment, has carried her too deep to rise.

25

IRONCLAD MEN

War is the province of audacity. For two young men — enemies — audacity leads to a desperate midnight encounter at the wharf of a small river town in eastern North Carolina. Both are ironclad men: one believes he can build a modern warship in a cornfield; the other believes he can destroy it with a handful of men and a dash of derring-do.

It is a strange fact of this war that, while there are very few major naval battles, both the blockading U.S. fleet and its river navy are crucial in deciding the fate of the Confederacy. The Confederacy never sails a deepwater navy to fight it out with the U.S. Navy fleet, yet by its ingenious innovations it changes the very nature of seaborne battle.

First, it spurs the development of the fastest steamships on the oceans, mostly built in Scotland on the banks of the River Clyde.

Second, in February 1864, in the css *Hunley*, named for one of its developers, Horace Lawson Hunley, the Confederacy pioneers submarine warfare. Never again can a warship assume safety just because the horizon is clear of enemy vessels.

Third, to protect their rivers, Confederate engineers rig elaborate underwater defenses of mines and torpedoes strung across vital channels.

But the real naval arms race is about the fourth weapon: ironclads. The Confederates armor the captured hull of the uss *Merrimack* and rechristen it the css *Virginia*. The *New York Times* paints a word-portrait of the ship that does no justice to its lethal firepower — and its ability to withstand shot and shell, steaming "like a submerged house, with the roof only above water."

Meanwhile, the U.S. Navy develops a flat-topped ironclad with a rotating turret, the *Monitor*. On March 8, 1862, the *Virginia* runs rampant in Hampton Roads, sinking the uss *Cumberland* and running the uss *Congress* onto a sandbar, where it burns. More than 240 U.S. sailors are killed. The deep-draft frigate uss *Minnesota*, maneuvering to get out of range, also runs aground, an easy target when the ironclad returns.

The following day, the *Monitor* arrives on the scene, and the two ironclads slug it out for more than four hours in a torrent of iron shot. Neither can vanquish the other, and they fight to a draw, both vessels heavily damaged. But it is clear to all observers that the ironclad is the warship of the future.

THE SHIPBUILDER

Gilbert Elliott is born on a river, the Pasquotank, of a shipbuilding family. His father dies when he is just seven years of age. As a young man, he reads law at the office of Col. William Francis Martin, in Elizabeth City. Martin also builds ships. When the colonel is captured with his regiment at Fort Hatteras in August 1861, Elliott assumes management of his shipbuilding enterprise.

Elliott is mature beyond his years. His audacity lies in having the confidence to take on daunting challenges with a cool head and a steady hand.

The shipyard—with an unfinished hull on the stocks—needs a government contract to remain solvent. Martin's older brother, James, is adjutant general for North Carolina. On Elliott's behalf, he approaches the government in Richmond, and in October 1861, Elliott is awarded a contract for an ironclad gunboat: "The length of keel of said boat is to be one hundred and thirty feet, the breadth twenty-five feet, the depth of hold seven feet." Elliott would be paid "the sum of fifty dollars per ton of Carpenters Measurement." The design is provided by John Luke Porter, the architect of the css *Virginia*, under construction at Portsmouth, Virginia.

Thus at the age of nineteen, Elliott begins constructing an armored ram for the Confederacy at the Martin Shipyard in Elizabeth City.

Like its sister ship, this gunboat will be slow and ungainly, but its massive armor should render it invulnerable to the shallow-draft Union gunboats. It will be the perfect river battleship, an invincible object standing in the way of Union control of the water.

But scarcely has Elliott begun assembling men and materials when the city is threatened with capture. By February 1862, he has moved all his equipment and workers to a new site at Norfolk, some fifty miles away. The Martin shipyard is burned.

Only a couple of months later, when Norfolk, too, comes under threat, Elliott must disband his workers, crate his equipment, and head back to North Carolina. He briefly enlists in the 17th Regiment of North Carolina Infantry under his old boss, William Martin. But his talents lie elsewhere. Secretary of the Navy Stephen Mallory plucks him from the ranks and gives him a two-year furlough to resume the building of a gunboat. After stints at

Tarboro and Halifax, Elliott sets up a shipyard in a cornfield on the William Ruffin Smith Jr. Plantation at Edward's Ferry, above Plymouth on the Roanoke River.

Elliott is determined and resourceful. His crews scavenge the countryside for tools and parts. Iron is especially hard to come by—most of it is hoarded by the railroads. He badgers officials, pleading relentlessly with the governments in both Richmond and Raleigh.

In 1863, Governor Zebulon Vance authorizes 400 tons of North Carolina Railroad iron to be used for construction of ironclads, but more than a year passes before the Tredegar Iron Works in Richmond can transform it into armor plates. The delay in completing the ram incites accusations and counterclaims about who is responsible and who is owed what. Amid the controversy, against Elliott's wishes, the vessel is towed twenty miles upriver to Halifax for completion.

The vessel turns out to be considerably larger than the original design: 158 feet long and more than 35 feet wide, its topsides planked with four-inch-thick yellow pine sheathed in an additional four inches of armor plate. The ram protrudes 18 feet. Two 6.4-inch Brooke rifled cannons can be shifted between six gunports as needed. Before the last of its armor is fastened, the vessel is launched and proceeds about fifty miles downriver to Hamilton.

At last, on April 17, 1864, the ironclad is formally commissioned CSS *Albemarle* and begins the slow journey downriver toward battle under the command of James W. Cooke, a North Carolina native who oversaw the fitting out. Determined to shepherd his project through to the finish, Gilbert Elliott serves as his volunteer aide.

Much work is left to be done. Blacksmith's forges are set up on the ship's flat fore- and after-decks. Mechanics swarm over the hull, still fitting and hammering iron plates. Twenty veteran sailors come aboard to swell its crew to 150 as it drifts downriver.

At Williamston, hundreds of spectators turn out in carriages and small boats to watch the leviathan pass. By suppertime, it is a blur sliding downriver. At ten o'clock, the drive shaft comes unseated, and progress halts for major repairs.

Farther on, it is reported that sunken ships block the way downriver. Commander Cooke and Elliott investigate and find a channel ten feet deep—more than sufficient for passage. The great ram slides through in the dead of night, and at dawn it goes into ferocious action against the enemy flotilla at Plymouth.

The gun crew of ironclad ram CSS *Albemarle* in action.
(Courtesy of the State Archives of North Carolina)

Blocking the *Albemarle*'s way are two gunboats, the USS *Southfield* and the USS *Miami*, chained together in the channel, commanded by Lt. Cmdr. Charles W. Flusser. The *Albemarle* charges toward them and rams the *Southfield*, which sinks quickly—still impaled by the ironclad's ram. On board the *Miami*, gun crews fire at point-blank range. Flusser yanks the lanyard of a nine-inch gun. His shot ricochets off the *Albemarle*'s sloping armor, careens back, and explodes above Flusser's gun, killing him and several crewmen. The U.S. squadron retreats downriver, and Confederates troops stream into Plymouth—their victory assured by the indomitable ironclad.

THE DAREDEVIL

William Barker Cushing—Will to his friends—is restless almost from the day he is born in Wisconsin. His father, a physician, dies of pneumonia when Will is just five years old. His widowed mother moves the family to Fredonia, New York, where they reside on the bottom rung of the social ladder, dependent on the largesse of uncles. Will is egotistical and hot tempered, headstrong and quick to take offense at any casual insult, with an almost pathological craving for danger. He is also insanely brave. Friends speculate that the loss of his father drives him to prove himself.

Appointed to Annapolis by his uncle Francis, a congressman, he shares classes with the likes of future naval legends George Dewey and Alfred Thayer Mahan.

But he is impatient with his teachers, chafes at the necessity of sitting still indoors. Midway through his plebe year, he has already racked up 147 demerits. When he fails his Spanish exam, his professor reports, "Deficient in Spanish. Aptitude for Study: good. Habits of study: irregular. General conduct: bad. Aptitude for Naval Service: not good."

Cushing is summarily dismissed from the academy, only to be reinstated in the navy when war begins. He is insubordinate to officers he considers too timid. But the very traits that sabotage his career as a scholar and a subordinate make him a daring and unconventional warrior.

After leading several audacious raids in Virginia and North Carolina, he is denied by his commanding officer permission to land and take the battery at Smith's Island, thereby pinching off one entrance into the Cape Fear. So Cushing conceives another plan: "My object was to take the commanding general from his bed, in the midst of his men, and to take him out of the harbor in one of his own steamers."

But Brig. Gen. Louis Hébert, commandant of Fort Caswell, is not at home when the raiders arrive, so Cushing carries off Capt. Patrick Kelly, Hébert's chief engineer.

In April 1864, Rear Adm. Samuel Phillips Lee, commander of the North Atlantic Blockading Squadron, awards Cushing a "roving commission" to capture or destroy prizes on his own initiative. Cushing is just twenty-one years old.

In May 1864, Cushing sets his sights on the ironclad ram CSS *Albermarle*. He intends to strike far up the Roanoke River and destroy it. Charles Flusser was one of his oldest friends. Will Cushing vows, "I shall never rest until I have avenged his death." He acquires two small wooden picket boats. Cushing's plan is simple and bold: "I intended that one boat should dash in while the other stood by to throw canister and renew the attempt if the first failed."

But one of his boats suffers engine trouble, runs aground, and is captured. His remaining boat, christened simply Picket Boat No. 1, is about thirty feet long with a small engine, a screw propeller, and a twelve-pound howitzer at the bow. Its most potent weapon is a spar torpedo rigged to a fourteen-foot boom and unleashed against an enemy ship by a complicated system of pulleys, lines, and pins—then detonated by a percussion cap.

The picket boat is manned by fourteen volunteers, chosen from among dozens of eager men. One of them, Assistant Acting Paymaster Francis Swan, describes his commander as he prepares to engage the ironclad: "He was a young man about twenty-one years of age, tall, very erect, with light brown hair flowing down to his shoulders. . . . His exploits on the coast of North Carolina had preceded him, and he was fully up in style and manner to the picture we had drawn of him."

Just before midnight on October 27, 1864, shielded by clouds and rain, Cushing's force—the picket boat towing an escort cutter, twenty-seven men in all—enters the mouth of the Roanoke. Picket Boat No. 1 steams upriver quietly, engine muffled by a tarpaulin, hugging the south bank and taking advantage of the cover of overhanging trees.

The stealth tactics work. By 3:00 A.M., Cushing has reached his target unobserved and casts off the cutter to serve as a rear guard. But almost immediately, guards on the moored *Albemarle* spy the picket boat and open fire. Cushing's coat is shredded by buckshot. He maneuvers his boat head-on at the ironclad, bumping it over the protective log-boom, and amid all the shooting, his crew manages to lower the torpedo boom to the *Albemarle*'s waterline.

Meanwhile, inside the *Albemarle*, the gun crew is frantically loading a round, the muzzle of its rifled cannon scarcely ten feet away from Cushing. Like some figure out of an adventure romance, Cushing stands upright in the bow of the picket boat, right hand clutching the release line of the torpedo, left hand holding the trigger pin.

At the same moment the ironclad's cannon fires, Cushing detonates the torpedo, and all hell breaks loose. A geyser of water and fire erupts between the boats. Men fly out of the picket boat. Cushing sheds his coat, shoes, and sword and dives underwater.

The *Albemarle* is fatally wounded—a six-foot hole blown in its underbelly. In the ensuing chaos and gunfire, two of Cushing's volunteers drown. Eleven are captured, and just one other escapes. The twelve men in the cutter row downriver to safety. Cushing swims to the swamp downriver, steals a skiff, and after twelve hours of rowing reaches the mouth of the river, where he is taken aboard the picket boat *Valley City*.

Will Cushing is a hero of the Union, enjoying the thanks of both Congress and President Lincoln. His hometown of Fredonia throws a gala for him at the concert hall and welcomes him with a standing ovation. He tours Northern cities, famous and fortunate, and in January 1865 he rejoins the fleet for its second assault on Fort Fisher. He will lead a detachment of sailors across the beach in a desperate and doomed frontal charge.

After the war, Gilbert Elliott resumes his profession of attorney and resides for periods in Norfolk, St. Louis, and New York City, where he dies suddenly at the age of fifty-one.

The *Albemarle* is raised and towed to Norfolk, where it is auctioned off to the highest bidder, who pays $2,500 for its iron.

WRITING THE WAR

Jacob Nathaniel Raymer is a literary adventurer: a lean, handsome young man with a long, angular face, a strong nose, and intense eyes. At age twenty-one, he leaves his home in Catawba County and strikes out for the west—Arkansas—his mind set on seeing the world beyond the mountains. At Swannanoa Gap, east of Asheville, he lingers for a last look homeward, "and from that lofty pinnacle, the dividing line between home and strangers," he writes in his diary, "I did take a long farewell."

Well-read and already erudite, he composes a wistful poem of 201 lines, preoccupied with death and loss, that he titles, "A Last View of Home." "Knowing that / Life at best, is uncertain as the wind," he writes, "And man, with death's ghostly messengers / On all sides is beset—. Nor leaves behind / A memento of his existence. . . . Fame dies with the individual."

His Arkansas sojourn lasts just a couple of years, and by 1860 he is back home, living with his parents and teaching at the Common Schools. On June 7, 1861, soon after North Carolina secedes from the Union, Raymer crosses the county line into Iredell to join Company C of the 4th North Carolina Infantry as a private soldier and musician. Before setting off for training at Garysburg, he visits his schoolhouse one last time. The young scholars strike up a chorus of "Mount Vernon," and Raymer joins in. "But when we began 'Unity,' my voice failed—I could not sing—I felt so sad! So strange!"

His company is nicknamed the Saltillo Boys, since it includes some veterans of the Mexican War. Raymer begins a journal he will keep faithfully throughout four years of war, chronicling nearly every major battle in the east: the Peninsula Campaign, the Seven Days Battles, Sharpsburg, Chancellorsville, Gettysburg, the Wilderness, Spotsylvania Court House, the Shenandoah Valley Campaign of 1864, the siege of Petersburg, and the last stand at Appomattox.

Raymer draws from his copious, detailed notes to write letters home—not to his parents, but to a public audience. By choice, he becomes one of the

Confederacy's corps of a hundred-odd war correspondents. Many of them, like Raymer, are soldiers who send home letters to their local newspapers as circumstances allow. In the Confederacy, a letter may take a month or more to reach its destination, and the 50,000 miles of telegraph lines in the eastern states, like most other resources, are heavily concentrated in the North.

Some paid correspondents work as part of a ragged consortium called the Press Association of the Confederate States — counterpart to the newly formed Associated Press in New York — but with few of AP's resources.

The Northern newspapers, by contrast, field more than 500 paid correspondents, although they are not *well* paid. The *New York Herald* alone sends 63 correspondents into the field, and its sister papers, the *Times* and the *Tribune*, each send 20. Mostly young, untrained, and inexperienced on a battlefield, the correspondents earn only $10 to $25 per week, including expenses, which can be exorbitant in the war zone. Some earn bonuses from regimental commanders or generals to write glowing reports about their leadership, thus advancing their careers. Others leak news of upcoming battles to financial speculators, who use the insider knowledge to play the markets for a profit. The correspondents style themselves the Bohemian Brigade. The work is so physically and emotionally taxing that fewer than 10 of those 500 will last out the whole war.

For Northern newspapers, the war is a bonanza. News of any major battle increases circulation fivefold. Correspondents are driven by their editors to file stories of heroism and slaughter, atrocity and intrigue, and always, always victory — the more lurid, the better.

Neither side is much concerned with objectivity. Stories are printed rife with hyperbole and misinformation. Any minor skirmish is reported as an apocalyptic battle. A small advantage is turned, by journalistic alchemy, into a stunning victory for the cause of right. Pressured for timely news, correspondents who are nowhere near the scene of battle concoct detailed narratives of heroic charges and desperate last stands where none occurred. Since newspaper technology can make no use of photographs, sketch artists draw scenes of combat and destruction — sometimes witnessed firsthand, other times conjured up in the safety of camp.

Wilbur F. Storey of the *Chicago Times* instructs one correspondent, "Telegraph fully any news you can get and when there is no news send rumors." Thus Atlanta is reported captured a full week before Sherman's army arrives there.

Though conscientious reporters work on both sides, the reporting tends toward the partisan, the inflammatory. The numbers of enemy casualties are always inflated, while those of the correspondent's side go undercounted. And correspondents are not treated as neutral noncombatants. At least two are incarcerated in Salisbury Prison and lead a daring overland escape.

From London, as early as November 1861, Henry Adams complains in the *New York Times* that "people have become so accustomed to the idea of disbelieving everything that is stated in the American papers that all confidence in us is destroyed." Indeed, the British and European papers are brimming with stories of the American war. The *Times* of London sends William Howard Russell, celebrity veteran of the Crimean War and the Indian Mutiny, to report, then recalls him because he contends that the Union will inevitably prevail. The *Times* management is rooting for America to pull itself apart and thus quell calls for greater democracy in England.

This war becomes the most thoroughly reported war in history. Because of the telegraph and the railroad, in most Northern cities, news of battles is available within twenty-four hours of the event. Even in the South, news finds its way to the most isolated backwoods settlement within a few weeks. Yet much of the news is unreliable, exaggerated, misrepresented, or simply wrong. In the meantime the U.S. War Department does its best to censor any stories that might cast it in an unflattering light, such as the rout at First Manassas.

The great apparatus of reporting produces a brilliant, confused, and epic masterpiece of fiction.

Especially in the South, a war correspondent sees his job as being a champion of the Cause. Southern reporters cast their stories in tones of optimism even in the face of cascading disaster. Deserters are rarely mentioned; they are "absentees" or "stragglers." Yankees are "infidels," "foreigners," and "drunkards." No Confederate force ever retreats. Instead, it makes a "retrograde movement." Rarely mentioned are war profiteering, incompetent or drunken generals, the hideous nightmare of army hospitals, or the hell-on-earth of prisoner of war camps. Stories of victories almost invariably begin by praising God for his hand in routing the unholy enemy.

When the war opens, Southern newspapers are at least a generation behind their counterparts in the industrial cities of the North in resources and professional practice. They operate with small staffs, enjoy a limited local circulation, and can't afford to put correspondents in the field. Their pages mix news, opinion, speeches, political arguments, propaganda, civic announcements, and commercial advertisements willy-nilly.

And it is not long before newsprint and ink become as scarce as any other manufactured commodity. Some newspapers are reduced to a single sheet. Others, such as the *Pictorial Democrat* in Alexandria, Louisiana, resort to printing issues on the blank side of wallpaper.

One of the most prominent newspapers in the Confederacy is the *Richmond Dispatch*, located near the scenes of so many major battles. In North Carolina, dozens of newspapers reprint letters and reports from the Richmond paper, while contributing their own. The *Fayetteville Observer*, led by editor Edward Jones Hale, enjoys the largest circulation in the state and is such a force for promoting the Cause that Maj. Gen. William T. Sherman, who famously loathes even the Northern press, vows to burn it down when he arrives in North Carolina.

By contrast the *North Carolina Standard*, edited by William Woods Holden in Raleigh, becomes the voice of the Peace Party and a vexation to the Confederate government in Richmond.

The *Wilmington Daily Journal* exhorts citizens to beware of profiteers. It runs breathless headlines of the glorious victory at Richmond and erroneous reports of U.S. general McClellan's death. The issue for August 8, 1862, like many others, includes reward notices for deserters and runaway slaves:

ABSCONDED

AND SUPPOSED TO BE IN HIDING in town, MARIA, a bright mulatto girl, about 25 years old, 5 feet 5 inches high, stout and good looking, neat in appearance and well dressed. Twenty-five dollars reward will be paid for her apprehension, and Twenty-five for the detection of any person harboring her.

ELIZA M. WALKER.

Jacob Nathaniel Raymer enters the journalistic fray as both a typical, biased amateur and a principled exception. In an early dispatch to the *Carolina Watchman* in Salisbury, he reveals his credo as a reporter: "All I promise is an account of what came under my immediate observation, and such incidents as I can prove to be actual facts."

He sends home to the *Watchman* and to the *Iredell Express* regular, detailed dispatches of astonishing length, given that he must write them in such rough circumstances — under a tent he shares with best friend and bandmate James Columbus Steele, after a day's hard marching or during the lull after a battle. He writes by the light of a candle stuck in the socket of a bayonet, long after his fellow soldiers have lapsed into exhausted sleep. His letters are reprinted in other papers across the state, such as the *Fayetteville Observer* and the *Statesville American*.

He begins nearly all his dispatches the same way: "From the 4th North

Carolina" or "From the Saltillo Boys." Most of what appears in any newspaper is without byline, unsigned, or signed with a classical Greek or Roman pseudonym. At first, Raymer signs off as "Scribbler," but he soon settles on "Nat."

Raymer takes on one of the most important and difficult duties of the war, and he performs it faithfully and with diligence: reporting the casualties in his unit. In this arena, he must be absolutely accurate, for a mistake in his dispatch means heartbreak and anguish back home.

Soldiers on neither side carry uniform identification — no badge or card with name and unit. Before major battles, many pin papers to their shirt backs listing their names, units, and hometowns, so they can be identified if they fall. Late in the war, sutlers following the Union army offer engraved metal badges for $1 — or $3 for gold. But in truth, bodies are often mangled by cannon fire, burned, or blown to bits. Men go lost in the wilderness of battle, drown in rivers and creeks and are washed away. Dazed or overwhelmed, they are captured. In the aftermath of battle, it is commonplace for hundreds of unidentified bodies to be dumped into mass graves. Especially among Confederate troops, as the war wears on and units find themselves mixed together in retreat, often the only way to know for certain if a man has been killed or wounded is for someone who knows him personally to miss him and go looking.

Neither side has any procedure for notifying a dead or wounded soldier's next of kin. So Raymer includes the litany of the fallen, by company, in each dispatch. After Gettysburg, he writes: "Com A — Killed — Privates M B Mayhew and R.M. Brawley wounded, Eli Day, thigh severe; J Massey, left leg amputated; M.T. Clark, both legs fractured below the knee; J A Cohen, side slight; M. Snow, shoulder slight; F M Morrison, head slight." And on through Companies B through K. He confesses, "The best writer in the universe could not give the faintest idea of the horrible conflict."

As a bandsman, he helps clear the battlefield of wounded, then assists in the operating theater — a grisly scene of amputation and screaming agony. After Chancellorsville, he writes with characteristic truthfulness: "Here is where we could see the melancholy fruits of war. Never since the war began have I seen so many men severely wounded or so many amputations necessary. The work of butchery began about noon on the same day and continued with little intermission until ten o'clock the following day. Arms and legs were scattered and tossed about with utmost indifference, wounds probed and dressed, balls extracted, and the sufferers made as comfortable as the nature of the case would possibly admit."

Jacob Nathaniel "Nat" Raymer becomes a fighting war correspondent,
reporting news of his comrades wounded or killed in action.
(Courtesy of Nancy Moss Miller)

In the same long dispatch, he rails against soldiers caught in the act of stripping the Union dead and recounts a tender scene in which he comforts a dying enemy soldier. Elsewhere he addresses all the taboo subjects: deserters, the plight of prisoners, the grief of soldiers who have lost their pals, the horrific wails of the wounded at the Wilderness as they burn to death in a forest fire ignited by artillery.

Raymer is both observant and reflective. He quickly understands that the war is not about glory, that Yankees are not cowardly infidels, and that the wanton sacrifice of so many young men is a tragedy that will haunt the nation for generations to come.

He writes not only of the battlefield but of anything else that catches his fancy. "For my part, I desire to see the strange, the wonderful and the beautiful." He takes his readers on a tour of a "lunatic asylum" and the state capital, where he is appalled to find the place teeming with "an amalgamation of two races, the extremes of color and intellect — Raleigh Seminoles, or what will convey the idea better, Mongrels — in short, good reader, Mullatoes." He is, then, possessed of a native bigotry. And at times his prose can be as florid as the worst sentimental novel of the day.

He makes no apology for penning an impassioned plea for new recruits. Only after the slaughter at Gettysburg does he express any doubts that the Confederacy will prevail. "Fighting does not seem to do a particle of good, for no sooner is one bloody struggle over than preparations are made for another." Fresh Federal "armies spring up like Jonah's gourd vine, in one night . . . while we might as well expect reinforcements from the moon."

Yet, amid the horror of battle, he is able to compose passages of stunning vividness, nuance, and beauty.

Near Strasburg, Virginia, drawn up in line of battle on a cold November night to await an onslaught by Federal troops, he writes, "The sun went down and the night grew dark and cheerless. The vast amphitheater of mountains around us were dark and dismal, except a few spots occasionally illuminated by a few straggling rays from the half moon, which now seemed more distant and colder than ever."

In April 1864, in winter quarters awaiting the coming campaign season, he confides to his readers, "The enthusiasm of our soldiers, and also of those at home, is at such an extravagant pitch, that if we should meet with misfortune, the tumble from hope almost realized, to absolute despair, would be so great that I fear we would hardly ever recover from its effects."

Raymer's wartime dispatches accumulate into the length of a book titled

Confederate Correspondent, a comprehensive chronicle of four years of brutal war and remarkable compassion in the company of his fellow North Carolinians. After Appomattox, he walks home, accompanied by his friend Steele. Once again, he becomes a private citizen, a schoolteacher. But in the end, he proves himself wrong: his fame — embodied in his words — outlives the man.

OCCUPYING ARMY

For Joseph B. Morgan, owner of a prosperous farm at Indian Ridge, in coastal Currituck County, the war brings the strange and unpredictable ordeal of occupation.

Strange because the occupying army represents the same government under which he has lived his whole life—the United States of America. But North Carolina has seceded, and Morgan is a wholehearted Confederate now. So the familiar blue troops—wearing the same uniform as those who manned coastal forts before the war—take on the aspect of a horde of foreigners.

Unpredictable because the rules are rarely clear, the requirements always shifting, the behavior of the blue soldiers at times orderly, at other times capricious and wantonly destructive. They can be cordial and respectful or threatening and thieving.

On the coast, invasion comes early and fast. In August 1861, an expedition led by Maj. Gen. Benjamin F. Butler captures Hatteras Island and holds it for the duration. By February 1862, under Maj. Gen. Ambrose E. Burnside, the Federals have taken Roanoke Island. In March they advance on Beaufort at night, and the citizens awaken to the sight of Union patrols.

A fierce battle at New Bern costs more than a thousand casualties and leaves the Federals in control of that crucial stronghold, now the capital of Union North Carolina. Washington falls, and the Federals lay siege to Fort Macon, which is surrendered the following month. Carolina City, Havelock Station, and Morehead City all come under occupation. Meanwhile, expeditions probe west toward Kinston, Plymouth, Elizabeth City, and the critical Wilmington and Weldon Railroad. Dozens of skirmishes take place along crucial crossing points of creeks. Gunboats duel on the shallow rivers.

By the summer of 1862, U.S. forces control the coast from the Virginia border to the White Oak River. Beaufort becomes a coaling station for the blockading fleet.

Like most in the Confederate South before the war, Joseph Morgan had very limited interactions with the federal government in Washington, D.C., other than sending letters via the U.S. Post Office and voting in elections. It neither taxed him nor policed his activities. Now the federal government is an armed presence, restricting travel, controlling commerce, dictating nearly every facet of daily life.

At the outbreak of war, one of Morgan's sons, Patrick, is far away in the Shenandoah Valley, attending Virginia Military Institute, once a prestigious training ground for U.S. Army officers. Now most of its living alumni are serving in the army of the rebellion.

Morgan keeps up a regular correspondence with his son. In January 1863, he writes, "Your Uncle James has again been driven from his home by the shelling of his premises, and together with his family is now residing with us." In the same letter, he describes the unsettled state of the country-side: "The enemy occasionally makes raids upon us & plunder & destroy our property. A few weeks ago they came over to Indian Town & burned all the buildings on Dr. Marchant's place, opposite where he used to live, together with the academy, & plundered several citizens, taking horses, carts, negroes, salt & c."

And disease is ever present, respecting no military lines, carried by the hordes of soldiers and sailors passing through crowded encampments: "The Diphtheria has been very prevalent this winter. . . . All of us have had sore throats and your Ma has been doctoring for diphtheria." His wife suffers one debilitating illness after another.

Able-bodied white men caught in the zone of occupation enjoy only bad choices. They can take a loyalty oath and bide their time, making the best of it; they can steal across the lines and join or be conscripted into the Confederate army; or they can collect a $300 bounty by enlisting in the Union volunteer regiments. Meanwhile thousands of slaves free themselves or are liberated by Union troops. Some live off the countryside. Others congregate inside the Union lines. When the U.S. War Department authorizes the raising of U.S. Colored regiments, many enlist.

The war on the coast is one of guerilla actions against both regular U.S. Army troops and volunteer units raised from local men, derisively called "buffaloes." Many buffaloes behave more like gangs of bushwhackers and thugs than disciplined troops. They plunder at will, settling old scores and terrorizing local farmers like Morgan.

The situation remains fluid. Men are arrested for treasonous activities. Some are hanged. Others are later freed without explanation. Pickets are ambushed in the dark. Spies cross the lines carrying precious information about

Occupying Army

troop movements. Punitive patrols target local rebels, steal or slaughter their livestock, and even burn their homes.

With too few troops to mount a major offensive, the U.S. army of occupation fortifies its lines and settles for a series of ineffectual raids. At first, the Confederate commander in the East, General Lee, won't spare troops from the Virginia front to retake the coastal plain. Then in early 1863, forces under Maj. Gen. D. H. Hill attack New Bern and Washington, both unsuccessfully.

In February 1864, Maj. Gen. George E. Pickett leads 13,000 troops in an attempt to capture New Bern, but incompetence and poor communication turn the expedition into a fiasco. Brig. Gen. Robert F. Hoke recaptures Plymouth and Washington in April 1864, but he can hold them only until the autumn, when once again they fall to Union forces.

North Carolina is now two states: the mountains and the Piedmont, controlled by the secessionist state government, and a large swath of the coastal plain — not including Wilmington — under control of the U.S. Army and, as of May 19, 1862, an appointed military governor: Edward Stanly. A follow-up to his appointment letter from Secretary of War Edwin M. Stanton reads in part, "It is obvious to you that the great purpose of your appointment is to re-establish the authority of the federal government in the State of North Carolina."

Stanly is a New Bern native, a lawyer and former congressman, tall and lanky with a long, kindly countenance. He faces an impossible mandate. He must govern a war zone with shifting boundaries and multiple commanders jockeying for prominence. He is a man of upright character and good intentions but blind to the need to abolish slavery. Among other futile tasks, he attempts to keep slaves from being set free from their local masters. He is no abolitionist. He opposes the education of freed slaves, honoring a state law that is at odds with a principal aim of the war. He persuades "a gentleman of good Samaritan inclinations" in New Bern to close his school for educating black children on the grounds that, once they are returned to their masters at the end of hostilities, "those negroes who have been taught to read and write would be suspected and not benefited by it." He clearly envisions a postwar state in which slavery is restored.

Stanly's task is complicated in May 1862 by an order issued by Brig. Gen. John G. Foster, the new presiding military authority in eastern North Carolina, to establish a Freedmen's Colony on Roanoke Island. The task falls to Rev. Horace James, an army chaplain of the 25th Massachusetts appointed "Superintendent of all the Blacks" in the Department of North Carolina. He diligently collects funds and implements to undertake the daunting project.

Within eighteen months, he has laid out a grid of streets and established 591 families on one-acre plots of uncultivated land with plain wood homes. The plan is for the colony to be self-sufficient, but so many of the able-bodied men have been recruited into the U.S. Army that most of the remaining 3,000 people are women and children, who must be fed and clothed.

The settlement comes to a heartbreaking end. In 1865, the U.S. government orders that the land be surrendered to any original owner who can prove title.

Meanwhile, Stanly is appalled by the plundering of roving squads of buffaloes, as well as bands of free blacks. He complains, "Had the war in North Carolina been conducted by soldiers who were christians and gentlemen, the state would long ago have rebelled against rebellion. But instead of that, what has been done? Thousands and thousands of dollars worth of property were conveyed by the North."

For the people of Winton, a small town on the Chowan River, Union occupation brings much worse. In February 1862, an expedition of six gunboats carrying 1,000 troops under Cmdr. S. C. Rowan sets out to burn two railroad bridges above the town. But the flotilla is driven back by the heavy fire of Confederate artillery and muskets. Returning downriver, the expedition sends a landing party ashore at Winton under command of Col. Rush C. Hawkins of the 9th New York Zouaves. The town is deserted and the troops meet no resistance, but Hawkins orders it burned anyway. As his order is carried out, the troops go on a looting spree. A volunteer of the 4th Rhode Island recounts, "The boys found plenty of everything and soon came flocking back to the boats loaded down with household goods, books, articles of food, and anything they found that suited their fancy."

A soldier in the 10th Connecticut, stationed in New Bern, observes, "This whole country for purposes of maintenance for man or beast, for the next twelve months is a *desert* as hopeless as *Sahara* itself. If this *war* continues another twelve months this country will be little else than a 'howling wilderness' and the 'abomination of desolation' will be written on every 'gait post.'"

After scarcely a year in office, Governor Stanly resigns on January 15, 1863, explaining his reasons in a letter to a friend:

My chief hope & aim in coming here was to protect loyal men, and to encourage the people to return to their allegiance to the Union. I have protected loyal citizens in numerous instances you know, and have induced many to take the oath of allegiance & to keep away from all connexion with Secessionists.

I have told our people that the Government would restore property to loyal men & would secure all their constitutional rights. How can I say so, after the Proclamation of the First of January?

He refers, of course, to the Emancipation Proclamation, freeing slaves in the states in rebellion.

No one is appointed to succeed him as governor. From now on, the zone of occupation is under the control of generals. Every time things calm down, some new act of violence against the occupying army—which includes not only regiments from New York, Rhode Island, and other Northern states but North Carolina troops recruited from local counties—causes a backlash.

In September 1863, Morgan reports to his son, "We have just heard that the guerillas had attacked the enemy in Pasquotank killing Tim Cox & probably some others. We hear that the Capt. Commanding in E. City has ordered all the people white & black to report to him, & it is said he intends to compel them to take up arms. The whole country is in a perfect ferment. The people are growing desperate & the inhuman conduct of our enemies seems to be driving every man capable of bearing arms into the bushes or into the army. How long such a state of things is to exist the Lord only can determine."

For many inhabitants, the last straw is the raising of U.S. Colored Infantry from locally freed slaves. Brig. Gen. Edward Augustus Wild arrives at the head of the 55th Massachusetts Colored Volunteers and, with the help of a local black leader, Abraham Galloway, recruits the 1st North Carolina Colored Volunteers.

In January 1864, Morgan writes his cadet son, "It has been a long time since we have had a letter from you. I wrote you a short time since giving a short statement of our troubles & the devastations & excitement produced by a Brigade of negro troops under Gen. Wild passing through our country. But it is utterly impossible for me to give you anything like a correct idea of the state of things in our midst." He recounts how he has been appointed to a committee that will treat with the U.S. commander at Old Point Comfort, Virginia, "for the purpose of ascertaining what was required of the peaceful inhabitants to secure their property from destruction & their dwellings from the flames."

The three-day journey brings them face-to-face with the commander of the Department of North Carolina, Maj. Gen. Benjamin F. Butler, a dumpy, bald-headed, sour-faced state senator from Massachusetts whose political savvy has propelled him to high command. He voted for Jefferson Davis to be the Democratic candidate for president in 1860. His iron-handed tenure as military governor of New Orleans earned him the moniker among Confederates as "the Beast."

But on this occasion he is gracious. "He received us very respectfully and treated us courteously, and after hearing our statement conversed with us some half an hour or more very pleasantly. He said nothing was required of us only to remain peaceful and use our influence to put down guerillaing & blockade running; that being accomplished we should not be further molested by his troops."

Morgan and his delegation return home, still wary of the buffaloes and unable to learn reliable information about the progress of the war. Most of the "news" turns out to be unfounded rumor, and most of the reliable news is bad. "Everything is excitement & suspense & God only knows how we are to get along. All is gloom and doubt around us, but God governs in the affairs of men & will bring all things right in the end."

Thinking his son Patrick safely ensconced at the academy, Morgan writes him again in May with family news and rumors. But unbeknownst to him, on the night of May 10, 1864, the cadets are roused by drums; dress in their gray trousers, tunics, and kepis; and form up in columns. Maj. Gen. John C. Breckinridge, who ran unsuccessfully against Abraham Lincoln in the 1860 presidential election, has summoned them to reinforce his outnumbered Confederate force opposing Maj. Gen. Franz Sigel's 6,500 troops marching from Winchester to New Market. Sigel's mission is to drive the rebels from the Shenandoah Valley—the breadbasket of the Confederacy.

The youngest Virginia Military Institute cadet is fifteen years old. Most are between seventeen and twenty-one. They trudge along the rugged Staunton road as far as Midway, eighteen miles north of Lexington, and camp for the night in the rain. Next day they continue on to Staunton through torrential rain, slogging through mud and water-filled ruts. On the following day, they reach Harrisonburg. On May 14, they advance to within seven miles of New Market.

After midnight on Sunday, May 15, Patrick Morgan and the other cadets are again roused to march into battle. They advance through intermittent thunderstorms to New Market by sunrise. All told, the cadets have marched almost eighty miles along mountain roads through mud and drenching rain.

Some ten hours after having been awakened, the cadet corps, 257 strong, forms into line of battle in four companies.

Hard pressed by the enemy, but wracked by doubt to the last, Breckinridge orders, "Put the boys in, and may God forgive me for the order."

They enter the battle at the moment of crisis and hold a crucial position in the line under withering fire from shells, caseshot, and musketfire—then charge the enemy and capture two guns. Ten cadets are killed and fifty-seven more are wounded, a staggering casualty rate of more than one in four in their first engagement. Behind them they leave a sight that will come to symbolize the glorious and futile sacrifice of brave boys to the Cause: a field of lost shoes, sucked off their feet by the glutinous mud in the trampled wheatfield.

His line broken, General Sigel retreats.

By the time word of his son's fate reaches Joseph Morgan back on Indian Ridge, the battle is long over. This time, at least, the news is good: Cadet Patrick Morgan has survived the killing field.

But at home, the occupation goes on.

28

A MERCIFUL REPRIEVE
AT POPLAR GROVE

While the war wreaks havoc on occupied coastal towns and western settlements engage in their own brutal war between neighbors, a few favored places remain virtually untouched by the cataclysm. One island of peace and plenty in the storm is Poplar Grove, in Scotts Hill, fifteen miles northeast of Wilmington on the coastal plank road linking the city to Topsail Sound.

There, on a small rise shaded by towering white poplars and live oaks, Joseph Mumford Foy builds a manor house on cleared land in the midst of 2,025 acres. He inherited the land—lush with longleaf pine woods, pocosins, and saltmarsh—from his father. Originally it had been owned by the widow of Cornelius Harnett, the revolutionary firebrand, called the "Sam Adams of the South," who conferred the name Poplar Grove on the plantation, one of several he owned. It was to Poplar Grove that Harnett returned to die amid the tranquility of the spreading fields and seaborne breezes.

When the original house burns, Joseph M. Foy designs a new one, grander, almost 4,300 square feet. He personally supervises construction between 1849 and 1853. The house remains a consistent sanctuary through the war, even as its residents perish.

Joseph Foy is a sturdy, thick-browed, handsome man with a prominent widow's peak. He is ambitious and energetic, a hard worker who doesn't shy from physical labor. He is also a staunch Unionist, outspoken against the talk of secession.

In October 1860, he writes to his eldest son, David Hiram, "Should political demagogues succeed in severing the bonds of this glorious union it will be the duty of every patriotic citizen to prevent such an event and restore peace and harmony once more." He sees a grave crisis coming—fomented by avowed secessionists such as John D. Bellamy and other planters in the Cape Fear region—and fears the consequences. He continues: "The question is should Lincoln be elected, (which I fear will be the case) will the South secede, and how shall it be prevented? My motto is Union Forever."

On his views about slavery—the very issue dividing the Union—he keeps his own counsel. He is reputed to be liberal in his treatment of his slaves, by the standards of the region, allowing them to hire out for wages that they themselves keep. During one rough patch, when his hold on Poplar Grove is threatened by falling markets, he actually borrows money from his slaves to remain solvent. He later pays it back.

He buys many slaves but never sells a single person. He records such transactions matter-of-factly in a diary, betraying no more emotional or moral considerations than when he is buying lumber for his house. The entry for March 3, 1857, is typical: "Attended Collins sale bought two girls Selia and Ellen $1925." Likewise, a week later he records, "Fair & cold 4 plows & 4 carts Went to town Bought David $1180." The slaves are known by first names only, including Winslow, Izaz, Bill, Sam, Isaac, Peter, Bob, and Abel.

The Foy manor house contains twelve rooms, each with its own brick fireplace and painted mantel of pine and poplar woods. Because he is an amateur, he builds his mistakes into the house, so that chandeliers are off-center with fireplaces, the brick columns supporting the rear porches look strangely delicate for such a robust Greek Revival–style facade, and the whole place exudes a slightly unbalanced, asymmetrical, yet charming feel.

The artisans who work on the place include his own slaves and those from some of the eleven other family plantations in Scotts Hill, hired out for their expertise as stonecutters, brickmasons, plasterers, and finish carpenters. His neighbors include Shepherds, Kings, and Sidburys. The adjoining property is owned by Nicholas Nixon, who keeps a barracks of skilled enslaved artisans in Wilmington—men such as William B. Gould, a master brickmason and plasterer, who works on the Bellamy mansion on Market Street before escaping during the yellow fever epidemic of 1862.

The main staircase is constructed of black walnut, which also panels some of the walls. The floors are heart pine, dense with resin that repels insects. A full raised basement features eight-foot ceilings, and on the first and second floors, the rooms are twelve and ten feet high, respectively, with numerous high sash windows. Broad, airy balconies on the rear look out over the three-chimney detached kitchen and cook's house, the woodshed, the mule barn and horse stables, the wash house, the "necessary," the sawmill and gristmill, the turpentine distillery and blacksmith shop, the wine press, the sheep and hog pens and chicken coops, and rolling acres of corn, sweet potatoes, grapes, and melons. And most of all, "ground peas"—peanuts—the golden cash crop of Poplar Grove.

Far enough from the manor house for mutual privacy, beyond all the outbuildings, stands a row of twelve rude board-and-batten cabins that house the slaves. In 1850, the U.S. Census enumerates the thirty-two Foy slaves: half of them are under the age of sixteen, ten men are of working age, and the other six are either female or too old to work. By 1860, fifty-nine slaves work the plantation. Many toil in the fields, tend and slaughter the hogs, work as blacksmiths to make tools and iron fittings, or drive teams of mules hauling the produce to town in heavy slab-sided wagons. Before the plank road was built, they hauled peanuts and sweet potatoes and melons to the sound and stowed them aboard barges and small schooners for the trip to the market in Wilmington, where the fruits of the fields would be shipped far and wide. Some live in the manor house and attend to Foy's wife, Mary Ann Simmons Foy, and their six children: David Hiram, Henrietta, Joseph Thompson, James William, Henry Simmons, and Francis Marion.

After her last childbirth, Mary Ann is paralyzed, likely by polio, and there is no treatment. Then in April 1861, her husband dies suddenly, leaving her an invalid widow with only one grown son to help her run the plantation.

In his will, Foy declares his intention that his wife should not sell any slave unless he or she becomes "unmanageable." He offers no more direction than that, no hint of why he desires that they should all be kept together at Poplar Grove. Some speculate that what he really desired in death was to free them all. But even had he wanted to free his slaves through his last will and testament, his decision likely would have been invalidated by a probate court.

In many Southern states, after the American Revolution, legislators eased their restrictions on "manumission"—the legal term for the process of freeing a slave—by the deceased owner's will. Not so North Carolina. In fact, a succession of North Carolina laws have made it extremely difficult for an owner to free slaves under almost any circumstances.

The state's position is that free blacks are a menace to a community. As early as 1777, the legislature decrees in a preamble to An Act to Prevent Domestic Insurrections, and for other Purposes, "Whereas the evil and pernicious Practice of freeing Slaves in this State, ought at this alarming and critical Time to be guarded against by every friend and Wellwisher of his Country."

If a slave were allowed by his master to hire himself out for wages, "such Slave may be taken up by any Magistrate or Freeholder, and kept to hard

Labour, for the Use of the Poor of the County, for any Time not exceeding Twenty Days."

By 1826, free blacks are forbidden entry into North Carolina under penalty of a $500 fine or worse. In the decades following, the North Carolina Supreme Court, under Chief Justice Thomas Ruffin and others, invalidates many cases of manumission by last will and testament. They even make it legally difficult for Quakers and others to buy slaves with the intention of freeing them, though some find clever ways around the laws.

In 1829, David Walker, a free black native of Wilmington who fled north to Massachusetts, issues his notorious "Appeal," urging blacks to rise up against slavery because "America is more our country than it is the whites — we have enriched it with our *blood and tears.*"

Within months, the North Carolina general assembly passes the most draconian antimanumission law to date. It stipulates that a slave can be freed only for documented "meritorious service," which is deemed to be so unusual that it can never be granted to more than one slave at a time. Furthermore, the applicant must apply for a license at a state superior court, then advertise — for a minimum of six weeks in the *State Gazette*—his or her intention to free the slave. For each slave freed, the owner must submit a bond of $1,000. Finally, the slave must be at least fifty years old and leave the state within ninety days of manumission, never to return, or be auctioned by the state to the highest bidder, back into slavery.

This last provision makes freedom a bittersweet achievement, for the slave must leave his or her home, friends, and any family still enslaved, then start over in a new place without money or means at an age when many are all but broken by a lifetime of hard labor.

So upon Joseph M. Foy's death, his slaves remain slaves.

Mary Ann, unable to run the place, takes her young children to live with relatives inland in Sampson County, leaving her eldest son, David Hiram, in charge. In a photograph taken about this time, David Hiram wears a mournful expression, his eyes downcast, his face sagging with apparent grief. Almost as soon as secession is declared, David hires an overseer and leaves Poplar Grove. He enlists in Company A, 41st North Carolina Troops. But he does not survive long enough to see combat; he succumbs to typhus in 1862 at the age of twenty-one.

So, just seventeen years old, Joseph T. Foy takes over management of Poplar Grove.

Across the plank road, Confederate infantry encamp to guard the salt works along the sound. Only a few miles north, the Topsail Battery repulses an attempt by the blockading U.S. Navy to raid the salt works, so crucial to the preservation of pork and beef for the troops. Just offshore, two blockade-runners are sunk in sight of land by Federal gunboats.

But except for the death of the eldest Foy brother far from home, the war does not touch Poplar Grove. The place remains charmed. For the duration, the plantation remains self-sufficient, able to feed and clothe its own, able to build what it needs, isolated from the violence of cannons and muskets.

While the rest of the state suffers worsening food shortages, even starvation, food remains plentiful on the plantation. Indeed, Poplar Grove becomes a strategic asset to the war effort, supplying thousands of pounds of pork to Confederate troops in the field by way of the Wilmington and Weldon Railroad. Mary Ann's greatest anxiety is that the war will claim her next eldest son, Joseph T., who has proven so adept at managing the large livestock and farming operation.

In a canny, politically astute letter to Confederate president Jefferson Davis, on October 13, 1864, she urges him to exempt her son Joseph T. from conscription into the army by reason of his value in managing Poplar Grove and, in so doing, feeding the beleaguered Confederate troops: "In the kindness of your heart to widow and orphan Please send me an exemption for Joseph T. Foy. . . . There is no way for me to carry on a farm without him. . . . I will work hard (or have it done) to help support the Government if you will share this son to my help. . . . Please don't overlook my place for it is my love for my Country and the support of myself and little children that I presume to write to you."

Davis, who this late in the war is no longer exempting even university students, is persuaded by her cool logic and charm and grants her wish. Joseph T. remains safe at Poplar Grove.

At war's end, Sherman's Final March misses Scotts Hill by many miles. Only a few mules and horses are commandeered by the occupying U.S. Army in Wilmington. In a miracle of luck and location, Poplar Grove has come through the violence of war unscathed. Mary Ann signs a loyalty oath in June 1865, and the land and manor house remain solidly in the possession of her family.

Only the slaves no longer belong to them. All but one remain at Poplar Grove, now free by law to work the land that has become their home.

A Merciful Reprieve at Poplar Grove

THE IRON LIFELINE

Late on the bright, clear afternoon of September 12, 1862, Col. William Shepperd Ashe is supervising the salt works on Masonboro Sound, east of Wilmington at the mouth of Whiskey Creek. He is forty-nine years old, a large, active, cheerful man long in the habit of being in charge. A messenger arrives bearing an ominous telegram: Ashe's youngest son, Samuel A'Court, has been captured at Manassas, Virginia.

Samuel is the spitting image of his father, even to the wry turn of his mouth, and shares his temperament and zeal for efficient organization. Just weeks ago, Samuel was appointed adjutant general to Brig. Gen. William Dorsey Pender's brigade at the rank of captain, responsible for all the myriad details of troop movements, logistics, and supplies. Pender considers him "A very nice modest young man."

The day following Samuel's promotion, Pender's brigade was engaged heavily. All Ashe knows is that his son has been captured, his fate otherwise unknown. Ashe hurries to the depot of the Wilmington and Weldon Railroad on the east bank of the Cape Fear River and commandeers a handcar and two men to help propel it. He can do such things—he is president of the line. He mounts the car, and they roll north through the beautiful balmy evening on a three-hour journey to his home in Rocky Point, a distance of just under twenty miles.

Ashe is dressed in his customary dark coat and waistcoat, a stylish cravat at the collar. He is a little heavy, in the fashion of successful businessmen. His thick brown hair is combed back, his long whiskers razor-cut at his jawline, his face bare of beard or moustache. His countenance can appear stern, but friends and employees find him congenial and kind-hearted.

Ashe follows a route he knows well, almost exactly due north over his company's tracks. The handcar is propelled by two men alternately pumping on horizontal bars running through a fulcrum at the center of the deck—strenuous physical labor.

Though he could wait for news in the city, this impetuous drive to be

William Shepperd Ashe, president of the vital Wilmington and Weldon Railroad, inspires both respect and affection among peers and workers alike.
(Courtesy of the State Archives of North Carolina)

in motion toward his goal is typical of him. Ashe is a man who gets things done: a dynamo with a vision, grandson of Governor Samuel Ashe, a former state senator and congressman who became president of the line in 1854. As a state senator, Ashe championed the expansion of railroads to connect the far-flung regions of his own state with one another and with the lucrative world of commerce beyond. He envisions a fully integrated system of Southern railroads, depots, ports, and shipping.

Some of that vision has already come true: in just a dozen years, the state's railroads have grown from 283 miles to nearly 1,000. The Wilmington and Weldon alone now runs 26 locomotives and 182 coaches and freight cars. Still, Ashe has not been able to secure funds to build a bridge across the Cape Fear River. A steam ferry connects his railroad to the Wilmington and Manchester line on the other side — a bottleneck that is costly and inconvenient in peacetime, and in wartime, downright dangerous.

From the moment in the summer of 1861 when Brig. Gen. Thomas J. Jackson entrains his troops in the Shenandoah Valley and delivers them right onto the battlefield at Manassas — a rail junction — it becomes apparent that this is a new kind of war. Troops and guns can shift positions in days, rather than marching for weeks. Already in the North the federal government has established the U.S. Military Railroad System, a unified web of more than 20,000 miles of track, hundreds of locomotives, and thousands of boxcars, flatcars, and passenger coaches.

Ashe was an ardent supporter of secession, but like many of those who favored disunion, he did not really expect war. He imagined a new Southern nation, irresistibly — but peacefully — pulling away from the Union to command its own destiny, united in purpose and culture and bonded by efficient railroads.

President Davis personally enlisted Ashe: "By direction of the President you are assigned to the duty of superintending the transportation of Troops and Military stores on all the Rail Roads, north and south, in the Confederate States."

A full year ago, in order to speed supplies to troops in Virginia, Ashe attempted to commandeer locomotives and boxcars from Georgia. Governor Joseph E. Brown reacted with furious threats. "If you seize our cars or engines," he declared, "I will, by military force if necessary, make counter seizures." Secretary of War Judah P. Benjamin backed the governor, on the grounds of states' rights. Ashe has strenuously advocated for an interconnected railroad system, but Davis has demurred, allowing each state to set priorities. Therein lies the conundrum of trying to unify a band of states whose guiding principle is the sovereignty of the individual state over the national government.

Even now, depot managers and station managers are constantly harangued by nagging officials representing various states and arms of the Richmond government, all demanding that their particular freight or contingent of troops be given priority.

Only two reliable routes connect the deep South with Virginia, where much of the heaviest fighting occurs and hundreds of thousands of troops need to be supplied with everything: Enfield rifled muskets from England; pork and corn from the Piedmont; powder from the works at Augusta, Georgia; tents, uniforms, haversacks, and a myriad of other camp equipment; even gold and whiskey. Both routes run through North Carolina.

From Augusta, trains can travel to Manchester, South Carolina, and thence on the Wilmington and Manchester line through Florence to Wilmington. From Wilmington, trains run to Goldsboro junction, then either to Weldon to join with the Petersburg and Richmond line or to Raleigh. From Raleigh, troops and freight arriving from either Charlotte or Wilmington can move west on the North Carolina Railroad through Greensboro, then north to Danville — but the last forty miles of track connecting the line to Danville has never been laid.

Governor Vance agrees to allow construction of the final leg connecting Danville in 1862, but he does not make it a priority. He engages in a persistent feud with Davis to provide troops and guns to defend the eastern part of the state, where Union forces periodically stage raids on the Wilmington and Weldon line. Vance fears that if an alternate line is finished, Richmond will devote even fewer troops to defending the coastal railroad.

Meanwhile, the scarce supplies of pig iron are being diverted to construct ironclad warships at Wilmington, Halifax, and White Hall, upriver of Kinston. By the time the last forty miles of track are laid two years later, it's too late to change the outcome of the war.

Worse, there is no standard gauge for railroads. The Wilmington and Weldon's gauge matches the emerging national standard of 4 feet 8½ inches, inherited from the old English measurement between wagon wheels. So does the North Carolina Railroad's. But two crucial connecting lines, the Richmond and Danville Railroad and the Charlotte and South Carolina Railroad, run on a 5-foot gauge. Davis urges Vance to retool the North Carolina Railroad tracks to the Virginia gauge, but Vance refuses such an impractical request. And the heavy military usage was never planned for. Running more and more trains loaded with troops, ammunition, and other essentials is wearing out the track.

Even manpower is a problem. Most of the rail corridors were laid by slaves, who still maintain them, working in gangs housed at various junctions along the line. But owners who contract the slaves to the railroad have had to lend many of their best workers to build coastal forts. White supervisors and engineers find themselves conscripted for military duty.

Frustrated at the lack of cooperation between state governments, Richmond, and the railroads, Ashe stepped down as quartermaster and devotes himself to his own railroad. In addition, he oversees the salt works, a multimillion-dollar operation that is vital to the war effort.

But this evening, Ashe is preoccupied with another worry. Tomorrow young Captain Ashe will celebrate his twenty-second birthday—but where? And in what condition? Ashe wheels his way through the gathering gloom of the forested track, hoping that some further word awaits him at home. There he must also comfort his invalid wife, Sarah Ann. The sun has been down for nearly an hour. The three men cross the river trestle and labor on through the tree-tunneled Low Country forest. Inside the narrow right-of-way, hemmed in by dense thicket and tall longleaf pines, the darkness is dense as water.

Ashe is aware that the southbound mail train from Goldsboro to Wilmington will pass the Northeast Cape Fear River turnout near Castle Haynes at 7:30 P.M., barreling head-on down the same track, but he has made the trip often enough to time his passage. And in any case, they will see the towering locomotive headlamp coming for miles. In his haste to leave, he brought no lamp for the handcar. But he can't get lost: the track runs only one way.

But he has not counted on the mail train's engine breaking down along the route. The mail train is towing a second, faster locomotive newly purchased from the Seaboard and Roanoke Railroad. When the regular engine gives out, the Seaboard locomotive is moved to the front of the train to haul it down to Wilmington, making up lost time along the way. The powerful Seaboard locomotive has no headlamp.

The mail train speeds south into the darkness. The handcar cranks its way north. Just a few hundred yards shy of the Northeast Cape Fear River turnout, the blacked-out locomotive erupts out of the darkness and smashes into the handcar. Its enormous cowcatcher flips the handcar off the tracks. Ashe's two companions are thrown clear, miraculously unhurt, but Ashe is catapulted onto the tracks right under the wheels of the onrushing locomotive.

Ashe is so mutilated that the crew of the mail train does not at first recognize him. He is carried to a doctor in Wilmington, but it is clear that his condition is dire.

The *Weekly Raleigh Register* describes the "painful accident" in all its grisly particulars: "We learn that last evening, about 7½ o'clock, a most painful accident occurred on the Wilmington and Weldon Railroad, a short distance this side of the North East Bridge, resulting in severe, if not fatal injuries to Hon. W. S. Ashe, President of the road, whose left thigh was broken—his right leg shattered below the knee, and his right foot almost crushed off, besides other injuries. The right leg has since been amputated just below the knee."

The *Wilmington Journal* reports on September 15, "He lingered, however, until last night about eight o'clock, when he passed off quietly and calmly, and apparently without pain, from sheer exhaustion of his system consequent upon the terrible stroke it had received." The *Journal* declares, "We shall seldom look upon his like again; nor can this community and the State . . . soon cease to mourn the loss of the noble, generous, big-hearted gentleman, the ardent patriot and the useful citizen." And in truth, the railroad has lost its fiercest advocate, the one man who understands that success on the battlefield is impossible without a reliable, unbroken railroad. The Wilmington and Weldon continues without Ashe's leadership, but his vision remains unfulfilled.

The war will be long over before the Cape Fear is spanned by a railroad bridge connecting the Wilmington and Weldon with the Wilmington and Manchester. Meantime, for the remainder of the war, each railroad in the state continues to operate independently, rather than under a central authority, and the result is continued—often heartbreaking—inefficiency. Stockpiles of food and clothing rot in warehouses or alongside depots, exposed to the elements, while troops in the field starve. Ammunition remains safely in the rear, where it cannot help beleaguered soldiers. Whole regiments elect to march rather than surrender themselves to the uncertain timetables of the railroads.

In the North, the trains deliver troops, ammunition, and provisions with industrial precision. Hospital trains carry the wounded from battlefields such as Chancellorsville and Gettysburg to safe havens in Washington. Flatcars mount leviathan mortars that bombard Petersburg and other fortified Southern cities.

Nevertheless, by 1864, a single iron road, the Wilmington and Weldon, supplies Lee's Army of Northern Virginia with 60 percent of its supplies.

As long as Wilmington holds out and the line is not cut, the Confederate army remains unvanquished. But the rails are at last wearing out. Trains must creep along at speeds as slow as five miles per hour. On a good day, the single northbound track can deliver just 200 tons of supplies, not nearly enough to stave off disaster.

Repeated raids by Union troops cut the line, destroy vital bridges. The retreating Confederates themselves destroy portions of the railroad—trains, equipment, and depots—leaving the enterprise a shambles.

By war's end, of thirty-one locomotives, just seven will be reported to Wilmington and Weldon stockholders as being "in good order." Others will be written off as "Totally unfit for service" and one "In the Roanoke River."

Samuel A'Court Ashe languishes in Old Capitol Prison for two months after the calamitous death of his father. Then he is exchanged for a Union officer. When Sherman invades North Carolina, Ashe is second in command of the Fayetteville Arsenal, one of Sherman's prime targets.

He endures the humiliation of surrender and lives to be ninety-seven. When he passes away in 1938, he is the last surviving commissioned officer of the Confederate States of America.

30

GETTYSBURG

North Carolina's Darkest Hour

The darkest hour of the war lasts for three days.

It is an hour named for a place, the wholesale slaughter of North Carolina troops spelled out in the name of a small crossroads town 350 miles north of Raleigh—far beyond Richmond, Washington, and even Maryland: *Gettysburg*. The name becomes shorthand for death on a massive scale, for blunder and miscalculation, for unimaginable courage. And for defeat.

July 1–3, 1863. It is an hour whose penumbra burns for weeks and months afterward, the breaking point between *before* and *after*.

Before Gettysburg, the 26th North Carolina Regiment is the largest in the Army of Northern Virginia. After Gettysburg, it has virtually ceased to exist, a legion of ghosts and wounded and a handful of shocked survivors.

Before Gettysburg, the war seems winnable; the Confederate army is invincible under legendary commanders. After Gettysburg, it has been shaken to its core, many of its best commanders dead or grievously wounded.

Even in the chronicle of this bloody war, Gettysburg is extraordinary. It exceeds all other battles in the number of casualties—more than Shiloh, Sharpsburg, or Chancellorsville.

More extraordinary is the absoluteness of the Confederate defeat in the absence of an absolute victory for the Union. Ultimate victory seemed so tantalizingly close just weeks earlier, when Lee celebrated a stunning defeat of the U.S. Army at Chancellorsville. He has invaded the North to force the issue, to place his army between the Federal army and Washington and thus give President Lincoln no alternative but to sue for peace and guarantee the sovereignty of the Confederate States of America.

Along the route of march through Maryland and Pennsylvania, his troops systematically abduct as many as a thousand free blacks and escaped slaves, to be transported south into slavery.

Lee's army, spread out in three corps, blunders into battle as one regiment advances on the town, searching for shoes. But Gettysburg has neither a shoe factory nor a shoe warehouse. And Lee's cavalry, under its storied commander, J. E. B. Stuart, is unaccounted for somewhere in the Pennsylvania countryside. Thus Lee's army marches blind in enemy territory straight into the Army of the Potomac.

The regiment searching for shoes is set upon by Union cavalry blocking the road. Within hours, the first divisions of an eventual total of nearly 170,000 soldiers are locked in a desperate fight.

Other figures tell the tale with numbing clarity. Over the next three days, as many as 51,000 men are killed, wounded, captured, or missing in action—many of the missing simply obliterated by artillery.

Of these, some 28,000 are Confederates, fully one-third of the army.

The numbers are staggering, and every state in the Confederacy mourns its dead—nearly 5,000 in total. But North Carolina endures a special grief: one in four of the dead is a North Carolinian.

On the first day, nearly 14,000 Tar Heels march into battle: thirty-two regiments of infantry, four regiments of cavalry, one attached battalion, and four batteries of artillery. By the third day, some 6,000 of them lie wounded or dead on the field.

All the numbers are approximate, for it is impossible to keep track of the fates of so many men in violent motion—especially once the Army of Northern Virginia retreats south, leaving behind its dead and many of the wounded, who disappear into hospitals and prison camps, many to die there, others giving false names to their captors. Meanwhile Lee's retreating troops shepherd a train of makeshift ambulances seventeen miles long.

Each of the three days is counted off in brutal assaults.

On the first day, the 26th North Carolina advances against the Iron Brigade—resolute veterans from Michigan, Indiana, and Wisconsin—at McPherson's Ridge.

Charging uphill into the murderous fire of seasoned troops, Henry King Burgwyn Jr., "the boy colonel" of the 26th North Carolina, is shot through the lungs while bearing the colors of his regiment. He dies after two hours of agony. He is twenty-one years old. Thirteen other color-bearers are shot down, yet the regiment never loses its banner.

Command passes to Col. John Randolph Lane. He turns to rally his men, shouting, "Twenty-Sixth, follow me!" and almost at once is shot in the back of the head, the Minié ball passing out his mouth. He is two days shy of his twenty-eighth birthday, for like his illustrious brigade commander James Johnston Pettigrew, he was born on the Fourth of July. Miraculously, he will survive the war, suffering four more serious wounds.

One by one every colonel, major, and captain on the field goes down, except Capt. H. C. Albright — so he now takes command of the whole regiment.

Capt. J. J. Young, assistant quartermaster, sends an after-battle report to Governor Vance, who once led that same regiment into battle: "We went in with over 800 men in the regiment. There came out but 216, all told, unhurt." One company now musters a single sergeant and no one else, and he falls on the third day.

Captain Young dutifully catalogs the dead and wounded: Burgwyn, Capt. McCreery of Pettigrew's staff shot through the heart; adjutant James B. Jordan in the hip; Capt. J. T. Adams in the shoulder; Capt. William Wilson killed; Lieutenants John W. Richardson and J. B. Holloway dead of wounds. And "It is thought Lieut. [M.] McLeod and Capt. [N. G.] Bradford will die."

"Our whole division numbers but only 1,500 or 1,600 effective men, as officially reported, but, of course, a good many will still come in. . . . It was a second Fredericksburg affair, only the wrong way. We had to charge over a mile a stone wall in an elevated position."

To Colonel Burgwyn's namesake father, Captain Young writes, "How beautiful he looked even in death. There was none of the usual hideous appearance generally apparent in those killed while contending in mortal strife, but he looked like one just fallen asleep." Young and his comrades bury Burgwyn near a walnut tree: "Capt. Iredell of the 47th is on his left side & Capt. Wilson Co B of the 26th on his right. I was fearful to put his uniform coat on knowing if the vandal Yankee knew it they would disinter him. I wrapped him closely in his red woolen blanket to preserve the body as much as possible."

Tom Setser, a twenty-one-year-old private who survives the battle unhurt, writes home, "You may talk of this big fite and that big fite, but tha hante bin sutch fiting as was dun over their for the first days fite. I could all but walk over the field on dead and wounded. I never hav seen the like before."

The 43rd North Carolina, under Col. Thomas S. Kenan, joins eight other North Carolina regiments in the attack that drives the Federals from Seminary Ridge west of the town.

At nightfall, the heights farther on remain in Union hands.

On the second day, other regiments assault Little Round Top on the southern portion of the battlefield, a mile from the town. Attacking straight up the rough boulder-strewn slopes, they *almost* take the hill.

Pvt. Louis Leon of the 53rd North Carolina, held in reserve throughout the day after a hard fight on July 1, describes advancing under an artillery barrage: "Just at dark we were sent to the front under terrible cannonading. Still, it was certainly a beautiful sight. It being dark, we could see the cannon vomit forth fire." Leon is so exhausted that, despite the thunder of the guns, he falls asleep.

On the third day, seven North Carolina regiments, including once again the 53rd and 43rd, assault Culp's Hill at the north end of the Union line under withering crossfire. Private Leon, one of two sharpshooters in his company to survive, records the slaughter: "Here we stayed all day — no, here, I may say, we melted away."

Repeatedly, the North Carolina troops charge downhill through a swale in order to charge uphill, and the result is murderous. "It was truly awful how fast, how very fast, did our poor boys fall by our sides. . . . You could see one with his head shot off, others cut in two, then one with his brains oozing out, one with his leg off, others shot through the heart," Leon writes in his memoir. "I know that our company went in the fight with 60 men. When we left Culps Hill there were 16 of us that answered the roll call."

Meanwhile 15,000 Confederate troops nominally under the command of Maj. Gen. George E. Pickett assault the center of the Federal line on Cemetery Ridge. The troops include the remnants of the 26th North Carolina in the brigade led by the celebrated scholar Pettigrew. North Carolina troops under Pettigrew reach the stone wall atop the ridge and *almost* take the position; then, they are repulsed by a sudden point-blank torrent of canister shot and a swarm of reinforcements.

Pettigrew is wounded, his brigade decimated, and 100 more men of the 26th fall. More than 3,000 Confederate bodies, including the dead from the Pickett-Pettigrew-Trimble charge, lie on the battlefield, unburied for days. Almost 1,000 of them will never be identified.

Col. Edward Porter Alexander records the grim search for fallen officers: "Negro servants hunting for their masters was a feature of the landscape that night." More than 6,000 slaves have accompanied Lee's army, in addition to free blacks captured on the march north, who will be taken south with the army and into bondage. Alexander brought along two slaves. Col. Isaac Avery's slave, Elijah, retrieves his master's body from the field and buries him along the line of retreat in Maryland.

On the first day of battle, Tillie Pierce, a pretty fifteen-year-old blonde

Pickett's Charge—an uphill frontal assault on the center of the
Union line—results in a wholesale slaughter of North Carolina troops.
(Painting by Edwin Forbes; courtesy of the Library of Congress, LC-DIG-ppmsca-22570)

who lives in Gettysburg and attends the Young Ladies Seminary, takes refuge in the home of Jacob Weikert, the father of a schoolmate, near Little Round Top. When the fighting surges around the house on the second day, they flee again. Of her return after the din of battle has receded, she writes, "Upon reaching the place, I fairly shrank back aghast at the awful sight presented. The approaches were crowded with wounded, dying and dead. The air was filled with moanings and groanings. As we passed on toward the house, we were compelled to pick our steps in order that we might not tread on the prostrate bodies." Like many homes in Gettysburg, the Weikert house is filled with wounded soldiers from both sides, many of them with mangled limbs. Surgeons work their saws and knives in plain sight, amputating arms, legs, hands, and feet. They probe for bullets while an assistant holds a cow-horn over the patient's face to administer chloroform.

For months after the battle, the stench from the unburied or shallowly buried corpses remains so pungent that locals carry bottles of peppermint oil or pennyroyal to blunt the smell.

A Vermont soldier describes the condition of bodies left on the field in the July sun for days on end: "The faces of the dead, as a general rule, had turned black—not a purplish discoloration, such as I had imagined in read-ing of the 'blackened corpses' so often mentioned in descriptions of battle-grounds, but a deep bluish *black*, giving to a corpse with black hair the ap-pearance of a negro."

On the Forney farm, overrun on the first day of the fight, the bodies of seventy-nine North Carolinians lie side by side in a neat row exactly where

Gettysburg

Dead Confederate soldiers lie in ranks on the battlefield at Gettysburg.
(Courtesy of the Library of Congress, LC-DIG-stereo-1s02691)

they fell, cut down by a surprise volley fired from soldiers concealed behind
a stone wall.

Because the battle has been fought well beyond the reach of Confederate authority, there is no practical way to recover the bodies of the dead
North Carolinians and bring them home for burial, though some families try.

The retreat of Lee's army turns into a series of running skirmishes, with
more casualties.

Meanwhile, on the now-peaceful battlefield, the U.S. government commissions a Gettysburg merchant, Samuel Weaver, to locate the bodies of
Union soldiers buried in shallow graves. During the next four and a half
months of meticulous daily labor, he personally supervises the exhumation
of 3,354 bodies. He reports how conscientiously he searched out the identi-
ties of the decomposing corpses: "I examined all the clothing and everything

about the body to find the name. I then saw the body, with all the hair and all the particles of bone, carefully placed in the coffin."

An African American subcontractor named Basil Biggs does the physical labor of digging and preparing the bodies for re-interment in the national cemetery, which pays $1.59 for each corpse delivered. The U.S. government provides a sturdy pine coffin for each fallen soldier. But Weaver is strictly forbidden from burying Confederate dead in the cemetery, now—after President Lincoln's dedication—considered sacred patriotic ground.

Before Gettysburg, Governor Vance manages to keep his state staunchly supportive of the war effort, even though it has remained bitterly divided between Unionists and Secessionists. After Gettysburg, he understands all too well that a growing majority of North Carolinians have had enough of war.

Beginning only weeks after Gettysburg, the Peace Movement sweeps the state. The first of 100 rallies is held, at first protesting the conduct of the war, then calling for an outright peace. Companies of North Carolina soldiers vote resolutions in favor of a separate peace with the Union. They desert in gangs.

At war's end, after Samuel Weaver dies in a railway accident, his son takes over the hunt for bodies. Rufus Weaver is a young physician training to be an anatomist in Philadelphia. It is the women of the Wake Ladies Memorial Society in Raleigh who first seek him out. He responds with a sense of sacred duty to the dead, whom he has seen tumbled into ditches, hastily disposed of in farmers' fields, and gawked at by the influx of visitors eager to ogle the grisly battlefield dead for themselves: "If all could see what I have seen and know what I know, I am sure there would be no rest until every Southern father, brother and son would be removed from the North."

Other memorial societies join the ladies from Raleigh in their effort, and Rufus Weaver spends years scouring the battlefield for Confederate dead, including all those North Carolina boys.

He writes, "It required one with anatomical knowledge, to gather *all* the bones. And regarding each bone important and sacred as an integral part of the skeleton, I removed them so that none might be left or lost."

In 1871, he sends 137 sets of remains to Raleigh, along with other shipments to Savannah and Charleston. Two years later, at the request of the Hollywood Cemetery Memorial Association, he ships the remains of 2,935 soldiers to Richmond. Three hundred and twenty-five of those soldiers fell on the third day in Pickett's Charge. They have arrived in twenty-seven boxes labeled simply with the letter P. This was determined by where they were discovered on the battlefield. And it means that many of them are undoubtedly North Carolinians, but they find their final rest on Gettysburg Hill in Hollywood Cemetery.

Stevedores spend an entire day unloading the crates of remains from a steamboat of the Powhatan line. Then more than 1,000 Confederate veterans led by four generals, including Pickett, march in the funeral cortege past crowds of solemn onlookers.

At last, in 1867, the remains of "the boy Colonel" are carried home to Oakwood Cemetery in Raleigh for a proper burial.

But many of the dead from North Carolina never make it home. Their loved ones are left to wonder what became of them, how much they suffered, whether they died alone or in the solace of friends, and what ground, in what faraway state, is now their final resting place.

31

THE SCHOLAR-WARRIOR

In the summer of 1859, while hotheads in the Carolinas are debating whether to secede from the United States, a young planter's son from Tyrell County is tramping through the hills of Spain, gathering material for a book. He is James Johnston Pettigrew, known by family and friends as "Johnston": thirty-one years old, independently wealthy, a slave owner, a graduate of the University of North Carolina, former assistant at the U.S. Naval Observatory in Washington, D.C., a licensed attorney in Charleston, South Carolina, and a former state legislator.

Pettigrew is a champion fencer, a mathematical wizard, and fluent in five languages. At age fourteen, he entered the University of North Carolina and later graduated valedictorian of a thirty-six-member class.

He has traveled to Europe to join the Sardinians in fighting for independence from Austrian domination. Part of him, chafing at the scholar's mild life, craves adventure and glory. Before the first shots are fired, however, the French emperor intervenes and the war is called off. Pettigrew treks though the pass from France to Italy along a mountain road built by Napoleon. "It was my birthday; but far more, it was the day that ushered into life my native land—a day ever memorable in the history of the world—not so much because it had added another to the family of nations, as because it had announced, amid the crack of rifles and the groans of expiring patriots, the great principle, that every people has an inalienable right of self-government, without responsibility to aught on earth, save such as may be imposed by a due respect for the opinions of mankind."

Pettigrew retreats to Spain, a country he's always fancied and once visited. He admits, "I went to Spain actuated by the purest motives of selfishness—to gratify myself." There, he writes a book, *Notes on Spain and the Spaniards, in the Summer of 1859, with a Glance at Sardinia*. The book's byline reads, "By A Carolinian," followed by Pettigrew's initials (J.J.P.). He is flippantly self-dismissive.

So accomplished, and yet Pettigrew laments that his life lacks purpose. "I live for nothing that I am aware of," he writes to his older brother, William. On another occasion: "I believe I should turn my head toward getting rich: one must have some object in view; that would be better than nothing; this floating along is rather unsatisfactory." He struggles to find a practical purpose for his life, a useful way to apply his dazzling intellectual skills and all he has learned.

He is slender and mildly handsome, with a receding hairline and a sickly constitution. He endured many childhood ailments: as a young man he contracted an eye infection that blinded him for a time; later he managed to survive a raging bout of yellow fever. Yet he is physically agile, even graceful, and loves the open air. His steady, penetrating eyes seem at odds with his careless, insouciant manner. In the company of strangers, he appears relaxed, even listless, but in fact he is capable of masterful concentration and focus, and he lives an intense, active interior life. He is considered by many acquaintances to be socially backward, declining to participate in the kinds of revelry that the other young men pursued at New Hope Chapel Hill. Instead of rowdy socializing, he prefers to spend studious hours in reading and contemplation.

His sense of honor is notorious, grounded in a romantic ideal of chivalry, and he is quick to feel slighted. At the university, in response to a perceived insult, he set upon a much stronger boy with his fists, and no one ever insulted him again.

He has issued several challenges to engage in duels, played a part in at least one fatal shooting—of a newspaper editor who insulted a friend. He is a fatalist, careless of his own life. He is ambitious but lacks a focus for that ambition. He declines many honors for fear of being seen as a self-promoter. For Pettigrew, reputation is all.

He returns to Charleston, his adopted home, as South Carolina moves toward secession. Pettigrew becomes the chief military aide of South Carolina governor Francis Pickens. During the tense standoff between Federal forces manning the forts at Charleston harbor and the state troops, he advises the governor not to move on Fort Sumter. Thus, when Federal troops reinforce the fort from another garrison, Pettigrew feels responsible. He negotiates with Maj. Robert Anderson, the commander of Fort Sumter, urging him to abandon the fort, to no avail. To satisfy his honor, Pettigrew vows that his regiment will be the first to assault the island fortress.

With no military experience at all but bearing a prominent family name, he is appointed colonel of the 1st Regiment of Rifles. Leading 200 troops from the Citadel, he takes possession of Castle Pinckney, one of the Federal harbor forts.

His 1st Regiment takes up positions on Morris Island, nearest Fort Sumter. Though he has no formal training as an engineer, using cotton bales, railroad iron, and whatever other materials he can muster, Pettigrew supervises the building of gun batteries and ramparts with such zeal and efficiency that he quickly establishes a reputation as a gifted military leader.

A relative of Pettigrew and his law partner, James Louis Petigru, notes in a letter to his own grandson, "Your cousin Johnston is no longer a pale intimate of the obscure building in St. Michael's Alley, where he used to pore over dusty books in a foreign tongue; but bestrides a gallant steed. With gay trappings, long spurs, and bright shoulder knots."

His mentor, Petigru, is troubled by what he sees as an infatuation with danger, a courting of glorious death: "He is just in the vein to 'seek the bubble reputation' where he is more apt to find his grave than ever to tell the story."

After a spectacular bombardment, in which, miraculously, no one is killed, Fort Sumter surrenders. Pettigrew's regiment shifts to Sullivan's Island, to fend off an attack they are sure will follow. But Charleston goes quiet and the 1st Regiment is relieved. Pettigrew is offered and declines the position of adjutant general for South Carolina, among other offers of commissions as a captain and even a major. He declines them all and instead enlists as a private in Wade Hampton's legion.

Even so, his heart lies with his native state, North Carolina. Before long, he is pulled from the ranks and commissioned colonel of the 22nd North Carolina Regiment.

Johnston Pettigrew is not the only scholar who marches off to war. On the eve of secession, in April 1861, sophomores and juniors at his alma mater present a petition to former North Carolina governor Charles Manly, secretary of the board of trustees, asking that they be allowed to enlist: "In presenting this petition we have been actuated by no desire to be released from our studies but by a thorough conviction that the present perilous condition of our country and our own interest demand it." Most of the seniors have already joined the army. But their petition is denied.

At the outset of the war, the Confederate government exempts university students from conscription. However, as battle and disease deplete the army, the exemption is rescinded. Conscription agents round up young scholars and carry them off to fight. By 1862, only about 50 students remain

James Johnston Pettigrew, the restless scholar who
becomes a daring, even reckless soldier.
(Courtesy of the North Carolina Museum of History)

on a campus that, just months ago, was home to 456 students, the second-largest student body in the South after the University of Virginia.

A year later, the senior class numbers just nine young men. Three are combat veterans, including one who is permanently disabled, and two others have purchased substitutes to enlist in their stead. The junior class has dwindled from thirty to fourteen, two of them veterans. Only nine sophomores remain, two of them disabled. The freshman class counts only three members over the age of eighteen. The rest have all enlisted, and some already lie dead upon the field of battle.

From Durham County, Trinity College sends a cadre of students and teachers, the Trinity Guards, to serve as wardens at Salisbury Prison. Wake Forest, a Baptist institution in Wake County, shutters its doors to its seventy-six students for the duration of the war. Many of them join the army along with their teachers, and in time the college reopens as a military hospital.

In 1860, North Carolina is home to sixteen colleges and universities, divided by sex and serving a range of ages. Ninety-five teachers instruct more than 1,599 students. The University of North Carolina was the first public university in the newly formed United States of America to admit students. Hinton James of New Hanover County, near the coast, walked to New Hope Chapel Hill, a site chosen for its location in the center of the state, and was the first student to enroll in 1795.

With its high illiteracy rate—more than 70,000 whites over the age of twenty and nearly all blacks—North Carolina has struggled to educate its citizens. Some 3,500 public schools and private academies enroll more than 13,000 pupils, but school sessions may be as short as three months per year. Some criticize the University of North Carolina as an enclave of privilege. But for many, the university, built upon the commanding heights of Prospect Point, symbolizes progress and enlightenment, the aspirations of many state leaders to raise North Carolina out of poverty and ignorance and toward a prosperity fueled by ideas. James Johnston Pettigrew is the embodiment of the educated leader.

On May 31, 1862, he enters battle at Seven Pines, Virginia, where a Minié ball catches him in the throat and tears through his shoulder, severing an artery. Convinced he is going to die, he chooses to remain on the field of battle, a fallen hero. Retreating soldiers spot Pettigrew's motionless body and send word to his family that he has been killed in action. But in fact, Union soldiers discover him alive and carry him to a field hospital. By August, his wounds have healed and he is exchanged.

On July 1 of the following year, Pettigrew's brigade joins the Army of

Northern Virginia invading Maryland and Pennsylvania. Outside the quiet crossroads of Gettysburg, his brigade blunders into first contact with dismounted troops of U.S. cavalry. The division commander, Maj. Gen. Harry Heth, is badly wounded, so Pettigrew assumes command. On the third day of Gettysburg, Pettigrew personally leads his division of nearly 5,000 men — conspicuous for their bloody bandages — into battle alongside Pickett's division. One of Pettigrew's four brigades consists of North Carolinians. The other three brigades are made up of Virginians, Alabamians, Mississippians, Tennesseans, and the 55th North Carolina.

At two o'clock in the afternoon, after a thunderous, sustained barrage by as many as 170 Confederate cannons has shaken the ground and deafened them, they step out of the tree line and cross a mile of cornfields under heavy fire, then advance up the steep slope of Cemetery Ridge, toward the stone wall at the center of the Union line. Because of its position on the extreme left of the Confederate line, Pettigrew's division has to cross several hundred more yards of deadly ground than Pickett's.

As thousands fall around him, Pettigrew advances. His horse is shot, and he dismounts, sending it to the rear. On foot now, miraculously he leads troops through a deadly hail of fire that one survivor calls "that storm of death." Pettigrew's right hand is shattered by grapeshot, but he presses on. His line stands and delivers a volley, then charges forward to within a few yards of the stone wall.

But Union troops swarm into the line. The Virginia brigade on the far left flank of Pettigrew's division breaks first — it never reaches the Emmitsburg Road. Flanked by the 8th Ohio, the ranks dissolve, the troops turn and run. The Federals smash the North Carolina brigade with relentless massed musket and cannon fire. With no support coming up behind him, Pettigrew falls back with the other battle-shocked survivors across a rutted landscape littered with bodies. He is one of the last soldiers to quit the field.

As Pettigrew rallies his men to defend against a counterattack, General Lee, who ordered the assault, approaches him, bereft and stunned. He takes Pettigrew's good hand and tells him, "General Pettigrew, it is all my fault."

But within hours the Richmond papers are calling the foolhardy assault "Pickett's Charge," lauding the bravery of the Virginia troops and blaming the failure on the "cowardly" North Carolinians. Yet in the single North Carolina brigade in Pettigrew's division, every colonel, lieutenant colonel, and major has been killed or wounded, save one, who was captured at the wall. One of its regiments, the 26th, went into battle on the first day with 800 men. At the close of the third day, it musters 3 officers and 64 privates.

On his thirty-fifth birthday, the fourth anniversary of his crossing from France into Italy along a Napoleonic road, Pettigrew retreats with the remnants of his brigade down the backside of Seminary Ridge through torrential rain, along mud-sloppy roads. They march all night to South Mountain, Maryland, heading for the safety that lies beyond the Potomac in Virginia.

Now Pettigrew commands part of the rear guard of the shattered Army of Northern Virginia. Though his right hand is splinted and his arm hangs in a sling, he tirelessly rallies his men, through ten days of hard marching and constant skirmishing. At Falling Waters, Maryland, on July 14 — at camp with his brigade — he is standing under a tree in a barnyard, conferring with General Heth and a gathering of officers, when a troop of U.S. cavalry bursts out of the woods.

At first, Heth mistakes them for Confederate cavalry, dressed in captured blue coats. But then they charge into the middle of the camp. Pettigrew attempts to mount his horse one-handed, but the horse shies and throws him to the ground. His men fire back, club some of the Yankee troopers out of their saddles with rifle butts. One big trooper shoots down several Confederates with his Colt revolver. Pettigrew advances on him, draws and raises a small pistol from his breast pocket, aims at the charging cavalryman, and pulls the trigger — but the weapon misfires. The trooper shoots him in the stomach.

Confederates swarm after Pettigrew's assailant, chase him into a barn, and finally batter him to death with a rock. It has not been a glorious battle, just a brutal melee that has decided nothing.

The Federals are driven off. The surgeon advises Pettigrew to remain behind and be captured, since the Union surgeons will be better equipped to treat him. He refuses and is carried eighteen miles over rough roads to Bunker Hill, now part of the newly formed state of West Virginia. He lingers for three days in agony. His military career has been as remarkable as the rest of his life: he has advanced from private to general, has been wounded twice, was captured and exchanged, survived the massacre at Cemetery Ridge, and now has fallen again. He is a long way from the classroom.

On July 17, he confides to a fellow officer, "It's time to be going," and gives up the ghost. His body is borne back to North Carolina, lies in state at the capitol in Raleigh, and is buried nearby.

At war's end, the University of North Carolina is bankrupt, owing debts of $100,000, and by 1871 is forced to close. Like so many other institutions, it invested heavily in Confederate securities and bank bonds, all of which are now worthless. The new state constitution of 1868 declares that it will have an "inseparable connection to the Free Public School system of the State," under the oversight of the Board of Education. The old trustees, many of them ex-Confederates, are ousted so that it can become the "people's university." It reopens in 1875.

In November 1865, honoring his wishes that in the event of his death he be returned to the family plantation, Pettigrew's family arranges to move his remains to Bonarva, overlooking Lake Phelps. The wandering scholar found his purpose and has, at last, come home.

32

THE AFTERLIVES OF THE DEAD

It is a father's saddest duty. In August 1864, it falls to William Harding, the father of two sons serving together in Company I, 28th North Carolina Regiment, which has just taken part in the bloody Confederate victory at Ream's Station, on the Wilmington and Weldon rail line outside Petersburg, Virginia.

The battle costs almost 3,500 casualties, among them Samuel Speer Harding, killed in action. William Harding, accompanied by his youngest son, nine-year-old Thomas Renny Harding, travels north to retrieve Samuel's body and carry it home to Yadkinville for burial in the family plot. For the long wagon journey home, the body is said to be preserved using the new method of embalming: injecting fluids into the veins in order to slow decomposition. The remains are sealed in a lead coffin. If true, this is unusual treatment for a Confederate soldier; it is much more common among Union officers.

Many in both armies are buried in unmarked graves on the battlefields where they fell. The Confederate dead retrieved by family or friends often make the long journey home in canvas sacks, "body baskets," or wooden boxes filled with sawdust—whatever is available.

The Charleston, South Carolina, *Tri-Weekly Mercury* offers a helpful recipe for those who face the grisly task without the aid of an embalmer: "The following preparation, which has been used on many occasions for thirty or forty years, comes highly recommended for the preservation of dead bodies. It will, in great degree, prevent the offensive odor from corpses; and, while the remains of so many of our deceased soldiers are being transported from the camps homeward, it may be of service to publish: Take two pounds of common salt, two pounds of alum, one pound of saltpeter—dissolve in six gallons of water and keep the shrouding wet with the mixture."

Since most of the fighting occurs in warm weather, the final journey is often plagued by vultures and the stench of the decomposing corpse, a morbid race against time to preserve the dignity of the loved one and inter him in his homeplace, where he can be honored, remembered, and even visited in death.

Decades before the war, in rural areas of both the North and the South, "cemeteries"—derived from the Greek for "sleeping chamber"—replaced the more straightforward "burying grounds" to identify the deceased person's final resting place. The word conjures up an image of the loved one peacefully asleep in the arms of the Savior, connoting not death but eternal life.

On the headstones themselves, the stark and menacing images of mortality—skull and crossbones, skeletons, and the like—have gone out of fashion in favor of angels and cherubs, promising reminders that the loved one is forever safe in heaven.

The markers have also grown more elaborate, no longer just flat slabs bearing dates and a brief epitaph. At least for the more affluent, the gravestone becomes a sculpture, memorializing the dead with both words and symbols. An anchor can signify hope; an oak leaf, strength; an acorn, victory.

Local cemeteries become gardens, sectioned off into family plots bordered by ornamental fences, often shaded by dogwood or live oak trees, and navigated by winding footpaths and carriage tracks that link to main roads. They are not macabre places to avoid but, rather, scenes of both private and communal ceremony and leisure. Families not only tend to their plots—planting flowers, trimming brush, and raking off leaf litter—but they also gather to picnic beside the graves of their loved ones. In this way a beloved spouse, parent, or child is not entirely gone but remains, both in memory and in fact, a part of the family's life.

Even in peacetime, death is no stranger. Farm and factory labor is dangerous. Carriage and railway accidents are all too common. Illness is a constant threat, especially to the very young and the very old. In the decade preceding the war, one in five white babies dies in infancy. As many as one in three babies born to slaves dies before reaching age four. The passing of a child is commonly sentimentalized in verse, such as "The Child's Last Sleep," which appears in the *North Carolina Whig* in December 1862. In it, the poet celebrates the dying child's new birth in Paradise, finishing,

> So faint was each expiring breath,
> And to the last we thought it sleep—
> It was the sleep of death.

Slowly she closed, without a pain,
Her loving eyes of cloudless blue,
And when her vision cleared again,
Her heaven was cloudless too.

Especially when memorializing the death of an innocent child, poems, letters, cartes-de-visite, and epitaphs emphasize an end to suffering, the loving comfort of God in heaven, and eternal peace.

It is the custom among those with means to have their dead child photographed in peaceful repose as a keepsake. Indeed, certain photographers advertise this as their specialty. One soldier of the 4th North Carolina Infantry carries such a memento in a gilt oval frame: his infant daughter, posed in a tiny crepe-lined casket, her curly golden hair neatly combed, her slight body clothed in a white dress, her little bare arms crossed and clutching a bouquet of flowers, her eyes closed as if she is only sleeping.

Images of a favorite toy are sometimes etched into the headstone of a child's grave. Sometimes, on visitation days, real toys are left there.

Home crafts become a popular way to memorialize lost loved ones. Watch fobs, bracelets, and earrings are woven from the hair of the deceased. Intricate patterns are woven with long hair, sometimes framing a portrait of the deceased. Professional jewelers encase locks of hair under crystal in brooches and lockets.

A detailed etiquette of mourning develops, eventually codified in tracts such as Arthur Martine's *Hand-Book of Etiquette and Guide to True Politeness*. Naturally, the higher the class of the mourner, the more elaborate the requirements—including behavior, dress, and even jewelry.

A woman mourns her lost parent or child for six months to a year, dressing only in black. She may mourn a brother or sister, a grandparent, or a relative who has left her an inheritance for just six months. Uncles and aunts, and nieces and nephews require just three months of wearing black, and the mourning dress may be trimmed with white lace.

A widow mourns her husband for a full two and a half years, divided into heavy mourning, full mourning, and half-mourning. Each phase follows a strict regimen of dress and behavior: all-matte-black and heavy veils give way to gray and lavender and lighter veils, shiny jewelry is at last allowed, and seclusion among immediate family yields to decorous public visitation. In North Carolina, as in most Southern states, Canton or English crepe and silk or linen clothing—and the appropriate jewelry fashioned from black jet— must be imported.

A widower mourns his dead wife for just three months to a year, wearing plain white shirts and business suits, sometimes festooned with a black crepe armband. Especially if he has young children, etiquette allows — even encourages — him to remarry reasonably soon.

Slaves follow their own mourning rituals, one of which is to decorate a fresh grave with items recently used by the deceased — bottles, pottery, dolls — all broken, symbolically breaking the tie with the living world and protecting the survivors from early death.

With the war comes wholesale death. No longer do communities mourn their dead one at a time. The *Greensborough Patriot* of April 10, 1862, carries a story that becomes all too typical in communities around the state: "Died. — In Wilkesboro, on the 13th ultimo, Leander B. Carmichael, Esq. He was a brother of Maj. A. B. Carmichael who was killed the day following in the battle below Newbern. Three grown brothers of this family have died in the last twelve months."

No longer do families enjoy the luxury of discarding used crepe clothing as unlucky. Now they save it, in the near-certainty that they will need it again before long. Women confide to their diaries that there are far too many widows and not enough crepe to clothe them all. Mourning periods are shortened, women share their mourning dresses with their families and neighbors, and the protocols of death and mourning require improvisation. Finding it impossible in the maelstrom of war to satisfy the stringent etiquette of grief, mourners do the best they can.

If the body of a beloved son, husband, or father cannot be carried home from a distant battlefield, then the next best thing is to recover the story of how he died, who was with him to offer comfort and prayer, and with what care and honor he was laid to rest. In their letters home to grieving families, soldiers are careful to provide such details, knowing their own families would crave the same emotional comfort.

Lewis Warlick of Table Rock writes to his "dearest friend," Cornelia McGimsey, from his camp near Orange, Virginia, in April 1864, "I staid with Mat the night after I left home, arrived at Richmond Saturday morning, went to the Hospital where brother died and found on the books his death recorded 28th Dec., I inquired where his remains rested, was told at Oakwood Cemetery 2½ miles. . . .I was told that he was neatly buried in a raised lid coffin and that the grave was marked."

For Warlick, as for so many soldiers, the news of death often carries to the front lines from home. Just the previous year he wrote Cornelia, "I received two days since the sad intelligence of my sister, sorry was I to hear it but God's will be done. It is a debt we all owe and have some day or other to pay. Our family has been distressed greatly for the past four years for in that time I have lost a mother, brother and two sisters. I do hope that there will not be another death in the family while the war continues as that gives sorrow and sadness enough to be borne; but we know not the day or the hour we are to bid adieus to this world."

His letter reflects the prevailing fatalism about death, an attitude grounded by a solid faith in Divine Providence and an eternal afterlife. In January 1862, Larken Kendrick writes in a heartfelt letter from his camp at "Goalds Burough" to his wife, Mary, "I helpt to put a man in his coffen this morning by the name of Gilbert Bell he was from Rutheaford he Died in a ful Triumph of a living faith." This news is comfort to the man's family, and it illustrates the reason why chaplains follow the army, conduct prayers before battle, persuade unbelievers to be "plunged" or baptized, and bless the fallen: to ensure that any man who dies is received by the Almighty into his everlasting reward. How else could a man face such appalling odds in battle?

Kendrick continues in the same letter, "I often look at the moon and the countless stares and wonder if my belove ones is a behold the same seen my Dear companion I never Shal forgit you for my love to is as costant as the Wheales of time the time es a huring us on to a neve ending eturnty I hope if we never meat on earth we may meat where the Sound of the Drom and war whoop ie heard no moar I will cloas by saing I want you to Rite as Son as you Get this and Give me the news So nothing moar at this time but Still Remaines yor husban untill Deth."

Most of the men who fall in battle or succumb to illness are ordinary, even anonymous, known only to friends and family, their names mere letters on a company roster of casualties. Some are famous: the "Boy Colonel," Henry King Burgwyn Jr.; Brig. Gen. James Johnston Pettigrew; Lt. Gen. Leonidas Polk. They pass into legend, and one day their names will adorn monuments.

And there is one ordinary man whose very death rescues him from obscurity: Pvt. Henry Lawson Wyatt, nineteen years old, shot in the forehead at Big Bethel on June 10, 1861, while charging a sharpshooters' nest. Wyatt is immortalized by Maj. Jedediah Hotchkiss, one of Stonewall Jackson's staff officers: "It is generally admitted that young Wyatt was the first Confederate soldier killed in action in Virginia during the civil war." Others dispute this distinction, but certainly he is the first North Carolinian to die in battle.

The stories of death in battle are often colored with descriptions of manly virtue and upright moral character. A comrade, Pvt. John H. Thorpe, paints a word picture of Wyatt's glorious, seemingly painless death: "He never uttered a word or groan but lay limp on his back, arms extended, one knee up and a clot of blood on his forehead as large as a man's fist. . . . To look at Wyatt one would take him to be tenacious of life; low, but robust in build, guileless, open, frank, aggressive."

Capt. Matt Manly of the 2nd North Carolina relates the death of Col. Charles Courtenay Tew, struck down in the charge of Brig. Gen. Thomas F. Meagher's Irish Brigade at Sharpsburg: "He was shot through the head and placed in the sunken road. . . . Here he was found, apparently unconscious, the blood streaming from a wound in the head, with his sword held in both hands across his knees. A Federal soldier attempted to take the sword from him, but he drew it toward his body with his last remaining strength, and then his grasp relaxed and he fell forward dead."

But as the war wears on, the sacrifice begins to seem too much, the valor wasted. Lt. Col. James M. Ray of the 60th North Carolina writes of his men lost in the slaughter at Chickamauga—an Indian word, he reminds his reader, that signifies "river of death": "Of the color guard, every man save one, George Lindsey, was killed or wounded. The bearer of the flag, Sergeant Baily, though mortally wounded, called Sergeant Lindsey to him, told him he was shot, showed him the wound and said: 'I turn over to your keeping the colors.' . . . Here again is another instance of great victory, at an expense of almost a deluge of the best blood of the country and apparently nothing achieved." The 60th contributes its bloody share of the nearly 35,000 casualties.

For the grieving families waiting at home, usually without a body to bury in a sanctifying funeral, the dead live on in their letters, the stories told by their comrades, and another ritual: singing at the piano in the family parlor. The songs are sentimental, keyed to the range of ordinary voices, memorials to both the courage of the fallen brother, son, or husband and the joy he brought to others. "The Vacant Chair," with lyrics by H. S. Washburn, becomes a favorite. Written about a fictional Union soldier, it nevertheless speaks to the hearts of families on both sides made bereft by war. It celebrates his courage:

> At our fireside, sad and lonely, Often will the bosom swell
> At remembrance of the story How our noble Willie fell.
> How he strove to bear the banner Thro' the thickest of the fight
> And uphold our country's honor In the strength of manhood's might.

But the chorus tells the harder story of sadness and loss:

We shall meet, but we shall miss him. There will be one vacant chair.
We shall linger to caress him While we breathe our ev'ning prayer.

And off on distant battlefields, in crude outdoor camps and crowded hospitals, the dying goes on.

33

CAUGHT BETWEEN BLUE AND GRAY

The invading force of five brigades moves by train into eastern North Carolina from the north in the last days of a bitter cold January 1864: 13,000 infantry and cavalry troopers, fortified by artillery batteries and including a special detachment of 100 marines for an amphibious assault. They are mostly Virginians but include the 43rd North Carolina Regiment.

This is a strange and paradoxical moment in the war: a Confederate army invading one of the states of the Confederacy to fight citizens of that state. In the conflict to come, North Carolinians will fight on both sides.

The expedition takes the field under the nominal command of Maj. Gen. George E. Pickett, a Virginian of the planter class who bears the stigma of the fatal last charge at Gettysburg. But the real commander is Brig. Gen. Robert F. Hoke, a handsome, brash North Carolinian, soon to be—at age twenty-seven—the youngest major general in the Confederate army. In six months, Hoke will be the hero of Cold Harbor, the man whose stubborn troops stop Grant's bold advance, sparking rumors that he is Lee's hand-picked successor, should Lee ever succumb to illness or wounds.

Although Lee issues the order, Hoke is the author of the complicated plan of campaign. The army stages at Kinston, a river town, then proceeds thirty-two miles to New Bern in three columns, each with designated objectives:

Pickett and Hoke's main body will follow the corridor between the Trent and Neuse Rivers, knock out the star fort, and descend on the town in a surprise attack.

Brig. Gen. Seth M. Barton's column, the most formidable in numbers and guns, will capture the vital railroad and cut the telegraph lines to prevent the regiments at Morehead City from reinforcing the garrison. Barton's force will then capture the Neuse River bridge, attack across it, and take the Union position from the rear.

Col. James Dearing's column will carry Fort Anderson, the anchor of the whole Union defense.

The night before the attack, a fleet of small boats carries the marines down the Neuse River close to the moored Union gunboats so they can be scuttled.

Hoke has another objective: to capture North Carolina troops serving in the U.S. Army, many of them rumored to be Confederate deserters.

Desertion has become the scourge of the Confederate army, and North Carolina troops are notorious for absenting themselves at will from their units. Many simply respond to the pleas of the families they left behind: wives who cannot get the crops in, aged parents caught between Unionist neighbors and marauding outliers. Some return to their units, but many do not. The rugged western mountains provide one refuge. The Eastern Seaboard, since 1862 occupied by Union troops, provides another: Hatteras Island, Roanoke Island, New Bern.

Hoke has convinced Lee that New Bern is ripe for the taking. He even has a spy roaming the city dressed as a Union officer to scout the garrison and report on how and where the troops are deployed. Lee advises President Davis, "I can now spare troops for the purpose which will not be the case as spring approaches. . . . A large amount of provisions and other supplies are said to be at New Bern, which are much wanted for this army."

The Confederate force arrives in Kinston, still scarred by a battle the previous year, when a force of Federals under Maj. Gen. John G. Foster overran it. They routed the defenders and looted the town, set fire to buildings, and left behind charred souvenirs of their visit and bitter memories among the inhabitants. Then, as quickly as they came, they withdrew downriver to New Bern.

Kinston has a raucous, boomtown feel, thriving with war trade—factories that manufacture shoes, uniforms, and hardtack—but lawless and mobbed by strangers, speculators, refugees, and all the opportunists of war. An enterprising community of prostitutes inhabits Sugar Hill. Whiskey is freely available at all hours. Now Pickett's troops overwhelm the town. Like many towns in the state, Kinston is divided by the war, and for many residents, the occupation by Confederates is no more bearable than the brief, violent stay by the Yankees.

But Hoke's plan, though bold, is doomed from the start.

Union forces shattered Pickett's division at Gettysburg the preceding July—fully half his command was killed, wounded, or captured. Seven of his veteran colonels are now dead. Pickett himself, recently married to his third wife, is reluctant to take the field from his comfortable headquarters in Petersburg, Virginia. Winter campaigning is the hardest duty, and many officers in Lee's army suspect that Pickett will never be the same after the bloody debacle at Cemetery Ridge. Haunted by monumental failure, he has become both timid at command and bitter, even cruel, toward his enemies.

Pickett is something of a self-made dandy and makes sport of the fact that he graduated dead last in his class of fifty-nine at West Point. He has proven his bravery on the field. But he does not have a keen mind for strategy or tactics. He relies on subordinates like Hoke to provide him with detailed plans and "sometimes stay with him to make sure he did not go astray," one staff officer records.

This overly complicated plan unravels on a stage three years in the making and carries Lee's admonition: "Everything will depend upon the secrecy, expedition, and boldness of your movements. . . . Commit nothing to the telegraph that may disclose your purpose. You must deceive the enemy as to your purpose, and conceal it from the citizens."

Among the troops waiting to receive the attack is the 2nd North Carolina Union Volunteer Regiment, one of four loyal North Carolina regiments, one of eighty-five Union regiments recruited from the states of the Confederacy. Eastern North Carolina is ripe territory for the recruiters. The poor farmers and fishermen along this apron of Low Country by the sea never really support the rebellion. In fact, many of them harbor bitter resentment against the slave-owning class who started the war and then made themselves exempt from conscription.

These poor men find themselves caught between the Confederate conscription agents, who would march them away from their farms and families to become cannon fodder on the deadly battlefields in Virginia, and the occupying U.S. Army troops, who promise amnesty, protection, and food. Faced with this choice, many of them cross into the blue lines and claim an enlistment bounty of $300, a fortune to a poor farmer. The recruiters promise them that they will be stationed in their home county on safe garrison duty. The Confederates call them "buffaloes"—not a compliment. They are lackluster in their performance, considered unreliable in their loyalty.

Maj. Gen. John Peck, U.S. commander of the District of North Carolina, complains: "Mere boys, children, some of them weak, puny, scrofulous, have been enlisted, passed by the surgeon, and mustered in by the mustering officer. And again, old men, eaten by disease or utterly incapacitated by old age and general infirmity, have been enlisted, fed, and accepted into the service as able-bodied soldiers."

The *New York Times* weighs in with its own commentary on the motives of the North Carolina enlistees: "But it is so more from natural necessity than anything intelligent and voluntary. This is found among the poor whites. A few days since, we saw at the Provost-Marshal's office, thirty-five of this class, mostly deserters from the rebel army, all having taken the oath, and desirous of going to New-York. . . . Perhaps six hundred of this class have taken the oath since the 1st of January, and daily squads of them come in for that purpose. . . . They are not bound to the Confederacy by the pride of opinion, and interest and culture."

Thus the ranks of the 2nd North Carolina Volunteers swell with local men, sick of the war, many of them simply trying to survive it in a safe place, close to home, where they enjoy regular meals. Most exhibit no more zeal for glory than the mules that pull their commissary wagons.

They are garrison troops, not combat troops. But in Lincoln's strategy of encouraging Unionist resistance, none of these drawbacks makes any difference: once in the Union army, they are removed from the ranks of the enemy's army as completely as if they have been captured or killed. The paymaster's bargain is far easier on both the conscience and the army than the transaction in blood.

Some of the new recruits are deserters from Home Guard or Railroad Guard units. Some have already been conscripted for service in line regiments but sneak off into the woods before being formally sworn in. This nicety will matter later: Home Guard and Railroad Guard are state organizations not subject to the military law of the Confederacy, and as far as the state of North Carolina is concerned, desertion from a Confederate unit is not a crime. If a man has not been duly sworn in to the ranks of a Confederate regiment, then he, too, is exempt from the rules of war that apply to soldiers who have taken the oath.

On January 30, Pickett's command marches on New Bern, advancing slowly through deep sand and swamp. The march quickly deteriorates into an ordeal. A grass fire ignited by a careless match threatens to blow up the artillery powder and sends the gunners scurrying to rescue their caissons. The cannons bog down in the deep sand and must be manhandled forward. The relentless northeast wind sears the men with damp, biting cold.

The battle opens at midnight. The flotilla of small boats arrives in New Bern to find only a single enemy gunboat to scuttle: the 325-ton side-wheeler USS *Underwriter*. The marines board it and set it ablaze, with no effect on the outcome of the expedition. Barton's cavalry, scouting ahead to secure the railroad and cut telegraph lines, runs into stiff resistance and retreats. The various forts and batteries prove too formidable to take by storm. The intelligence is all wrong. Seven hours of fierce fighting drives Hoke's column to within a mile of New Bern, where it is stopped in its tracks at sunrise.

The column led by General Barton does not attack at all. Awed by the strength of the defenses, he refuses to give the order to advance. Pickett is furious.

The *New York Times* reports on February 11, through a correspondent on the scene, "The enemy proposed to themselves the recapture of Newbern. They probably expected to surprise us, get possession of the gunboats, carry the fortifications by storm, and then feed on the 'fat of the land.' In all this they have been nicely checkmated."

But one masked battery at Beech Grove on Batchelder's Creek is cut off in the dense woods and vulnerable to attack: a blockhouse fort mounting just two artillery pieces. It stands eight miles from the main garrison at New Bern. A small force, including the ninety-seven men of Company F, 2nd North Carolina Union Volunteers, defends it. Hidden in the dark, foggy woods, the battery was invisible to the advancing Confederates, but now it has been found out. Two couriers slip out to report the battery surrounded, but both are shot dead.

With a far superior force of Confederates poised to attack, the locally recruited volunteers at Beech Grove face a moment of truth. They are commanded not by one of their own but by Lt. Samuel Leith of the 132nd New York Infantry—an arrangement that carries fatal consequences.

An officer of their own regiment writes in the *New York Times* about what happens next:

> When it became evident that the position could not be held against the overwhelming force of rebels, which was rapidly approaching, the men of this company, having the certainty of an ignominious death before them if they should be captured, proposed to the officer in command to pilot the force at the outpost in safety to Newbern, by paths through the woods known only to themselves. But unfortunately, they were temporarily in charge of officers not belonging to their own regiment, who were either ignorant of the blood-thirsty character of the enemy, or too timid to fight to the death, if flight were deemed impracticable. Had these men been commanded by officers of their own regiment, they all would have escaped, or, as preferable to their inevitable doom if taken prisoners, would have found a more honorable death on the field. As it was,

they were sternly forbidden to leave the ranks, and, without a shot being fired, or the stipulation secured that they should be treated as prisoners of war, they were surrendered.

Capt. John G. Smith of the 8th Georgia writes, "We flushed them like a covey of birds."

The prisoners include Joseph L. Haskett, twenty-six, a farmer from Carteret County, and David Jones, twenty-one, of Craven County—both deserters from Company B, 10th Regiment, North Carolina Artillery, which assists in their capture.

Some of the defenders defy orders and slip away into the woods. But fifty-three men of Company F, 2nd North Carolina Union Volunteer Regiment, now find themselves at the mercy of Pickett, a troubled, unstable commander who has led the largest independent command of his career to yet another grand failure, a man who notoriously lacks the one quality that might spare their lives: mercy.

Pickett withdraws his disorganized forces back toward Kinston, prisoners in tow. They halt on February 4, 1864, to spend the night at Dover, well beyond the reach of the U.S. Army forces at New Bern. In the clearing beyond Pickett's tent, his officers interrogate some of the Union prisoners beside a campfire. Sgt. Blunt King, a forty-six-year-old veteran of the Mexican-American War, recognizes two of them, former members of his own Company B. King asks his lieutenant, H. M. Whitehead, whether these men are indeed Joe Haskett and David Jones.

The lieutenant tells him that is exactly who they are.

"Good evening, boys," King greets them, and, sullenly, they wish him good evening too.

But Pickett, humiliated once again on the field of battle, is not in the mood for pleasantries. He stalks out of his tent, where he has been conferring with Brigadier Generals Hoke and Montgomery Corse. He confronts the prisoners. "What are you doing here? Where have you been?"

The young soldiers, dressed in Union blue, haven't got a good answer.

Pickett's fatal anger is roused. "God damn you, I reckon you will hardly ever go back there again, you damned rascals; I'll have you shot, and all other damned rascals who desert."

Jones is defiant and tells Pickett that he does "not care a damn whether they shot him then, or what they did with him."

On Pickett's orders, soldiers hustle the men away. He turns to his sub-

Caught between Blue and Gray

ordinate generals and declares, "We'll have to have a court-martial on these fellows pretty soon, and after some are shot the rest will stop deserting."

"The sooner the better," Corse says.

Before they leave the Dover camp, Pickett convenes a court-martial headed by a Virginia officer, Lt. Col. James R. Branch. Jones and Haskett admit that they are indeed deserters, but they claim they were conscripted into the Union army against their will. But the outcome is never really in doubt. The court finds them guilty and sentences them to death by hanging—not by firing squad, the time-honored military method. Hanging is for cowards and criminals, not soldiers.

The officers march all the prisoners to Kinston and lock them up in the Lenoir County Courthouse, where they sleep on the floor without blankets and subsist on a diet of one cracker a day. Outside on the sandy lot behind the jail, they can hear the gallows being hammered together. The next day, February 5, 1864, Jones and Haskett receive a visit from the Reverend John Paris, chaplain of the 54th North Carolina, a thin-faced man with close-set eyes. He reports, "They were the most unfeeling and hardened men I have ever encountered. They had been raised up in ignorance and vice. They manifested but little, if any, concern for eternity."

The hangman is recruited from a gang of soldiers playing cards at the railroad depot: their old company sergeant, Blunt King, volunteers for the duty, though he later claims he was forced to do the odious chore. There's no rope to be had in the army, so he scrounges a coil from the CSS *Neuse*, an ironclad ram moored on the river.

The two unfortunates are marched outside to the gallows and mount the scaffold. Hoke, their fellow North Carolinian, orders his brigade to form up in ranks to witness the hanging. Barton's brigade completes the hollow square of gray-clad soldiers surrounding the scaffold. Another North Carolinian, Lt. John G. Justice, Hoke's aide-de-camp, reads out the charges and the sentence. No one remarks that many of the officers present, including Pickett himself, once swore allegiance to the United States and are, at this very moment, guilty of "taking up arms for the enemy"—the same crime for which these men have been condemned to death.

Sergeant King hoods each man's head in a corn sack, then pulls the lever that drops them into the next world. After they are cut down, King slices off their brass "US" tunic buttons for souvenirs.

In the wake of the first executions, desertions increase. Two dozen men evaporate into the Union lines at New Bern.

On February 8, Maj. Gen. John J. Peck, U.S. commander of the Department of North Carolina, is appalled to read an article in the *Richmond Examiner* about the hanging of a captured "negro soldier." He sends a letter to Pickett through a truce pouch reminding him of President Lincoln's order that for every U.S. soldier executed in a manner contrary to the laws of war, a Confederate captive will be executed. Peck—unaware of the Kinston hangings—informs him that he believes this must have happened without Pickett's knowledge and urges the general to take prompt action to bring the offenders to justice. He concludes, "I shall refrain from executing a rebel soldier until I learn your action in the premises."

Pickett responds that he has captured 450 Federal soldiers, "and for every man you hang, I will hang 10 of the US Army."

Peck then sends across the lines a roster of the fifty-three men captured at Batchelder's Creek, and Pickett sarcastically thanks Peck for help in identifying the rest of the Confederate deserters.

The court-martial doesn't skip a beat. A duplicitous captured Union sergeant helpfully provides a company roster, identifying all the former Confederates who joined the 2rd North Carolina. Next to be tried are Amos Armyett, Lewis Bryan, Mitchell Busick, William Z. Irving, and John L. Stanley. All are sentenced to death, to be carried out "in twenty-four hours after the publication of the sentence."

But before these five can be executed, the court-martial convenes again on February 11, this time at Goldsboro, where Pickett has shifted his headquarters. Thirteen more men are sentenced to be hanged at Kinston: Andrew J. Brittain, John J. Brock, Joseph Brock, Charles Cuthrell, William H. Daughtry, John Freeman, Lewis Freeman, William Haddock, Calvin Hoffman, Stephen Jones, William Jones, Jesse James Summerlin, and Lewis Taylor.

With eighteen more men now under sentence of death, Pickett orders a larger scaffold erected. On February 12, it stands ready to receive the five men convicted in the second round.

Again the chaplain, Paris, attends the condemned men, this time baptizing two of them—John Stanley and William Z. Irving. At the gallows, Amos Armyett, the oldest of the men at forty-four, speaks on their behalf. He confesses that they have "done wrong and regret it. And warn others not to follow our example."

By the time Peck's letters reach Pickett, these men are already dead. The two generals exchange other letters, but Peck cannot persuade Pickett to stop hanging prisoners. Barring a miracle, which is not likely, the remain-

Caught between Blue and Gray

ing thirteen will die on Monday, February 15. Chaplain Paris visits the jail on the fourteenth to offer spiritual solace. He writes in a letter to the *Wilmington Journal*, "They had only twenty-four hours to live. . . . Here was a wife to say farewell to a husband forever. Here a mother to take the last look at her ruined son, and then a sister who had come to embrace for the last time the brother who had brought disgrace upon the very name she bore by his treason to his country." Paris baptizes eight of the men. Two others are escorted to the Neuse River, where they are baptized by immersion.

Paris conducts a prayer service. Then he exhorts the prisoners to tell him the names of the "men who had seduced them to desert and go to the enemy." They name five men from Jones County. Paris immediately reports the names to Hoke so they can be arrested and tried.

The day is so cold that the assembled troopers complain. The thirteen men climb the scaffold and leave behind no record of their last words, save a general protest that they are not guilty. A brass band plays the death march. This time the executioner is a mysterious cross-eyed stranger from Raleigh. For his trouble, he strips clothing off some of the corpses, cuts buttons from the coats of the others. Now some of the dead lie naked to the biting February cold. Others are stripped down to longjohns.

Families brave enough to dare Pickett's wrath claim the bodies of their men. "Plenty would have been willing to have assisted me, but did not dare for fear of being called Unionist," laments the widow of William Jones, who lies dead wearing only his socks. Other bodies are buried in a shallow grave at the foot of the scaffold.

Morale among the Confederate ranks sinks to a dismal low. Witnessing the hangings gives some would-be deserters second thoughts, but many of the ordinary soldiers find the spectacle disgusting and unnerving.

Six more men are put on trial. Of those, two are sentenced to be branded with the letter D for "deserter" on their left hip and sent into hard labor with a ball and chain attached to their leg. One is spared the death penalty and confined at hard labor on account of his "extreme youth . . . physical disability and mental imbecility." A fourth, Sgt. William Clinton Cox, is found not guilty because he was a railroad guard in the North Carolina Bridge Guard Company, not technically enlisted in the Army of the Confederacy. Nonetheless he remains in custody, to be tried for simple treason.

His acquittal may be a tacit recognition of his role in betraying so many of his fellow captives.

But two more men are sentenced to be hanged: Elijah Kellum and William Irving Hill. Kellum is an illiterate conscript who twice tried to enlist in the Confederate service but was turned down by reason of physical deformity. Then he was "sent to a conscript camp by some persons who wished to scare him; he hearing of it deserted to the Union lines." Notwithstanding, he is hanged along with Hill on February 22, 1864.

In all, Pickett hangs twenty-two North Carolina men. Their Union army careers were short lived. None lived past ninety days from enlistment. Not a single one received the promised bounty of $300.

Six days after the hangings, Paris, who acted as a spy and interrogator among the prisoners, delivers a long, fiery sermon to Hoke's assembled brigade founded on the gospel of St. Matthew—the passage that recounts Judas Iscariot's betrayal of Christ: "And I now lay down the Proposition, that every man who has taken up arms in defence of his country, and basely deserts or abandons that service, belongs in principle and practice to the family of Judas. . . . I hold, gentlemen, that there are few crimes in the sight of either God or man, that are more wicked and detestable than desertion." He could be addressing every West Point officer in the Confederate army.

The remaining thirty-one prisoners captured at Batchelder's Creek disappear into Confederate prisons in Richmond and Georgia. Twenty-five die of disease and malnutrition within two months of the hangings. Three are eventually granted a parole. The remaining three are unaccounted for. Two months after his acquittal as a deserter, William Clinton Cox, the railroad guard, succumbs to fever at Andersonville Prison.

The mass executions shock the citizens of Kinston, even solid Confederate sympathizers, many of whom witnessed the hangings. As word leaks across Union lines on the coast, the loyalist North Carolina troops are driven to a state of near-panic. Col. Edward Ripley reports, "Indeed they are already looking to the swamps for the protection they have so far failed of getting from our Government. . . . I believe they will inevitably, in case of a fight, become panic-stricken and have a bad effect on the rest of this slim command."

Peck will not let the matter drop. Though his correspondence with Pickett saved no one, he reports the executions to Maj. Gen. Benjamin F. Butler, his superior, who argues Peck's case with Grant himself. Grant is reluctant to act: "I would claim no right to retaliate for the punishment of deserters who had actually been mustered into the Confederate Army and afterwards deserted and joined ours."

But not all the hanged men swore the oath to the Confederacy, though all took the oath of allegiance to the Union.

After the war, an assistant quartermaster in New Bern, Capt. W. H. Doherty, pursues the matter with zeal. He convinces Secretary of War Edwin M.

Stanton to seat a board of inquiry composed of three officers, with Doherty in charge. Between September 13 and November 14, 1865, the board hears from twenty-eight witnesses in New Bern and Kinston. It determines that half the men who were executed had served—not in the regular Confederate army, but in state militia and guard units not subject to Confederate military justice.

Therefore under the law, the hangings constituted a war crime, and the two men with the greatest culpability are Generals Pickett and Hoke. Doherty sends his findings to Washington, where they are criticized. The investigation stalls—until Pickett's letters to Peck are forwarded to Judge Advocate General Joseph Holt. He is outraged by their haughty tone and murderous threats. He concludes, "Not only does the imperious and vaunting temper in which these letters . . . indicate his readiness to commit . . . any . . . atrocity, but his boastful admissions that he was in command at the time that the twenty-two men had been executed . . . all tend to show that he was in responsible command and furnish evidence upon which it is believed charges can be sustained against him."

Holt convenes a second board of inquiry in Raleigh on January 23, 1866. This one holds hearings not just in Kinston but also in Salisbury, Goldsboro, New Bern, Halifax, and Beaufort. A host of luminaries is called to testify, including William Woods Holden and former governor Vance.

The board concludes that Pickett alone is culpable. He is excluded from the presidential pardon of 1865. In July 1866, Holt calls on Secretary of War Stanton to put Pickett on trial.

Pickett flees the country to Montreal, where he lives for a time with his new wife Sally (Lasalle Corbett) under the name of Edwards. Meanwhile, his case goes before Congress. Grant, still in charge of the army and a favorite to succeed President Andrew Johnson, intervenes on Pickett's behalf.

In part he acts on principle: the parole he granted to the officers who surrendered at Appomattox remains in force unless they commit some unlawful act *after* the parole. There are no exceptions for crimes committed prior to the surrender. But in fact, other officers have been prosecuted for war crimes, and many believe it is simply Grant's long friendship with his old West Point comrade that saves Pickett.

Pickett, now a civilian, returns to Virginia, where he lives until 1875, selling insurance. He is snubbed by former comrades, notably Lee. The hard-drinking general dies of an abscess of the liver at age fifty in a Norfolk hospital.

His body is returned to Richmond, to be interred at the Hollywood

Cemetery among other famous officers. He is eulogized as one of Virginia's "noble sons." His funeral is grand, but the *Richmond Dispatch* delays printing a story about it for two days. For those two days, the paper devotes itself to coverage of the new statue erected on Monument Avenue — of a much more successful and revered general: Thomas J. "Stonewall" Jackson.

34

WILD'S AFRICAN LEGION

The planters of eastern North Carolina have long lived in fear of a slave uprising. Many of the 35,000 slave owners in the state make their homes in the
broad coastal plain and the eastern Piedmont, where a good many of the
state's 330,000 enslaved people are concentrated on the large farms and plantations of the rich river basins.

An 1831 law prevents the education of slaves because "the teaching of
slaves to read and write, has a tendency to excite dissatisfaction in their
minds, and to produce insurrection and rebellion, to the manifest injury of
the citizens of this State." Other draconian laws allow slave catchers to inflict
cruel and violent punishments on recaptured fugitives.

The white slaveholders' fear is partly a result of numbers. In coastal
counties such as Brunswick, New Hanover, Onslow, Craven, and Beaufort,
slaves make up one-quarter to one-half of the population. In the adjoining
counties farther inland—Jones, Lenoir, Pitt, Greene, and Bertie—slaves
constitute a majority of the inhabitants.

Over the long history of slavery, occasionally rebellious slaves in Virginia and the Carolinas have murdered their masters, and these rare violent
episodes have only fueled white paranoia. In 1863, the war takes a turn that
makes the white landowners' worst nightmare come true: black men with
guns march into their home counties, bent on righteous reprisal. They number almost 2,000. They are trained and disciplined and act with the full might
of the U.S. government behind them. Once utterly powerless, the former
slaves now wield the power of life and death.

In January 1863, President Lincoln's Emancipation Proclamation is derided by the *Chicago Times* as "a wicked, atrocious and revolting deed." But
abolitionists across the North widely hail the move as a new definition of war
aims: the Civil War has now become not just a violent sectarian conflict but
a crusade to free enslaved human beings. The proclamation, in freeing slaves
in the areas under rebellion, sets the stage for recruiting all-black regiments
officered by whites. In North Carolina, that duty falls to Brig. Gen. Edward

Augustus Wild, a steely one-armed Union veteran sent to work with local free black leaders such as Abraham Galloway to raise three regiments.

In the Union ranks, many soldiers are outraged by the move. Cpl. Felix Brannigan of the Army of the Potomac is typical. "We don't want to fight side by side with the nigger," he confides in a letter to his sister in New York. "We think we are a too superior race for that." But others welcome the new recruits—anything to break the back of Confederate resistance and deprive the enemy of the capacity to wage war. Another soldier says of the proclamation, "I'd thought of it myself, but I didn't think Linken'd hev the grit to up and do it. It's an all-fired good move, so far's the army's concerned."

In due course, the regiments are raised in New Bern, mostly manned by freed slaves, many of them from the local districts. To the 1st North Carolina Colored Volunteers and the other regiments, soon to be reclassified as U.S. Colored Troops, fall the labors of digging entrenchments, building roads and forts, hostling wagons, wrangling mule trains, and performing other fatigue duties. General Foster, commander of the Department of Virginia and North Carolina, has little faith in the fighting mettle of the black troops and fears they will prove only a provocation to North Carolina Unionists to joint the Confederate cause.

But some of their white officers are eager to prove the black soldiers' worth in combat. One such officer is Col. Alonzo G. Draper of the 2nd North Carolina Colored Volunteers, a hard-driving field officer and strict disciplinarian. With Wild's and his own regiments temporarily posted to Virginia by Foster, Draper conceives and executes a raid into the heart of territory infested with irregulars—guerilla forces that have been sniping at pickets, ambushing patrols, and smuggling provisions out of New Bern and Beaufort to Confederate forces. Draper is a strong supporter of the U.S. Army's new hard policy regarding guerilla troops—an increasing problem in and around all zones of occupation. Wild orders Draper that, in the event his troops are fired upon by irregulars, "you will *at once*, hang the man who fired." The bodies of such miscreants are to be hung with a sign proclaiming their crime. Wild is clear: "Guerillas are not to be taken alive."

In late November, Draper selects 118 officers and men from the 800 in his regiment and heads south. In nine days, they cover 250 miles and liberate almost 500 slaves, with other contraband borne back to Norfolk on captured livestock and wagons. For Draper's black troopers, the raid presents their first chance to return to their home ground and free family members and friends left behind, while exacting a measure of justice and revenge.

Many of the soldiers in Draper's command escaped from the same plan-

U.S. Colored Troops under General Wild liberate slaves on their
former plantations. (Courtesy of Wilson Special Collections
Library, University of North Carolina at Chapel Hill)

tations they are raiding and can identify who is a Unionist and who is a Confederate partisan — and therefore should be punished. Draper makes it clear that he believes the liberated slaves have a right to their masters' property and encourages their widespread confiscation of horses, mules, and wagons on which to ride to freedom.

Draper's minor foray is so successful in its mission of freeing slaves and suppressing the guerillas that Wild quickly conceives of a much larger expedition in force, this one focused on the Great Dismal Swamp Canal, a trading conduit between Virginia and North Carolina tracing its usage back to the days when it was developed by a consortium headed by George Washington.

Maj. Gen. Benjamin F. Butler, who succeeds the more timid Foster as overall commander of the Department of Virginia and North Carolina, offers a straightforward rationale for the raid: "Our navigation on the Dismal Swamp canal had been interrupted, and the Union inhabitants plundered by the guerillas."

Wild's force of nearly 2,000 includes troops from the 1st and 2nd N.C. Colored Volunteer Regiments, the 1st U.S. Colored Troops, and the 55th Massachusetts. Again, many of the black troops find themselves going into their home districts as armed liberators—in Currituck, Camden, Pasquotank, Perquimans, and Gates Counties. It is the first time in history that U.S. Colored Troops conduct a significant operation on their own, not as part of a larger enterprise.

The column marches along the canal path deep into the heart of the swamp. One man records, "We were in the dreariest and wildest part of the Dismal Swamp, the darkness was dense, the air damp, and the ghostly silence was broken only by the hooting of owls and crying of wild cats. For two hours we rode through the Stygian darkness of the forest, when we arrived at South Mills."

Two shallow-draft steamers are outfitted to shadow the raiders, bringing up fresh provisions and ammunition; but they somehow get lost in the fastness of the swamp, and Wild's troopers must now live off the land. "Here we left the canal and descended into another swamp of Hades," the same trooper writes. "The narrow crooked road was flooded with water and crossed with innumerable little rickety bridges, over which our horses made their way with great caution and reluctance."

From South Mills, they strike overland and cross the Pasquotank River, and when they arrive at Elizabeth City, they inspire widespread panic: the citizens there have never seen armed black troops before. Whatever action the black troopers take, it is magnified, embellished, and distorted by wild rumor and the panicky exaggeration born of a fear going back many generations.

From their base at Elizabeth City, the troops sortie as far as the Chowan River in search of recruits and guerillas. "Finding ordinary measures of little avail," Wild reports, "I burned their houses and barns, ate up their live stock, and took hostages from their family." He tallies four guerilla camps destroyed, guns and ammunition captured, and two dozen homesteads burned, along with two distilleries. By his reckoning, his forces liberate some 2,500 enslaved blacks from their bondage—many of whom will now be recruited into the ranks of the U.S. Army.

All but one of the twenty prisoners they capture are either released, retained as hostages, or sent to Norfolk for trial and imprisonment. The lone exception is Daniel Bright, a Pasquotank County man. The general tries him before a drumhead court-martial, and he is found guilty of guerilla activity. Bright is hanged, a placard around his neck proclaiming, "This guerilla hanged by order of Brigadier General Wild."

Confederate colonel Joel R. Griffin, posted in Virginia, is outraged by Wild's raid and the summary execution of an irregular soldier who, though acting on his own, was in fact a private in a Georgia cavalry regiment. Griffin writes, with barely tempered anger, "Probably no expedition, during the progress of the war, has been attended with more bitter disregard for the long established usages of civilization of the dictates of humanity than your late raid into the country bordering the Albemarle. Your stay, though short, was marked by crimes and enormities. You burned houses over the heads of defenceless women and children, carried off private property of every description, arrested non-combatants, and carried off ladies in irons, whom you confined with negro men."

At last Griffin arrives at the crux of the matter, the hanging of Daniel Bright, which he recounts in detail. "Therefore," he declares, ignoring the savage irony of his own response, "I have obtained an order from the General commanding, for the execution of Samuel Jones, a private of Company B. Fifth Ohio, whom I hang in retaliation." It is a sad measure of how far the generals have come from the quaint notions of chivalry and honor that laced their heroic speeches in the spring of 1861.

The first independent action conducted by black troops attracts all manner of commentary far exceeding its limited value as a military operation. A newspaper reporter who accompanies Wild into the Great Dismal Swamp has nothing but praise for the actions and behavior of the black troops: "By it the question of their efficiency in any branch of service has been practically set at rest." By his testimony, the soldiers behaved with admirable discipline, obeying orders smartly. They "performed all the duties of white soldiers — scouting, skirmishing, picket duty, guard duty, every service incident to the occupation of hostile towns, and best of all, fighting."

Wild himself confirms that his men "marched wonderfully, never grumbled, were watchful on picket, and always ready for a fight. They are most reliable soldiers."

But it doesn't take long for Confederate voices to raise their own clamor. The *Southern Recorder* of Milledgeville, Georgia, runs a story of how "the negro ran riot during the Yankee stay in the Albemarle country." Worse, it reports, under enemy fire black troops "fled like wild deer."

Other newspapers follow suit, decrying alleged atrocities and barbaric behavior they claim is natural conduct for an inferior race. They do not mention the many instances in which captured, disarmed black troops have been executed by Confederate victors.

General Butler recognizes the weapon he has helped to forge, which borrows its power partly from ingrained bigotry and unreasoning fear. He threatens the inhabitants of the region with more "visitations from the colored troops" if they do not drive the "Partisan Rangers" out of their home counties. He declares, "You will never have any rest from us so long as you keep guerillas within your borders."

Delegations in Chowan, Gates, Currituck, Perquimans, and Pasquotank Counties draft resolutions to resist Confederate conscription and expel guerillas. More than 500 residents of Pasquotank County alone petition Governor Vance to disband the guerilla units operating in the coastal counties.

As for Wild, the crusading champion of black troops, he has fulfilled the prophecy he made when presented with the hand-sewn silk battle flag of the 1st North Carolina Colored Volunteers by 400 cheering members of the Colored Ladies Relief Association the previous summer. The front of the flag features the Goddess of Liberty stomping a copperhead snake. The reverse is ornamented with a brilliant sun rising above dark clouds toward the word "Liberty," underscored by the motto, "The Lord is our sun and shield."

Receiving the flag on that sunny July afternoon, Wild said, "I thank Him who has enabled you to give and us to receive this emblem of the future destiny of your race." He ended his remarks to the hundreds of assembled free black men and women with a gesture: "I will now consign it to the care of those who I know will never disgrace it."

35

SISTERS OF MERCY

The nine women arrive at Beaufort on a steam tug, rescued from the *Cahawba*, run hard aground in Pamlico Sound with its cargo of 500 cavalry remounts. The women are dressed in long black habits, their hair covered, only their faces visible. All are sodden from the passage, their heavy serge clothing made heavier with drenching rain and salt spray. It is July 19, 1862, late afternoon, and they land to oppressive heat and humidity. But they bear hardship patiently. It is the life they have chosen. Five are Irish-born, two are New Yorkers, and the remaining two are Canadian and English.

They teeter up the narrow gangplank single file onto the ramshackle wharf, followed by two men. One wears a priest's black cassock: Father Bruhl, sixty, a Hungarian-born veteran of the Crimean War, his face masked by an extravagant gray beard. The other man wears a formal suit and strides with the confident bearing of a man in charge, a doctor: John Baxter Upham, the officious new medical superintendent of the Hammond Hospital, housed in the old Atlantic Hotel.

From the windows of the Atlantic Hotel, overhanging the water, scores of sick and wounded soldiers watch the women and wonder out loud who they are. The answer seems obvious to many of them: these are grieving widows come in search of their husbands' bodies.

But they are not. They are Sisters of Mercy, volunteers enlisted by Secretary of War Stanton on behalf of the War Department to do what they have been doing in America since 1846 and before that in Ireland: ease suffering. They have been sent here under direct orders from Gen. John G. Foster, commander of the Department of North Carolina. His own wife and daughter arrive with them on the *Cahawba*.

The Sisters of Mercy are not alone in their calling. More than 600 women from twenty-one religious communities serve in military hospitals throughout the theater of war.

When the sisters left New York, their friends and families feared they would die on the battlefield. Well-wishers provided linen for bandages and escorted them to the wharf. The great bell of St. Catherine's convent, their New York home, mournfully tolled their departure.

Before the war, the Atlantic Hotel in Beaufort was a palace of porches and breezy guest rooms, three elegant stories faced in planks painted to mimic stucco and extending on pilings over the harbor. Josiah Pender, a wealthy artist, soldier, and entrepreneur from Edgecombe County, bought it only four years before the outbreak of hostilities. It is the largest resort hotel on the coast of North Carolina, catering to visitors arriving on the newly extended rail line to bathe in salt water and enjoy the sea breeze.

Now it is a shell of its former grandeur, ransacked by Union troops after the capture of the port. What couldn't be hauled away was vandalized. Gone are the comfortable couches and easy chairs, the parlor pianos and paintings. Even the kitchen has been looted, only a few pots and pans and a handful of cutlery and silverware remaining.

In the late afternoon swelter, the sisters haul their meager belongings ashore to the eight rooms that have been reserved for their use—only to discover that the rooms are filthy and stripped of all comforts.

Dr. Upham orders the black cook, "Aunt" Clarissey, "See that these nurses have a fine dinner and as soon as possible." The sumptuous welcome meal, served in the orderlies' room, consists of cold, moldy pork and beans, soggy bread saturated with sea salt, and bitter coffee sweetened with molasses. For utensils, the sisters share a single fork, two knives, and one big iron spoon. After running aground, being drenched on their wild ride over the shoals in a steam tug, finding squalid quarters and now an inedible meal, one sister can't help but laugh. She is joined by another, and soon the orderlies' room fills with their raucous laughter.

Without even candles for light, they retire at sundown.

Next day, July 21, despite the fact that he professes a horror of "lady nurses," Dr. Upham summons them to accompany him as he makes his rounds of the hospital to determine how best to care for the 200 wounded and sick soldiers. Each ward seems worse than the last. Patients lie in filth, their dirty bandages unchanged for weeks, walls and floors stained with blood, only hardtack and salt beef for food. Medicine of any kind is scarce, and the only nurses are other patients, untrained and unwashed, many of them too ill to stand.

In the whole hospital, there is not one lamp or candle. The cleaning supplies consist of a single straw broom.

Besides Clarissey, the kitchen staff includes a strapping six-foot-tall soldier named Trip, who shadows the nuns as they move about their chores and is convinced they are agents of the pope come to poison them all, and Edward the baker, who rolls out pies and bread on the stripped marble top of the billiards table. At least one of the workers becomes their ally: Bob Sprawl, a young, recently liberated black man, attaches himself to the sisters and takes on any job at hand with gusto. They reward him with a handsome red flannel shirt, which he wears cinched at the waist, Cossack-style, declaring, "I'm the best-dressed man in North Carolina."

But even with the enthusiastic help of recently freed blacks, the situation is untenable. How can they care for so many suffering men with no supplies? The sisters catalog an extensive list of what they need, from medicine and instruments to brooms and scrub brushes to kerosene, soap, tubs, and cooking utensils. Dr. Upham and his staff assure the sisters that they have asked repeatedly for medical supplies and other necessities, to no avail.

But Mother Mary Madeline Tobin, a Canadian by birth, the superior of the nuns, sends her list directly to General Foster, with one additional item: if the supplies are not forthcoming, she will take her eight sisters and return to New York.

Mother Madeline also demands the keys to the storehouse, held by the current "superintendent" of the building, a short, pudgy, illiterate soldier from Maine with a tangled, tobacco-stained beard, who is typically found lounging barefoot in a wheelbarrow at the kitchen door. His name is Kit Condon, and he stubbornly refuses to give over the great ring of keys he wears on his belt, the badge of his authority.

A short time later, a small miracle steams into the harbor: a supply ship full of food, medical supplies, cleaning tools, and kitchen equipment. Convalescent soldiers, supervised by the "North Ladies"—the name they are called by their patients—unload the cargo. And the ship brings something else: orders from General Foster. From now on, the Sisters of Mercy are to have complete charge of the hospital, excepting only Dr. Upham's medical department. Mother Madeline takes the keys from Condon.

In short order, the sisters scrub the place clean of bloodstains and filth and reorganize the kitchen to provide nutritious meals under the direction of Sister Mary Augustine McKenna, who pledged her novitiate at St. Catherine's after fleeing the great Irish famine of 1848. They institute a regimen of bathing for the patients and regularly clean wounds and change dressings. Gone is the air of misery and neglect. The suffering patients now are infected with hope.

Many of the soldiers are at first leery of the sisters; they've never laid eyes on one before, and up until now they have been nursed only by men.

When one sister leans over to sponge the face of a patient, he recoils. "Great heaven—are you a man or a woman?" he blurts out. "Your hand felt like a woman's—not a bit rough—what are you anyway?"

The sister tells him, "Just a servant of Our Lord come to care for you."

Some of the medical staff also remain wary of the sisters, unsure of their motives. One of them asks Foster how much the sisters are being paid for their work. Foster assures him, "They receive no money at all, but work entirely for love of God and their fellow man." All the sisters have taken vows of poverty.

Many of the sick and wounded, now enjoying healthy meals and clean dressings, revive under their diligent care. Instinctively, and as part of the discipline of their order, the nuns have practiced the three most effective tools to heal the sick and wounded: good nutrition, cleanliness, and gentleness—and their gentleness is what the young soldiers will remember most vividly about the sisters' care. Often the soldiers who recover leave a token of gratitude for the sisters: a brass button, a seashell.

Some of the mortally wounded call upon the sisters to pray with them. One of them says to Sister Mary Augustine McKenna, "I want to be what you are."

When Father Bruhl is summoned to the bedside of a dying man who wishes to be baptized, he inquires about the man's faith. "What the Sisters believe, that is what I believe," he says.

Before long, however, the heat and rigors take their toll on the nuns. Two of them, Sister Agatha McCarthy and Sister Mary Paul Lennon, fall ill with fever. Next to succumb is Sister Mary Elizabeth Callahan, who is so near death that she is given the last sacraments. And before long Mother Madeline herself is too ill to work.

Dr. Upham inquires of her who will now take her place as superintendent. "Do I know her?"

She replies at once, "Of course you do. It is Mother Augustine, the tall dark Sister who prepares the soldiers' food."

He is dumbfounded. "What—the cook? Is that the way you do business?"

"Yes," she tells him flatly. "Every sister must be prepared to discharge any duty that may be entrusted to her." Sister Mary Augustine McKenna is no mere cook. She is educated, tireless, unflagging in her zeal for her patients, and a natural leader who inspires respect in the nuns and the patients alike. There is a reason she has been put in charge of the kitchen, for good nutrition is key to bringing the wounded and ill back to good health. Sister Mary Calla-

Irish-born Sister Mary Ignatius Grant is one of a dedicated band of Sisters of Mercy who tend the sick and wounded soldiers of both armies. (Courtesy of the Institute of the Sisters of Mercy of the Americas, Mercy Heritage Center)

han recovers—to the surprise of everyone—and when she and the other sick nuns are strong enough to travel, they sail for New York. But shortly after their arrival, Sister Mary Paul Lennon dies—the first of the New York Sisters of Mercy to lay down her life.

In their places come the first of several replacements, Sister Mary Ignatius Grant and Sister Mary Francis Murray, both Dubliners, along with six Irish girls from the House of Mercy in New York to help with housekeeping and other chores.

In October 1862, the Sisters of Mercy are ordered to leave Beaufort for New Bern, to be stationed in the Stanly House, where George Washington spent two nights on his Southern tour after the Revolutionary victory.

Sister Mary Augustine McKenna writes of their new post,

The house is fine and in perfect order, having been used until a short time ago as headquarters for General Burnside of Rhode Island. A spacious lawn is in front of the mansion, covered with the plant which we Irish call periwinkle, here, I have heard it called myrtle—although by no means the myrtle of the poets. The largest, greenest, finest cedars I ever beheld grow within this enclosure, and as berries are now ripening flocks of mocking-birds are rejoicing. . . . The magnificent drawing room in the Mansion is now our chapel.

Gorgeous roses cluster around and climb into the windows and mocking-birds flittering through the branches serenade the Sisters at their prayers, while two majestic trees, "The Pride of India" — stand sentinels of honor before the grand entrance.

The hospital is housed in three well-equipped buildings not far from the Stanly house, now home to the patients transferred from Beaufort and other soldiers wounded in the constant skirmishing from New Bern inland.

In December 1862, General Foster launches a raid on the railroad bridge at Goldsborough. The raid is successful, but it comes at a cost of 220 casualties on both sides. Many of the wounded make the trek home to New Bern — a journey of eight days — with little food. The medical supplies were lost in the fighting, and many of them arrive in bloody uniforms, their wounds unbandaged and suppurating.

A soldier named Sherman was shot in the lower face, his jaw shattered, and the surgeons decline to work on him — his wound appears fatal. But the sisters gently loosen the rags binding his face, sponge away the blood, and prepare him for surgery anyway. Though disfigured, he eventually enjoys a full recovery.

Hiram Hubbard, a sixteen-year-old volunteer from the 44th Massachusetts Infantry, is stricken with "camp fever." His condition is worsened by an old folk remedy, the application of a fly-blister on the back of his shoulder. The blister has turned into a bad sore, and his shirt is stuck painfully to the raw tissue. A sister hears the young man's agonized screams as one of his fellows tries rubbing the shirt out of the wound with a coarse wet towel. She finds him face down on a pillow, moaning pitifully. With a sponge and warm water, she carefully swabs the wound and removes the shirt, offering him relief at last.

The soldier lifts his head and asks, "Who is doing that?"

The nun tells him, "A Sister of Mercy."

"No," Hubbard insists. "No one but my mother could do it."

The sister dresses the wound with liniment, then wraps the shoulder in clean linen.

Hubbard at last faces his nurse and is taken aback at her black habit and veil. "What sort of woman are you?" he wants to know. "What are you at all?"

She does her best to explain, but Hiram Hubbard makes his own pronouncement: "I don't care what you are, you're an angel to me."

Another fevered patient grows delirious, and on his deathbed he says to Sister Mary Augustine McKenna, "Mother, thank you, Mother," and she can't be sure he was not seeing his own mother's face leaning over him at the end. It is common for soldiers in their last extremities of suffering to see in the faces of the sisters the faces of their own mothers — a small, illusory consolation.

The sisters are by now well acquainted with death. David Brout, an eighteen-year-old, collapses after a forced march. Sister Mary Ignatius Grant has his boots cut away. His boots are full of blood. In one leg an artery has burst. The young soldier dies of blood loss and shock.

The sisters tend the wounded from both armies, and when the Confederate soldiers recover, some stay on as prisoner orderlies.

In February 1863, Mother Mary Madeline returns, bringing with her Sister Martha Corrigan and Sister Gerard Ryan, both Irish natives. A little more than a year later, on March 11, 1864, Sister Gerard dies of "hardships" — the second of four Sisters of Mercy to die in the service of soldiers in North Carolina, out of fifteen sisters who serve in the Beaufort and New Bern hospitals.

By May 1863, the sisters are no longer needed in New Bern, and, taking with them four of the free black girls who worked alongside them, they return home to New York, where they are greeted as heroes. In honor of their service, the city grants them a ninety-nine-year lease on a plot of land at Eighty-First Street and Madison Avenue. There the sisters construct St. Joseph's Industrial School, "intended for the protection of young girls and female children . . . and in a special manner for the children of deceased or disabled soldiers."

For their role in tending wounded Confederate soldiers, Jefferson Davis offers his personal thanks to the Sisters of Mercy.

The Atlantic Hotel is refurbished, and in August 1879, it hosts Governor Thomas J. Jarvis, a wounded veteran of Confederate service, and a convention of the North Carolina Press Association. Despite storm warnings, the hotel is not evacuated. A hurricane with 125-mile-per-hour winds demolishes the structure with great loss of life, erasing the last vestiges of the old hospital structure.

The "Nuns of the Battlefield" are remembered on a stone monument in Washington, D.C., inscribed,

THEY COMFORTED THE DYING,
NURSED THE WOUNDED,
CARRIED HOPE TO THE IMPRISONED,
GAVE IN HIS NAME A DRINK OF WATER TO THE THIRSTY.

36

THE CRATER

In a war full of absurdity and horror, six North Carolina regiments take part in perhaps the most bizarre and horrific slaughter of the eastern campaign — named for a place that doesn't even exist until after the battle opens: the Crater.

The stage is set in the late spring of 1864 with a surprise maneuver by Lt. Gen. Ulysses S. Grant. He marches his massed forces around the flanks of the Army of Northern Virginia, crosses the James River without a fight, and moves on Petersburg, Virginia, a vital railroad junction only twenty miles from the capital of Richmond. If Grant can take Petersburg, Richmond must fall.

On June 15, 10,000 Union soldiers assault the entrenched Confederate garrison, a motley collection of old men and boys, only a few thousand strong, hurried into the front lines. Commanded by Gen. P. G. T. Beauregard, they make a gallant stand and stave off the attackers. Now Grant has lost the initiative.

Pvt. William A. Day marches with Company I, also known as the Catawba Marksmen, of the 49th North Carolina Infantry, a unit mustered in Garysburg and composed of men from McDowell, Rutherford, Chatham, Cleveland, Iredell, Moore, Rowan, Mecklenburg, Gaston, Catawba, and Lincoln Counties. The 49th is a seasoned outfit, veterans of Malvern Hill, where their first commander, Col. Stephen Dodson Ramseur, suffered a debilitating wound; Sharpsburg, where they stood up to an infantry charge and then counterattacked successfully; and Fredericksburg, where they suffered heavy casualties from artillery.

Now they march at the quickstep toward Petersburg. Day recounts,

> We started about dark and moving up the James river crossed on the pontoon bridge and marched the whole night, arriving at Petersburg at daylight very tired and sleepy. . . . Pretty soon the artillery opened in front and we were ordered to move off in It double quick and came

upon the Militia fighting like regulars, They were falling back slowly contesting every inch of ground. When we arrived on the field the enemy turned their guns on us. We moved on into the field and lay down in an old road and waited for the Militia to form on our right. At every discharge from the enemy's guns they threw themselves flat on the ground and about the time they got on their feet another charge of grape and canister would fly and down they would go again.

Lee hurries his army into position overnight, as 100,000 U.S. troops mass on the outskirts of the city. Each time the bluecoats attack, they are driven off. And as they extend their lines south and west, Lee moves in more troops to meet them. Behind formidable entrenchments, linked by a chain of forts, even outnumbered, the defenders can't be dislodged. The two armies fight to a bloody stalemate. Every attempt to break through the Confederate line is thwarted. The toll of dead and wounded mounts, but no ground is gained and nothing is decided.

The 49th is rotated in and out of the front line, as Private Day records: "The enemy charged our lines on the 18th and the dead had not been buried but lying in the hot sun they had begun to smell so badly we could hardly stay in the breast-works. The sharpshooters and artillery kept up a continual fire on both sides. . . . We remained in the works until the 26th — we were then relieved and sent back in reserve. We lay in a ditch, or covered way as it was called."

But even in reserve, the North Carolinians come under pounding fire from mortars — stubby, thick-barreled artillery pieces that launch projectiles weighing between twelve and sixty-four pounds in a high arc so that they plunge steeply down from their apogee. They fall in behind even the heaviest breastworks.

Day writes, "The next day they had their mortars ready and about ten o'clock they began throwing twenty-four pounders into our works. Among the first they threw landed in our Regiment. I was lying down in the covered way when I heard one coming. I sprang to my feet to give it room. It fell in the ditch but never bursted but rolled along on the ground and lodged against my haversack. I waited a reasonable time then picked up my haversack and moved out to another place."

Day writes, "On the 13th [of July] was the great mortar day. . . . They opened on us soon in the morning and kept it up all day." At sundown, when the barrage at last is lifted, the regiment counts forty dead and scores more wounded and mutilated. But all the killing accomplishes nothing. The defenders of Petersburg stubbornly hold out, and the Union army digs in deeper, equally stubborn.

And then a daring plan is hatched, the revival of a technique once used in medieval siege warfare to undermine thick-walled castles. The ranks of one of the Union regiments, the 48th Pennsylvania, are full of coal miners. They get to talking about how close their own lines are to Elliott's Salient, the nearest Confederate battery. One of the enlisted miners remarks, "We could blow that damned fort out of existence if we could run a mine shaft under it."

Their commander, Lt. Col. Henry Pleasants, himself a mining engineer, endorses the bold tactic. He persuades Maj. Gen. Ambrose E. Burnside, the commander of the Ninth Corps, to give it a try. In December 1862, waiting for pontoon boats to arrive, Burnside delayed his advance across the Rappahannock at Fredericksburg long enough to allow the Confederates to deploy behind impregnable fortifications on Marye's Heights. As Burnside ordered one after another Union brigade to charge up the long hill, an appalling slaughter ensued. Now he is eager to restore his reputation. Though he is skeptical of the miners' plan, he backs it anyway.

Maj. Gen. George G. Meade, commander of the Army of the Potomac, also approves the plan. The generals confer with Grant, a hardheaded realist. A breakthrough would scatter the thin gray line. Defenseless, Petersburg would fall, Richmond would be doomed, and the war might end this summer. Grant approves the plan.

Pleasants mobilizes his 400 men. His official report reads like an engineering manual: "It was commenced at twelve P.M., the 25th of June, 1864, without tools, lumber, or any of the materials requisite for such a work. The mining picks were made out of those used by our pioneers; plank I obtained, at first by tearing down a rebel bridge and afterwards by sending to a sawmill five or six miles distant, and the material excavated was carried out in hand-barrows, constructed of cracker boxes." Colonel Pleasants, reverting to his prewar profession, calculates depth and direction using an old-fashioned surveyor's theodolite.

A week later, the timbers give way under the weight of rain-sodden ground, and "the roof and the floor of the mine nearly met." The miners shore up the shaft and dig through a layer of putty-like marl. They craft an ingenious mechanism for drafting fresh air into the long tunnel: an airtight canvas door seals the tunnel entrance, except for a wooden pipe to let in fresh air. Far inside the tunnel, a constant fire draws bad air from the digging end and drafts it up a ventilating chimney.

Pleasants notes the progress: "On the 17th of July the main gallery was completed, being five hundred and ten and eight-tenths feet in length."

By the end of the month, the Pennsylvania miners have bored out a tunnel seventy-five feet long, perpendicular to the main shaft, forming the top of a T and running twenty feet under the Confederate breastworks. Directly above that shaft, thirty gunners man Richard G. Pegram's four-gun battery of twelve-pounder Napoleons, supported by companies of the 22nd and 18th South Carolina Infantry—nearly 300 men.

The plan is simple. At the appointed day and hour, the engineers will blow the four tons of black powder in the mine. Immediately, a specially trained regiment—Brig. Gen. Edward Ferrero's Fourth Division of U.S. Colored Troops (USCT)—will rush into the gap created by the blast, with reinforcements in support to exploit the breakthrough.

Ferrero's troops have been schooled for two weeks in the use of scaling ladders and instructed to wheel right and left in double column *around* the blast pit on either side—*not* down into it. His nine regiments are well-rested, but they are green troops, their only experience gained in guard duty and labor details. And they have not been spared fatigue duty during the run-up to the assault; they spend most of their time digging trenches, not drilling for battle.

Private Day underscores the danger to Lee's forces, should the plan succeed: "It was the intention of the enemy to blow up Pegram's battery on the crest of the hill, charge through the breach and take possession of a long high ridge, known as Cemetery Ridge, half a mile in rear of our works. On reaching this ridge the whole country around would be at the mercy of their guns."

Pleasants records in precise detail the planting of the mine: "The charge consisted of three hundred and twenty kegs of powder, each containing about twenty-five pounds. It was placed in eight magazines, connected together by wooden tubes half filled with powder. These tubes met from the lateral galleries at the inner end of the main gallery, and from this point I placed three lines of fuses for a distance of ninety-eight feet. . . . I received orders from corps headquarters, on the 29th of July, to fire the mine at half past three A.M., July 30th."

But detonating the mine proves tricky. Pleasants lights the fuse, but after an hour of tense waiting, nothing happens. Lt. Jacob Douty and Sgt. Henry Rees volunteer to go into the mine. They relight the fuse from where it burned out, and at 4:44 A.M., the mine explodes.

Pleasants continues his official account: "The size of the crater formed

The Crater: Pennsylvania miners succeed in detonating a mine under Confederate fortifications—and create a deathtrap for onrushing U.S. infantry.
(Courtesy of the Library of Congress, LC-USZ62-72890)

by the explosion was at least two hundred (200) feet long, fifty (50) feet wide, and twenty-five (25) feet deep. I stood on top of our breastworks and witnessed the effect of the explosion on the enemy. It so completely paralyzed him, that the breadth of the breach, instead of being only two hundred feet, was practically four or five hundred yards."

One rebel commander describes it as "bursting like volcano at the feet of the men."

Day witnesses the cataclysm: "It raised the ground and sent the men whirling in the air and lumps of earth as large as barrels were thrown a hundred yards. One of the guns, a brass twelve pounder was thrown to within thirty feet of the enemy's breastworks."

Signaled by the detonation of the monstrous mine, the Union artillerymen open fire with 110 cannons and 54 mortars, creating a hell on earth for the defenders. Surely a breakthrough is imminent. But there has been a last-minute change in the plan.

Generals Meade and Grant decide not to allow the U.S. Colored Troops to lead the assault. Both are skeptical of the fighting ability of the black soldiers. Less than twenty-four hours before the attack, Meade has the division commanders draw lots for the honor. Brig. Gen. James H. Ledlie "wins" the lottery. His division will be followed by two other white divisions led by Brig. Gen. Robert B. Potter and Brig. Gen. Orlando B. Willcox.

But no one has briefed Ledlie's brigade commanders on the plan to capture Cemetery Hill, nor have his men been trained to go around the Crater. Instead, they rush headlong into it and find themselves trapped in a helpless mob at the bottom, unable to claw their way up the near-vertical sandy sides.

Only now, after the disaster has been unfolding for an hour and a half, does Burnside order the Fourth Division of U.S. Colored Troops into the breach. The first four regiments, led by Col. Joshua K. Sigfried, actually manage to cross the Crater and capture 200 prisoners. But they are hemmed in by counterattacking Confederate troops filling in on either side of the breach. The 35th and 56th North Carolina hold the north flank, the 61st is blocking the middle behind the Crater, and other regiments are forming on the Union left.

The remaining USCT regiments advance down into the Crater, shouldering their way through retreating white soldiers, and they too are trapped there. Lt. Robert Beecham of the 23rd USCT records with bitterness, "Our generals had pushed us into this slaughterpen and then deserted us." As the carnage begins, none of the four Union division commanders is on the field. Ferrero and Ledlie are hunkered in a bombproof drinking whiskey.

The 49th and 24th North Carolina rush to the Crater, form on the right, and watch Union troops converge on the Crater and overwhelm the works on either side. "When we reached our position we counted twelve United States flags in the works, and the whole field in front of the Crater was full of Yankees," Day writes.

White and black Union troops are mixed together in a charging mob. "Oh, they looked black and ugly," Day recalls. "It was said they were drunk, but I don't know whether they were or not. We plainly saw the position we were in, to be captured by negro troops meant death. It meant the capture of Petersburg, and the slaughter of helpless women and children, we knew the negroes would spare neither sex. . . . We had the whole field full of negroes to shoot into, at about seventy-five yards distance. Good breast-works, and plenty of ammunition, and we made every shot tell."

The 28th Regiment USCT loses seven of eleven officers. Ninety-one of 224 men fall, a casualty rate of greater than 40 percent. Inside the Crater, hundreds of men are trapped. Day and his comrades fire down on them. Soon mortars open fire, dropping shells directly into the Crater. The officer corps of the 29th USCT suffers nearly 100 percent casualties, its commander killed. One surviving officer reports, "The 'crater,' where we were halted, was a perfect slaughterpen."

Enraged by the instantaneous annihilation of nearly an entire regiment and its guns, the Confederate counterattackers show no mercy. And the sight of hundreds of black soldiers among the attacking enemy only fuels their killing frenzy.

Lt. Col. Delevan Bates of the 30th USCT records that "many a dusky warrior had his brains knocked out with the butt of a musket, or was run thru with a bayonet while vainly imploring for mercy."

Confederate brigadier general E. Porter Alexander reports, "Some of the Negro prisoners who were originally allowed to surrender . . . were afterward shot by others, & there was, without doubt, a great deal of unnecessary killing of them."

Alerted by Lee, Brig. Gen. William Mahone launches his division into a counterattack at 8:00 A.M. His five brigades of infantry from Florida, Georgia, Alabama, Mississippi, and Virginia sweep the field.

The 25th North Carolina, raised from the mountain counties, also arrives on the scene with a South Carolina regiment to reinforce the shattered Confederate line. "They halted on the brink and fired one volley into the surging mass, then turned the butts of their guns and jumped in among them," Day records. "How the negroes' skulls cracked under the blows. . . . I, boy like, ran up the line to see them. When I got there they had the ground covered with broken headed negroes, and were searching about among the bomb proofs for more, the officers were trying to stop them but they kept on until they finished up."

Before long, the surviving white and black Union troops are routed, mobbing toward the rear. By day's end, nearly 4,000 Union troops are killed, wounded, or missing in action, including nearly 1,300 of the USCT. The casualties among those manning Elliott's Salient above the blast are almost 100 percent — some 300 men gone in an explosive instant. The Confederates have suffered about 1,500 total casualties. For his role in the disaster, Ledlie is dismissed from the army. Burnside too is later removed from command, never to hold another.

Grant calls the butchery "the saddest affair I have witnessed in this war. Such opportunity for carrying fortifications I have never seen and do not expect again to have." He explains his and Meade's fatal decision in testimony before the congressional Joint Committee on the Conduct of the War: "If we put the colored troops out front . . . and if it should prove a failure, it would then be said, and very properly, that we were shoving those people ahead to be killed because we did not care anything about them. But that could not be said if we put white troops in front."

The Crater, an artifact of the terrible power of human engineering, endures as a fixture in the landscape outside Petersburg—a great scar in the earth that becomes an emblem for this consuming war that features efficient modern weapons of destruction wielded by men behaving at their most savagely primitive.

DESERTERS AND OUTLIERS

At the outbreak of war, W. H. Younce is just eighteen years old. He reports that among his neighbors in northeastern Ashe County, he has been "marked and spotted as a Lincolnite." So he keeps his head down, suppressing his honest views on slavery and the war. By October 1862, the militia—made up of men over thirty-five—encamps a mile from the Younce home to enforce the new Conscription Act.

Younce, his older brother, and two companions ride stealthily across the Tennessee border, just six miles away, bound for Union territory in Kentucky. Their route takes them past the home of a young woman, the youngest of three sisters, whom Younce has been courting. Against the advice of his brother, he stops there for the night while the others lie low in the countryside. She guesses that he is fleeing the draft. "You can not only be turning your back upon your own country in the darkest hour of its peril, but by this act blasting every hope for an honorable and useful life in the future."

He declares his loyalty in no uncertain terms: "Miss Edith, you talk very prettily and grow quite eloquent but you represent a wicked and unjust cause.... I owe my allegiance to that country only that is represented by that beautiful emblem of the free, the Stars and Stripes. It is true this is my native land, and I love its mountains, but I cannot and will not fight for a government that seeks to enslave me, and whose cornerstone is slavery."

But late that night, he is surprised by a band of eight Home Guardsmen led by Maj. George Washington Long. Younce is arrested and taken back home under close guard. There he is persuaded to enlist in Company L of the 58th North Carolina, commanded by Capt. James M. Gentry, a family friend, in order to avoid a worse fate. He leads fifty new recruits on a forty-mile march to the train that will take them to the regimental camp at Tazewell, Tennessee.

Within two weeks of arriving there, he attempts to desert, but a family that has offered Younce and his companions a meal and a bed betrays them. Younce is convinced that the Confederate army cannot shoot or hang all its deserters without becoming decimated, and he convinces the authorities that he and his cohort were only attempting to visit family for a few days, intending to rejoin the regiment. In fact Younce has taken a private, sacred oath that he will not raise arms against his country, the United States of America. But keeping it will not be easy.

Desertion undermines the Confederate army, and North Carolina regiments have been made infamous for the number of their soldiers who desert. In some regiments, guards armed with pistols are delegated to watch over their fellows. As early as March 1862, a company of soldiers is dispatched to Chatham County to round up the numerous deserters. But there is no state law against desertion, so not much can be done with the men once they are in custody except try to repatriate them to their units. Governor Vance consistently invokes writs of habeas corpus to secure the release of North Carolinians arrested by Confederate authorities for disloyalty, including many imprisoned at Salisbury.

In April 1863, Lee complains to Secretary of War James A. Seddon of "frequent desertions from the North Carolina regiments." In truth, this reputation seems an unfair slur. Tar Heels are generally stationed far from home, and many take unauthorized leave to visit their families, help with crops, or attend to sick relatives and then return to duty. And desertion is a rapidly growing problem in virtually all Confederate regiments.

But on the eve of a new offensive to invade the North, the numbers alarm Lee's generals. General Pender reports that during the previous month alone, at least 200 soldiers from the 24th North Carolina have deserted. He partly blames the constant stream of letters from home exhorting the men to abandon the army and return to protect their own loved ones from the outliers, bushwhackers, and Home Guardsmen roaming a lawless country.

Lee writes Seddon the following month that thirty-two Ashe County men of Company A, 37th North Carolina Volunteers, have deserted, taking with them their arms and ammunition.

By the fall of 1863, after the great slaughter at Gettysburg, western North Carolina becomes a safe haven for hordes of deserters from all states. They congregate in bands of 30, 50, 100, armed and defiant. In Randolph County, 300 to 400 deserters dare the conscript patrols to molest them. Five hundred deserters are said to gather in a makeshift regiment in Wilkes County, conducting disciplined drills.

Even the men who remain in the ranks are not necessarily loyal. Maj. Gen. Simon Bolivar Buckner reports that "fully half of the East Tennessee and North Carolina troops from the mountain districts are not to be relied upon." It is those mountain districts, mostly devoid of plantations and slave-holders, that most bitterly opposed secession.

By May 1863, the problem has become so acute that Governor Vance issues an impassioned proclamation condemning desertion as treason: "I therefore appeal to all good citizens and true patriots in the State to assist my officers in arresting deserters, and to frown down all those who aid and assist them. Place the brand upon them and make them feel the scorn and contempt of an outraged people."

Vance must walk a fine line between threat and persuasion or else his state's regiments might never recover the strength of numbers they need. So he includes an inducement: "Though many of you rejected the pardon heretofore offered you, and I am now not authorized to promise it, yet I am assured that no man will be shot who shall voluntarily return to duty. This is the only chance to redeem yourselves from the disgrace and ignominy which you are incurring."

In the mountainous west, deserters are often welcomed back into the ranks with little fanfare. There simply aren't enough able-bodied men to allow the luxury of execution. In other commands, justice is arbitrary and often capricious.

John Redman, a young farmer from the coastal plain, writes to his wife from military prison in Kinston, where he has been condemned to be shot for desertion. His crime was to slip back to his farm for a few weeks to help his starving wife harvest their crops. Then he rejoined his unit out of duty. But he is to be made an example of. He writes, "My dier wife, if I see you no more on erth donte grieve for mee nether lamente nor morne. I hope I shall with my jesus bee while you are left alone."

This time, Younce has no intention of going back and risking military justice. By February he is on the run again, playing hide-and-seek with rebel cavalry, at last making his way to Doe Mountain. He spends a miserable rainy night in the open there and then proceeds to Mountain City, Tennessee, just across the border from home.

He recalls,

> I will not attempt to describe the condition of things that existed
> there at that time. My vocabulary is too limited to attempt a
> portrayal of the horrors and the sufferings of those poor Union
> people. Civil law and courts of justice had been abolished, monarchy
> and ruin reigned supreme; men and neighbors, who had always

passed for good men, who had turned to be rebels, were transformed into demons, murderers and savages. Conscripts were hunted like wild animals, and often shot and murdered. Their homes were often destroyed by the torch, and if spared were robbed of everything they had, and their families left without a crust of bread.

The local Home Guardsmen know him and continually search the Younce homestead looking for him. He hides out in the woods, making furtive visits to the house for food.

Two weeks after his arrival home, on March 23, 1863, Younce learns firsthand of an atrocity that inspires in him both outrage and fear.

Jesse Price is harboring his sons Hiram and Moses—deserters—in the woods near his gristmill. The Home Guard stakes out the place and captures all three, along with Price's nephew Solomon, then jails them in the Jefferson courthouse.

Younce describes the scene the next morning, as a mob led by a Major Long takes the men forcibly from jail to a locust tree on the snowy courthouse lawn. "They would tie one of the poor fellows hands behind him, put a rope around his neck, place him on a horse behind one of the mob, who would ride under the limb of the tree, throw the end of the rope to a man on the limb, who would tie it, and then on the horse would ride out from under him, leaving him dangling in mid-air."

Jesse Price, fifty-five years old, is the last to be hanged.

"In the crowd that went out to witness the hanging was Dr. James Wagg, a prominent physician, and also a Methodist preacher, a man well and favorably known throughout all the country, and be it to his credit, was trying to quell the mob and save the lives of these men," Younce recalls.

After the three young men had been hanged, Dr. Wagg approached the old man, whom he had known for many years, and told him he could do nothing for him: that he had no influence with these men, and they were going to hang him. "And now," he said "you are unprepared, and in a few minutes more your soul will be ushered into eternity. I am here to try to do you good. Shall I not stay the hand of death, while I pray with you?"

The old man replied: "Doctor, I have done nothing to be hung for. I am old—not even subject to military duty. I have committed no crime. I have only been loyal to my country, and if it is for this you intend to murder me, I will go into eternity as I am. I want no rebel, such as you are, to pray for me."

In a moment his hands were pinioned, and he was swinging beside the three boys.

Incredibly, Younce reports, one of the sons—twenty-year-old Moses—survives his hanging. Dr. Wagg rubs snow on his face to revive him. Moses recovers and is eventually sent back to the front. But he deserts again, this time enlisting in the U.S. Army, and for the rest of the war he fights against the Confederacy that killed his father and brother, carrying the nickname "Scape Gallows" Price.

One of Jesse's nephews, Thomas, embarks on an odyssey of vengeance, tracking down and killing five of the men who hanged his uncle.

Many Unionists are equally guilty of heinous acts of violence against their own neighbors, for the war in the mountain counties devolves into a blood feud that is fueled by long-standing local animosities and carried on in ever-escalating acts of violent retaliation and vengeance. One of the many victims is Isaac Wilson, a forty-one-year-old Confederate lieutenant on furlough to his home in North Fork, in Watauga County. He is out plowing his field when he is gunned down in cold blood. His death may be a fatal case of mistaken identity: Unionist "scouters," called "bushwhackers" by the Home Guard, are hunting his cousin, "Big Ike" Wilson, for killing one of their own.

With the Home Guard tracking him, Younce decides he must leave North Carolina for good. Once again he crosses into Tennessee, but there again he feels trapped by the constant cavalry patrols. He makes a deal with a young artillery captain named Oliver to enlist with his company, if Oliver will guarantee his safety from the authorities who want to hang him.

In due course Captain Oliver is appointed provost marshal, and by April, Younce is posted to Dublin, assigned as an armed escort aboard passenger coaches on the Norfolk and Western Railroad. His duty is to examine the papers of all travelers and arrest any suspected deserters. Younce proudly reports, "During all the time I did duty on that road, I never made a single arrest." In fact, he openly aids at least one deserter in escaping capture.

But he winds up in the thick of the fighting at the rail junction of Wytheville, where the Confederates are routed. Oliver is shot and killed. Younce and many of his fellows scatter into the countryside and hole up in bands, determined not to rejoin the fighting. But surviving that way is hard, and by August he finds his way back to his company, which is now posted just forty miles from his home. He still intends to desert, but opportunity has not

Deserters and Outliers

favored him. More deserters rejoin as the company rests in camp through the waning weeks of summer.

With the company still understrength, Younce convinces his commander that, if only he were granted a short leave of absence, he could recruit more men from the conscripted deserters among whom he was hiding out. Once again his glib tongue wins over his superiors, and off he goes alone hunting up new recruits. And before long, he does indeed persuade twenty-five men to join him—to fight for the Union.

They make their headquarters in the Unionist stronghold of Johnson County, Tennessee. Many of the men want to take revenge on the Home Guard and other Confederate sympathizers who have ransacked and burned Unionist farmsteads and done violence to their families, but Younce argues strongly against retaliation. He fears that will only incite further depredations against the families they leave behind.

Younce enjoys one last furtive nocturnal visit to his family—and another clandestine midnight rendezvous with Edith, who warns him that Major Long has determined to kill him outright.

Now escape is urgent. He leads his men on an arduous journey through the mountains to the Union lines at Jonesboro, Tennessee. They collapse exhausted in a barn on the outskirts of town. At daybreak, they rouse themselves. "We started up town altogether," he remembers, "and the first thing that attracted our attention was the flag—the Old Stars and Stripes, floating over the courthouse."

Until this moment, his patriotism has been an abstraction, an ideal. Now it surges through him as a wave of heartfelt emotion. "The boys began to cheer. We formed them in line double file, and marched around the courthouse square, cheering and hallooing like wild men." Men toss their hats into the air and cheer until they are hoarse. Others weep openly. Younce writes, "This was Monday morning the 30th of September [1863], and it marks an epoch in the history of my life."

Younce never sees his sweetheart Edith again, and she marries another. Long after the war, he visits the scene of so much bloodshed and strife. "But few of the friends of my youth are there, and only the hands of strangers greet me in my native land."

38

THE LAST HURRAH OF THE SLAVERS

By the fall of 1864, the war is going badly for the Confederate cause. The Army of Northern Virginia finds itself in desperate straits in Petersburg, starved for food, ammunition, and supplies. Sherman has taken Atlanta and is poised to march to the sea. Maj. Gen. Philip H. Sheridan has routed Lt. Gen. Jubal A. Early's army at Cedar Creek in the Shenandoah Valley. Union forces occupy Knoxville and eastern Tennessee, just across the mountains.

Privation and ruin afflict much of the South, including North Carolina, which has endured partial occupation for more than two years and has become a haven for deserters.

At the center of the conflict are the slave owners, who agitated for war and now find their way of life threatened by it. As early as February 1861, The *North Carolina Standard* warns that if war comes, "the negroes will know, too, that the war is waged on their account," making them "become restless and difficult to manage." The whole economic system will begin to break down.

Four of the forty largest slaveholders in the western counties die violently during the course of the war — not on distant battlefields, but on home ground.

In 1863, John W. Woodfin is shot from the saddle leading a contingent of North Carolina cavalry into Warm Springs, in an attempt to dislodge Union cavalry raiders.

William Waightstill Avery, the most prominent advocate of secession in Burke County, is killed in a skirmish with Col. George W. Kirk's cavalry raiders at Brown Mountain, fourteen miles west of Morganton.

In June 1864, Andrew Johnstone, a wealthy rice planter, allows a gang of six deserters into his home, a stone estate called Beaumont. After he gives them food and drink, one of them shoots him dead in front of his young son, who picks up his father's pistol and shoots three of the bushwhackers.

The first to die, Col. George Bower of Ashe County, drowns when his carriage overturns in the rain-swollen Yadkin River. A slave driving the carriage warned the colonel not to attempt the crossing. The slave survives. But as the story appears in the *Standard*, the slave becomes the cause of the fatal accident, which provides him the opportunity to run away to freedom. This is the contradiction. For certain rich owners and the economy they support, the slaves are essential, but the fear of betrayal and attack, even uprising, pervades the culture.

It might seem obvious from outside events that slavery's days are numbered, yet in the western counties, from the Piedmont into the mountains, the slave trade flourishes. Since 1808, U.S. law has made it illegal to import slaves, but an uncounted number, likely in the tens of thousands, were smuggled into the South between then and the outbreak of war. But the trade has mainly been interstate, conducted from auction houses in large cities such as Charleston and Richmond, or between local owners.

By 1864, with U.S. troops occupying the swath of coastal counties and the Freedmen's Colony on Roanoke becoming a magnet for runaways and recruits for the new U.S. Colored regiments, Governor Zeb Vance declares, "It is the duty of all slaveowners immediately to remove their slaves able to bear arms." And so begins a forced exodus of slaves into the interior counties. One consequence is that families are broken up: able-bodied men are removed temporarily or sold outright to owners and dealers from the Piedmont to the west, while their wives and children remain behind.

John W. Woodfin's brother, Nicholas Washington Woodfin—a lawyer and planter from Asheville and the largest slave owner in Buncombe County—sees in this upheaval an opportunity for profit. Before the war, he recruited slave labor from owners across the state to build the Western North Carolina Railroad. By 1862, he and his consortium have hired 150 "able-bodied negroes."

Nicholas Woodfin, a handsome, likable man with a shock of upswept graying hair and a thick, well-groomed beard, sets himself up as a slave broker, arranging work-for-hire for idle slaves—wages to be paid to the owner, minus his commission—or outright sale. He propositions David L. Swain, former governor and president of the University of North Carolina: "Now upon the subject of your negroes, If you will send them up to this country, I can yet hire to advantage for the rest of the year. The men especially will command high prices, particularly before harvest commences. There is a great demand for labor indeed. . . . It won't be as easy to place women & children, but it can be done."

With the shortage of men lost to the ranks of the army, the slave labor market becomes lucrative. Calvin Cowles of Wilkes County casts his net even farther afield, writing to slave owners as far away as Mississippi, promising them that he can hire out adult males for up to $150 per year — $18 more than the wage earned by a private soldier.

So desperate is he for slave labor that he enjoins his brother in the eastern part of the state, "Can't you catch me a Negro or two and send them up?" He can get a premium for skilled craftsmen — carpenters and blacksmiths — but is willing to take any slaves he can get. During a trip to Charleston, he buys Nancy, a forty-year-old "cook, washer, and house servant," for his wife, at a price of $805, but he is disappointed that he can't find a suitable "boy" for himself. For, as he confides to his sister, "prices rule high here."

And so it goes. From middle Tennessee, Georgia, South Carolina, and the coast, slaves are transported to the highlands of North Carolina in a lucrative trade that goes on vigorously until the spring of 1865.

One irony is that the mountain counties, which had relatively few slaves at the start of the war and relied mostly on a wage and subsistence economy, now become a region heavily dependent on slave labor. And as the number of slaves increases, so too does fear of "Negro ravages." An Asheville man, reflecting the general concern, writes Governor Vance requesting protection from the growing population of enslaved blacks working for hire.

But the numbers only increase, because the shortage of free labor grows ever more severe. An adult male slave of Joseph Corpening of Caldwell County fetches a yearly rate of just $28 in 1861. By 1865, he is worth $525 per year to his owner.

Part of the increase is due to the depreciation of the Confederate currency, but speculators focus only on the dollar value. Cowles, always a dealer with a cold eye for the main chance, advises his sister on how to dispose of two of her slaves, recaptured runaways. "Robert could have been sold in Charleston for $2,500," he writes, "but I presume you allowed your philanthropy to influence you in marketing him — he is with old friends. In Wash's case, I advise you to put him on the block in Richmond . . . get the most you can for him."

Financial matters also weigh on the minds of the Lenoir brothers, Thomas, Walter, and Rufus. When their prominent father, Col. Thomas Lenoir, dies just before secession, they inherit Fort Defiance Plantation in Caldwell County, a large farm in Haywood County called the Den, a considerable sum of money, and sixty-one slaves.

As eldest brother, Thomas manages Fort Defiance, while his youngest brother, Rufus, moves to the remote Den. The middle brother, Walter, goes off to war. It takes two years to settle the estate, and by then the war is already a catalog of slaughter: Big Bethel, First Manassas, First Winchester, Seven Pines, the Seven Days Battles, Second Manassas, Sharpsburg, Fredericksburg.

And President Abraham Lincoln has issued his Emancipation Proclamation, declaring all slaves residing in states in rebellion to be free. But the buying and selling of slaves goes on, a matter of shrewd investment.

From Kinston, in April 1862, Walter advises Rufus to be wary of investing in property that is overpriced on account of the war, "but there are two kinds of personal property which form exceptions in this respect, negroes and cotton." So, "for long investment and in a mere pecuniary point of view, I would prefer buying negroes or cotton near the point where they are in the greatest present danger & removing them to the mountains to any other investment in personal property." Indeed, when Walter returns home—having lost a leg to amputation—he finds that his own slaves have doubled in value.

Like many slave owners, Walter is torn between his zeal for profit and his ambivalence about the means. Before the war, he confided to his eldest brother, Thomas, an attitude shared by his wife, Nealy: "I feel determined at present never to own another slave. Both Nealy and I have concluded after our limited experience with slaves that the evil of being a master and mistress of slaves is greater than we are willing to bear unless imposed upon us by some sterner necessity belonging to our lot." He does not favor secession, but when war comes, he ardently embraces the Confederate cause, including slavery. Thus he dutifully bears his inheritance of more slaves, but like his brothers, he increasingly chafes under what they all come to recognize as a burden as much as an investment.

They share their inheritance with their sister Julia's husband, James Gwynn, who wants as much of his share in slaves as possible, especially young slaves, which he considers a capital long-term investment. He purchases two additional slaves from a widow, crowing about the bargain price he pays. Gwynn complains that he sold off one slave, only to see her market value go up dramatically after the sale: "I had to sell one of Byram's and Betsey's children (Polly) which I disliked very much but she got too far along in the sleight of hand to keep; I only got $1250 for her—could now get $1800. I also sold Lark a few weeks ago for $2000 which I then thought an exorbitant price but it seems there is not telling what property will go for."

From now on he holds out for top dollar and increasingly distrusts the Confederate currency. "I have had several persons to see me to buy George and his family," he writes, "but I have not sold them yet and I hardly think I will for awhile at least, altho' I do not think I will keep them, but maybe they are as safe as the money I would get for them."

After the carnage at Gettysburg and the forced retreat of Lee's army, some slave owners begin to doubt the durability of the institution. "I have never thought that the Yankees would succeed in liberating our slaves," Walter Lenoir writes his brother Rufus. He always believed that "God will not suffer the Yankees to perpetrate so great a crime as that against us and our species."

But recent events have changed his mind. Slavery may well be doomed, and this will not necessarily lead to the "horrid massacre and butchery" that he and the slaveholding class have long feared would come hand in hand with emancipation. He goes on, "There will be no rising upon the non-combatant men, women, or children. Those of us who live to see it will see their Yankee masters set the negroes free and then govern them and their fellow citizens, their late masters and mistresses, as well as subjugated peoples are governed by other enlightened nations."

In the final months of the war, sales are brisk. Families like the Cowleses sell off slaves in a market that is peaking. But this is no reflection that they fear either imminent invasion by U.S. troops or forced emancipation. They sell off "troublesome" slaves, of whom there seem to be more and more — the runaways, those caught stealing, the unruly, the slackers, the malcontents — with no notion that these individual cases of rebellious behavior indicate a more general belief among the enslaved that salvation is near. And it will arrive dressed in a blue coat and carrying a musket.

Yet the owners are aware of a growing agitation and defiance among the slaves now crowded into the mountain region. Rufus Patterson writes in late 1864, "A general spirit of devilment is thro' the country. I deem it best to be constantly on the lookout. Our negros need watching."

And indeed, one of the most subversive activities of all is taking place right under the slave owners' noses: aiding and abetting fugitive slaves, deserters, and escaping Union prisoners of war, many of them trekking over the mountains toward the safety of the Union strongholds in Tennessee. One U.S. cavalry captain calls the enterprise "an underground railway, as systematic and as well arranged as that which existed in Ohio before the war." Unionists and local blacks act as "conductors."

Albert Richardson, a correspondent for the *New York Tribune*, escapes from Salisbury Prison and makes his way with other escapees through Wilkes County. He observes, "By this time we had learned that every black face was a friendly face. So far as fidelity was concerned, we felt just as safe among the negroes as if in our Northern homes. Male or female, old or young, intelligent or simple, we were fully assured they would never betray us."

Other escaping prisoners express their gratitude to the slaves who helped them find their way home. Writes one, "It would have been impossible . . . to make an escape without the aid of negroes."

So by importing slaves into the west to safeguard them from being liberated, slave owners and speculators have unwittingly strengthened a subversive network that undermines the Confederate war effort. For the slave owners of the western counties, the end comes not gradually but in a storm of U.S. cavalry. One day they are wealthy in slaves. The next, their "investment" has walked away and they are ruined.

Some owners bow to the inevitable, but only at the eleventh hour. Mary Anderson is an enslaved child on the plantation of Sam Brodie in Wake County, which features a big house of twelve rooms and slave cabins of two rooms each. One day she hears a distant *booming*. She recalls, "Next day I heard it again, boom, boom, boom. I went and asked missus, 'Is it going to rain?'"

Of course it isn't thunder she is hearing but the concussion of cannon fire as Sherman's army advances. Brodie summons all the slaves on the plantation. Anderson has a clear memory of what happens next: "At nine o'clock all the slaves gathered at the great house and marster and missus came out on the porch and stood side by side. You could hear a pin drop everything was so quiet. Then martser said, 'good morning,' and missus said, 'Good morning, children.' They were both crying. Then marster said, 'Men, women and children, you are free. You are no longer my slaves. The Yankees will soon be here.'"

Brodie and his wife then sit on the porch and wait for the Yankees, who gallop into the yard in a cloud of dust and camp there, taking hams from the smokehouse and brandy from the storeroom and setting out a feast for themselves and the liberated slaves.

Anderson recounts, "The Yankees stayed there, cooked, ate, drank and played music until about night, then a bugle began to blow and you never saw such getting on horses and lining up in your life. In a few minutes they began to march, leaving the grove which was soon as silent as a grave yard."

In a single day, life has forever changed for Mary Anderson and the other former slaves—and for the slave owners, who imagined that their privileged way of life could survive such a shattering passage of arms.

39

CONFEDERATE GIBRALTAR

At precisely 1:40 A.M. on the chilly morning of Christmas Eve 1864, Confederate soldiers asleep in their blankets at Sugar Loaf, a sandy bluff just south of Wilmington, are jolted out of their slumber "like pop-corn in a popper" by a booming concussion.

Farther south, on the parapets of Fort Fisher overlooking the channel into the Cape Fear River from the sea, artillerymen stare, entranced, at a display of pyrotechnics half a mile offshore—serial explosions and flames shooting high into the cold night for more than an hour.

Upriver in Wilmington, district commander Maj. Gen. William H. C. Whiting—a dashing but diminutive officer affectionately known to his men as "Little Billy"—is awakened by the blast. He telegraphs the young commander of Fort Fisher, Col. William Lamb, for an explanation. Lamb replies, "A blockader got aground near the fort, set fire to herself and blew up." In fact the burning ship is a secret weapon gone awry: the hulk *Louisiana*, stuffed with 215 tons of powder and detonated by a small band of volunteer daredevils. Maj. Gen. Benjamin F. Butler and Rear Admiral David D. Porter, the feuding commanders of the army and navy forces massing offshore, expect that the concussion will level the walls of the fort—but it does no damage at all. The bomb ship is a noisy farce that nonetheless signals the opening salvo against Fort Fisher.

Nine forts and batteries guard the lower Cape Fear River, anchored by Fort Fisher, the "Gibraltar of the South," at Confederate Point, the sandy spit where the river meets the sea. The river has two outlets: the main channel past Smith's Island, and the shallower New Inlet preferred by the fast blockade-runners. Fort Fisher is the guardian of New Inlet.

With New Orleans and Norfolk in Union hands and Charleston harbor bottled up by a close blockade, the port of Wilmington has taken on more and more importance as the gateway to the Confederacy for seaborne commerce. Despite the blockade, more than three-quarters of the blockade-running ships successfully reach Wilmington harbor.

In one year alone, beginning in November 1863, they bring into the struggling Confederacy more than 6 million pounds of meat and 400,000 pounds of coffee, as well as war materiel: 1.5 million pounds of lead for musket balls; close to 2 million pounds of saltpeter for making gunpowder; tons of iron, tin, and zinc; and hundreds of thousands of rifles, carbines, boots, shoes, buttons, buckles, tools, blankets, and other gear. The bulk of this precious cargo steams past Fort Fisher and into Wilmington, there to be loaded onto freight cars of the Wilmington and Weldon Railroad and hauled to the battlefields of Virginia.

In a single five-week period, nineteen ships make it through, carrying tons of the supplies needed to keep the war going. During the course of the war, nearly 100 of the sleek side-wheel steamers slip in and out of Wilmington, usually by night. The port is ideally located to take advantage of transshipment of European goods from neutral ports such as Nassau, in the Bahamas, just under 600 miles southeast, and Bermuda, 100 miles farther to the east. One shipload can maintain a fighting regiment in the field for a whole month.

During this critical period, Gideon Welles, U.S. secretary of the navy, does his best to persuade President Abraham Lincoln to attack Fort Fisher. "Could we seize the forts at the entrance of Cape Fear and close all illicit traffic," he argues, "it would be almost as important as the capture of Richmond on the fate of the Rebels, and an important step in that direction."

Unlike Fort Caswell across the channel, a typical masonry fort that could be reduced to rubble by heavy-caliber cannon fire, Fort Fisher is made of sand. During the first year and a half of the war, ten different commanders worked to create the fort. One of those officers was Seawell Fremont, a West Point friend of Gen. William T. Sherman, who as a young lieutenant attended a wedding in Wilmington along with Lt. Abner Doubleday. It is Fremont who names the peninsular bastion Fort Fisher, in honor of Col. Charles Frederick Fisher, who died leading the troops of the 6th North Carolina Infantry at First Manassas.

But for all that time the fort remains a shambles of unconnected ramparts and missing armaments. It requires an officer with vision and practical skill to turn the sandy outpost into a true fort.

The man turns out to be Lamb, a twenty-nine-year-old artillery officer with no previous engineering experience. He is a Virginia native, born to a prominent and wealthy slaveholding family. His father was once mayor of

Norfolk, where the family's estate, Kermure, occupies an entire block along the waterfront. His military experience consists of a stint at the Rappahannock Military Academy and commanding a company of local militia, the Woodis Rifles. As an officer in the state guard, he was present at the hanging of the abolitionist John Brown. When war comes, he is co-owner of a secessionist newspaper, the *Southern Daily Argus*. Fair-haired and charming, handsome with a stylish moustache and wispy goatee, he looks more poet than warrior.

But in the design and construction of military fortifications, Lamb is a prodigy—mentored by his commander, Whiting, considered by Lee to be the finest engineer in the Confederacy. But many of Whiting's superiors find him arrogant and intemperate. Lee respects and admires him but does not like him. President Davis finds him insufferable, and persistent rumors about his drunkenness sabotage his prospects. Thus Whiting has been moved from a combat command in Virginia to the relatively quiet Cape Fear district.

Lamb's other inspiration comes from books. He has carefully studied the accounts of Sevastopol in the Crimean War, and he intends nothing less formidable for his own fort.

He arrives at his new post on July 4, 1862, and is appalled by the lack of preparedness he finds. The fort is only partly constructed. Many of the guns have not been mounted. The garrison—cut off by nearly twenty miles of sunbaked sand, marsh, and pine forest from Wilmington—is ill-disciplined and prone to desertion. Lamb instills a sense of purpose in his men, and they respond with enthusiasm. One writes, "I like him splendid, and all the rest of the men likes him." They build a small private cottage just north of the fort on the river for Lamb, his wife Daisy, and their children.

The garrison is too small for the giant fort. The two battalions of heavy artillery—the 1st and the 3rd—are augmented by gunners from the 10th and the 40th North Carolina troops and the 13th battalion, along with companies of the 36th North Carolina, and four battalions of Junior Reserves—teenaged boys, many of them hardly tall enough to load and aim a musket. All in all, Lamb commands just 800 troops.

Using the conscripted labor of 500 slaves and Lumbee Indians, along with his own troops, Lamb sets about redesigning the fort into the shape of a number 7 on a grand scale. The short stroke of the 7 extends for about 500 yards across the peninsula to the north, forming the land face. The long leg of the 7 constitutes the sea face. On the river side, the fort is open. A line of rifle pits south of the land face, inside the fort, offers a line of defense from amphibious landings on the point, as well as a fallback position for the gunners on the land face.

The ramparts rise from a base that is twenty-five feet thick to a height of twenty-three feet, anchored by marsh grass to keep them from blowing away in the incessant blustery winds. At the foot of the land face, Lamb builds a stubborn nine-foot-high palisade out of axe-sharpened pine logs. He orders half a mile of trees and shrubs cleared from the approach to the land face, then plants a minefield on the cleared land. The mines can be detonated electrically from inside the fort. His engineers tunnel a sally port into the land face, so sharpshooters can deploy outside the fort to rake advancing enemy troops.

The firepower of the fort is massive: in its sixteen gun chambers are mounted an assortment of eight- and ten-inch cannons called Columbiads, each weighing many tons and heaved into place by teams of sweating slaves and white laborers; seven-inch Brooke rifled cannons; and twenty-four-pounder Coehorn mortars, backed up by smaller mortars and fieldpieces.

Thus Fort Fisher rises out of the sandy peninsula separating the river from the ocean as a line of thick, sandy berms, with gun emplacements carved into the earthworks in a line from river to sea on the north side and another facing the sea to the east. To the south, Battery Buchanan mounts its two massive ten-inch Columbiads and two eleven-inch Brooke smoothbore cannons to cover the channel through New Inlet.

The hundreds of tons of piled sand can absorb artillery blows that would flatten a conventional brick or stone fortress. Bombproof caverns tunneled into the sandy berms and reinforced by thick timber can shelter troops from harm during the shelling. The capacious powder magazine is also safely secreted under many tons of sand.

The ongoing fortification of Confederate Point is no secret — spies and escaped slaves bring word north. One Union officer writes that, based on what he has heard, the fort "is a work of more labor than the pyramids." It is an unfortunate metaphor, since Fort Fisher is not intended as a tomb. One of the engineers at work on its battlements reports, "I have seen no works anywhere in the Confederacy that can compare with them." He claims they can "withstand an indefinite hammering from any ordnance now known."

That test is now at hand. In the gray light of dawn, the defenders of the far-flung garrison on the edge of the sea witness a sight for which they have been preparing for more than three years: a fleet of fifty-six warships accompanied by transports and tenders, including the dreadnoughts of the Atlantic

A stereopticon card shows an English Armstrong gun—just one of many massive artillery pieces mounted on the sandy ramparts of Fort Fisher. (Photo by Timothy H. Sullivan; courtesy of the Library of Congress, LC-DIG-stereo-1s02551)

fleet: *Colorado, Minnesota, Powhatan, Susquehanna,* and *Wabash*. Grant calls it "the most formidable armada ever assembled for concentration upon one given point." The ordinarily flat horizon has become a cityscape of masts and superstructures.

And all at once it blooms with fire. For the next five hours, the ships unleash a bombardment of 10,000 projectiles on the fort, including fifteen-inch cannonballs that weigh 300 pounds each. There has been nothing like it in history.

By mid-afternoon, the wooden barracks inside the fort are burning,

Confederate Gibraltar

Lamb's brick headquarters reduced to rubble. The gunsmoke hangs so thick over the fort that ships' gunners have a hard time tracking their targets and fire blind, often undershooting their marks or overshooting the fort completely and lobbing their shells harmlessly into the river beyond. One witness recalls, "The ironclads and their consorts thundered away at Fort Fisher with such stunning violence that the ocean fairly trembled."

Meanwhile, the outgunned defenders fire back—but only once every half hour, by Colonel Lamb's order, so they can preserve their precious stock of ammunition, a total of just 3,600 rounds. Firing the massive ten-inch Columbiads is a dicey business. The gunners stand on tiptoes with their mouths wide open. Pvt. George Washington Benson later explains, "If you didn't, it would knock you silly and jar your teeth out."

Aboard the bombarding ships, the gunners fare even worse, at least those assigned to the wrought-iron Parrott rifled cannons, their barrels reinforced with iron bands. Several blow up in their gunners' faces, killing or maiming some forty sailors.

The firing continues long after dusk, the brilliant flashes lighting up the sea.

As Christmas morning dawns gray and windswept, wooden gunboats pound the shoreline three miles north of the fort in advance of a landing by army troops. Dr. David W. Hodgekins, a surgeon aboard the *Ben De Ford*, observes, "How sadly have we fallen that the anniversary of the day of the birth of Jesus Christ, who came to declare peace on earth and good will to men, should be spent in endeavors to take the lives of our fellow creatures in war."

Upriver at St. James Episcopal Church in Wilmington, congregants flinch at the steady concussion of the great naval guns while their minister prays, "From battle and murder and sudden death, Good Lord, deliver us."

Opposing the landing are troops from Sugar Loaf: regiments of Brig. Gen. William W. Kirkland's brigade, force-marched from Wilmington after a long train journey from Virginia, and 800 Junior and 400 Senior Reserves— teenaged boys and men well beyond the age of conscription. One of them is William Pettigrew, brother of Johnston Pettigrew, the scholar-soldier killed during the retreat from Gettysburg. Scores of them fall under the terrific pounding of the naval guns. One of Kirkland's staff officers observes, "It was pitiful to see some of those gray-haired patriots dead in the woods, killed by shells from the fleet."

Eighty boatloads of troops snake toward shore, fanning out to make landfall. First to step ashore is Brig. Gen. N. Martin Curtis, who cuts a heroic figure among the blue throng: 6 feet 7 inches tall, well-muscled, with a thick black beard—leader of the 1st Brigade of Brig. Gen. Adelbert Ames's division.

Battery Anderson, cut off from the Sugar Loaf line to the north and Fort Fisher to the south by waves of blue troops storming ashore, surrenders. Hot skirmishing drives away the rest of the Confederate defenders, some of whom are killed or captured, but Curtis's forces are stopped a few hundred yards from the fort. The fleet turns its guns on the fort once again, delivering two shells per second against its sandy ramparts. Inside Fort Fisher, Lamb knows an infantry assault is imminent.

Only 2,300 of the 6,500 troops in the armada have made it to shore. As the afternoon wears on, the weather worsens—the wind kicks up steep, heavy seas. Thousands of troops remain stranded on their transports. Curtis is undaunted, confident he can take the fort, even as the naval barrage ceases and Confederate riflemen begin firing from behind the wooden palisade on the land face.

General Butler, who has carried on a running feud not just with Admiral Porter but also with many of his own subordinates, has remained offshore with the fleet. The new firing from the fort makes him fearful about being blamed for a defeat, and he calls off the attack. About all Curtis has to show for his brave effort is the capture of 200 malnourished Junior Reserves, who are deemed so harmless that they are allowed to keep their muskets as they are marched off to captivity. One Union soldier recalls, "I never saw such a lot of spindle shanks as they were."

Curtis and 600 of his men, along with their prisoners, are stranded on the beach without blankets, overcoats, or provisions while a howling gale thrashes the peninsula.

Unaccountably, Gen. Braxton Bragg, overall commander in Wilmington, does not order the remainder of his nearly 4,000 troops at Sugar Loaf to attack the Federals. They remain on the beach until December 27, and Curtis, seething at the lost opportunity, is the last to step into a boat.

Lamb decries Bragg's inaction as "incomprehensible": "He had the force and the position."

When the fleet sails away, leaving the walls of Fort Fisher unbreached despite more than 20,000 rounds of naval gunfire, Colonel Lamb's gunners fire a parting salute.

PART II

In January 1865, the fortunes of war are changing fast.

Lt. Gen. Ulysses S. Grant supported the first assault on Fort Fisher on Christmas Eve only reluctantly. But now, south of Wilmington at Savannah, Gen. William Tecumseh Sherman has refitted his army of 60,000 campaign-hardened veterans. Instead of embarking them on transports to steam north — the original plan — Sherman has fixed on a bold new strategy: he will march them through the Carolinas, wrecking railroads and supply depots as he goes, aiming for the railroad junction at Goldsboro. There he can unite his army with troops marching in from the coast, then head north. His army will become the hammer, Grant's the anvil, with the Army of Northern Virginia crushed in between.

Grant wants a seaport through which to resupply his favorite general. The Cape Fear River is navigable all the way to Fayetteville, 100 miles northwest of Wilmington, and could provide an excellent means of supply and reinforcement. Now the taking of Fort Fisher is a prime objective, and an even larger invasion force is assembled, nearly 9,000 soldiers in twenty-two transports escorted by fifty-nine warships, this time under the competent leadership of Brig. Gen. Alfred Howe Terry, who gets along splendidly with Rear Admiral Porter.

In addition to the brigades from the first assault and an additional brigade of white soldiers, Porter is charged with transporting two brigades of U.S. Colored Troops (USCT). He complains to his aide, "We want white soldiers here — not niggers."

White and black soldiers crowd aboard the hard-used transports, embarking light and heavy artillery, and endure a rough passage down the coast. Off Cape Hatteras, violent storms buffet the leaky vessels, and confined in the stinking wet spaces below decks, the men endure a misery of pitching and rolling. But the armada sails on. By now, its target is no secret.

Both Col. William Lamb, the commander of Fort Fisher, and his mentor, Gen. William H. C. Whiting, second in command of the Wilmington district, fully expect a second assault to come soon. Yet in the face of this threat, Bragg, commander of the Department of North Carolina, withdraws most of his formidable force of 6,000 men up the peninsula beyond Sugar Loaf to Wilmington, leaving Fort Fisher once again vulnerable.

Bragg, a striking figure with hooded, brooding eyes and a famous temper, suffers from chronic migraines and is almost universally reviled for his overbearing manner and his inability to make up his mind. When it was announced he would replace Whiting as commander, the *Richmond Enquirer* trumpeted, "General Bragg is going to Wilmington. Goodbye Wilmington."

Before dawn on January 13, 1865 — just three weeks after the first assault — Union gunboats begin shelling the beach north of Fort Fisher. Two hundred boatloads of assault troops hit the beach unopposed. In the rough seas, landing a boat laden with troops and gear requires deft maneuvering. Just shy of the breaking surfline, a sailor heaves out a small anchor behind the craft. Other sailors leap over the side and, with the help of the anchor, steady the boat enough so that the men can then clamber out and wade ashore in "knee-deep water, carrying knapsacks and the sacred ammunition high up on fixed bayonets."

Out on the uncontested beach, General Terry immediately constructs a defensive line. The 37th USCT and the 5th USCT march through swampy terrain and dig in two miles north of the fort. Seven other black regiments join them, and soon they have formed a line stretching from river to sea. Their mission is to beat back any attack from Sugar Loaf to reinforce the fort.

Maj. Gen. Robert F. Hoke's regiments, dug in behind Sugar Loaf just to the north, watch them land. They see U.S. Colored Troops entrenching in a line across their front. Many of Hoke's officers want to attack the Federals while they are most vulnerable, on the beach, especially the colored troops; but Hoke fears the gunboats will make short work of any Confederate force caught in the open, and he refuses to order an attack. He awaits instructions from Bragg. He waits in vain.

Once the Union assault force is safely ashore, the fleet turns its guns on the fort. Unlike the bombardment of Christmas Eve, when many shells overshot the fort and fell harmlessly in the river beyond, this time the naval firing is deadly accurate. Lamb records that in the space of a single minute, 100 shells explode inside the fort. One after another, the heavy guns in the chambers dug into the sandy ramparts are wrecked. Projectiles rain down on the beleaguered defenders, blasting men to bits as they venture out of the bombproofs to return fire. One defender recalls, "It was the most terrible storm of iron and lead that I have ever seen during the war."

In the first half hour, the shelling knocks out the telegraph connection to Wilmington. But in the midst of the horrific barrage, Whiting and his staff find their way downriver to the fort aboard a steamer, and so do about 700 reinforcements, raising the garrison to a strength of about 1,500 — still outnumbered more than four to one by U.S. troops, and by even more counting the gunners aboard the ships.

Whiting has no faith that Bragg, ever indecisive, will commit his troops

The second naval bombardment of Fort Fisher: "It was the most terrible storm of iron and lead that I have ever seen during the war." (Courtesy of the Library of Congress, LC-DIG-pga-01164)

at Wilmington and Sugar Loaf to aid the defense of the fort. He declares, "Lamb, my boy, I have come to share your fate. You and your garrison are to be sacrificed." Indeed, the sacrifice has already begun.

In the open sand flats behind the ramparts, the dead and wounded lie everywhere. Severed limbs litter the ground behind the gun chambers. The living huddle in bombproofs under a seemingly endless rain of shells. Lamb waits for Bragg to come to his rescue. He knows that Bragg considers the fort impregnable. Both Lamb and Whiting understand now that it is not.

As daylight fades, the bombardment slackens, but it keeps up intermittently all through the night, to demoralize the defenders and deprive them of sleep. Next day, the bombardment resumes with full force. By late afternoon, more than 200 Confederates lie dead or wounded. All but three of the land-face cannons have been knocked out of action.

Brig. Gen. N. Martin Curtis, the bearded giant who commands the 1st Brigade of Gen. Adelbert Ames's division, has landed with his troops for a second try at the fort. He maneuvers his men to within 175 yards of the fort and sets them to digging rifle pits. He deploys forty sharpshooters where they can pick off any man who shows his head above the ramparts.

All of this is reported to Lamb. Certain that an assault is at hand, he determines to attack the Federals before they can launch their own attack, thus breaking their momentum. He telegraphs Bragg at Sugar Loaf to attack from the north while he comes up from the south, trapping the Union forces in the middle. He will lead his regiments out of the fort at the first sound of gunfire from Sugar Loaf. But Bragg dithers, already planning to evacuate Wilmington. At daylight, Lamb orders his advance regiment back inside the fort.

The main attack is scheduled to step off at 4:00 P.M. the following day, Sunday, January 15. The bombardment begins with renewed fury, shells "falling and bursting faster than the ticking of a watch."

In a deadly show of derring-do, 2,261 sailors and marines—including Lt. Cmdr. William B. Cushing—armed with cutlasses and pistols assault the "pulpit" where the land and sea faces meet. As they charge along the narrow, open beach, they are cut to ribbons by sharpshooters and cannoneers firing canister shot from the parapets. They never get close enough to fire their pistols with any effect. In less than half an hour, almost 300 sailors and marines fall dead or wounded. But even as their attack dissolves into a rout, it has provided a diversion for the main assault, led by Curtis, reinforced by two other brigades.

At 3:25 P.M., the bombardment abruptly ceases and every steam whistle in the fleet shrills out the signal to attack. Curtis orders, "Forward First Brigade, forward," and his men follow him in silence, tramping through the deep sand with stubborn purpose. They force a breach at Shepherd's Battery flanking the gated sally port to the Wilmington Road, overwhelming the defenders by sheer force of numbers. Many shell-shocked Confederates find refuge in the bombproofs, refusing to come out and fight.

At the sally port, defended by half a company from the 36th North Carolina, the attackers are at first cut down by volley fire and canister shot from a cannon, earning it the nickname "Bloody Gate." But Curtis's men will not withdraw. They fling themselves at the position again and again, and at last they are inside the walls.

The fighting inside the fort is savage. Men clamber across the traverses from chamber to chamber, firing down into the mass of defenders, so thick that the dead scarcely have room to fall, pinned upright by their living comrades. Men swing their rifles like clubs, hammer each other with fists, stab with bayonets. Any man who reaches the summit is shot down almost at once.

At the third gun chamber, Whiting fights hand to hand with a Union standard-bearer, attempting to wrest away his colors. He is shot twice in the right leg, critically wounded.

Lamb recoils at the carnage he sees: "Great cannon broken in two, their carriages wrecked and among their ruins the mutilated bodies of my dead

Union infantry storms the land face of Fort Fisher in a deadly and overwhelming assault. (From an 1865 woodcut in *Le Monde Illustre*; courtesy of Dr. Chris Fonvielle)

and dying comrades." On the shell-blasted parade ground, in a remarkable display of cool-headed courage, Lamb organizes troops to stage a counter-attack. Turning to the enemy troops swarming down the backside of the ramparts toward him, he mounts a breastwork and shouts, "Charge bayo-nets, forward, double quick, march!" Hardly are the words uttered when a volley of musketfire rips into his men. A Minié ball punches him in the left side and knocks him to the sandy ground, and the counterattack falters, his best officer down, the survivors scattering for cover.

From across the river, a group of soldiers' wives and mothers— evacuated before battle—watch the violent spectacle, trying to make out details through the haze of gunsmoke. Mrs. Thaddeus C. Davis, whose hus-band is a sergeant in the 40th North Carolina inside the fort, recalls, "At times my imagination would tell me that my anxious eyes were resting upon him in that little group of heroic defenders. The next instant a monster shell would explode in their midst, enveloping everything in smoke and dust. At such moments I would feel as if my heart would burst."

The end appears inevitable, even to those anxious ladies: "When the smoke would lift, we could see distinctly the lines engaged often in hand-to-hand fighting: but O! we could see so distinctly that the thin gray line was growing thinner, and that the dark, heavy masses were growing heavier."

As afternoon turns into evening, the battle rolls across the fort. The Confederate defenders are exhausted, but fresh attackers keep joining the fray. Now, to turn the tide, five regiments of U.S. Colored Troops are ordered into the fort.

The remaining four regiments of black troops facing Sugar Loaf, reinforced by the surviving marines and sailors on the beach, fend off a probing attack by Hoke's men—too little, too late, to save Fort Fisher.

With his commanders out of action, Maj. James Reilly gathers a band of thirty-two men and withdraws south across the parade ground to Battery Buchanan, the last redoubt at the extreme southern end of Confederate Point. Lamb and Whiting are sent ahead on stretchers.

Reilly has served on both sides of the conflict. Almost exactly four years before, as a U.S. ordnance sergeant, he surrendered Fort Johnston on the Smithville side of the river to the Cape Fear Minute Men. Once North Carolina seceded, he enlisted in the Confederate army and earned a reputation as one of its best—and toughest—artillery officers. His men call him "Old Tarantula" Reilly. At Battery Buchanan, Reilly is furious to discover that the naval contingent stationed there has fled, taking its boats, the only means of retreat from the fort. Hundreds of shell-shocked soldiers make their way to Battery Buchanan, but since most of his men are unarmed, Reilly bows to the fortunes of war and surrenders. He records, "It was a distressing time to me and the brave officers and men under my command."

Prisoners, including Thaddeus C. Davis, whose wife watched the battle from across the river, are rounded up and put under guard. Everyone on both sides is exhausted, thirsty, and cold. Hundreds nurse wounds from bullets, bayonets, and shrapnel, and in the darkness of full night, men collapse and fall asleep wherever they can find a place.

Guards are posted at the entrances to the bombproofs, but, unaccountably, none has been posted at the entrance to the main powder magazine, in which is stockpiled 13,000 pounds of black powder. A few curious soldiers explore the subterranean cavern, lighting their way with candles.

At 7:30 the following morning, while most are still asleep, a great explosion rocks the fort. One witness recalls the scene: "The entire structure, with a dull heavy sound that shook the surrounding country, went up into the air like an immense water-spout, with timbers, debris, and human forms flying against the sky."

Dr. J. A. Mowris, the surgeon of the 117th New York, which fought in the front line at Shepherd's Battery at the sally port, has just entered the fort, searching out his regiment's dead and wounded, and is caught in the blast. "I felt myself an atom amid the clash of the worlds," he recalls. "I felt the grave rudely closing round me, and realized the horrors of being buried alive." The main powder magazine has gone up, with horrific loss of life: Dr. Mowris revives, but at least 130 Union soldiers and Confederate prisoners are dead, wounded, or missing, according to General Terry's official report. A correspondent on the scene numbers the casualties at 265.

The assault that began with the harmless blast of a bombship weeks ago on Christmas Eve has ended with a lethal explosion in the heart of the fort, adding to the roll call of sacrifice. The toll is never calculated exactly, but the two battles for Fort Fisher have cost as many as 1,700 dead and wounded from the U.S. Army and Navy and about 600 Confederates.

Colonel Lamb, the fair-haired young commander of Fort Fisher, is down. Gen. "Little Billy" Whiting is mortally wounded. The Gibraltar of the South has fallen and will not rise again. The river to Wilmington—and Fayetteville 100 miles beyond—is open to the Union gunboats, closed for good to the blockade-runners so vital to keep the Confederate army in the field.

The idle troops at Sugar Loaf watched the battle unfold, powerless to go to their comrades' relief while their commander, Bragg, stalled. Now they brace for the five brigades that will soon march up the peninsula against them. The war has come home.

The Cape Fear River is now closed to the blockade-runners that have been supplying Lee's Army of Northern Virginia through the railroad nexus at Wilmington. Starved of rations and materiel, how much longer can it carry on? The answer can be measured in weeks.

40

WILMINGTON FALLS

The morning after a six-hour battle at the mouth of the Cape Fear River, Fort Fisher lies in ruins under a chilly drizzle. The mysterious explosion of the main powder magazine at dawn has left a yawning crater in which are entombed hundreds of men who survived the battle, blue and gray alike.

The Federal commanders—General Terry and Rear Admiral Porter—envision a quick thrust up the peninsula to capture Wilmington while its shipyards and railroads are still intact, before ammunition and stores can be spirited away into the countryside, before its garrison can escape and its hundreds of Union prisoners can be evacuated.

Secretary of War Stanton arrives on January 16, 1865, bearing a round of promotions and is presented with the battle flag that flew over the Mound Battery, where the fort's surrender took place. President Lincoln sends his congratulations. In Virginia, Grant orders a 100-gun salute fired by each of the U.S. armies in the field. Then he travels to the Cape Fear for a council of war.

But the fight has been horrific, and the victors are exhausted and demoralized. Even by the grisly standards of this war, the battlefield is a vision of hell: body parts are strewn everywhere from the massive sustained bombardment and the blown magazine. Scores of the victims are bluecoats, caught in friendly fire. One Union survivor writes, "Headless trunks, shattered limbs, and bodies lay thick on the parapets, in the traverses, as well as everywhere all over the fort."

Union army and navy forces have suffered as many as 1,000 casualties in the second battle—among them some of their most valuable field officers. Brigadier General Curtis, the imposing commander who led the land-face assault that turned the tide, was blasted in the face by shellfire on the traverse and blinded in his left eye, part of his face shot away.

Meanwhile the captured Confederates are shipped north to Fort Delaware, Fort Monroe, Elmira, and other grim prisons. Among them is Maj. James Martin Stevenson of the 36th North Carolina, who commanded the lower sea-facing batteries. His son, signalman James Chapman Stevenson, escapes Battery Buchanan in a small boat. He turns back to find his wounded father, but rockets signal that the fort has fallen. He will never see his father again.

It is a campaign of family separations. The day after the surrender, Daisy Lamb, wife of the wounded commandant of Fort Fisher, approaches the Federal lines facing Sugar Loaf under a flag of truce, seeking her husband. She is sent away.

From Richmond, Jefferson Davis, alarmed by the fall of the fortress that Bragg assured him was unassailable, telegraphs Bragg, "Can you retake the fort?" But Bragg, indecisive and irascible as ever, won't even entertain the idea. Residents fear he has already determined to abandon Wilmington. He orders a complete blackout of all war news. He withdraws all his remaining forces on the east bank to Sugar Loaf, about six miles north of Fort Fisher, under Maj. Gen. Robert Hoke.

On the west bank, Fort Holmes on Smith's Island and the garrisons at Smithville and Fort Caswell downriver are evacuated, leaving behind precious guns and ammunition. Forces under Brig. Gen. Johnson Hagood concentrate at Fort Anderson, directly across the river from Sugar Loaf. Hagood, a lean aristocrat from South Carolina, is also a veteran of Petersburg, where his brigade lost six men in ten. He is known as an unlucky commander. Now he is woefully short of troops and soon will be outnumbered by at least three to one.

On both banks of the Cape Fear, Bragg fields a combined force of fewer than 7,600 soldiers, and in the course of the next few weeks, about 900 desert their posts, disappearing into the swamps and woods. But the *Wilmington Daily Journal* stubbornly maintains, "The cause is not gone up. . . . Now is the time to try our manhood."

The 9,000 Union assault troops have been badly cut up. Terry sends one foray toward the Confederate lines at Sugar Loaf: the 4th, 6th, 30th, and 39th U.S. Colored Troops (USCT). But in a hot three-hour firefight they cannot breach the Confederate position and withdraw. One officer explains that the entrenchments at Sugar Loaf are "as strong as Lee had at Petersburg or Richmond & from water to water."

Now the Union troops endure the raw, primitive conditions of the sandy peninsula for a full month before reinforcements arrive and they begin their march on Wilmington.

The main fleet disperses, but monitors—flat-hulled ironclads with revolving turrets—and other gunboats remain to support the Union advance up the river. Porter orders that all the signal lights at the fort be maintained, to lure in unsuspecting blockade-runners.

On the night of January 16, Capt. John Newland Maffitt slips his side-wheeler *Owl* through the inlet to Smithville, where he is warned off. *Owl* sails back out to sea.

Porter assigns the job of entrapment to Lt. Cmdr. William B. Cushing, the wily young daredevil who destroyed the ironclad CSS *Albemarle* on the Roanoke River. In a single night, Cushing snares the *Stag* and the British steamer *Charlotte* out of Bermuda, and a few nights later, the *Blenheim* en route from Nassau. In the words of one Yankee sailor, "This is the kind of blockading that I like, where the prizes come to us, instead of our going out for them."

Grant has decreed that Wilmington must be taken to supply Sherman with an open port. Sherman marches north from Savannah on February 1. Grant orders Maj. Gen. John M. Schofield to transport his Twenty-Third Corps—21,000 strong—from Alexandria to the Cape Fear and assume command.

A three-pronged attack pushes upriver along both banks, with the gunboats plowing upriver in the middle and providing covering fire against Confederate artillery. They keep up nearly constant shelling, wreaking havoc, while the Confederate shells bounce off the monitors' iron plating.

On February 11, Brig. Gen. Charles J. Paine leads the assault on the line at Sugar Loaf. His Third Division, consisting of nine regiments of USCT plus an artillery brigade, has among its ranks nine Medal of Honor recipients. Maj. Gen. Jacob D. Cox, one of many white officers who have never seen black men fight, observes with admiration, "They were disciplined and well led, and went forward with alacrity in capital form, showing that they were good soldiers."

One of those "good soldiers," a former slave, captures a Confederate officer and leads him to the rear, declaring, "He's my prisoner, old massa is." And indeed, the prisoner confirms he once was slavemaster to the solder herding him toward the holding pen. It is the first of several remarkable reunions.

The USCT push back parts of the line at a heavy cost: almost a hundred men killed or wounded. But the main Confederate line holds.

Six thousand five hundred Union troops are ferried over to the west bank, under the command of Cox, a bookish former divinity student with no formal military training who has nonetheless developed into a shrewd battlefield tactician. As they march northward, liberated slaves come "running out . . . singing and shouting with joy and thanksgiving."

The blue troops advance through the marshy pine flats. Guided by a local black man named Lem Brown, Cox outflanks Hagood, coming in behind Fort Anderson—built on the two-sided model of Fort Fisher with no battlements in the rear. The monitor *Montauk* and a fleet of wooden gunboats fire more than 2,700 shells into the fort. The Union forces prepare for a dawn assault. Outgunned and outflanked, Hagood withdraws to Town Creek, a deep, unfordable tributary of the Cape Fear, leaving his dead laid out in the ruins of St. Philip's Church.

With Fort Anderson directly across the river in Union hands, Hoke cannot hold Sugar Loaf. He falls back on the junction of Confederate Point Road and a small local lane, later called Forks Road, some three miles south of the city. His men entrench behind heart-pine breastworks fortified with mounded sand.

Terry's troops chase the retreating Confederates up the peninsula and pause to regroup about halfway between Sugar Loaf and Forks Road. Cpl. Jacob Horne asks permission to fall out and visit a nearby home. The request is granted, and as the *Philadelphia Inquirer* reports, the soldier is "soon clasped in the arms of his overjoyed mother. She said, 'your brother was here yesterday; he stopped as the Confederates marched past.'"

Now his brother, Cpl. Hosea Horne, of the Wilmington Horse Artillery, is posted with his two-gun battery at Forks Road. During the battle to come, while one son attacks the other, their mother will listen to the cannon fire from her front porch.

Again the USCT strike in the vanguard, the 5th USCT leading the way, taking heavy casualties but unable to dislodge the stubborn defenders.

But events across the river decide the fate of Wilmington.

The only two bridges across Town Creek are sited with deadly accurate artillery and rifle fire. But a local slave shows Cox's scouts the whereabouts of a cotton barge, and—seventy-five men at a time—two of Cox's brigades cross Town Creek east of Hagood's lines and once again outflank them. Three thousand Federals charge with bayonets across a field of sedge broom grass, and the firing rises to such a "perfect roar" that it sets the grass on fire.

Hagood's men fall back, leaving open the road to Wilmington. The retreating Confederates burn their bridges behind them—soon repaired by Union engineers—and reach the city in darkness on February 21. Some remain on Eagles Island, separating the Cape Fear and Brunswick Rivers, site of the Beery shipyard, a cotton compress, warehouses, docks, and the depot of the Wilmington and Manchester Railroad. They methodically burn the railroad trestle and destroy everything else of value.

Across the river, cotton bales are burning and tobacco is being dumped into the tannin-brown current. Warehouses and docks are aflame as the easterly wind carries the fire from rooftop to rooftop, stopping only at the river itself.

As the 16th Kentucky and 65th Illinois advance onto Eagles Island, a battery of artillery across the river at the foot of Market Street opens fire. The rifled guns of Battery D, 1st Ohio Light Artillery, return fire, slamming accurate shots into riverfront buildings, and Hagood quickly orders his own guns to cease fire. He does not want the Federals to level the city.

Before dawn on February 22, a reconnaissance party finds that the Confederates have abandoned Forks Road. General Schofield wastes no time. He orders Terry to advance on Wilmington.

The Reverend L. S. Burkhead, assigned as pastor of the Front Street Methodist Episcopal Church in December, arrived in time to preach his first sermon to the sound of the naval guns bombarding Fort Fisher on Christmas Eve. He writes, "This was the first time in my life I had attempted to preach the blessed gospel of PEACE with the sound of WAR ringing in my ears." Now he waits at the foot of the steps of City Hall with John Dawson, the mayor. "Then came General Terry at the head of a column up Market Street, with the strains of martial music, and colors flying," he reports. Meanwhile U.S. Colored Troops, "with burnished barrels and bayonets gleaming in the bright sunshine," sing a hearty rendition of "John Brown's Body."

Though the USCT fought in the vanguard of the assaults at Sugar Loaf and Forks Road, they march in the rear of the white troops. But they are cheered by white and black citizens alike, though the wealthy class is conspicuously absent from the throng. One USCT veteran marches into Wilmington in triumph and spies his mother standing on the sidewalk. Beaming, she remarks that he left enslaved and returned a soldier and a free man.

A Union soldier records the jubilation of the black crowds thronging the sidewalks as the regiments parade past: "They all seemed to have an intuitive knowledge that their shackles were broken; that henceforth and forever, they were free."

General Terry dismounts his magnificent bay warhorse and approaches Dawson. "Is this the mayor?" he inquires.

"It is," Dawson replies.

Terry and Dawson remove their hats and climb the steps to arrange the details of the occupation. Meanwhile, as Burkhead watches, "The troops came pouring through the City, white and colored, and marched directly towards 'Northeast' in pursuit of General Hoke's braves."

It is February 22, the birthday of George Washington, the secular saint of the southern Confederacy whose portrait hangs in the war room of the Confederate White House in Richmond. To the Union troops flooding into the city, the anniversary is a fortuitous omen of destiny. At noon, the river fleet fires a thirty-five-gun salute, one for each state in the Union.

Before long, emaciated Union prisoners from Salisbury and Andersonville stream into the city at the rate of 1,400 per day for a whole week, nearly 10,000 in all. One of them, Benjamin F. Booth, will publish a shocking indictment of his jailors at Salisbury, taken from his detailed diary.

The prisoners are joined by as many as 25,000 "contrabands"—blacks freed by Sherman's army advancing through the interior.

The Stars and Stripes flies over the U.S. Army headquarters of occupation, in the finest mansion in the city, constructed by slave labor: the home of John D. Bellamy, who once sponsored a torchlight parade to celebrate the secession of the Old North State.

Bellamy returns from Floral College in Robeson County, where he and his family have been waiting out the war attended by nine household slaves, well-supplied with provisions from his plantations. He applies to Brig. Gen. Joseph R. Hawley, Terry's chief of staff, newly appointed commandant of occupied Wilmington, for permission to enter the city.

Hawley, a no-nonsense North Carolinian and Radical Republican, writes, "Having for four years been making his bed, he must lie in it for a while."

Permission is denied.

41

SHERMAN'S FINAL MARCH

He is a plain boy named by his parents William Tecumseh, the middle name after the fearsome Indian war chief from his native Ohio.

When the boy is just nine years old and his father dies suddenly, leaving behind eleven children, he is taken in by a family friend, Thomas Ewing, a politician and lawyer. Ewing arranges for the boy to receive an appointment to the United States Military Academy at West Point, where his fellow cadets, including a champion rider called Sam Grant, nickname him Cump, the name by which his friends will call him ever after. And the staunchest of those friends will be Grant.

He grows up to be a man of average height and wiry build, recognizable by his receding, unkempt red hair and beard and the intensity of his glaring eyes. He is smart and nervous, speaking in quick, often ill-considered outbursts. His attention darts from one idea to another. He writes almost compulsively — candid, passionate, even intemperate letters.

Like his friend Grant, he takes up the habit of cigars and smokes furiously, lighting the next cigar off the glowing butt of the one in his teeth.

When he is thirty years old, he marries Ewing's daughter, Ellen.

By the time South Carolina secedes from the Union, Sherman has long since resigned his U.S. Army commission and done stints as a banker and a manager. At last, in Alexandria, Louisiana, he finds his calling: superintendent of the Louisiana State Seminary of Learning and Military Academy.

He intends to bring his wife, Ellen, and their three children from Ohio to settle permanently there. He loves the South and its genteel customs. He has no moral compunctions about slavery. "I would not if I could abolish or modify slavery," he tells his brother-in-law. "I don't know that I would materially change the relation of master and slaves. Negroes in the great numbers that exist here must of necessity be slaves."

In the contentious presidential election of 1860, he does not vote for Abraham Lincoln. He does not vote at all. But when the state secedes, he speaks plainly and prophetically: "I see every chance of a long, confused and disorganized Civil war, and I feel no desire to take a hand therein."

He admonishes a pro-secession faculty member at the academy, "You, the people of the South, believe there can be such a thing as peaceable secession. You don't know what you are doing." He goes on, "The country will be drenched in blood. . . . Oh, it is all folly, madness, a crime against civilization!"

The South's cause is hopeless from the start, he maintains. The North can forge steam engines and the South can hardly make a pair of shoes. "You are rushing into war with one of the most powerful, ingeniously mechanical and determined people on earth—right at your doors. You are bound to fail." Worse, to Sherman, secession is treason. He resigns his teaching post and heads north.

There is nothing in his character, background, or training to indicate that in a very short time he will command a relentless and disciplined army of veterans, liberate tens of thousands of slaves, and write the final chapter of the war. But in the winter of 1864–65, having reclaimed an officer's commission and risen quickly to command the victorious Union armies in the West, he conceives a bold plan to restage his army in the East and support Grant's final move on the Army of Northern Virginia.

It is, in fact, his signature asset: the ability to go all in, to go for broke, to risk everything on a bold move and then follow through on it come hell or high water. And he will see plenty of both.

He cuts a wide path across Georgia, from Atlanta to the coast, systematically destroying any resource that can aid the enemy. In his army's wake lie the ruins of railroads, storehouses, bridges, government buildings, and even homes—though far fewer than he will be accused of later. He presents Savannah to President Lincoln as a Christmas present. Grant wires him to ferry his army up the coast on transport ships, but Sherman calculates that this will take two full months, and on his arrival many of his troops will be weak and sickened from the journey.

He proposes to Grant, instead, that he turn north and *march* his army toward southern Virginia. "We can punish South Carolina as she deserves, and as thousands of the people in Georgia hoped we would do," he argues. "I do sincerely believe that the whole United States, North and South, would rejoice to have my army turned loose on South Carolina, to devastate that state in the manner we have done in Georgia, and it would have a direct and immediate bearing on the campaign in Virginia."

He will lead his combined forces — the Army of the Tennessee and the Army of Georgia, more than 60,000 strong — 450 miles through Fayetteville, site of one of the Confederacy's last arsenals, to Goldsboro. There, at the junction of the Wilmington and Weldon and the Atlantic and North Carolina railroads, he can refit his army, then move on Virginia. On Christmas Eve 1864, as the first naval shells are exploding against Fort Fisher, Sherman receives Grant's telegram: *March.*

Sherman spends a month culling out the sick and wounded, procuring fresh horses and mules, and restocking ammunition, food, and medical supplies. His quartermaster and commissary train of 2,500 wagons is freighted with plenty of ammunition but carries just twenty days' rations. After that, his men will live off the country.

Mostly his troops are men who reenlisted after hard campaigning. The slackers and green conscripts are long gone. And they regard their commander as invincible, almost godlike. One soldier writes, "There never was such a man as Sherman or as they call him (Crazy Bill) and he has got his men to believe they cant be whiped."

On February 1, Sherman's army begins its inexorable progress north. It pushes up the coast in two wings: Maj. Gen. Oliver Otis Howard commands the right wing, the Army of the Tennessee; Maj. Gen. Henry Warner Slocum commands the left wing, the Army of Georgia; Brig. Gen. Judson Kilpatrick — "Little Kil" — commands the cavalry, about 4,400 troopers, many of them armed with repeating carbines that can deliver massive firepower against single-shot muskets.

Sherman's army surges through the Low Country in a track forty to fifty miles wide, the wagon trains, drawn by 10,000 mules, nose to tailboard for twenty-five miles.

Pointing his two wings in a Y formation, with a reserve held in the center, Sherman feints toward both Charleston and Augusta, forcing the Confederates to defend both cities. But instead he arrows due north for Columbia, the capital — the seat of secession and home of Gen. Joseph E. Johnston. Over the strenuous objections of Jefferson Davis, Confederate general in chief Robert E. Lee has called on Johnston to stop Sherman. Johnston writes, "Be assured . . . that knight of old never fought under his king more loyally than I'll serve under General Lee."

Like many Confederates, Lt. Gen. William J. Hardee, commander of Charleston, doesn't believe Sherman's army can possibly forge a road through the Low Country swamps, but Johnston knows his old stubborn adversary better: "When I learned that Sherman's army was marching through the Salkehatchie swamps, making its own corduroy road at the rate of a dozen miles a day or more, and bringing its artillery and wagons with it, I made up my mind that there had been no such army in existence since the days of Julius Caesar."

The going is tortuous, in steady rain, but time and again the pioneers rise to the task, hauling wagons out of mud, shouldering limbers and cannons across creeks, chopping trees and laying down the ever-lengthening corduroy roads.

Meanwhile Kilpatrick's cavalry runs rampant across the countryside, burning houses and stores, and the legions of "bummers" strip the countryside clean of livestock, grain, and any valuables they can find.

Columbia falls with barely a fight, and the first blue troops rush in skirmishing with Wade Hampton's retreating cavalry. And here one of the most shameful episodes of the war plays out, inciting recriminations and accusations and denials for the rest of Sherman's lifetime: Columbia burns. Cotton bales are fired — by either Hampton's cavalry or U.S. soldiers — and then more fires are ignited by freed Union prisoners and other bluecoats. Because Columbia was thought safe from the advancing Union army, its warehouses and homes are stuffed with all kinds of goods brought here for safekeeping, including hundreds of barrels of whiskey and thousands of bottles of wine and brandy. The occupying troops lose all discipline and degenerate into a drunken mob on a spree. They loot and burn private homes and shops, the Methodist church, and even the Ursuline convent. A number of them seize enslaved girls and women, rape them in gangs, and beat and even kill them afterward.

Sherman's conclusion about the burning of Columbia is characteristically candid: "Though I never ordered it and never wished it, I have never shed any tears over the event, because I believe it hastened what we all fought for, the end of the war."

On February 20, Sherman resumes his march. Soon his army crosses into North Carolina — to Sherman, friendlier territory. A member of his staff writes, "Our men seem to understand that they are entering a state which has suffered for its Union sentiment, and whose inhabitants would gladly embrace the old flag again if they can have the opportunity."

Sherman now orders restraint. Slocum counsels his subordinates, "It should not be assumed that the inhabitants are enemies to our Government, and it is to be hoped that every effort will be made to prevent any wanton destruction of property or any unkind treatment of citizens." While foraging to feed the army and its livestock is as necessary as ever, strict protocols are

Sherman's Final March: *Sherman's March through South Carolina —
Burning of McPhersonville, February 1, 1865*, by William Waud.
(Courtesy of the Library of Congress, LC-DIG-ppmsca-21756)

now in force. Soldiers are forbidden from entering private homes under any circumstances. Only food, livestock, and forage for horses and mules may be commandeered.

But among the contraband of war are naval stores: tar, pitch, and turpentine camps in the great forests of longleaf pine. Warehouses stacked with barrels of tar, turpentine stills, and tools and equipment are all put to the torch, and inevitably the thick stands of highly volatile pine trees catch fire. The route of the march is marked by gouts of flaming forest and plumes of thick, tarry smoke.

All along the way, newly freed blacks appear in great numbers, as if springing from the land itself. They sing and shout their liberation and fall in behind the marching soldiers.

The blue columns cross the Pee Dee, the Lumber, and the Cape Fear, the cavalry scouting ahead. At Monroe's Crossroads on March 10, fifteen miles south of Fayetteville, Kilpatrick's cavalrymen are surprised in their beds by the dawn attack of Wade Hampton's cavalry, buying time so Johnston's main force can concentrate ahead of Sherman. In the fierce skirmish that follows, the Union cavalry first is routed, then regroups and counterattacks.

Sherman's Final March

Before it becomes General Sherman's headquarters, the Fayetteville Arsenal grounds provide a shady park for citizens and grazing livestock. (Courtesy of the NC Dept. of Natural and Cultural Resources and the Museum of the Cape Fear)

The Union troopers fend off one of the last great cavalry charges of the Confederacy. Both commanders exaggerate the enemy's casualties and minimize their own, but by any count the dead, wounded, and captured number in the hundreds.

The following day, Sherman occupies Fayetteville and establishes his headquarters at the arsenal. The arsenal is a magisterial structure, both beautiful and functional, occupying almost 100 acres of meadows shaded by stands of hardwood. The main citadel, which took more than twenty years to build and was only completed on the eve of war, is a fortress 500 feet by 500 feet, with guard towers rising four stories high at the corners. The brick and sandstone walls are painted in a yellow wash, and inside the doors are mahogany strapped with brass hinges and locks—not the usual wrought iron. It is a showplace, but also a factory that has turned out for the Confederacy 10,000 Fayetteville model rifled muskets and nearly a million paper-wrapped cartridges, along with gun carriages, artillery fuses, and ramrods. Four thousand people work at the arsenal, including the women who make the cartridges.

The people of Fayetteville regard it as a civic monument, and on weekends and holidays the grounds are crowded with picnickers and strolling couples.

Sherman writes Secretary of War Stanton, "I cannot leave a detachment to hold it, and therefore I shall burn it, blow it up with Gunpowder, and then with rams Knock down its walls. I take it for granted the United States will never again trust Carolina with an arsenal to appropriate at her pleasure."

He is wary of his old adversary, Johnston, who even now is concentrating the remnants of the Army of Tennessee, coastal artillery units from Charleston and elsewhere, Hoke's and Hagood's Wilmington troops, and Junior Reserves on ground in Sherman's path. Johnston, the highest-ranking U.S. Army officer to resign his commission at the start of the war, fought Sherman from Chattanooga to Atlanta, defeating him at Kennesaw Mountain, Georgia, and inflicting 3,000 casualties. Sherman calls it "the hardest fight of the campaign up to that date."

To Col. Orlando M. Poe and the 1,000 men of the 1st Michigan engineers falls the task of destruction. They spend March 12 smashing with sledgehammers whatever equipment they can find inside the walls; the rest has been spirited off to be secreted in coal mines in Egypt, in Chatham County. Next day they rig railroad ties as battering rams and knock down the walls. Finally on the third day, they dynamite the remains and set them on fire. The flames burn so high and hot, the wind whips the fire to neighboring homes and they, too, burn. The arsenal's outbuildings burn.

Sherman's men fire warehouses and cotton mills, confiscating whatever they can use. An army comrade from prewar days seeks out Sherman at his headquarters, pleads with his old friend to spare his property. Sherman tells him, "You are here a traitor, and you ask me to be again your friend, to protect your property. . . . Turn your back to me forever."

And Sherman, no friend of even Northern newspaper reporters, holds the *Fayetteville Observer* in special contempt. Not only has it been a loud champion of the Confederate cause, but its stories have been reprinted far and wide across the South.

Editor Edward Jones Hale manages to rescue plates and some printing equipment, but his son, Edward Joseph Hale, writes what happens next: "His office with everything in it, was burned by Sherman's order—Slocum, who executed the order, with a number of other Generals, sat on the verandah of a hotel opposite watching the progress of the flames, while they hobnobbed over wines stolen from our cellar. A fine brick building adjacent, also belonging to my Father, was burned at the same time."

Hale continues his damning account:

You have doubtless heard of Sherman's "bummers." The Yankees
would have you believe that they were only the straggling pillagers
usually found with all armies. Several letters written by officers
of Sherman's army, intercepted near this town, give this the lie.
In some of these letters were descriptions of the whole bumming
process; & from them it appears that it was a regularly organized

system, under the authority of Genl. Sherman himself; that 1/5 of the proceeds fell to Gen. Sherman; another 1/5 to the other Genl. Officers; another 1/5 to the line officers; & the remaining 2/5 to the enlisted men. There were pure-silver bummers, plated-ware bummers, jewelry-bummers, women's-clothing bummers, provision bummers, &, in fine, a bummer or bummers for every kind of steal-able thing—no bummer of one specialty interfering with the stealables of another. A pretty picture of a conquering army, indeed; but true.

The steamboat *Davidson* arrives from Wilmington, now in Union hands, and Sherman opens regular communication with General Terry, whose troops plan to rendezvous with Sherman in Goldsboro, along with General Schofield's regiments from New Bern. By steamboat and mule train, he sends 25,000 camp followers—mostly liberated slaves—downriver to Wilmington. He writes to Terry, "They are dead weight to me and consume our supplies."

Meantime, he orders Terry, "I want you to send me all the shoes, stockings, drawers, sugar, coffee and flour you can spare, finish the loads with oats or corn. Have the boats escorted, and have them run at nights at any risk."

The retreating Confederates burn the Clarendon Bridge across the Cape Fear, but in less than a day Union engineers lay down pontoon bridges. After a three-day sojourn, Sherman quits Fayetteville—now a ruined city—and leads his army across the river, where the enemy is waiting.

42

JOHNSTON'S LAST STAND

Sherman's massive army streams across the Cape Fear River at Fayetteville on pontoon bridges and surges in two muscular columns northeast, threatening Raleigh to the north and the Goldsboro railroad junction to the east. Sherman's force of 4,400 cavalry and nearly 56,000 infantry seems unstoppable.

It falls to Gen. Joseph E. Johnston to stop it.

He is fifty-eight years old, of slight stature, his high forehead crowned with thinning silver hair. He favors side whiskers and a goatee. He is naturally reticent, even aloof, but his gray eyes can suddenly light up with humor. He pursues any objective with single-minded intensity. He does not like to lose. Many of his fellow officers consider him the best fighting soldier of his generation. But two flaws of character sabotage his career: he is often prickly and irritable, and he is oversensitive about matters of personal honor.

At the outbreak of the war, Johnston resigns his commission as quartermaster general of the U.S. Army to fight for the Confederacy. At First Manassas, he commands the Confederate forces as the highest-ranking officer in the army. Then President Davis reorganizes the high command, demoting Johnston to fourth in rank. He takes this as the gravest insult to his honor and enters a feud with Davis that comes to a head after he is wounded in the chest by a shell fragment at Seven Pines. When Johnston recuperates, he is posted to the western outlands of the war, far from Richmond.

But now, with Lee's army surrounded in Virginia and so many other generals dead or incapacitated, old feuds matter less than fighting spirit and competence. Johnston faces the ultimate test of his generalship: to defeat a well-equipped, seasoned army almost three times as large as his own. His only advantage is the cavalry, three divisions under Maj. Gen. "Fighting Joe" Wheeler and a fourth under Lt. Gen. Wade Hampton—all thoroughly battle-tested and superior in numbers to the U.S. cavalry under Kilpatrick.

His only chance for victory is to force one of Sherman's columns into battle separately on prepared ground—and to do this before the other two

Union corps in New Bern and Wilmington can link up with Sherman. "I will not give battle with Sherman's united army," he advises Lee, "but will if I can find it divided."

But all of Johnston's forces aren't assembled yet. Not knowing whether Sherman is aiming for Raleigh or Goldsboro, he intends to unite his troops at Smithfield, halfway between the two cities: Hoke's division under Bragg; the ragged remnants of the Army of Tennessee; Hardee's mixed column of coastal artillery and garrison units from Charleston, some 6,000 men armed with obsolete muskets; and the horse troopers — altogether, about 20,000 fighting men.

On March 6, Bragg's force of nearly 10,000 is deployed to hold off a Union advance of 13,000 infantry marching from New Bern under Maj. Gen. Jacob D. Cox. At Wyse Fork near Kinston, the Confederates battle doggedly for three days, mounting a series of fierce assaults on the Federals. But they cannot break the Union line, and Bragg once more retreats.

Now that Sherman knows the enemy lies in wait somewhere ahead, he breaks out four divisions from each wing to march without supply trains, ready for battle at a moment's notice. But he doesn't want to fight in North Carolina if he can avoid doing so. His objective is to link the armies and provide Grant with overwhelming force in Virginia. His columns continue to move fast, and on March 15, Kilpatrick's cavalry catches Hardee's troops four miles south of Averasboro. Hardee's orders are to hold up Sherman's advance long enough for Johnston to unite and position his army.

The first skirmish is inconclusive, and both sides entrench, waiting for dawn. "Hardee is ahead of me and shows fight," Sherman records. "I will go at him in the morning with four divisions and push him as far as Averasborough before turning to Bentonville." Hardee's troops occupy the boggy bottleneck between the Cape Fear and Black Rivers, blocking the Raleigh Road, and Sherman wants that road.

On the rainy morning of March 16, over sodden ground, the blue troops attack. Acting on Sherman's order, Col. Henry Case, leading a brigade of the Twentieth Corps through dense woods, emerges on the Confederate right flank and turns the tide. One bluecoat writes, "The johnnies showed their heels as fast as God would let them."

Only the sudden arrival of Wheeler's cavalry stems the Confederate rout, and again the two armies dig in for the night. But as the Union commanders lay their battle plans, Hardee's troops quietly abandon their line and night-march to link up with the rest of Johnston's force.

Janie Smith, seventeen years old, records her experience of the fighting in a letter to her friend Janie Robeson: "I just felt like my heart would break when I would see our brave men rushing into battle and then coming back so horribly mangled." A parade of ambulances delivers the wounded to barns and sheds on her family's farm, where operating tables have been hastily erected. Some are set in the open shade of great oak trees. "The scene beggars description, the blood lay in puddles in the grove, the groans of the dying and the complaints of those undergoing amputation was horrible," she writes. "The painful impression has seared my very heart."

Wrongly believing that Sherman's two columns are separated by at least a day's march, Johnston plans to make his stand at Bentonville. First to arrive at the rendezvous point is the division commanded by Hoke, the young North Carolinian: five brigades, fielding regiments from South Carolina, Georgia, and North Caronia, including 1,200 teenaged Junior Reserves and soldiers who escaped Fort Fisher.

Next on the field is the Army of Tennessee — hardly an army at all, since it numbers only 4,500 men. They are filthy and exhausted, and even their old commander, Lt. Gen. John Bell Hood, believes the fight has gone out of them. But at least one young staff officer, Capt. Bromfield Lewis Ridley, holds different: he writes in his diary, "Our army in high spirits and ready to brave the coming storm."

Hardee's troops are still a ways off, and the cavalry meanwhile are scouting and preparing to screen Johnston's army as it deploys in ambush of Sherman's advancing left wing. Hampton positions his cavalry at the house of Willis Cole, a couple of miles south of Bentonville at the junction of the Averasboro-Goldsboro and Smithfield-Clinton roads. The cavalry and Hoke's brigades will block the Union columns, forcing them to form into line of battle and then goading them to attack a carefully chosen entrenched position. When that attack fails and the enemy is reeling, the brigades will counterattack hard and drive them off.

The Goldsboro road, running east-west, defines the battlefield. To the north, the Confederates deploy on elevated ground with down-sloping open fields of fire across the Cole farm. South of the road, the country turns boggy and nearly impassable, a swampy blackjack thicket. Hoke's division blocking the road east is the anvil. Onto it will swing the Army of Tennessee — the hammer — deployed in an arc north and west.

Having scarcely rested at all, Hardee's corps begins its six-mile march at 3:00 A.M. in pitch darkness to be on the scene by dawn, the hour of the attack.

As the Army of Tennessee moves into battle lines at daybreak on Sunday, March 19, Johnston can be spied "sitting on his horse . . . with head un-covered bowing to the small remnant of the noble army." The sky is clear, and it promises to be a beautiful spring day.

The first Union skirmishers advance across the field blindly, squarely into the center of the Confederate line, and at a distance of forty yards, the 42nd Georgia rises up as one man and "a sheet of fire blazed," withering the Federal line.

Meantime, up the Goldsboro road, more blue troops feel their way through the swamps and along the cleared northern edge in a series of sus-tained attacks, each harder than the last. Bragg, Hoke's commander in the Department of North Carolina, fears a breakthrough and pleads with John-ston to send reinforcements. Johnston concedes and dispatches Hardee's strongest division, commanded by Maj. Gen. Lafayette McLaws, to aid Hoke.

Johnston lives to regret taking counsel of Bragg's fears. He later writes to Hoke, "I believe that Genl Bragg's nervousness when you were first attacked at Bentonville, was very injurious—by producing urgent applications for help—which not only made delay, but put a large division out of position."

The anvil has been strengthened, but the hammer is now much weaker—and this is exactly the moment to strike. The Federals are in disarray, caught in the open fields and flung back from the stubborn regiments firing down on them. This is the opportune moment to swing the hammer into their flanks and trap them against Hoke's division. But instead, the Confederates stand fast, and the blue troops attack uphill yet again. And a Confederate deserter helps to change the fate of the armies. He is a young soldier from Syracuse, New York, who crosses into Union lines with two fellow Northerners, "gal-vanized Yankees," who chose to enlist in the Confederate army after capture to avoid prison.

The soldier requests to see Brig. Gen. William P. Carlin, commander of the First Division, which made the attack. He claims that Johnston's whole army is arrayed on their front, preparing to swoop down and destroy them. In an odd coincidence of war, one of General Slocum's staff officers recog-nizes his old neighbor from New York and vouches for his character. The intelligence travels up the line, and now the Federals dig in hard, throwing fresh regiments into the line, while Slocum sends a courier for reinforce-ments from Howard's right wing, a hard ride of about a dozen miles away.

Johnston at last orders a massive counterattack. At 2:45 P.M. the Army of Tennessee steps off in two lines in a chorus of keening rebel yells. Offi-cers "led the charge on horseback . . . with colors flying and line of battle in such perfect order . . . it looked like a picture." The attack breaks the line and drives off Brig. Gen. George P. Buell's 2nd Brigade, along with three additional brigades. The Federals fall back through the trees in confusion, even as reinforcements try to move through them to the front. One reports that he "saw the rebel regiments in front in full view, stretching through the fields to the left as far as the eye could reach, advancing rapidly and firing as they came."

Now the North Carolinians join the attack down the Goldsboro road, catching the Federals in a crossfire. Before long, the Confederates sweep the bluecoats beyond the Goldsboro road into the blackjack thickets, where reserve troops are building breastworks. One recalls, "Just as we had got a few rails piled up, the whole *14th corps* broke pannick stricken, throwing away guns, knapsacks & everything and all running like a flock of sheeps."

But a stubborn contingent under Brig. Gen. James Dada Morgan, a fifty-four-year-old Boston Yankee, takes the field. He is a deliberate, independent-minded officer, beloved by his men. He deploys his Second Division at the crossroads. One Union officer reports, "Just as we passed the underbrush Morgan's men were swinging into line with all the precision of a dress parade. Morgan always went into battle that way."

Morgan calls up a reserve brigade to strengthen his position, deploys scouts, and orders his men to dig in deep. In less than an hour, log and dirt breastworks are thrown up, trees axed into abatis to stop advancing troops.

When the center and left collapse under the furious Confederate onslaught, one of Morgan's brigades is ordered to plug the gap, leaving him with just two brigades to hold the crossroads. The Confederate attack surges around and past them, as they collapse into an elongated square, a rock amid the maelstrom.

Twice Hoke's North Carolinians throw themselves into Morgan's brigades, whose rifles are so hot they can barely hold them.

One of Morgan's brigades, led by Brig. Gen. John Grant Mitchell, is completely surrounded, his troopers repeatedly crossing and recrossing their own breastworks to fire at the enemy. Nearly out of cartridges, they fix bayonets. Pvt. William C. Robinson writes his father, "Some Jump the Works and Hand to Hand Fight with the Rebs. Many of the Rebs are Dressed in Our Blue Clothes which Deceive us. . . . Bloody garments and bloody men strewed the ground."

But Morgan's brigades hold fast.

And six batteries of Union guns, hastily emplaced across the Goldsboro road, pour havoc into the onrushing Confederates as they come out onto the road, at last breaking their momentum.

Meanwhile a brigade under twenty-six-year-old William Cogswell rushes to the front from his position guarding the supply train. Cogswell's regiments emerge out of the dense woods and take the Confederates by surprise, counterattacking against the troops pressing Morgan. The fighting goes on until 8:30 P.M., and the weary survivors plug their ears against the moans and cries of the wounded lying scattered across the field.

On Monday, as Howard's wing arrives on the battlefield, the fighting is renewed, but the only outcome is more slaughter.

On Tuesday, the rain that has dogged Sherman's march from Savannah returns as a steady downpour. He concentrates his forces and prepares for an all-out battle he does not want. Howard's right wing deploys from the east, nearly behind the lines of Hoke's division, and the troops dig in, some occupying rifle pits dug by their enemies, in driving rain. Determined attacks push the rebels back half a mile or more. By four in the afternoon, the lines have stabilized.

But Sherman's favorite subordinate general, Maj. Gen. Joseph A. Mower, strikes out on his own. Leading two brigades, he punches through the thin left line of Johnston's army, penetrates all the way to his headquarters, and threatens to capture the lone bridge across Mill Creek—Johnston's single avenue of retreat.

Hardee gathers a force of cavalry and assorted infantry, including the 8th Texas Rangers; among their ranks is sixteen-year-old Willie Hardee, son of the general. They counterattack Mower's brigades and drive them back in a glorious and deadly charge. Willie Hardee is shot in the chest, mortally wounded.

All through the night, in driving rain, Johnston's army retreats across the Mill Creek Bridge—artillery, supply train, infantry, and cavalry in the rear guard.

The battle has ranged over 6,000 acres of farm, woods, and swamp, leaving wreckage, burned out woods and homes, hundreds of dead mules and horses, and hundreds of corpses. As many as 4,000 men have been killed or wounded or are missing in action, in a battle Sherman never really wanted to fight.

The farmhouse of John and Amy Harper is turned into a field hospital. Col. William D. Hamilton of the 9th Ohio Cavalry describes the scene: "A dozen surgeons and attendants in their shirt sleeves stood at rude benches cutting off arms and legs and throwing them out the windows, there they lay scattered on the grass. The legs of infantrymen could be distinguished from those of the cavalry by the size of their calves, as the march of 1,000 miles had increased the size of the one and diminished the size of the other."

Sherman does not pursue Johnston but pushes on toward Goldsboro. Union victory now appears inevitable. At Goldsboro, the finish line of his 450-mile final march, he links up with Generals Schofield and Terry and now commands an army of nearly 90,000 men. His ragged troops parade in trousers that are torn to the knees. As they file past, one of his corps commanders remarks, "See those poor fellows with bare legs."

Sherman replies, "Splendid legs! Splendid legs! I would give both of mine for any one of them."

Just weeks before, in Charlotte, Mary Boykin Chesnut observed Lt. Gen. Stephen D. Lee's corps heading off to battle with the ragged Army of Tennessee: "There they go, the gay and gallant few, doomed; the last gathering of the flower of Southern pride, to be killed, or worse, to a prison. They continue to prance by, light and jaunty. They march with as airy a tread as if they still believed the world was all on their side, and that there were no Yankee bullets for the unwary. What will Joe Johnston do with them now?"

After Bentonville, what indeed?

43

THE GREAT SURRENDER

The unthinkable has become the inevitable.

On April 6, 1865, Maj. Gen. William T. Sherman, encamped near Goldsboro with his entire army of nearly 90,000 troops, receives the stunning news: Richmond has fallen. Jefferson Davis and his cabinet are fleeing south and west toward Greensboro. Lee's Army of Northern Virginia also is pushing west toward the supply depot at Amelia Courthouse—with the combined armies of the Potomac and the James under Grant in relentless pursuit.

With Richmond fallen, Sherman's mission to aid in its capture becomes moot, and now he turns to a new and pressing objective. He writes to his old friend Grant, "On Monday at daylight all my army will move straight on Joe Johnston, supposed to be between me and Raleigh, and I will follow him wherever he may go."

Johnston stages a stubborn rearguard action as he moves his army from the vicinity of Smithfield toward Durham Station. At last his troops push across the Neuse. The Federals move through Smithfield and continue their pursuit.

Meanwhile, up in Virginia, Lee hopes to march south and unite his army with Johnston's for a final campaign. But Sheridan's hard-riding cavalry catches his army at Sailor's Creek and deals a shattering blow, capturing nearly 8,000 troops and eight generals, including the commander's son, George Washington Custis Lee.

On the morning of April 12, 1865, a courier brings news that Lee has surrendered the Army of Northern Virginia to Grant at Appomattox Court House, Virginia. At dawn Sherman writes Grant, "I hardly know how to express my feelings, but you can imagine them." He goes on, "The terms you have given Lee are magnanimous and liberal. Should Johnston follow Lee's example, I shall of course grant the same."

More ebullient than Grant—a famous study in inscrutability—Sherman proclaims to his troops, "Glory to God and to our Country, and all honor to our comrades in arms, toward whom we are marching." His men celebrate with a riot of cheering, drinking, and song. "The band struck up the 'Star-Spangled Banner' which they turned into 'Yankee Doodle' the martial bands struck up (13 of them) cheers upon cheers!" reports one Illinois volunteer. "When quietude again occurred the band gave us 'Home Sweet Home' and I will tell you there was many a quivering lip and glistening eye but the order is march!"

Among the loyal veterans of Johnston's army, determined to fight it out to the end, the news of Lee's surrender comes as a body blow. Men weep like children. Some of them curse and swear. Some — like Wade Hampton — vow to flee the country and continue the war from Mexico.

Many — like Pvt. Daniel E. H. Smith of Parker's battery — simply refuse to believe it is true. When a retreating veteran tells him of Appomattox, he says, "You are a damned liar!"

The veteran answers forlornly. "I only wish it were a lie."

Sherman exhorts his men, "A little more labor, a little more toil on our part, the great race is won, and our Government stands regenerated after four long bloody years of war." And therein lies the rub: the war is not over.

Though Lee is commander in chief of the entire Confederate army, he has surrendered only about 29,000 troops — surrounded and facing slaughter by Grant's far superior forces. Three times that many troops remain in the field under the overall command of Johnston — an army that is not surrounded. If his infantry can make it to the mountains, they can disperse and wage a guerilla war for years to come.

Johnston is summoned to a meeting with President Davis in Greensboro, where the Confederate government has halted. Boarding a train at midnight, he travels all night to make the seventy-five-mile journey over the worn-out North Carolina Railroad. Joining him for the meeting is Gen. P. G. T. Beauregard, with whom he served in the opening battle of Manassas. The generals confer in Beauregard's headquarters, a converted boxcar, then meet Davis at noon at a house rented by his nephew and aide, Col. John Taylor Wood.

Davis announces plans to recruit a new army from among the many deserters in the region, as well as conscripting those men previously exempt, and launching a new bold offensive. To Johnston this scheme is "inexpressibly wild" — sheer madness.

Sherman is bearing down on Raleigh. Maj. Gen. George Stoneman and 6,000 cavalry are raiding across the border from Tennessee as near as Salisbury. Farther south, the Federals have captured Selma, Alabama, and are threatening Montgomery. Mobile is likely to fall any day.

At a second conference the next day, April 13, having been briefed by Confederate secretary of war John C. Breckinridge, Davis announces, "Of course, we all feel the magnitude of the moment, the late disasters are terrible; but I do not think we should regard them as fatal." Incredibly, he continues, "I think we can whip the enemy yet, if our people will turn out."

But there are no more people to turn out. One in four men of military age in North Carolina has died in the war—a ratio shared throughout most of the Confederacy. Johnston's own army is melting away daily; exhausted men are simply quitting and quietly going home.

Johnston plainly summarizes the woeful state of the Confederate army and bluntly declares that "it would be the greatest of human crimes to continue the war." He has decided enough is enough. The war must end. He recounts, "I therefore urged that the President should exercise at once the only function of government still in his possession, and open negotiations for peace."

Beauregard adds, "I concur in all that Genl. Johnston has said."

Davis bows to the overwhelming pressure of his generals and his cabinet and dictates a letter for Johnston's signature to be conveyed to Sherman, asking for a "temporary suspension of active operations," explaining, "the object being to permit the civil authorities to enter into the needful arrangements to terminate the existing war."

In other words, he is not necessarily seeking a path to surrender but only a truce to open negotiations—and negotiations have already been tried by the Confederate government, in vain. Davis expects them to fail again; he anticipates fighting on.

It falls to Wade Hampton, adamantly opposed to any terms of surrender, to deliver the letter. He entrusts it to Capt. Rawlins Lowndes, who rides accompanied by a single private in order not to draw fire from Union pickets.

Meanwhile, Davis orders that supplies be stockpiled along the southwestern route to the mountains, through Asheboro and Salisbury, the planned avenue of retreat of Johnston's army. He still intends to carry on the war.

In Washington, D.C., President Lincoln awaits news from Sherman. On April 14, he confides to Gideon Welles, secretary of the navy, that he has once again dreamed of sailing fast on a ship toward an unknown shore. Always in the past, the dream has portended a Union victory. Now he is confident that victory will be Sherman's.

Meanwhile, in Chapel Hill, former governor Charles Manly has expressed his anxiety to David L. Swain, also a former governor and president of the University of North Carolina: "I think it is pretty certain that Johnston & Sherman will both pass over this place. Utter and universal devastation & ruin will follow inevitably. There is no difference in the two armies as to making a clean sweep wherever they go of provisions, stock & and everything dead or alive." Manly buries a packet of university papers and other valuables in the woods near Raleigh.

Swain agrees. He writes to Confederate senator William A. Graham, "North Carolina has never passed through an ordeal more severe than that which we are about to undergo." If events are allowed to take their predictable course, "suffering, privation and death—death on the battlefield, and death in the most horrible of all forms, the lingering death of famine, is imminent to thousands, not merely men, but helpless and innocent women and children."

The two confer with Governor Vance in Raleigh, urging him to seek a separate peace for the state in order to spare it the devastation that further armed resistance will surely bring. Vance dispatches them to Sherman with a letter that reads in part, "I have to request, under proper safe-conduct, a personal interview, in such time as may be agreeable to you, for the purpose of conferring upon the suspension of hostilities, with a view to further communications with the authorities of the United States, touching the final termination of the existing war."

But their train is intercepted by Hampton, who has received orders countermanding their safe conduct through the lines. As the train heads back toward Raleigh, it is captured by troopers of the 9th Michigan Cavalry. At length the commissioners are conveyed to Sherman's headquarters. By the time they make it back to Raleigh, events have overtaken them. The mayor has surrendered the city.

Sherman has taken Raleigh, evacuated by Johnston to spare it the torch. On the morning of April 14, as Lincoln recounts his dream to Secretary Welles, Sherman reviews the Army of the Tennessee in Capitol Square. "As far as the eye can reach is a sea of bayonets," marvels Maj. Gen. Carl Schurz, one of Sherman's lieutenants.

Nearby a young townswoman openly weeps. "A few days ago, I saw General Johnston's army, ragged and starved," she says between sobs. "Now when I look at these strong, healthy men and see them coming and coming—it is all over with us!"

Johnston's letter requesting a truce reaches Sherman at midnight on

The Great Surrender

April 15. He replies immediately: "I am fully empowered to arrange with you any terms for the suspension of further hostilities as between the armies commanded by you and those commanded by myself, and will be willing to confer with you to that end." He promises that Stoneman's cavalry will stop its raiding. Grant gave Lee generous surrender terms — acting on his own authority, without consulting Washington, confident he was carrying out President Lincoln's desire for reconciliation, not retribution. Sherman writes, "I undertake to abide by the same terms and conditions as were made by Generals Grant and Lee at Appomattox Court-House, on the 9th instant."

Sherman interprets the letter as an overture of surrender, and he loses no time in writing a reply. It is the morning after Good Friday. Due to a holdup at Kilpatrick's picket line, Sherman's reply doesn't reach Johnston until Easter Sunday morning, April 16. The general rides to Greensboro to confer with Davis, but he and his entourage have departed without notice, bound for Charlotte. Johnston will have to negotiate the surrender on his own authority.

For political cover, at the urging of Beauregard he sends for Breckinridge — a cabinet member — to accompany him. Hampton again is directed to act as intermediary and arrange a conference with Sherman. He pulls back all his troops a safe distance from the Federal lines so as not to provoke an accidental skirmish. This includes evacuating Wheeler's cavalry rear guard from Chapel Hill.

"A few hours of absolute and Sabbath stillness and silence ensued," writes Cornelia Phillips Spencer, a journalist and poet who would be instrumental in reopening the University of North Carolina in Chapel Hill, a little village that sacrificed the lives of thirty-five young men to the war.

The faculty and students of the university have also suffered: more than a quarter of the eighty-four graduates of the class of 1860 have died in service. Altogether, thirty-two alumni have given their lives to the Confederate cause.

"We sat in our pleasant piazzas and awaited events with quiet resignation," Spencer writes. By the time Sherman's troops arrive, just a dozen students remain. University president Swain meets the advance guard of Ohio cavalry as they jog into the village, to make sure they honor Sherman's promise of protection. They do. Chapel Hill is Sherman's last conquest.

Spencer's own loyalties are clear: "Peace we had longed for, but not this peace."

At last, after a series of miscarriages and delays, on April 17, Sherman and his staff board a train for Durham Station to meet with Johnston. Sherman, forty-five, wears the years of war on his seamed face. His red hair is disheveled, his chin and cheeks stubbled with gray-flecked whiskers. He is dressed in his hard-used blue field coat, unbuttoned over a blue vest. One observer reports, "An old, low crowned, round topped, faded black felt hat sat clapped close on his head."

His special two-carriage train is delayed for half an hour while the Raleigh telegraph operator decodes for him an urgent message. The train at last pulls out.

At Durham, Sherman mounts a white charger. He and his entourage, trailed by a company of cavalry troopers, follow the Hillsborough road for five miles. To his staff, Sherman appears "quite cheerful and at his ease, having the air of one who felt himself indubitably 'master of the situation.'"

Maj. George W. Nichols, one of his staff officers, recounts the scene: "As General Sherman rode past his picket line that sunny spring morning, the fresh breeze came laden with the fragrance of the pine, of apple blossoms, of lilacs, roses, and violets. . . . The scene was symbolic of the new era of peace then just beginning to dawn upon the nation."

Johnston rides to meet him. His silver beard neatly trimmed, his gray dress uniform pressed and buttoned to the throat, Johnston looks more like the victor than the vanquished, except for the exhaustion and care furrowed into his high brow.

Each party is preceded by a rider bearing a flag of truce. At noon, the two flag-bearers meet. The generals are summoned. They shake hands cordially, inquire after mutual friends. Sherman suggests they confer in private, and Johnston directs him to a nearby farmhouse, the home of James and Nancy Bennitt. They cannot know that the Bennitts have been made destitute by the war, have lost two sons and a son-in-law.

In the main room, which features a couple of beds, a drop-leaf table, and chairs, Sherman hands Johnston the telegram he received before leaving Raleigh: "President Lincoln was murdered about 10 o'clock last night in his private box at Ford's Theater in this city, by an assassin who shot him through the head with a pistol ball."

Sherman has not yet announced the tragic news to his own troops. "Mr. Lincoln was particularly endeared to the solders," he writes, "and I feared that some foolish woman or man in Raleigh might say something or do something that would madden our men, and that a fate worse than Columbia would befall the place."

Sherman offers immediate and generous terms for surrender—the same that Grant offered Lee. Johnston has understood that this meeting

The Great Surrender

was simply a preamble to a conference between the governments to arrange a peace. But Sherman reminds him that the United States has never recognized the Confederacy as a sovereign nation and therefore cannot negotiate with it as such. But the generals may do whatever duty requires.

Johnston recognizes the urgency of the moment, the fleeting opportunity to end the madness once and for all. But his army is not in the same dire position as was Lee's—he can still escape, and his men can fight on. He makes this clear, but in truth, he has no more heart for a war that he believes is irrevocably lost.

Now it is his turn to make a startling offer. He proposes to surrender not just the troops under his immediate command, but all the soldiers remaining in the Carolinas, Georgia, and Florida—about 90,000 men. In exchange, he wants amnesty for soldiers and officers, as well as for Davis and his cabinet. His proposal also includes restoring political and civil rights and recognizing the authority of state governments—a political as well as a military end to the war. He will secure Davis's approval.

Sherman is elated and moved by the proposal, declaring, as Johnston recounts, "that to put an end to further devastation and bloodshed, and restore the Union, and with it the prosperity for the country were to him objects of ambition." Sherman cannot guarantee amnesty to the Confederate president and his cabinet, but in all else the two soldiers agree. They will confer again tomorrow.

The night passes, blessedly, without violence, and the next day the two generals again meet at the Bennitt farmhouse. Johnston pushes for stronger guarantees that his soldiers will be restored full rights of citizenship, that officers will not suffer reprisals. He points out again that his army is far from being surrounded—as Lee's was at Appomattox—let alone defeated. He wants Breckinridge, in his capacity as a major general, to help sort out the legal details, and Sherman summons him. Tall, patrician, wearing a distinctive handlebar moustache, he walks the gauntlet of blue-clad gapers, and enters.

In the middle of their discussion, a courier arrives bearing a memorandum from John H. Reagan, postmaster general of the Confederacy, the "Basis of Pacification" from the Confederate government outlining the terms it authorizes for Johnston.

Sherman quickly reads the memorandum, then dismisses it—too "general and verbose." He sends for a bottle of whiskey from his saddlebag, pours himself a healthy shot. Breckinridge pours himself one large glass before Sherman takes away the bottle, then sits down at the table and begins to

General Johnston meets General Sherman along the Hillsborough road; it takes
more than a week of negotiating to conclude the terms of the Great Surrender that
effectively ends the Civil War. (Courtesy of the State Archives of North Carolina)

write. From time to time he takes a sip, but he offers no more to Brecken-
ridge, who later complains that Sherman was "a hog."

Along with a general amnesty, the document guarantees full political
and property rights to the citizens of the Confederate states and recognition
of their state governments.

Two copies are scribed, then both generals sign the document, confident that at last the cruel war is over. They dispatch copies of the agreement
to their respective governments. Sherman chides Breckinridge, a former vice
president, for his treason. "He answered me that he surely would give us no
more trouble, and intimated that he would speedily leave the country forever," Sherman writes later. "I may have also advised him that Mr. Davis too
should get abroad as soon as possible."

The waiting begins. In the tense interval of the armistice, Confederate
desertion increases. Gangs ransack state property and rob army baggage
trains. Governor Vance asks to be allowed to entrust the state archives to
Sherman, but Johnston will not allow it.

At daybreak on April 24, General Grant arrives in Raleigh unannounced
and surprises Sherman, still in his nightshirt. He has orders to relieve his old

friend of command, but he has not the heart to carry them out. He merely informs Sherman that Washington has denied the terms of the surrender. He does not tell him that some in the government, in particular Secretary of War Stanton, have accused him of treasonous ambitions. Sherman must offer Johnston only the terms offered to Lee at Appomattox, nothing more. Sherman writes two notes to Johnston: the first reminds him that the cease-fire will be up in forty-eight hours after receipt unless they reach a final agreement; the second notifies him of Grant's straitened terms.

Meanwhile, Davis has approved the terms in principle, but after their rejection by Washington, he orders that the infantry be disbanded, to reunite at a prearranged rendezvous. Through Secretary of War Breckinridge he asks if Johnston can mount as many infantry as possible on transport animals and join them with the cavalry; then they "could march away as far from Sherman and be strong enough to encounter anything between us and the Southwest." Johnston is appalled by the notion and disobeys the orders of his commander in chief — but his men are leaving the army by the thousands. He appeals to Sherman to meet one more time, and so on April 26, the two generals once again take up the contentious cause of peace.

They talk for hours but cannot agree. The sticking point: transportation. After Lee's army was disbanded with no provision for getting the men back home, the countryside became infested with gangs of pillaging veterans. Major General Schofield, already assigned to become commander of the department after the surrender, hits upon a simple, ingenious solution, one that will not violate Grant's directive. He writes out a second document, unconnected to the surrender terms, which simply spells out the logistical details for feeding and transporting the surrendered troops — including 25,000 rations for the malnourished Confederate troops.

In addition and unofficially, Sherman orders his army commanders to "loan" to the local farmers and merchants any captured horses, mules, or wagons not essential to the service. He makes good on his promise to halt Stoneman's ruinous raiding from the west, for which he is accused by Stanton of aiding the enemy, since Davis is still on the run. The Confederate president is captured on May 10, near Irwinville, Georgia.

General Kilpatrick's provost marshal sends a detail to buy the Bennitts' drop-leaf table, on which the surrender was signed. They offer $10 and a horse, but the debt is never paid. The Bennitt house "was being carried off piecemeal," writes a newspaper reporter, "and in due time there will be an excavation to mark the spot where the disappearing Bennett cottage now stands."

Sherman and Johnston, who never met face-to-face before negotiating surrender, become fast lifelong friends. They reunite with Grant one last time on August 8, 1885, escorting his casket through the streets of New York City.

In North Carolina, the vast tide of soldiers recedes. The hope and terror and heartbreak of Reconstruction will soon begin.

Cornelia Phillips Spencer, the poet and journalist, renders a private judgment that for many becomes the epitaph of history: "Looking back at our delusions, errors, and miscalculations for the four years of the war, the wonder is, that the Confederacy lasted as long as it did."

The long gray line has broken. The bright battle flags are furled. Out across the killing grounds of Fort Fisher, Averasboro, Wyse Fork, Bentonville, and a hundred other fields, all stained with blue and gray, a sigh of wind is the only sound, as night falls over day.

AFTERWORD

To write for more than six years about a long-ago war as if it were happening at the present moment — four composing the series and two more re-reporting and revising the material into this book — was exhilarating. The intensive immersion filled me with a depth of empathy I could hardly have imagined for the players on that epic stage — who more often than not were acting privately, out of the public eye, mostly invisible to history as it is usually written.

The experience also filled me with a kind of grief, so that, at the finish, I felt in some sense as if I too were coming home from war, having lost dear friends and loved ones, having seen my country sundered and my state devastated by violence. The voices in the letters and diaries were just that real and compelling, and the slow-motion, cumulative emotional ambush of their heartbreaking stories took me off guard and sometimes left me reeling.

Slavery — jimmied into our Constitution in a series of shameful, legalistic contortions — has rightly been called our nation's original sin, leading to the cataclysm we gently call the Civil War and trailing behind it even now a dark legacy of racial division. So part of my grief is that such an existential war should have settled the matter of equality once and for all — but it didn't. The war left us with a lot of unfinished business, including exactly how the people who fought and endured it should be remembered. I have done my best to remember them all with compassion and empathy. The ordeal they suffered was unique in our history, and we bear their legacy, morally complicated though it is.

And part of that grief comes from having stared into the face of what I have come to think of as our Great American Mystery: how so many millions of reasonable, decent people could have embarked on such a near-apocalyptic crusade, endured suffering that is unimaginable to most contemporary readers, and inflicted so much cruelty and death on fellow Americans, including their own neighbors.

I recoiled to learn of the deliberate execution of thirteen boys and men at Shelton Laurel; the wholesale massacre of surrendering black troops at the Crater at Petersburg; the capricious hanging of twenty-two captured North Carolina U.S. soldiers at Kinston; the burial alive of wounded Union prisoners at Salisbury; the savage slaughter of Pettigrew's brigade, including the 26th North Carolina, as they charged the stone wall on Cemetery Ridge at Gettysburg; and the nameless barefoot Alabama boys shoveled into a mass grave at Averasboro.

And almost more troubling were the individual deaths: Johnston Pettigrew, valorous to a fault, shot down by a Union cavalry trooper on the retreat from Gettysburg; William Shepperd Ashe, a kind father and husband, mangled to death by an oncoming locomotive while rushing home in the dark to learn the fate of his captured youngest son; William Henry Asbury Speer, homesick and dispirited, blasted in the head by an artillery shell at Petersburg; Sister Gerard Ryan, an Irish Sister of Mercy, killed by "hardships" while tending the wounded of both armies at Beaufort and New Bern; William Harding, the grieving father who traveled north to retrieve the body of his son, Samuel Speer Harding, and bring it home to Yadkinville for burial; Rose O'Neal Greenhow, the spy who drowned in the rough midnight surf off Fort Fisher, weighed down by the 400 gold sovereigns she was carrying as a donation to the care of Confederate veterans and buried in a city where she was a stranger.

But beyond the grief was also a feeling of transcendent admiration for so many of the people I came to know, who longed for their loved ones with fierce devotion, struggled with their consciences, endured physical suffering and want that we can hardly imagine, and showed breathtaking courage in their darkest hours.

Many of them, it must be said, were fighting for an abominable cause. The Confederate Constitution, ratified in North Carolina's Ordinance of Secession, contains several passages regarding slavery, including, "No bill of attainder, ex post facto law, or law denying or impairing the right of property in negro slaves shall be passed."

Alexander H. Stephens, vice president of the Confederate States of America, explained how the new constitution differed from the U.S. Constitution it was supplanting, in a speech in Savannah, Georgia, on March 21, 1861: "The new constitution has put at rest, *forever*, all the agitating questions relating to our peculiar institution — African slavery as it exists amongst us — the proper *status* of the negro in our form of civilization. This was the immediate cause of the late rupture and present revolution."

He proclaims explicitly, right at the outset, that the Civil War is being fought over slavery. There was no invasion by Federal troops, no new abhorrent tax, no unjust law passed, just the legal election of a president hostile to the institution of slavery, who took seriously the Declaration of Independence's bold assertion that "all men are created equal."

In case there be any misinterpretation, Stephens goes on: "Our new government is founded upon exactly the opposite idea; its foundations are laid, its corner-stone rests, upon the great truth that the negro is not equal to the white man; that slavery—subordination to the superior race—is his natural and normal condition. This, our new government, is the first, in the history of the world, based upon this great physical, philosophical, and moral truth."

So how are we to regard the reality of courage, sacrifice, and loyalty in service of such a cause? It is another facet of the Great American Mystery. The overwhelming majority of soldiers fighting for the Confederacy, especially from North Carolina, were not slave owners. That was for rich men, and Tar Heel boys were typically small farmers, laborers, and tradesmen. So why did they fight so readily on behalf of rich men, many of whom were exempt from service?

One answer is that a lot of them did not go to war willingly but were conscripted, and that a lot of them deserted—as many as 23,000, according to the U.S. provost marshal general at the close of the war, 70 percent of whom had served for at least a year. Another answer is that for each person the war was agonizingly personal. Each found in it what he or she needed to find: For some, enlistment was an expression of loyalty to homeplace, kin, or state, or a chance for a glorious adventure; for others, it was a holy crusade or a fight for freedom from bondage. For a few, it was the fast track to fortune, notoriety, or political power—or maybe just a chance to settle old scores with feuding neighbors. But for the rest, we stare into that Great American Mystery again. Their motives were as various as the men who fought.

Conventional wisdom holds that honorable men enlisted in the Confederacy out of loyalty to their state, which outweighed their loyalty to country. But this, too, is complicated. Prominent men like James Johnston Pettigrew and Leonidas Polk enlisted in the Confederate army long *before* North Carolina seceded, and at the time, there was no guarantee that it would. And whole Confederate regiments were raised from states such as Maryland and Kentucky that never seceded, just as Union troops were raised from North Carolina and other Confederate states.

What would have happened had North Carolina decided against secession, or even delayed it by a few months? The Confederacy would have been split—Virginia to the north and all the other states south and west.

The Army of Northern Virginia would have been hemmed in by Unionists in what would shortly become West Virginia and either a neutral or a hostile North Carolina below the long southern border—with only a tenuous, mountainous, western connection to Kentucky and Tennessee. The rebellion would not have been viable.

Historians generally agree that North Carolina was bound, sooner or later, to join the Confederacy for many reasons—Lincoln's call for troops to invade South Carolina chief among them—but it's plain the Old North State became a keystone to the whole rebellion. North Carolina was divided in its rebellion, a home front and a battleground, a critical nexus of supply trains to the Confederate armies, and a major source of troops to fight battles in Virginia, Maryland, Pennsylvania, and of course, North Carolina.

One in four men of military age in the state died of battle wounds or illness during the war—30,000 to 35,000 men. Many fell on faraway battlefields from where their bodies where never recovered. How many civilians died—women, children, free and enslaved blacks—is a calculation yet to be made with any accuracy.

And in a war in which about 10,000 named battles were fought over the course of four years, any North Carolina soldier, fighting on either side of the conflict, was likely to experience combat. All told, North Carolina fielded for the Confederacy some eighty regiments of infantry, cavalry, and artillery; more than eight additional regiments of Junior and Senior Reserves; William Holland Thomas's Legion of Indians and Highlanders; and assorted local defense companies, rangers, sharpshooters, railroad guards, prison guards, and militia companies.

For the Union, the state fielded four regiments of white infantry and four infantry and artillery regiments of what were designated U.S. Colored Troops.

The Civil War was not just an event; it was a state of life, after which private and public lives would be irrevocably changed. Even confined to North Carolina, the war was vast: Unionists in the Piedmont hanged their Confederate neighbors, Cherokees scalped Indiana troopers in the mountains, slaves on coastal plantations aided runaway slaves and Union captives, and full-scale battles erupted from New Bern to Bentonville.

Once, after a public reading of one of the episodes from this book, a man in the audience asked me, "Why should we care about all this stuff? It happened a long time ago." And the answer I found in the enlightening journey through the pages of diaries, letters, memoirs, and maps to this last battleground—the one we all inhabit—is that all the people in these pages are us.

Nearly every contemporary dilemma, political and social, was played out in this war by men and women who were far more like us than not. They loved their families, wanted to succeed at their jobs, tried their best to honor their convictions, struggled with faith and doubt, harbored prejudices, failed in ways large and small, committed acts of honor and atrocity, and finally went back to the earth—far too many of them in the bloom of young manhood.

If we wish to know ourselves, we must understand them, for we are living in the future that they created. We should know the story of that creation in blood and words.

Acknowledgments

I remain forever grateful to Elizabeth Hudson of *Our State* magazine for conceiving the idea for a Civil War sesquicentennial narrative series and reposing in me remarkable faith during four years of writing it, to publisher Bernard Mann for his commitment to the series, and to both for their ongoing encouragement. Also deserving of my gratitude are the conscientious and sharp editors who helped shape each installment: Todd Dulaney, Michael Graff, Sarah Perry, Katie Saintsing, Diane Summerville, and Jeffrey Turner. Hannah Wright, art coordinator for *Our State*, offered invaluable help locating images, as did Kim Andersen and William H. Brown of the State Archives of North Carolina, David Blum of the Moravian Music Foundation, Michelle Doyle of Old Salem Museum and Gardens, Sarah W. Carrier of the Wilson Special Collections Library, Caroline Gallagher and Bari Helms of Reynolda House Museum of American Art, David Reid of the Museum of the Cape Fear, Mrs. Leisa Greathouse of the North Carolina Department of Natural and Cultural Resources, Jim Steele of the Fort Fisher Historic Site, Nancy Ross Miller, and Barry Munson.

Time and again during the course of researching and writing, I turned for advice and guidance to my friend, colleague, and renowned Civil War historian, Chris Fonvielle, at the University of North Carolina Wilmington, and he always cheerfully obliged. At UNC Press, special thanks to Mark Simpson-Vos, who helped shepherd this book into being; associate editor Jessica Newman; Kim Bryant, director of design and production; John Sherer; Lucas Church; and Gina Mahalek, director of publicity. Katie O'Reilly took on the daunting task of fact-checking the manuscript with her typical, reassuring professionalism, ably assisted by Liz Granger. I extend a special note of gratitude to the eminent historian Mark L. Bradley, staff historian at the U.S. Army Center of Military History in Washington, D.C., who read the manuscript in draft and offered multiple suggestions to make it both more accurate and more fluent. Finally, my wife, Jill Gerard, has been my tireless supporter, reading endless drafts of stories, often taking on the role of research assistant, and always providing inspiration.

Others who helped along the way:

Heidi Appel, Burgwin-Wright House, Wilmington, N.C.;
Jan Barwick, director of special programs and events for
    the Chamber of Commerce of Kinston, N.C.;
Jeff Bockert, the North Carolina Civil War Sesquicentennial
    Committee and N.C. State Historic Sites;
Charles Broadwell, publisher emeritus of the
    Fayetteville (N.C.) *Observer*;
Dr. David S. Cecelski, independent scholar;
Samantha Crisp, Research and Instructional Service
    Department, Louis Round Wilson Special Collections
    Library, University of North Carolina, Chapel Hill;
Dennis Daniels, North Carolina Office of Archives and State History;
Al Denn, Sc.D., Burgwin-Wright House, Wilmington, N.C.;
Sister Paula Diann, archivist for the south central
    community of the Sisters of Mercy;
Michael Eury, historian and former executive director,
    Historic Cabarrus Association, Inc.;
Gareth Evans, executive director of the Bellamy Mansion
    Museum of History and Design Arts;
Grant Gerlich, CA, archivist at Mercy Heritage
    Center, Belmont, N.C.;
Betty Green, carolinakin.com, for information about
    Francis Marion and Martha Henley Poteet;
Gloria Gulledge, Averasboro Battlefield Commission
    Museum, Averasboro, N.C.;
John Guss, site manager, Bennett Place Historic Site, Durham;
Dennis Harper, guide to the battlefield at Wyse Fork;
Michael Hill, research branch supervisor, the North
    Carolina Office of Archives and History;
Josh Howard, research historian, the North Carolina
    Office of Archives and History;
Donald G. Johnson, M.D., M.A., M.P.H.,
    Brunswick Civil War Roundtable;
Tanya Jones, executive director of the Surry County Arts
    Council and great-great-granddaughter of Eng Bunker;
Dr. James R. Leutze, chancellor emeritus, University
    of North Carolina Wilmington;

Caroline Lewis, executive director of Poplar Grove Plantation;

Robert D. Maffitt for supplying materials relating to the
career of his great-grandfather, Capt. John N. Maffitt;

Candace McGreevy, executive director of the
Historical Society of the Lower Cape Fear;

A. Christopher Meekins, North Carolina Office
of Archives and State History;

Jerry Parnell, Special Collections, William Madison Randall
Library, University of North Carolina Wilmington;

Jane Phillips, president of the Historical
Preservation Group of Kinston, N.C.;

Kimberly Sherman, consulting historian at Poplar Grove Plantation;

Robert Moore Stockard Jr. for providing a copy of the family Civil
War history he compiled, "Six Stockard Boys Remembered";

Amy Thornton, state historic sites, site interpreter,
Fort Fisher Historic Site;

Dr. Harry Watson, University of North Carolina Center
for the Study of the American South;

Mac Whatley, adjunct curator of the American Textile
History Museum's machinery collection;

David Winslow, Winslow Associates, consultant to the North
Carolina Civil War and Reconstruction History Center.

Selected Sources

BOOKS

Anderson, Jean Bradley. *Durham County: A History of Durham County, North Carolina.* Durham, N.C.: Duke University Press, 1990.

Anderson, Lucy London. *North Carolina Women of the Confederacy.* Wilmington, N.C.: Winoca Press and Cape Fear Chapter #3, United Daughters of the Confederacy, 2006. First published under the name Mrs. John Huske (Lucy London) Anderson by Cumberland Printing Co., Fayetteville, N.C., 1926.

Bailey, Candace. *Music and the Southern Belle.* Carbondale: Southern Illinois University Press, 2010.

Barrett, John G. *The Civil War in North Carolina.* Chapel Hill: University of North Carolina Press, 1963.

———. *Sherman's March through the Carolinas.* Chapel Hill: University of North Carolina Press, 1956.

Bellamy, Ellen Douglas. *Back with the Tide.* Wilmington, N.C.: Bellamy Mansion Museum of History and Design Arts, 2002.

Bellamy, John D. *Memoirs of an Octogenarian.* Privately printed, n.d.

Berlin, Ira, Narc Favreau, and Stephen F. Miller, eds. *Remembering Slavery: African Americans Talk about Their Personal Experience of Slavery and Emancipation.* New York: New Press, 1998.

Blackman, Ann. *Wild Rose: Rose O'Neale Greenhow, Civil War Spy.* New York: Random House, 2005.

Booth, Benjamin F. *Dark Days of the Rebellion, or Life in Southern Military Prisons.* 1897. Reprint, Garrison, La.: Meyer Publishers, n.d.

Bradley, Mark L. *This Astounding Close: The Road to Bennett Place.* Chapel Hill: University of North Carolina Press, 2000.

Brown, Louis A. *The Salisbury Prison.* Wendell, N.C.: Avera Press, 1980.

Burton, Katherine. *His Mercy Endureth Forever.* Tarrytown, N.Y.: Sisters of Mercy, 1946.

Butler, Carroll B. *Treasures of the Longleaf Pines Naval Stores.* Shalimar, Fla: Tarkel Publishing, 1998.

Campbell, Edward D. C., and Kym S. Rice, eds. *A Woman's War: Southern Women, Civil War, and the Confederate Legacy.* Richmond: Museum of the Confederacy; Charlottesville: University Press of Virginia, 1996.

Carter, Alden R., ed. *The Sea Eagle: The Civil War Memoir of Lt. Cdr. William B. Cushing, U.S.N.* Plymouth, U.K.: Rowman & Littlefield, 2009.

Casstevens, Frances H. *The Civil War and Yadkin County, North Carolina: A History*. Jefferson, N.C.: McFarland, 1997.

Cecelski, David S. *The Fire of Freedom: Abraham Galloway and the Slaves' Civil War*. Chapel Hill: University of North Carolina Press, 2012.

———. *The Waterman's Song: Slavery and Freedom in Maritime North Carolina*. Chapel Hill: University of North Carolina Press, 2001.

Clinard, Karen L., and Richard Russell, eds. *Fear in North Carolina: The Civil War Journal and Letters of the Henry Family*. Asheville, N.C.: Reminiscing Books, 2008.

Cornelius, Steven H. *Music of the Civil War Era*. Westport, Conn.: Greenwood Press, 2004.

Day, William A. *A True History of Company I, 49th Regiment, North Carolina Troops, in the Great Civil War Between the North and the South, by A. Day, a Member of Company I*. Newton, N.C.: Privately printed at the Enterprise Job Offices, 1897.

Elliott, Robert G. *Ironclad of the Roanoke: Gilbert Elliott's Albemarle*. Shippensburg, Pa.: White Mane, 1994.

Faust, Drew Gilpin. *This Republic of Suffering: Death and the American Civil War*. New York: Knopf, 2008.

Fonvielle, Chris E., Jr. *The Wilmington Campaign: Last Rays of Departing Hope*. El Dorado Hills, Calif.: Savas, 1991.

Forbes, Ella. *African American Women during the Civil War*. New York: Garland, 1998.

Garafalo, Robert, and Mark Elrod. *A Pictorial History of Civil War Era Musical Instruments and Military Bands*. Missoula, Mont.: Pictorial Histories Publishing Co., n.d.

Gould, William B., IV. *Diary of a Contraband: The Civil War Passage of a Black Sailor*. Stanford, Calif.: Stanford University Press, 2002.

Govan, Gilbert, and James W. Livingood. *General Joseph E. Johnston, C.S.A.: A Different Valor*. Old Saybrook, Conn.: Konecky & Konecky, 1956.

Gragg, Rod. *Confederate Goliath: The Battle of Fort Fisher*. New York: HarperCollins, 1991.

Hadden, Sally E. *Slave Patrols*. Cambridge, Mass.: Harvard University Press, 2001.

Hagood, Butler. *Memoirs of the War of Secession from the Original Manuscripts of Johnson Hagood, Brigadier General, C.S.A.* Columbia, S.C.: The State Company, 1910.

Hardy, Michael C. *A Short History of Watauga County*. Boone, N.C.: Parkway Publishers, 2005.

Heaps, Willard A., and Porter W. Heaps. *The Singing Sixties*. Norman: University of Oklahoma Press, 1960.

Herron, Sister Mary Eulalia. *The Sisters of Mercy in the United States*. New York: Macmillan, 1929.

Hess, Earl J. *Into the Crater: The Mine Attack at Petersburg*. Columbia: University of South Carolina Press, 2011.

Hesseltine, William Best. *Civil War Prisons*. New York: Frederick Ungar, 1964.

Hughes, Nathaniel Cheairs, Jr. *Bentonville: The Final Battle of Sherman and Johnston*. Chapel Hill: University of North Carolina Press, 1996.

Inscoe, John C., and Gordon B. McKinney. *The Heart of Confederate Appalachia: Western North Carolina in the Civil War*. Chapel Hill: University of North Carolina Press, 2000.

Johnston, Frontis W., ed. *The Papers of Zebulon Baird Vance*. Vol. 1, *1843–1862*. Raleigh: State Department of Archives and History, 1963.

Jolly, Ellyn Ryan, CCD. *Nuns of the Battlefield*. 1927. Reprint, Whitefish, Mont.: Kessinger Publishing, 2010.

Joslyn, Mauriel P. *Immortal Captives*. Shippensburg, Pa.: White Mane, 1996.

Keegan, John. *The American Civil War: A Military History*. New York: Knopf, 2009.

Lawing, Carol, and Mike Lawing, eds. *My Dearest Friend: The Civil War Correspondence of Cornelia McGimsey and Lewis Warlick*. Durham, N.C.: Carolina Academic Press, 2000.

Leon, Louis. *Diary of a Tar Heel Confederate Soldier*. Santa Clara, Calif.: Stone Publishing Company, 1913.

Martin, Isabella D., and Myrta Lockett Avery, eds. *A Diary from Dixie, as Written by Mary Boykin Chesnut, Wife of James Chesnut, Jr., United States Senator from South Carolina, 1859–1861, and Afterward an Aide to Jefferson Davis and a Brigadier-General in the Confederate Army*. New York: Appleton, 1905.

Martine, Arthur. *Martine's Hand-Book of Etiquette and Guide to True Politeness*. New York: Dick and Fitzgerald, 1866.

McGowan, Faison Wells, and Pearl Canady McGowan. *Duplin's History and Government*. Raleigh: Edwards and Broughton, 1971.

McKinney, Gordon B. *Zeb Vance: North Carolina's Civil War Governor and Gilded Age Political Leader*. Chapel Hill: University of North Carolina Press, 2004.

McPherson, James M. *Marching toward Freedom: The Negro in the Civil War, 1861–1865*. New York: Knopf, 1965.

McWhirter, Christian. *Battle Hymns: The Power and Popularity of Music in the Civil War*. Chapel Hill: University of North Carolina Press, 2002.

Mitchell, Memory F. *Legal Aspects of Conscription and Exemption in North Carolina, 1861– 1865*. Chapel Hill: University of North Carolina Press, 1965.

Mobley, Joe A., ed. *The Papers of Zebulon Baird Vance*. Vol. 2, *1863*. Raleigh: Division of Archives and History, North Carolina Department of Cultural Resources, 1995.

Moore, John Hammond, ed. *The Confederate Housewife*. New York: Summerhouse Press, 1997.

Nolan, Alan T. *Lee Considered: General Robert E. Lee and Civil War History*. Chapel Hill: University of North Carolina Press, 1991.

Olson, Kenneth E. *Musket and Music*. Westport, Conn.: Greenwood Press, 1981.

Outland, Robert B. *Tapping the Pines: The Naval Stores Industry in the American South*. Baton Rouge: Louisiana State University Press, 2004.

Paludan, Phillip Shaw. *Victims: A True Story of the Civil War*. Knoxville: University of Tennessee Press, 1981.

Phifer, Edward W., Jr. *Burke County: A Brief History*. Raleigh: North Carolina Department of Cultural Resources, Division of Archives and History, 1979.

Reid, Richard M. *Freedom for Themselves: North Carolina's Black Soldiers in the Civil War Era*. Chapel Hill: University of North Carolina Press, 2008.

Roske, Ralph J., and Charles Van Doren. *Lincoln's Commando: The Biography of W. B. Cushing, U.S.N.* New York: Harper & Brothers, 1957.

Schneller, Robert J., Jr. *Cushing: Civil War Seal*. Washington, D.C.: Brassey's, 2004.

Scott, John Anthony. *The Ballad of America*. Carbondale: Southern Illinois University Press, 1983.

Sherman, William Tecumseh. *Memoirs of General W. T. Sherman*. New York: Library of America, 1990.

Silo, Mark. *The 115th New York in the Civil War: A Regimental History*. Jefferson, N.C.: McFarland, 2007.

Silverman, Jerry. *Just Listen to This Song I'm Singing: African-American History through Song.* Minneapolis: Millbrook Press, 1996.

Simpson, Brooks D. *Let Us Have Peace: Ulysses S. Grant and the Politics of War and Reconstruction, 1861–1868.* Chapel Hill: University of North Carolina Press, 1991.

Simpson, Brooks D., and Jean V. Berlin, eds. *Sherman's Civil War: Selected Correspondence of William T. Sherman, 1860–1865.* Chapel Hill: University of North Carolina Press, 1999.

Sisters of Mercy of New York. *The Golden Milestone, 1846–1896: Fifty Years of Loving Labor among the Poor and Suffering, by the Sisters of Mercy of New York City.* New York: Benziger Brothers, 1896.

Smith, John David, ed. *Black Soldiers in Blue: African American Troops in the Civil War Era.* Chapel Hill: University of North Carolina Press, 2002.

Soderland, Jean R. *Quakers and Slavery: A Divided Spirit.* Princeton, N.J.: Princeton University Press, 1985.

Southern, Ellen. *The Music of Black Americans.* New York: Norton, 1997.

Speer, Allen Paul, ed. *Voices from Cemetery Hill: The Civil War Diary, Reports, and Letters of Colonel William Henry Asbury Speer, 1861–1864.* Johnson City, Tenn.: Overmountain Press, 1997.

Spencer, Cornelia Phillips. *The Last Ninety Days of the War in North Carolina.* Watchman Publishing Company, 1866. Accessed through "Documenting the American South" digital archive, University of North Carolina, Chapel Hill.

Trotter, William R. *Bushwhackers.* Winston-Salem, N.C.: John F. Blair, 1988.

———. *Ironclad and Columbiads.* Winston-Salem, N.C.: John F. Blair, 1989.

———. *Silk Flags and Cold Steel.* Winston-Salem, N.C.: John F. Blair, 1988.

Viol, Dorothy Denneen, and James M. Volo. *Daily Life in Civil War America.* Westport, Conn.: Greenwood Press, 1998.

Wall, James W. *A Brief History of Davie County.* Raleigh: North Carolina Department of Cultural Resources, Division of Archives and History, 1976.

Watson, Alan D. *Edgecombe County: A Brief History.* Raleigh: North Carolina Department of Cultural Resources, Division of Archives and History, 1979.

Weinstein, Maurice A., ed. *Zebulon B. Vance and "The Scattered Nation."* Charlotte: Wildacres Press, 1995.

Witt, John Fabian. *Lincoln's Code: The Laws of War in American History.* New York: Free Press, 2012.

Yearns, W. Buck, Jr., and John G. Barrett, eds. *North Carolina Civil War Documentary.* Chapel Hill: University of North Carolina Press, 1980.

Younce, W. H. *The Adventures of a Conscript.* Cincinnati: Editor Publishing Co., 1901.

ARTICLES

Auman, William T., and David D. Scarboro. "The Heroes of America in Civil War North Carolina." *North Carolina Historical Review* 58, no. 4 (October 1981).

Browne, Maj. Gary D. "Prisoner of War Parole: Ancient Concept, Modern Utility." *Military Law Review* 156.

Bynum, Victoria E. "The Five Classes of Antebellum Women in North Carolina." *Tar Heel Junior Historian* 36, no. 1 (Fall 1996).

Collins, Donald E. "War Crimes or Justice?" In *The Art of Command in the Civil War*, edited by Steven E. Woodworth. Lincoln: University of Nebraska Press, 1998.

Heiser, John. "The Life of a Civil War Soldier." Gettysburg National Military Park.

Holmes, Michael I. "American Fretted Instrument Musical Instrument Makers, pre-Civil War to WWII." http://www.mugwumps.com/AmerInstMkr.html.

Honey, Michel K. "The War within the Confederacy: White Unionist of North Carolina." *Journal of the National Archives* 18, no. 2 (Summer 1986).

Norris, David A. "Clark, Henry Toole." In *The Encyclopedia of the American Civil War*, edited by David Stephen Heidler, Jeanne T. Heidler, David J. Coles, and James M. McPherson. New York: Norton, 2002.

Ruane, Michael E. "After 1863 Battle of Gettysburg, a Grisly but Noble Enterprise to Honor the Fallen." *Washington Post*, Local, September 13, 2013.

OTHER DOCUMENTS AND SOURCES

Dix, Maj. Gen. John A., USA, and Maj. Gen. D. H. Hill. "The Dix-Hill Cartel." July 22, 1862. In *The War of the Rebellion: A Compilation of the Official Records of the Union and Confederate Armies*, ser. 2, 4:265–68. Washington, D.C.: Government Printing Office, 1899.

Johnson, General Bushrod. "Report on Operations in SW Virginia and North Carolina: The Richmond Campaign." August 20, 1864. In *The Siege of Petersburg Online*, http://www.beyondthecrater.com/resources/ors/vol-xl/unpublished-reports-vol-xl/upr-18640616-bushrod-r-johnson-june-16-18-1864/.

Johnston, Cynthia. "Dixie." National Public Radio for the "Present at the Creation" series on *Morning Edition*. November 11, 2002.

A. J. Lineback papers, ca. 1861–1863, ca, 1914. Southern Historical Collection, Louis Round Wilson Special Collections Library, University of North Carolina, Chapel Hill.

ORGANIZATIONS

Averasboro Battlefield and Museum

Bellamy Mansion Museum of History and Design Arts, Wilmington, N.C.

Bentonville Battlefield Historic Site

Charlotte Mecklenburg County Library

Chimborazo Hospital, Richmond National Battlefield Park, Richmond, Va.

Department of Creative Writing and the College of Arts and Sciences, University of North Carolina Wilmington

Fort Anderson and Brunswick Town Historic Site

Fort Fisher Historic Site

Gaston County Public Library

Historic Cabarrus Association, Inc.

Historical Society of the Lower Cape Fear

Moravian Music Foundation, Salem, N.C.

Museum of the Cape Fear and Arsenal Park

National Park Service

North Carolina Department of Cultural Resources, Division of Archives and History

North Carolina Civil War and Reconstruction History Center
North Carolina State Museum of History
North Carolina Transportation Museum
Petersburg National Battlefield
Poplar Grove Plantation
Richmond National Battlefield Park
Special Collections at the William Madison Randall Library
    at the University of North Carolina Wilmington
Wilmington Railroad Museum
Wilson Library, University of North Carolina, Chapel Hill

Index

Page numbers in italics refer to illustrations.

208–9, 272, 291; surrender of, 62, 313; in
    Virginia, 1, 131
Army of Tennessee (CSA), 3, 146, 304, 307;
    at Bentonville, 308–12
Army of the James (USA), 313
Army of the Potomac (USA), 32, 246, 260,
    313
Army of the Tennessee (USA), 300, 316
artillery, 10, 76, 98, 106, 139, 194, 236, 259,
    270, 290; at Bentonville, 310–11; canister
    and grapeshot used by, 10, 43, 180, 213,
    223, 259, 288; at Chancellorsville, 59–60;
    coastal, 304, 307; Confederate, 8, 223,
    261; at Fort Fisher, 280, 281, 282, 287; at
    Gettysburg, 211, 213; mortars, 259, 263,
    281; types of, 281, 282, 283; Union, 30, 110,
    223, 262, 285
Arwood, James, 101
Ashe, Gov. Samuel, 205
Ashe, Capt. Samuel A'Court (CSA), 203,
    207
Ashe, Sarah Ann, 207
Ashe, Col. William Shepperd (CSA), 203–
    9; death of, 208, 324; portrait of, 204;
    Wilmington and Weldon Railroad and,
    203, 205, 207–8
Asheboro, 45, 315
Ashe County, 266, 267, 272
Asheville, 6, 20, 94, 95, 109, 183, 273
Ashland, Va., 142
Associated Press (AP), 184
Astoogatogeh, Lt. John (CSA), 97, 99–100
Atlanta, Ga., 153; Sherman takes, 110, 184,
    272, 299, 304
Atlantic and North Carolina Railroad, 300
Atlantic Hotel, Beaufort, N.C., 251, 252, 257
Augusta, Ga., 206, 300
Averasboro, 307, 322, 324; road to, 308, 310
Averell, Brig. Gen. William W. (USA), 125
Avery, Col. Isaac (CSA), 213
Avery, William Waightstill, 272

Bacot, Richard J. (CSA), 50
Bahamas, 163, 279
Baily, Sgt. (CSA), 231
Ball's Bluff, Battle of, 119
Baltimore, Md., 72, 75–76, 95
bands and musicians, 22, 44, 71–78, 241, 296,
    314; of 4th North Carolina, 183, 186, 187;

of 26th North Carolina Regiment, 64–70;
    buglers, 66, 76, 110; drummer boys, 10,
    66, 67; field musicians in command
    and control system, 66–67; fifers, 66;
    as stretcher bearers, 54, 67, 187. See also
    musical instruments; songs, hymns, and
    anthems
Baptist Gap, 99
Baptists, 87, 122, 135, 139, 145, 222
Barbados, 164
barbecues, 128, 129
Barhamville Academy (Columbia, S.C.), 12
Barnum, P. T., 120
Bartlett, Lt. Col. William C. (USA), 101, 102
Barton, Brig. Gen. Seth M. (CSA), 233, 236,
    237
Batchelder's Creek, 237, 240, 242
Bates, Lt. Col. Delevan (USA), 264
Battery Anderson, 26, 284
Battery Buchanan, at Fort Fisher, 281, 290,
    293
battle flags and regimental colors, 6–8, 10,
    211, 231, 288, 292, 322
Beaufort, 2, 153, 243, 251, 255, 324; seized by
    Union troops, 49, 191, 252
Beaufort, S.C., 51
Beaufort County, 245
Beaufort Inlet, 21
Beauregard, Gen. Pierre Gustave Toutant
    (CSA), 168, 169, 170, 258; Johnston and,
    314, 315, 317
Beecham, Lt. Robert (USA), 263
Beecher, Col. James Chaplain (USA), 116
Beech Grove, Batchelder's Creek, 237
Beery shipyard (Eagle Island, Wilmington),
    296
Bell, Gilbert, 230
Bellamy, John, Jr., 13
Bellamy, Dr. John D., 24, 26, 44, 198–99, 297
Bellamy, Marsden (CSA), 14
Bellamy, Mary Elizabeth ("Belle"), 12, 15
Bellamy, William (CSA), 14
Bellamy family, 11–12, 15
Bellamy mansion, 11–15; becomes Union
    headquarters, 44, 297; plasterwork in,
    24, 199
Benjamin, Judah P., Confederate secretary
    of war, 16, 205
Bennitt, Alphonso, 80, 84

Bennitt, Eliza. *See* Duke, Eliza Bennitt

Bennitt, James, 79–80, 82, 318; Johnston's surrender and, 84–85

Bennitt, Lorenzo (CSA), 80, 84

Bennitt, Martha Shields (Mrs. Lorenzo Bennitt), 80, 84

Bennitt, Nancy Leigh Pierson (Mrs. James Bennitt), 79–80, 82, 84–85, 318

Bennitt family, 79–80, 84

Bennitt Farm, 79–80; Johnston surrenders at, 3–4, 84–85, 101, 318–19, 321

Benson, Berry (CSA), 109

Benson, Pvt. George Washington (CSA), 283

Benton, Thomas Hart, 168

Bentonville, 307, 322

Bentonville, Battle of, 3, 307–12, 326

Bermuda, 279, 294

Bertie County, 245

Bethania, 94

Betsey (slave), 275

Betts, Rev. Alexander Davis (CSA), 141–46; portrait of, *144*

Betts, Eddie, 142

Betts, Mary, 141, 143, 145

Biblical Recorder, 139–40, 146

Big Bethel, Battle of, 230, 275

Biggs, Basil, 216

Bill (slave), 199

Black River, 307

blacks and African Americans, 55, 118, 216, 296; racism against, 20, 24, 285; as watermen, 25–26. *See also* black soldiers; free blacks; freed slaves; runaway slaves; slaves

black soldiers, 2, 112–18, 155–59, 240, 245–50, 285; slaughtered at Petersburg, 263–64, 324. *See also* United States Colored Troops

Bladen, 143

Blenheim, from Nassau, 294

blockade-runners, 2, 17, 27, 82, 105, 163–64, 167, 173, 196, 202, 294; Cape Fear River and, *161*, 291; Wilmington and, 14, 278–79. *See also* Confederate navy: *names of specific vessels*

Blue Ridge Mountains, 45

Blue Ridge Railroad, 94

Bob (slave), 199

Boetticher, Capt. Otto (USA), 34–35, *35*, 38

Bohemian Brigade (of Northern newspaper war correspondents), 184

Bonarva Plantation (Washington County), 225

Boone, 6

Booth, Pvt. Benjamin F. (USA): diary of, 42, 44, 297; on Salisbury POW camp, 41–43

Booth, John Wilkes, 140

Boston, Mass., 25, 36, 117, 120

Boucher, William, 72

Bower, Col. George (CSA), 272–73

Bradford, Capt. N. G. (CSA), 212

Brady, Matthew, 171, *172*

Bragg, Gen. Braxton (CSA), 3, 284, 285–88, 291, 293, 307, 309

Branch, Lt. Col. James R. (CSA), 239

Branch, Brig. Gen. Lawrence O'Bryan (CSA), 21

Brannigan, Cpl. Felix (USA), 246

Brawley, Pvt. R. M. (CSA), 187

Breckinridge, Maj. Gen. John C. (CSA), 196–97, 315; Johnston's surrender and, 317, 319–21

Brest, France, 165, 173

bridges, 256, 295, 299, 305; for railroads, 99, 194, 205, 208, 241, 256, 296

Briedz, Edward A. (CSA), 65

Bright, Daniel, 248–49

Bristoe, Va., 131

Bristol, Tenn., 86–87

Brittain, Andrew J. (USA), hanged by Pickett, 240–41

Brock, John J. (USA), hanged by Pickett, 240–41

Brock, Joseph (USA), hanged by Pickett, 240–41

Brodie, Sam, 277

Brout, David, 257

Brown, Capt. John, 164–65

Brown, John, abolitionist, 75, 155, 280

Brown, Gov. Joseph E. (Ga.), 17, 205

Brown, Lem, 295

Browne, Junius H., 41, 42

Brown Mountain, 272

Bruhl, Father, 251, 254

Brunswick County, 141, 245

Brunswick River, 295

Bryan, Lewis (USA), hanged by Pickett, 240

Cedar Creek, Battle of, 41, 100, 272
Cemetery Hill, Gettysburg, 133
Cemetery Hill, Petersburg, 263
Cemetery Ridge, Gettysburg, 32, 62, 223, 235; 26th North Carolina at, 69, 213, 324; North Carolina casualties at, 49, 213
Cemetery Ridge, Petersburg, 261
Chambersburg, Pa., 124–25
Chancellorsville, Battle of, 59–60, 134, 142, 208, 210; North Carolinians at, 32, 109, 133, 183, 187
Chancellorsville, Va., 57, 63
Chandler, Jasper, 88
Chanse, William, 23
Chapel Hill, 51, 80, 141–43, 146, 219, 222, 316–17. *See also* University of North Carolina
chaplains, 113, 116, 141–46, 193; in Confederate army, 137, 138, 230, 239
Chapultepec, Battle of (Mexican War), 9
Charleston, S.C., 11, 14, 51, 75, 160, 216, 218, 226, 278, 307; Pettigrew in, 219–20; Sherman and, 2, 300; slave trade and, 273, 274; Union siege of, 114, 117–18, 158. *See also* Fort Sumter
Charlotte, 2, 48, 312, 317
Charlotte, capture of, 294
Charlotte and South Carolina Railroad, 206
Chatham County, 258, 267, 304; Quakers and, 45, 135
Chattanooga, Tenn., 304
Cheraw, S.C., 109–10
Cherokee, Eastern, 92–104, 326
Cherokee, Western Band of, 93, 96
Cherokee language, 93
Cherokee Legion, 97–102, 326
Cherokee Nation, 97
Chesnut, Mary Boykin, 312
Chicago, 171
Chicago Times, 184, 245
Chickahominy River, Va., 30, 131
Chickamauga, Battle of, 231
Chickasaws, 97
children, 160; deaths of, 149, 152, 227–28; diseases and illnesses of, 86, 88, 219; as orphans, 92, 168; as slaves, 128, 153
Chimborazo Hospital (Richmond, Va.), 53, 55, 130, 142
chloroform, 56, 60, 110, 214

Choctaws, 97
Chowan County, 250
Chowan River, 25–26, 194, 248
Christ Episcopal Church (New Bern), 115
Christian Methodist Church, 135
Churchill, Rev. Orrin, 49
Citadel, The (Charleston, S.C.), 220
City Point, Va., 69
civil rights, 118, 319
Clarendon Bridge, 305
Clark, Gov. Henry T., 17, 18, 46–47
Clark, Pvt. M. T. (CSA), 187
Clark, Walter, 76
Clendennin, Monroe, 132
Cleveland County, 258
coffee, 81, 106, 110, 252, 279
Coffin, Abel, 119–20
Coffin, Thomas A., 51
Cogswell, William, 311
Cohen, Pvt. J. A. (CSA), 187
Cold Harbor, Battle of, 10, 33, 38, 54, 62, 142, 233
Cole, Willis, farmhouse of, 308
College of New Jersey (Princeton College), 128
Colored Ladies Relief Association, 250
Columbia, S.C., 12, 15; burning and looting of, 2, 301, 318; Sherman and, 110, 300
Columbus, Ohio, 125
Columbus County, 11
Committees of Safety, 52
Condon, Kit, 253
Confederacy, Confederate States of America (CSA): "breadbasket of," 100; capital of, 3, 313; communities in, 128; POWs and, 32; racial codes of, 116; sabotage against, 2; slavery and, 324; states' rights and, 205–6; war correspondents of, 184. *See also* Confederate government
Confederate army, 66, 91, 101–2; casualties in, 57, 210; chaplains in, 137, 138, 230, 239; courts-martial in, 101, 149, 239, 240, 248; engineers of, 176, 220, 280, 281; Medical Department, 53, 54; Quartermaster Corps, 17; uniforms of, 5, 17, 21, 65, 81, 124, 173. *See also* arms and ammunition; artillery; cavalry; Confederate military units; Confederate officers; Confederate

troops; conscription, conscripts; disease, diseases

Confederate government, 47; abandons Richmond, 313; "Basis of Pacification" by, 319; Congress of, 98; Constitution of, 5, 324; diplomatic relations of, 96, 173; "Dixie" as anthem of, 73–74; Eastern Cherokee ally with, 96–97; England and, 173; flags of, 7, 76; ignores U.S. copyright, 75; muddled policies of, 16; North Carolina's relationship with, 17–18, 45, 47–48, 50, 206, 267, 325–26; *North Carolina Standard* vs., 186; not recognized by United States, 319; POWs and, 39; prints currency, 108; salt policy of, 86; suspends habeas corpus, 10; taxation by, 149. *See also* conscription, conscripts

Confederate military units: 1st North Carolina Artillery Battalion, 280; 1st North Carolina Cavalry, 155, 247; 1st North Carolina Infantry, 7, 130; 1st Regiment of North Carolina Volunteers, 109; 3rd North Carolina Artillery Battalion, 280; 3rd North Carolina Regiment, 57, 58; 3rd Regiment of North Carolina Volunteers (became 13th Regiment of North Carolina Volunteers), 130, 131; 4th North Carolina Infantry, 183, 187, 228; 5th Regiment of North Carolina Volunteers (became 15th Regiment of North Carolina Volunteers), 129, 130–31, 132; 6th North Carolina Infantry, 279; 7th North Carolina Infantry Regiment, 48; 10th Regiment, North Carolina Artillery, 238; 10th North Carolina Troops, 280; 13th Regiment of North Carolina Volunteers, 130, 131, 280; 14th North Carolina Regiment, 20–21; 15th Regiment of North Carolina Volunteers, 129; 16th North Carolina Regiment, 108; 17th Regiment of North Carolina Infantry, 177; 18th Regiment of North Carolina Infantry, 14, 52, 59; 22nd North Carolina Regiment, 220; 24th North Carolina Infantry, 263, 267; 25th North Carolina Regiment, 264; 26th North Carolina Regiment, 2, 64–70, 66, 210, 211–12, 213, 223, 324; 27th North Carolina Regiment, 67; 28th North Carolina Regiment, 29, 32, 226; 30th North Carolina Regiment, 141–46; 33rd North Carolina Regiment, 47; 35th North Carolina Regiment, 263; 36th North Carolina, 280, 288, 292; 37th North Carolina Volunteers, 267; 40th North Carolina Troops, 280, 289; 41st North Carolina Troops, 201; 43rd North Carolina Regiment, 212, 213, 233; 46th North Carolina Infantry, 80; 47th North Carolina Regiment, 212; 49th North Carolina Infantry, 258–63; 49th Regiment of North Carolina Troops, 148; 53rd North Carolina Regiment, 213; 54th North Carolina Regiment, 138, 239; 55th North Carolina Regiment, 223; 56th North Carolina Regiment, 263; 57th North Carolina Regiment, 130; 58th North Carolina, 266; 60th North Carolina, 231; 61st North Carolina Regiment, 263; 64th North Carolina Regiment, 86, 87–91, 88; 8th Georgia Regiment, 238; 42nd Georgia, 309; 1st Regiment of South Carolina Rifles, 220; 1st South Carolina Infantry, 109; 18th South Carolina Infantry, 261; 22nd South Carolina Infantry, 261; 8th Texas Rangers, 311; 2nd Virginia Cavalry, 119; 37th Virginia Cavalry, 122, 124–25, 125, 126; renumbering of, 131

Confederate navy, 163–67, 176, 177; CSS *Alabama*, 164, 173; CSS *Albemarle*, 167, 177–79, 179, 181, 182, 294; *Cahawba*, 251; commerce raiders, 163–65, 167; *Condor*, blockade-runner, 173–74; CSS *Florida*, 163–64, 165; CSS *Hunley*, 176; ironclads of, 176–82; CSS *Neuse*, 50, 239; *Night Hawk*, blockade-runner, 174; officers of, 163; *Owl*, blockade-runner, 167, 294; *Phantom*, blockade-runner, 173; *Shenandoah*, commerce raider, 164; *Stag*, blockade-runner, 294; *Tallahassee*, commerce raider, 164; CSS *Virginia*, 176–77

Confederate officers, 16, 209; commissions of, 32; corruption and, 86, 90; Gettysburg and, 210, 212; horses of, 5; parole of captured, 31; pistols and swords of, 106; as POWs, 125; slaves of, 213; West Point and, 242

Confederate Point (formerly Federal Point), 26, 295; Fort Fisher at, 278, 281

Confederate troops, 9, 50, 73, 326; Bible reading by, 126; correspondence of, 108–9; disease and, 57; family connections of, 130; haversacks of, 105–9, 206, 259; identification of dead, 187; improper conduct of, 125; kit of, 53, 105, 107, 108–9; massacres by, 88–90; morale of, 241; payment of, 108, 149, 151; provisions and rations of, 106, 107–8, 109, 148, 151, 152, 252; punishments for, 150; recruitment of, 83; sharpshooters, 10, 213, 259, 281, 287, 288; treatment of enemy dead by, 189; treatment of wounded, 54–55; uniforms of, 5, 105, 107. *See also* arms and ammunition; Confederate army; Confederate military units; conscription, conscripts; desertion, deserters

Congressional Boarding House (Washington, D.C.), 168

Conley, Lt. Robert E. (CSA), 101

Connecticut, 158

Conner, J. J. Proser For Me D. Doctor DeVowell (CSA), 174

conscription, conscripts, 10, 18, 147, 148, 192, 207, 241, 325; agents of, 235; age of, 283; camps for, 242; Conscription Act and, 47, 81, 132, 266; exemptions from, 18, 47, 202, 220–21; patrols for, 45, 267; resistance to, 250; by Union army, 115, 239

USS *Constitution* ("Old Ironsides"), 160

contraband of war, 169, 302; slaves as, 27, 113, 118, 156, 246, 297

Cooke, James W., Capt. (CSA), 178

Corbett, Sgt. Boston (USA), 140

Corbett, Sally Lasalle. *See* Pickett, Sally Lasalle Corbett

Cornwallis, Charles, Lord, 6, 63, 147–48

Corpening, Joseph, 274

Corrigan, Sister Martha, 257

Corse, Montgomery, 238–39

Cottage Home Plantation (Lincoln County), 136

cotton: bales of, 220, 301; barges for, 295;

burning of, 296, 301; plantations of, 26, 153; presses for, 296; speculation in, 275

Cowan, Capt. John (CSA), 109

Cowen, Bill, 149, 150

Cowles, Calvin, 273–74

Cowles family, 276

Cowpens, Battle of (Revolutionary War), 9

Cox, Maj. Gen. Jacob D. (USA), 294–95, 307

Cox, Tim, 195

Cox, Sgt. William Clinton (CSA), 241, 242

Crater, Battle of the (Petersburg, Va.), 258–65; slaughter in, 263–64, 324

Craven, Dr. Braxton (CSA), 40

Craven, John A., 45

Craven County, 153, 238, 245

Creek Indians, 97

creole languages, 72

Crimean War, 185, 251, 280

Crossley, Sgt. William H. (USA), 36

Crouse, Dan T. (CSA), 65

Crusader, 162

Culp's Hill, Gettysburg, 62, 213

Cumberland County, 141

Currituck County, 248, 250; Union occupation of, 191–97

Curtis, Brig. Gen. N. Martin (USA), 283–84, 287–88, 292

Cushing, Lt. Cmdr. William Barker ("Will") (USA), 179–81, 288, 294

Cuthrell, Charles (USA), hanged by Pickett, 240–41

Daily Confederate (Raleigh), 49

Daily Conservative (Raleigh), 49

Danville, Va., 3, 206

Daughtry, William H. (USA), hanged by Pickett, 240–41

Davidson (steamboat), 305

Davidson County, 45, 46–47

Davie County, 9, 45

Davis, Jefferson, 16, 46, 50, 61, 75, 83, 98, 101, 139, 168, 169, 173, 196, 202, 205, 234, 257, 280, 293, 319; dissatisfaction with, 18, 132; flight and capture of, 313, 317, 320, 321; Johnston's negotiations and, 306, 314, 315, 321; Lee and, 300; North Carolina and, 47–48, 100, 206

Index

New Bern, 21, 64, 115, 153, 154, 193, 229, 234, 243; hospitals in, 255–57; recruitment of black soldiers in, 112–18, 158, 246; as refuge for freed people, 26, 113; Sisters of Mercy in, 255, 324; Union occupation of, 17, 30, 49, 116, 156, 191, 194, 305, 307

New Bern, Battle of, 2, 3, 67, 191, 233–44, 326

New Hanover County, 63, 222; slaves in, 13, 245

New Haven, Conn., 158

New Hope Chapel Hill, 80, 219, 222. *See also* Chapel Hill; University of North Carolina

New Inlet, 173, 278, 281

New Market, Battle of, 196–97

New Market, Va., 196

New Orleans, 36, 75, 76, 196, 278

newspapers, 17, 18, 49, 115, 126, 137, 184–85, 186, 219, 226, 249, 257, 280; European, 165, 185; in Fayetteville, 3, 22, 186; in Greensboro, 81, 229; in New York City, 164, 176, 184; in Raleigh, 2, 49, 95, 186, 208, 272–73; in Richmond, 223, 240, 244, 286; sacking of offices of, 50, 304; in Salem, 29; in Salisbury, 40, 83–84, 186; in Statesville, 186; in Tennessee, 88–89; in Wilmington, 116–17, 175, 186, 208, 241, 293. *See also* war correspondents

New York, 160, 195; baseball rules of, 34

New York City, 30, 36, 120, 170, 182, 184, 251; minstrel shows in, 72, 73; museums in, 120, 121; Sisters of Mercy in, 251–52

New York Herald, 50, 184

New York Times, 164, 176, 184, 185; on Battle of New Bern, 235–36, 237–38

New York Tribune, 184, 276–77

New York World, 136

Nichols, Maj. George W. (USA), 318

Nixon, Nicholas, 23, 199

Noah (slave), 129

Norfolk, Va., 177, 182, 243, 248, 278, 279–80

Norfolk and Western Railroad, 270

North Carolina: Confederate government vs., 16, 17–18, 45, 47–48, 50, 206, 267, 325–26; railroad tracks in, 205; slave population of, 25

North Carolina (steamer), 95

North Carolina Bridge Guard Company, 241

North Carolina Central Railroad, 84

North Carolina Press Association, 257

North Carolina Railroad, 178, 206, 314

North Carolina Standard (Raleigh), 17, 18, 49, 50, 186, 272, 273

North Carolina Whig (Charlotte), 227

North Fork, Watauga County, 270

nurses, 55, 143, 253–54, 256. *See also* Sisters of Mercy

Oakdale Cemetery (Wilmington), 167, 175

Oakwood Cemetery (Raleigh), 217, 229

Oconoluftee Indians, 92. *See also* Cherokee, Eastern

Oconoluftee Pass, 99

Oconoluftee River, 92

Ohio, 37, 73, 100, 125, 276, 298

Oklahoma Territory, 93

Old Capitol Prison (Washington, D.C.), 171, 172, 209

Old Cotton Factory (Salisbury), 39

Old North State, 16, 18, 45, 76, 168, 297

Old Point Comfort, Va., 195–96

Oliver, Capt. (CSA), 270

Olustee, Battle of, 117–18, 158

O'Neale, Maria Rosetta. *See* Greenhow, Rose O'Neal

Onslow County, 245

Orange, Va., 229

Orton Plantation (Brunswick County), 26

Outer Banks, 48

outliers, 100, 234, 266–71

overseers, 18, 24, 25, 73, 128, 201

pacifists, 41, 46. *See also* Peace Movement; Peace Party; Quakers

Paine, Brig. Gen. Charles J. (USA), 294

Palmer, Col. William (USA), 100

Pamlico Sound, 251

Paris, France, 120, 173

Paris, Rev. John, 138; as chaplain, 239, 240–41; as spy, 242

parole and exchange system, 31, 32, 39, 47, 70, 125, 133, 209, 242

Pasquotank County, 248, 250

Pasquotank River, 25–26, 177, 195, 248

Patterson, Rev. George (CSA), 61

Patterson, Rufus, 276

Peace Movement, 49, 216

Peace Party, 2, 186
Peale's New York Museum, 121
peanuts, as cash crop, 11, 13, 23, 72, 200
Peck, Maj. Gen. John (USA), 235, 240, 242, 243
Pee Dee River, 2
Pegram, Richard G. (CSA), 261
Pender, Brig. Gen. William Dorsey (CSA), 1, 203, 267
Pender, Josiah, 252
Peninsular Campaign, 183
Pennsylvania, 69, 74, 133, 142; Lee's invasion of, 124–25, 210, 223
People's Press (Salem), 29
Perquimans County, 248, 250
Peter (Cape Fear River pilot), 24
Peter (slave), 199
Petersburg, Va., 33, 109, 130, 152, 183, 208, 226, 234, 258, 324; Army of Northern Virginia at, 1, 3, 272; North Carolina troops at, 68, 69, 131, 151
Petersburg and Richmond Railroad, 206
Petersburg mine explosion, 261–62, 262. *See also* Crater, Battle of the
Peterson, Ed (CSA), 65
Petigru, James Louis, 220
Pettigrew, Gen. James Johnston, 68, 212, 218–25, 283, 325; death of, 1, 224, 230, 324; at Gettysburg, 62, 69; *Notes on Spain and the Spaniards, . . .* , 218; in Pickett's Charge, 213, 324; portrait of, 221
Pettigrew, William, 219, 283
Philadelphia, 26, 47, 113, 120, 126, 127
Philadelphia Inquirer, 295
Pickens, Gov. Francis (S.C.), 219
Pickett, Maj. Gen. George E. (CSA), 90, 193, 233, 234, 237; death and burial of, 243–44; hangs POWs, 238–42; instability of, 238–39. *See also* Pickett's Charge at Gettysburg
Pickett, Sally Lasalle Corbett (Mrs. George E. Pickett), 243
Pickett's Charge at Gettysburg, 32, 62, 213, 233; 26th North Carolina in, 69, 213; North Carolina casualties at, 49, 214; Pettigrew in, 1, 223; remains from, 216–17
Pictorial Democrat (Alexandria, La.), 186
Piedmont, 26, 43, 45, 48, 79, 135, 149, 193, 206, 245, 326
Pierce, Tillie, 213–14

Pierson, Nancy Leigh. *See* Bennitt, Nancy Leigh Pierson
Pine Mountain, Battle of, 139
Pinkerton, Allan, 170, 171
Pitt County, 245
Pittsburgh, Pa., 74
plantation culture and plantations, 26, 72, 138, 178; coastal, 23, 25, 326; escaped slaves return to as Union soldiers, 246–47, 247; networks in, 24–25
planter elite, 11, 95, 272; in Alamance County, 128–29; of eastern North Carolina, 17, 198, 245; resentment against, 47, 81, 235; women of, 81, 83
Pleasants, Lt. Col. Henry (USA), 260–62
Plymouth, 26, 49, 167, 178–79, 191, 193
Poe, Col. Orlando M. (USA), 304
poetry, poems, 183; "The Child's Last Sleep," 227–28
Polk, James K., 168
Polk, Lt. Gen. Leonidas (CSA), 138, 230, 325; death of, 1, 139
Polly (slave), 275
Poplar Grove Plantation, Pender County, 198–202
Porter, Rear Admiral David Dixon (USA), 164, 278, 284, 285, 292, 294
Porter, John Luke, 177
Port Royal, Battle of, 76
Portsmouth, Va., 177
Poteet, Alvis, 149
Poteet, Francis Marion, 147–52
Poteet, Martha Henley (Mrs. Francis Marion Poteet), 148–52
Poteet, Sydney, 152
Potomac River, 62, 124, 224
Potter, Brig. Gen. Robert B. (USA), 263
Presbyterianism, Presbyterians, 135, 136
Press Association of the Confederate States, 184
Price, George (runaway slave), 23
Price, Hiram (CSA), hanged as deserter, 269
Price, Jesse (CSA), hanged as deserter, 269–70
Price, Moses ("Scape Gallows") (CSA), hanged as deserter, 269, 270
Primitive Baptists, 135
Princeton College (College of New Jersey), 128

prisoner of war (POW) camps, 185, 211; Confederate, 3, 34–38, 39–44, 185, 242, 297, 324; Union, 30–31, 69–70, 125–26, 211. *See also names of specific POW camps*
prisoners of war (POWs), 31–32, 54, 69, 125–26, 133, 146, 165, 209, 292, 301, 309, 324; assisted by slaves, 276–77; blacks as, 114, 116–17, 264; Confederate deserters as, 238–39; escapes by, 42–43, 45; from Fort Fisher, 290, 292–93; at Salisbury POW camp, 34–38, 39–44; Speer as, 30–32. *See also* parole and exchange system
privateers, 164; in American Revolution, 163, 164
prostitution, prostitutes, 14, 171, 234
pseudonyms, in newspapers, 187
punishments: branding, 241; for recaptured slaves, 245

Quaker Belt, 45, 48, 135
Quakers, 29, 41, 49, 201; oppose slavery, 24, 135, 136
Quallatown, 92, 97, 102, 103
Queen, James Fuller, 157

Raccoon Creek (Haywood County), 92
racism, 69; against black soldiers, 116, 246, 285; of minstrel shows, 72
Radical Republicans, 297
Railroad Guard, 236
railroads, 54, 58, 70, 75, 130–31, 145, 170, 178, 185, 205, 207–8, 252, 258, 273, 285, 314, 317, 326; accidents on, 207–8, 216, 227, 324; Ashe and, 203–9; bridges for, 99, 194, 205, 208, 241, 256, 296; deliberate destruction of, 44, 299; depots of, 100, 146; guards of, 236, 241; junctions of, 3, 147, 270; raids against, 208, 233, 236; Salisbury and, 39, 44, 84; standard gauge of, 206–7; troops and supplies moved by, 2, 3, 17, 30, 43, 75–76, 109, 205, 233, 283; in western North Carolina, 94, 95; Wilmington and, 51, 203–8, 279, 292
Raleigh, 2, 4, 44, 45, 48, 73, 79, 81, 102, 138, 145, 178, 206, 210, 216, 224, 241, 243, 313, 316; bread riots in, 83; cemeteries in, 217; mustering camps near, 137, 147; newspapers in, 49, 95, 272, 273; parades in, 5–6; secession convention in, 5, 17;

Sherman and, 306, 307, 314; surrender of, 316; Thomas in, 94, 95
Raleigh Road, 307
Ramseur, Gen. Stephen D. (CSA), 1
Randall, James Ryder, "Maryland, My Maryland," 75–76
Randolph County, 45, 135, 267
Rappahannock Military Academy (Caroline County, Va.), 280
Rappahannock River, Va., 58, 260
Ray, Lt. Col. James M. (CSA), 231
Raymer, Pvt. Jacob Nathaniel ("Nat") (CSA): *Confederate Correspondent*, 189–90; dispatches of, 186–90; portrait of, *188*; pseudonyms of, 187; as war correspondent, 183–84
Read, Caroline. *See* Maffitt, Caroline Read
Reagan, John H., Confederate postmaster general, 319
Ream's Station, Battle of, 33, 226
rebel yell, 309
Reconstruction, 4, 322
recruitment, 83, 156, 192
Redman, John (CSA), as deserter, 268
Red Sulphur Springs, Va., 17
Rees, Sgt. Henry (USA), 261
regimental colors. *See* battle flags and regimental colors
Regular Baptists, 135
Reich, Gus (CSA), 65, 69
Reilly, Maj. James "Old Tarantula" (CSA), 290
religion, 135–40; baptism, 139, 230, 240–41, 254; Bible, 46, 73, 92, 108, 126, 135, 136, 242; blacks and, 159; *The Book of Common Prayer*, 139; *Chaplain C. T. Quintard's Balm for the Weary and Wounded*, 139; Christian hymns and, 74; church communities and, 128; Confederate troops and, 29, 36; death and, 230; Divine Providence, 135, 140, 230; nuns and, 251–57; politics and, 52; prayer, prayers, 137, 155, 241, 254; preaching, 148, 155; religious tracts, 137, 138, 146; revival meetings, 137; slavery and, 276; women and, 13. *See also* chaplains; *and names of specific churches, denominations, sects, and faiths*
Religious Military Press, 146
Republicans, 86, 297

Scots, 6, 29, 170; in Cape Fear River Valley, 135, 165

Scott, Thomas A., 170

Scott, Sir Walter, 147

Scott, Gen. Winfield (USA), 96, 169

Scotts Hill, Pender County, 196, 198–202

Seaboard and Roanoke Railroad, 207

secession, 12, 13, 20, 52, 86, 95–96, 128, 129, 137, 155, 162, 168, 183, 191, 198–99, 205, 218, 220, 268, 275, 290, 297, 324, 325; convention for, 5, 16–17, 20, 96; parades and pageantry for, 5–10, 12; secessionists and, 216, 272, 280; Sherman on, 298–99; South Carolina and, 2, 11, 219; splits North Carolina, 13, 16–17

Seddon, James A., Confederate secretary of war, 90, 267

Selma, Ala., 315

Seminary Ridge, Gettysburg, 62, 212, 224

Seminoles, 97

Semmes, Brig. Gen. Raphael (CSA), 16

Senior Reserves (CSA), 283, 326

Separate Baptists, 135

Setser, Pvt. Tom (CSA), 212

Sevastopol, 280

Seven Days Battles, 109, 183

Seven Pines, Battle of, 132, 222, 275, 306

Sevier County, Tenn., 99

Seward, William H., U.S. secretary of state, 168, 171

Seymour, Brig. Gen. Truman (USA), 158

Shakespeare, William, 23

Sharpsburg, Battle of, 10, 38, 47, 54, 61, 76, 139, 210, 231, 275; casualties at, 131; North Carolinians at, 142, 143, 183, 258. See also Antietam, Battle of

sharpshooters, 10, 41, 259; at Fort Fisher, 281, 287, 288

Shaw, Dr. Henry (USA), 63

Shaw, Lieutenant (CSA), 143

sheet music, 75, 77, 95

Shelton, Azariah, 88

Shelton, Bill, 87

Shelton, David (cofounder of Shelton Laurel), 87

Shelton, David (born ca. 1815), 88, 89

Shelton, David (born ca. 1850), 88, 89

Shelton, James, 88, 89

Shelton, James, Jr., 88, 89

Shelton, Martin, 87

Shelton, Mary, 88

Shelton, Roderick "Stob Rob," 88

Shelton, Sarah, 88

Shelton, William, 88

Shelton Laurel, Madison County, 86–91; massacre at, 87–91, 323–24

Shelton Laurel Creek, 87

Shenandoah Valley, Va., 61, 62, 100, 105, 133, 192, 205; as breadbasket of Confederacy, 196; Sheridan's army in, 1, 41

Shenandoah Valley Campaign (1864), 1, 41, 183

Shepherd family, 199

Shepherd's Battery, Fort Fisher, 288, 291

Sheridan, Gen. Philip H. (USA), 313; in Shenandoah Valley, 1, 41, 100, 272

Sherman, Ellen Ewing (Mrs. William T. Sherman), 298

Sherman, Gen. William Tecumseh ("Uncle Billy") (USA), 16, 186, 279, 294, 297, 298, 306–7, 316; in Georgia, 272, 299; Johnston and, 85, 320, 322; marches through Carolinas, 1–2, 3, 118, 146, 202, 277, 285, 294–95, 298–305; in North Carolina, 2, 109–10, 209, 301, 311, 312, 313, 314; physical appearance of, 317–18; surrender terms and, 316–19

Shields, Charles, 80, 84

Shields, Martha. See Bennitt, Martha Shields

Shiloh, Battle of, 54, 210

shipbuilding, 162–63, 176, 177, 206, 292

shoes, 81, 152, 211; shortage of, 107, 109

Siamese Twins, 119–27, 123

Sidbury family, 199

Siddall, Henry (CSA), 65

Sigel, Maj. Gen. Franz (USA), 196–97

Sigfried, Col. Joshua K. (USA), 263

signal corps, 76

Simmons, Mary Ann. See Foy, Mary Ann Simmons

Sims, Babe, 15

Singleton, William Henry (USA), 153–59, 158

Sisters of Mercy, 251–57, 324

slave brokers, 273–74

slave cabins, 200

slave catchers, 26, 154, 245

slave farms, as training centers, 153

slave labor market, 273–74

Taylor, George, 150
Taylor, Lewis (USA), hanged by Pickett, 240–41
Taylor, Thomas, 174
Taylor, Zachary, 92
tea, 82, 165
telegraph, telegraph lines, 184, 235, 293; destruction of, 233, 236, 286; military communication by, 278, 287; news and, 185, 318
Telford, Tenn., 100
temperance, 11
Tennent, Dr. Edward S., 14
Tennessee, 42–43, 86, 97, 102, 122–23, 272, 274, 276, 326; Cherokee Legion in, 99–100; as refuge, 42–43, 45, 47; Stoneman in, 3, 314–15; Younce in, 266, 270
Terrell, Lt. James (CSA), 97, 99, 103
Terry, Maj. Gen. Alfred Howe (USA), 291, 292, 305, 312; second assault on Fort Fisher by, 285, 286; Wilmington and, 3, 295–97
Tew, Col. Charles Courtenay (CSA), 231
Texas, 4, 36, 311
Thailand, 119
Theim & Fraps (Raleigh), 81
Thomas, Sarah Jane Burney Love, 92, 94–96, 98, 102, 103
Thomas, Temperance, 92, 93, 95
Thomas, Col. William Holland (Wil-Usdi; "Little Will") (CSA), 92–104, 326
Thomas, William Holland, Jr., 95
Thomasville, 47
Thornton, Margaret, 77
Thorpe, Pvt. John H. (CSA), 230–31
Times (London), 165, 185
tobacco, 108, 110, 150, 296; plantations of, 26, 80, 122
Tobin, Mother Mary Madeline, 253, 254, 257
Topsail Battery, 201
Topsail Sound, 198
Tories, Unionists as, 86
torpedoes, 163, 176; spar, 180–81
Town Creek, 11, 26, 295
Trail of Tears, 96
Transou, Charles (CSA), 65
Transou, Julius (CSA), 65

Trap Hill House of Siamese Twins (Wilkes County), 121–22
treason, 48, 50, 170, 192, 241, 268, 299, 320, 321
Treaty of New Echota (1836), 93
Tredegar Iron Works (Richmond, Va.), 178
Trent River, 26, 113, 233
Trimble, Gen. Isaac R. (CSA), 62, 213
Trinity College (Durham), 40, 222
Trinity Guards, 46–47, 222
Tri-Weekly Mercury (Charleston, S.C.), 226
truces, 54, 60, 85, 293, 315, 316, 318
Tuckaseegee River, 92
Tucker, George, 76
Tucker, Henry, 77
turpentine, 11–12, 13, 26, 199, 302
Tuscaloosa, Ala., 36
Tyler, John, 168
Tyrell County, 218

Ulster Scots, 20, 29
Uncle Tom's Cabin (Stowe), 116
Underground Railroad, 24, 46, 113, 155, 276
uniforms, 17, 196; Confederate, 65, 81, 105, 107; Union, 116
Union army, 2, 49, 54, 96; blacks and, 83, 114, 118, 245–46; occupies coastal North Carolina, 2, 17, 191–97; officers of, 16, 227. *See also* Union troops; United States Army units; United States Colored Troops
Unionists, 2, 8, 13, 20, 29, 41, 45–50, 48, 52, 198, 216, 234, 236, 241, 246, 266, 270, 276, 301; in Piedmont, 43, 45, 48, 326; in Tennessee, 3, 271; in western mountains, 48, 86, 99
Union Occupation, 191–97
Union troops, 91, 105, 209; amusements and pastimes of, 34–37, 35, 40; kit of, 41, 108; from North Carolina, 234, 325, 326; as POWs, 34, 39–44; racism of, 77. *See also* Union army; United States Army units; United States Colored Troops
United States Army units: 1st North Carolina Colored Volunteers, 116, 117, 158, 195, 246–50; 2nd North Carolina Colored Volunteers, 246–49; 2nd North Carolina Mounted Infantry Regiment, 101, 230–31;

268, 273, 274, 316, 320; as colonel of 26th North Carolina, 21–22, 64, 67; Davis vs., 206, 267; election of, 18, 50, 68; portrait of, *19*; Shelton Laurel massacre and, 89–91; Thomas vs., 94, 101

Vermont, 214

Vicksburg, Miss., 31, 39

Vincent, Rupert. *See* Livingstone, Robert

Virginia, 2, 14, 18, 37, 48, 76, 84, 105, 124, 128, 147, 180; Grant in, 299, 307; Lee in, 224, 306

Virginia Military Institute, 192, 196–97

Virginia Minstrels, 72, 119

Wagg, Dr. James, 269

Wake County, 222, 277

Wake Forest College, 222

Wake Ladies Memorial Society (Raleigh), 216

Wales, Albert, Prince of, 120

Walker, David, 25, 201

Walker, Eliza M., 186

Walker, Lt. Col. William C. (CSA), 100

Walter, Thomas U., 51

war, burdens of, 105–11

war correspondents, 183–90, 249; foreign, 185; at Salisbury POW camp, 41, 42, 276

war crimes, 44, 243

Ware, Charles Pickard, 72–73

Warlick, Lewis, 109, 229

Warm Springs, 272

War of 1812, 8, 32, 77, 160

Warren, Dr. John Collins, 121

Warrenton, Va., 143

Warsaw, 158

Washburn, H. S., "The Vacant Chair," 231–32

Washington, D.C., 48, 51, 62, 93, 162, 168, 170, 192, 208, 210, 218, 257, 315; Thomas in, 93–95

Washington, George, 108, 247, 255, 297

Washington, N.C., 26, 191, 193

Watauga County, 270

water, 107–8

Waynesville, 94, 101–2

Weaver, Rufus, 216

Weaver, Samuel, 215–16

Webster, Daniel, 168

Weekly Raleigh Register, 208

Weikert, Jacob, 214

Weldon, 149, 206; as railroad terminus, 130, 145

Welles, Gideon, U.S. secretary of the navy, 279, 315, 316

Wellington, Arthur Wellesley, First Duke of, 120

Wesley, Charles (runaway slave), 27

Wesleyan Methodists, 135

western mountains, 48, 86, 273; Cherokee Legion in, 99–100; Eastern Cherokee in, 92–93; economic development in, 94, 96; as refuge, 90, 234, 267

Western North Carolina Railroad, 94, 273

West Indies, 74, 162

West Point. *See* U.S. Military Academy at West Point

West Virginia, 224, 326

Wharton, Brig. Gen. Gabriel C. (CSA), 100

Wheeler, Maj. Gen. Joseph ("Fighting Joe") (USA), 306, 307, 317

whiskey, 80, 108, 110, 234; Salisbury distillery of, 43, 44

Whiskey Creek, 203

White, Martha, 88

White Hall, 206

Whitehead, Lt. H. M. (CSA), 238

White House, 168

White House Landing, Va., 30

White Oak River, 191

White Plains, N.Y., 160

White Plains Baptist Church (Mount Airy), 122, 127

White Sulphur Springs, 101

Whiting, Maj. Gen. William H. C. ("Little Billy") (CSA), 48, 51, 278, 280, 285–89, 291

Wild, Brig. Gen. Edward Augustus (USA), 112, 115–16, 118, 245–50, 247; raids Great Dismal Swamp Canal, 247–49; U.S. Colored Troops of, 2, 195. *See also* Wild's African Legion

Wilderness, Battle of the, 10, 38, 54, 70, 108, 139, 189; North Carolinians at, 33, 62, 131, 183

Wild's African Legion, 2, 112, 114, 245–50

Wilkesboro, 6, 122, 229

Wilkes County, 267, 273; Siamese Twins in, 121–22

Willcox, Brig. Gen. Orlando B. (USA), 263

Williamsburg, Va., 131